MĂNSING CHANDEN SING

A. Henry Savage Landor
and his two faithful servants

IN THE
FORBIDDEN LAND

AN ACCOUNT OF A JOURNEY IN TIBET
CAPTURE BY THE TIBETAN AUTHORITIES
IMPRISONMENT, TORTURE, AND
ULTIMATE RELEASE

BY

A. HENRY SAVAGE LANDOR

AUTHOR OF
"COREA, OR THE LAND OF THE MORNING CALM," "ALONE WITH THE HAIRY AINU," ETC.

ALSO VARIOUS OFFICIAL DOCUMENTS, INCLUDING THE ENQUIRY
AND REPORT BY J. LARKIN, ESQ., APPOINTED
BY THE GOVERNMENT OF INDIA

WITH A MAP AND TWO HUNDRED AND FIFTY ILLUSTRATIONS

IN TWO VOLUMES
VOL. I

LONDON
WILLIAM HEINEMANN
1898

I DEDICATE THIS BOOK

TO

MY FATHER & MOTHER

IN THE FORBIDDEN LAND

BY THE SAME AUTHOR

COREA, OR CHO-SEN

THE LAND OF THE MORNING CALM

With 38 Illustrations from Drawings by the Author, and a Portrait

In One Volume, demy 8vo, 18s.

LONDON

WILLIAM HEINEMANN

Reprinted 1983 from the 1898 edition.

Printed and bound by Brepols S.A.,
Turnhout, Belgium
ISBN: 7054 1509 0

PREFACE

In this book I have set down the record of a journey in Tibet undertaken by me during the spring, summer and autumn of 1897. It is illustrated partly from my photographs and partly from sketches made by me on the spot. Only as regards the torture scenes have I had to draw from memory, but it will be easily conceded that their impression must be vivid enough with me.

The map is made entirely from my surveys of an area of twelve thousand five hundred square miles in Tibet proper. In Chapter VI. the altitudes of such high peaks in India as Nanda Devi and others are taken from the Trigonometrical Survey, and so are the positions fixed by astronomical observations of the starting and terminating points of my surveys at the places where I entered and left Tibet.

In the orthography of geographical names I have adopted the course advised by the Royal Geographical

Society—viz., to give the names their true sound as they are locally pronounced, and I have made no exception even for the grand and poetic "Himahlya" which is in English usually distorted into the unmusical and unromantic word "Himalayas."

I submit with all deference the following geographical results of my expedition:

The solution of the uncertainty regarding the division of the Mansarowar and Rakstal Lakes.

The ascent to so great an altitude as 22,000 feet, and the pictures of some of the great Himahlyan glaciers.

The visit to and the fixing of the position of the two principal sources of the Brahmaputra, never before reached by a European.

The fact that with only two men I was able to travel for so long in the most populated part of Tibet.

In addition to the above, I am glad to state that owing to the publicity which I gave in the *Daily Mail* to the outrageous Tibetan abuses taking place on British soil, the Government of India has this year (1898) notified the Tibetan authorities that they will in future not be permitted to collect Land Revenue from British subjects there. This fact gives me special satisfaction, because of the exceptional courtesy and kindness bestowed on me by our mountain tribesmen, the Shokas.

The Government Report of the official Investigation of my case, as well as other documents substantiating the details of my narrative, are printed in an appendix.

A. H. S. L.

September 1898

CONTENTS

CHAPTER XV

CHAPTER XVI

CHAPTER XVII

CHAPTER XVIII

CHAPTER XIX

CHAPTER XX

CHAPTER XXI

CHAPTER XXX

CHAPTER XXXI

CHAPTER XXXII

CHAPTER XXXIII

CHAPTER XXXIV

CHAPTER XXXV

CHAPTER XXXVI

CHAPTER XLIV

CHAPTER XLV

CHAPTER XLVI

CHAPTER XLVII

CHAPTER XLVIII

CHAPTER XLIX

CHAPTER L

LIST OF ILLUSTRATIONS

PHOTOGRAVURE

COLOURED PLATES

FULL-PAGE PLATES

TEXT ILLUSTRATIONS

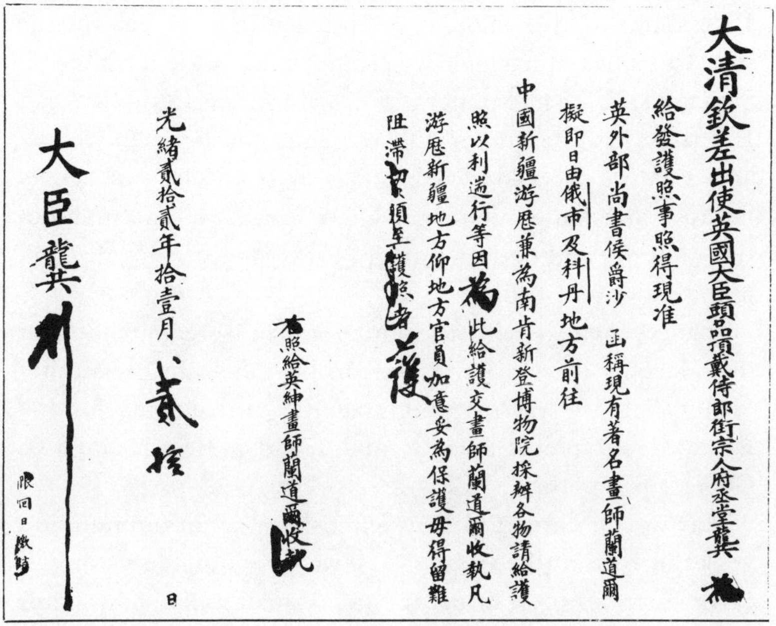
大清欽差出使英國大臣頭品頂戴侍郎銜宗人府丞堂龔 為
給發護照事照得現准
英外部尚書侯爵沙 函稱現有著名畫師蘭道爾
擬即日由俄市及科丹地方前往
中國新疆游歷兼為南肯新登博物院採辦各物請給護
照以利遄行等因為此給護交畫師蘭道爾收執凡
游歷新疆地方仰地方官員加意妥為保護毋得留難
阻滯切切須至護照者 護
右照給英紳畫師蘭道爾收執
光緒貳拾貳年拾壹月 貳拾 日
大臣龔
限回日繳銷

A CHINESE PASSPORT

CHAPTER I

FROM LONDON TO NAINI TAL

On leaving London, I intended to proceed *viâ* Germany to Russia, traverse Russian Turkestan, Bokhara and Chinese Turkestan, and from there enter Tibet. The Russian Government had readily granted me a special permission to take free of duty through their territory my firearms, ammunition, provisions, photographic cameras, surveying and other scientific instruments, and moreover informed me, through H.E. Sir Nicholas O'Conor, then our Ambassador in St.

Petersburg, that I should be privileged to travel on the military railway through Turkestan, as far as the terminus at Samarakand. I feel under a great obligation to the Russian Embassy in London for the extreme courtesy shown me, and I desire to acknowledge this at the outset, especially because that route might very likely have saved me much of the suffering and disappointment I was subjected to through going by way of India.

I was provided with introductions and credentials from the Marquis of Salisbury, the British Museum of Natural History, etc., I was carrying scientific instruments for the Royal Geographical Society, and I had a British and two Chinese passports.

Having forwarded all my explosives by an ammunition vessel to Russia (the German railways absolutely refusing to carry cartridges), I heard to my dismay, only a few days previous to leaving London, that the steamer had stranded just before reaching her port of destination, and that grave doubts were entertained as to the possibility of saving even a portion of her cargo. This was at the time of the outbreak of the Turco-Greek War, and the Russians were reported to be mobilising their troops along the Afghan frontier. I did not wish to delay my journey, and although my preparations were complete for going through Russia, I nevertheless decided to abandon that plan and go to India, with a view to penetrating over the Himahlya into Tibet. I sailed for India on March 19, on the P. and O. ss. *Peninsular*, and reached Bombay three weeks later.

It was my first visit to India, and my first impression was certainly not a good one. The heat was intense, and signs of the plague were discernible everywhere. The streets were deserted and the hotels bad and dirty for want of servants, who had abandoned the town in fear of the scourge.

Accompanied by a Parsee friend, I went to several of the districts of Bombay chiefly affected by the disease, but I noticed, wherever I went, little else than a strong odour of disinfectants. It is true there were few houses in those parts which had not ten, twenty, and even more circular red marks, denoting as many deaths, and on one door, which I photographed, I counted no less than forty-nine circles. But I was unable to gauge personally with any sort of accuracy the nature or extent of the disease, beyond seeing in the hospitals a few violent cases of bubonic attacks.

On the day following my arrival in Bombay, I proceeded by rail to Bareilly, which was reached in three days, and from there one more night brought me to Kathgodam, the terminus of the railway line. Travelling partly by Tonga (a two-wheeled vehicle drawn by two horses) and partly on horseback, I found myself at last at Naini Tal, a hill station in the lower Himahlyas and the summer seat of the Government of the North-West Provinces and Oudh, from whence I wrote to the Lieutenant-Governor, informing him of my intention to proceed to Tibet. I also called on the Deputy-Commissioner and made him fully acquainted with my plans. Neither one nor the other of these gentleman raised the slightest objection to my intended journey into the sacred Land of the Lamas.

CHAPTER II

Loads—A set of useful pack saddle cases—Provisions and scientific outfit—Clothes and shoes—Medicines—Under way—The first march—Servants—How I came to employ faithful Chanden Sing.

I KNEW that from Naini Tal, 6407 feet (sixty feet above lake level), all my loads would have to be transported on the backs of coolies, and therefore they had to be divided into equal weights not exceeding twenty-five seers, or fifty pounds. I packed instruments, negatives, and articles liable to get damaged, in cases of my own make designed especially for rough usage. A set of four such cases, of well-seasoned deal wood, carefully joined and fitted, zinc-lined, and soaked in a special preparation of mine by which they were rendered water and air tight, could be made useful in many ways. Taken separately, they could be used as seats; four placed in a row answered the purpose of bedstead; three could be used as seat and table; and the combination of four used in a certain manner made a punt or boat of quick, solid, and easy construction, by which an unfordable river could be crossed or soundings taken in the still waters of a lake. The cases could also be used as baths for myself and my followers (if I could induce these to so far indulge), and also in the developing of my negatives as tanks to properly wash my plates. I conjectured even that in case of emergency they might serve as water casks in arid regions, if I should have to traverse any. One of these boxes packed was exactly a coolie load, and two could be easily slung over a pack-saddle by means of straps and rings. It was due mainly to the stoutness and strength of these cases that, notwithstanding the amount of knocking about they got, my photographic and painting work, as well as my maps, instruments, etc., were really in no way injured until we fell into the hands of the Tibetans. Fortunately, the most important part of my work, from a scientific point of view, had already been accomplished. My provisions were prepared for me by the Bovril Company after instructions furnished by me, with a view to the severe Tibetan climate and the altitudes we should find ourselves in. They contained a vast amount of fat and carbonaceous food, as well as ingredients easily digestible and calculated to maintain one's strength even in moments of unusual stress. I had them packed in tin cases and skin bags. I carried in a water-tight box 1000 cartridges for my 256· Mannlicher rifle, besides 500 cartridges for my revolver, and a number of hunting knives, skinning implements, wire traps of several sizes for capturing small mammals, butterfly nets, bottles for preserving reptiles in alcohol, insect-killing bottles (cyanide of potassium), a quantity of arsenical soap, bone nippers, scalpels, and all other accessories necessary for the collection of natural history specimens. There were three sets of photographic apparatus in my outfit, and one hundred and fifty-eight dozen dry plates, as well as all adjuncts for the developing, fixing, etc. of the negatives as they were taken. The collecting materials were given me by the British Museum of Natural History, to which institution I had promised to present all specimens of fauna and flora I might collect during my journey. I had two sets of instruments for astronomical observation and for use in surveying (one of which had been furnished me by the Royal Geographical Society), such as the six-inch sextant, hypsometrical apparatus for measuring heights, with boiling-point thermometers specially constructed for very great altitudes ; two aneroids, one to 20,000 feet, the other to 25,000 feet ; three artificial horizons (one mercury, the others plate-glass with levels) ; a powerful telescope with astronomical eyepiece and stand ; a prismatic, a luminous, a floating, and two pocket compasses; maximum and minimum thermometers, a case of drawing instruments, protractors, parallel rules, tape rules, a silver water-tight half-chronometer watch and three other watches, section paper in books and in large sheets, Raper's and the Nautical Almanac for 1897 and 1898.

Not to neglect the artistic aspect of my expedition, I had provided myself with ample painting and drawing materials, and I trust to the appearance of my sketches in these volumes to prove that I did not carry them in vain.

I was provided with a very light mountain *tente-d'abri* seven feet long, four feet wide, and three feet high. Well accustomed to the sort of travelling I was in for, I decided that I required for myself only a camel-hair blanket in the way of bedding. I reduced my clothing also to a minimum and made no difference in it from start to finish. The only thing I ever missed was my straw hat, which I wore up in the Himahlyas just as I had worn it in the broiling plains, because it seemed to me always the most comfortable head-gear. It was rendered unwearable through the clumsiness of one of my Shokas to whom I had lent it to carry in it some swan eggs (presented by a friendly Shoka), and who fell with it, or on it, to the detriment and destruction both of vessel and load. After that I generally went about with my head uncovered, as I only had a small cap left, which was not comfortable. I wore medium thick shoes without nails, and never carried a stick, and I think it was due largely to the simplicity of my personal equipment that I was able, as will be seen presently, to climb to one of the greatest altitudes ever reached by a human being.*

My provision of medicines cost me only half-a-crown, firm as I am in the belief that man, living naturally under natural conditions, and giving himself plenty of exercise, can be helped very little by drugs.

And thus I started.

On the first day I rode from Naini Tal to Almora, thirty miles by the lower and well-known road *viâ* Khairna.

Almora (5510 feet) is the last hill station towards the frontier where I expected to find a European, or rather an Anglo-Indian, community, and I made it my headquarters for a few days. It was my intention to obtain some reliable hill men, possibly Gourkhas, to accompany me. I applied in vain for this purpose to the Lieut.-Colonel of the 1st 3rd Gourkha Regiment quartered in the station, duly showing letters, introductions, and documents from the highest authorities and institutions in England, plainly demonstrating the scientific object of my journey to Tibet.

The superior authorities seemed open to negotiations had I been able to afford a wait of several months; but, as this would have involved the postponement of my journey for a year on account of the passes leading into Tibet becoming impassable at the end of the summer, I decided to snap my

* See Appendix. Letter by Dr. H. Wilson.

fingers at all the red tape the job required, and to start on my journey without the Gourkhas.

As luck would have it, I came across a gentleman at Almora, a Mr. J. Larkin, who showed me great politeness and gave me much useful information with regard to the roads, the mode of travelling, etc. on the British side of the Tibetan frontier. He had himself travelled nearly up to the boundary the previous year, and knew that part of Kumaon better than any Anglo-Indian in the province. In fact, with the exception of Colonel Grigg, Commissioner of Kumaon, Mr. Larkin is the only other official who has any knowledge at all of the north-east of Kumaon, now so neglected by the Government of the N.W.P.

MY FAITHFUL COMPANION

Gourkhas being unobtainable, the question weighed heavily on my mind of obtaining plucky, honest, wiry, healthy servants, of whatever caste they might be, who would be ready for the sake of a good salary and a handsome reward to brave the many discomforts, hardships, and perils my expedition was likely to involve. Both at Naini Tal and here scores of servants and Shikaris (sporting attendants) offered themselves. They one and all produced

MY START FROM NAINI TAL

"certificates" of good conduct, irreproachable honesty, good-nature and willingness to work, and praises unbounded of all possible virtues that a servant could possess. Each certificate was duly ornamented with the signature of a General, a Captain, a Lieut.-Governor, or some other considerable personage, but each bearer of such testimonial seemed sadly neglected by those who had been so enthusiastically pleased with his services, for he invariably commenced by asking for a loan of several rupees to purchase boots and blankets, and to enable him to support a wife with or without a family whom he would be leaving behind.

I decided that my means did not permit of my supporting "the dear ones at home" of the two or three dozen followers I should require, and I made up my mind to wait and see whether I could not find men to suit me farther on my road without involving myself in the liability of supporting the entire population I left behind me. I made only one exception. I was sitting one fine day in my room at the Dâk Bungalow (post resting-house) when an odd creature entered and offered his services, salaaming me.

"Where are your certificates?" I asked.

"*Sahib, hum 'certificates' ne hai!*" ("Sir, I have no certificates.")

"Well, then I may employ you."

I had previously had a good look at the fellow His facial lines showed considerably more character and force than I had noticed in the features of other local natives. His attire was peculiar. He wore a white turban, and from under a short velvet waistcoat there protruded a gaudy flannel shirt in yellow and black stripes, which he wore oddly outside of his pyjamas instead of in them. He had no shoes, and carried in his right hand an old cricket stump, with which he "presented arms," as it were, every time that I came in and went out of the room. I at once decided to try him. It was about nine o'clock in the morning, when I, having many people to see, handed Chanden Sing, for that was his name, a pair of shoes and some blacking.

"Mind I find them clean when I return."

"*Acha, Sahib.*" ("All right, sir!")

"You will find some brushes in my room."

"*Bahut acha, Sahib.*" ("Very good, sir!")

I left. At six p.m. when I returned to my quarters I found Chanden Sing still polishing my footgear with all his might. He had been at it the whole day and had used for the purpose my best hair and clothes brushes.

"Oh, you *budmash! crab log, pagal!*" ("Oh! you bad character! bad man, fool!") I exclaimed, disgusted, making as much display as possible of the only three or four words I then knew of Hindustani. I snatched the blackened articles of toilet out of his hands, while he, with an air of wounded feelings, pointed out the wonderful results he had achieved.

It was clear that Chanden Sing was not much a valet, neither was he a master at opening soda-water bottles. He generally managed to give you a spray bath if he did not actually shoot the flying cork in your face. It was owing to one (by no means the first) of these accidents that Chanden Sing, having hit me full, was a few days later flung bodily out of the front door. I am very adverse to the habit of punishing the natives injudiciously and unjustly, but I believe that firm if not too severe a punishment administered in time is absolutely necessary with native servants, and generally saves much trouble and unpleasantness in the end. Anyhow Chanden Sing, none the worse, returned the next day to fetch his cricket stump which he had forgotten in his hurried and involuntary departure. He seized this opportunity to offer his humblest apologies for his clumsiness, and produced the following letter which he had got written in English by a Babu in the Bazaar :

"DEAR SIR,—I am a stupid man, but I hear you intend to take two Gourkha soldiers with you to Tibet. I am a good and very *stout* man and therefore far superior to any Gourkha. Please employ me.

"Your faithful servant,

"CHANDEN SING."

This was touching, and I forgave him and allowed him to stay. He improved as time went on, and after a while became quite tolerable. One morning Mr. Larkin called when Chanden Sing happened to be about.

"Who is that ?" said Larkin.

"That is my bearer."

"But he is not a bearer ! He was once a policeman, and a smart fellow too. He worked out a good case in his own village and had many people arrested and convicted for theft. As a reward they sacked him."

"I am thinking of taking him with me."

"He is a good lad," replied Mr. Larkin. "You can anyhow take him as far as the frontier, but I would not advise you to take him into Tibet."

Mr. Larkin counselled Chanden Sing to be diligent and attentive, and the ex-policeman beamed all over with joy when I told him definitely that he might accompany me to Bhot. He turned out to be the one plucky man among all my followers, and he stood by me through thick and thin.

CHAPTER III

Pithoragarh—Fakir women—A well-ventilated abode—Askote —The Rajiwar and his people.

THE country up to Bhot is comparatively well-known, therefore I will not dwell at length on the first portion of my journey.

On May 9 all my baggage, accompanied by two *Chaprassis*, left on its way to the frontier, and I followed on the next day. Two days' marching, at the rate of twenty-five miles a day, brought me to Shor, otherwise called Pithoragarh.

The road is good all the way, running through thick forests of pine and fir trees, and you get here and there pretty views of wooded mountain ranges. Nevertheless, it is tiring owing to the many ascents and descents, as will be seen from the following figures showing the principal elevations. From 5510 feet we climbed to 7650 feet, descended to 2475 feet, climbed again up to 6020 feet at Gangoli Hat, and re-descended by a steep incline to 2500 feet. The intense heat prevented me from walking at my usual pace, and I did not, therefore, reach my destination before sundown. Walking on in the dark, we saw the distant flickering forest fires crawling here and there like incandescent snakes along or up the mountain-side : these are caused by the igniting of the grass, shrubs, and undergrowth by the natives, the flames not unfrequently spreading and playing havoc among the finest trees of the forest.

At Pithoragarh (6650 feet) there is the old Loudon Gourkha fort to be seen, on a hilltop, also a well-kept leper

CASTLE AT PITHORAGARH

hospital, a school, and a mission-house. The soil is fertile and there are many stretches of well-cultivated land dotted with habitations. Water is plentiful, and though the scenery certainly lacks trees except in the immediate neighbourhood of the villages and houses, it has, nevertheless, a certain picturesqueness on account of its background of wooded mountains. I started from Pithoragarh at 6.30 A.M.; leaving the road to Tal on the left, I followed the track at a medium elevation of 6250 feet, arriving at Shadgora (6350 feet) just in time to witness the blessing of a calf by a Brahmin. Inside a diminutive shrine—into the door of which I was curious enough to peep—I discovered two skinny, repulsive old women, with sunken, discoloured eyes, untidy locks of scanty air, long unwashed, bony arms and legs, and finger and toe nails of abnormal length. They were clad in a few dirty rags, and were busily attending to the lights burning on several primitive stone candlesticks along the walls of the shrine. There were also some curiously-shaped stones standing upright among the candlesticks. The ceiling of this place of worship was not high enough to allow the women to stand, and they were compelled to crawl about inside on all fours. When they saw me they stretched out their angular arms towards me, begging for money. I gave them a silver coin, which they shoved under one of the peculiar stones, and then, turning round, immediately made violent gestures suggesting to me that I was to depart.

Farther on I came upon a point where three roads branched off to Deolthal (six miles) on the left, to Askote (twelve and three-quarter miles) in the centre, and to Pithoragarh (eleven and a quarter miles), a different route from the one followed, on the right. I took the middle one, and travelled on in a storm of hail and wind with a constant deafening roar of thunder and splendid flashes of lightning, which produced magical effects on the ever-changing and fantastic clouds and the weird mountain-sides along which I ploughed my way.

I arrived late in the evening at Askote, where there is neither Dâk Bungalow nor Daramsalla,* and found to my disgust that none of my carriers had yet arrived. I was offered hospitality by Pundit Jibanand, who put me up in his schoolroom, a structure consisting of a number of planks put together regardless of width, height, length, or shape, and supporting a roof of straw and grass. The ventilation of my abode was all one could wish for, and as during the night I lay wrapped up in my blanket under the sheltering roof, I could admire through the disconnected portions of the walls the brilliancy of the star-studded

* *Daramsalla*, a stone-walled shelter for the use of travellers and natives.

LEPERS

SHOWING STUMPS OF LIMBS

heaven above. When the sun arose, bits of scenery appeared between plank and plank, until by degrees the gaps were all stopped up by figures of natives, who took possession of these points of vantage to gaze to their hearts' content on the sahib, who, with signs of evident suspense on the part of these spectators, managed even to shave. Hilarity, on the other hand, was caused when I smeared myself all over with soap while bathing. Admiration followed at my putting on my last starched shirt and other mysterious garments, but the excitement grew almost to fever-heat when I went through the daily nuisance of winding up my watches and registering daily observations of temperature, etc. The strain was too much, I fancy, and a general stampede followed the moment I touched my unloaded rifle.

MY ABODE AT ASKOTE

The town of Askote is not unlike an old feudal castle such as are found in many parts of Central Italy. Perched on the crown of a central hill, the Rajiwar's palace overlooks a fine panorama of mountains encircling it on all sides. Among the higher peaks discernible from the palace are the Chipla Mountain and the Dafia. Then across the Kali River, forming the boundary of Nepal, is Mount Dooti. The "*gown*" or town itself numbers some two hundred houses scattered on the slope of the hill, and includes a school, a post-office, and two Mahommedan shops. The Rajiwar had on my arrival just completed building a new Court, a simple and dignified structure of brown stone, with fine wooden carvings on the windows and doors, and with chimneys in European fashion in each room. One wall in each room was left open, and formed a charming verandah, commanding a magnificent view of mountain scenery.

The Rajiwar of Askote occupies a unique position in Kumaon. Having repurchased his right to the tenure of land in the Askote Pargana as late as 1855, he now possesses the right of *zamindar* (translated literally, *landed proprietor*), and he is the only person to whom has been granted to retain this privilege in the Kumaon Division. Jagat Sing Pal, the Rajiwar's nephew, assured me that the people of the Askote Pargana are brave and good-natured. They never give any trouble to the Rajiwar, who, on the other hand, is almost a father to them. They apply to him in every difficulty, in sickness and distress, and he looks after them in true patriarchal fashion. The Rajiwar is not rich, probably because he spends so much for the benefit of his people and of the strangers who pass through Askote. Many of these are little more than beggars, of course, even when they travel as fakirs, or other religious fanatics, going to or returning from the sacred Mansarowar Lake in Tibet. The present Rajiwar,* Pushkar Pal, belongs to the Ramchanda family, and he is a descendant of the Solar dynasty. His ancestors lived in Aoudh or Ayodye (as it was formerly called), whence they migrated to the hills of Katyur in Kumaon, where they built a palace. The hill regions up to Killakanjia and the Jumna River were under the Raja of Katyur's rule, he assum-

* *Rajiwar:* head of kingdom.

ing the title of Maharaja. A branch of the family came from Katyur to Askote, its chief retaining the hereditary title of Rajiwar beside that of Pal, which each male assumes. The Rajiwar pays a yearly tribute of 1800 rupees to the Government of India. In the time of the Gourkhas he paid nothing except occasional gifts of *Nafas* or musk-deer to his neighbour the King of Nepal, with whom he is still in very close relation. He was then practically an independent king. Still Rajiwar Pushkar Pal has always been perfectly loyal to the Government of India.

"Are the people very obsequious to the Rajiwar?" I asked of Jagat Sing Pal.

"Yes, sir. For instance, when the Rajiwar sits on his *Karoka* (a kind of throne) he is saluted with a particularly respectful salaam. His subjects bring their hand up to the forehead and support the elbow with the left hand, as a sign that this salutation is so weighty that it requires the support of the other hand."

At Court functions, the male relatives, friends, and servants sit near the Rajiwar, his brother first, his son next, then his nephews, etc. Women are of course not admitted, and although no strict code of etiquette exists, the Rajiwar and his family are nevertheless always treated with Eastern deference.

CHAPTER IV

The Raots—A slippery journey—Superstitious notions—Anger and jealousy—Friends—To the homes of the savages—Photography—Habitations.

A YOUNG MAN

We had walked seventy-eight miles in three marches, and my men being footsore, I gave them a day's rest, which I employed in going to the haunts of the "Wild men of the forest," or *Raots* or *Rajis*, as they style themselves. They live in the woods several miles off, and to reach them I had to descend a steep incline covered by an uncommonly slippery carpet of dried grass and pine needles. I had to take off shoes and stockings to get along, and even bare-footed I found it difficult to maintain my hold. I was accompanied by one of my chaprassis and a man from Askote, and we were forced down more swiftly than comfortably till we reached a faint track, which we followed until we came upon a man hiding behind some trees. He was a wild-looking creature, naked and unkempt, with flowing hair and scanty beard and moustache, and, regarding us with an air of suspicion, he was most reluctant to show us

RAOTS

the way to the homes of his tribe. He was a Raot, and his reluctance to let us approach his home seemed justified enough when he said to my guide, "No white man has ever visited our home, and should one ever come we shall all die. The spirits of the mountains will prevent your progress—not we. You will suffer pain, for the spirit who watches over the Raots will let no one enter their homes."

RAOT ON TREE

I gave the man a rupee, which he turned and weighed in his hand.

"You can come," he muttered, "but you will regret it. You will have great misfortunes."

There was something so weirdly peculiar in the tone of voice in which the man spoke, as if he had been in a trance, himself only the channel through which the threat of some occult being was conveyed to us, that for some minutes I could not get his words out of my head. I followed him as best I could, for he climbed up huge boulders with the agility of a monkey. It was no easy job, for we bounded and leapt from rock to rock and vaulted over fallen trees. The track became more marked and went up along the incline of a steep ravine. We continued until, hot and panting, we arrived at a large hollow high up in the cliff of clay. There, on a semicircular platform with entrenchments of felled trees, were about a dozen men almost devoid of clothing, some sitting on their heels and resting their arms on their knees, others lying down flat. One fellow smoked dry leaves inside a pipe of Hindoo origin. I snatched a photo of the group as, with an air of suspicion mingled with surprise and sadness, but no apparent fear, they stared at the unexpected visitors. Two of the elder men having overcome their first stupor sprang to their feet and with mad gesticulations refused to let me come nearer. But I penetrated right into their circle, and found myself surrounded by a sulky and angry crowd.

"No man has ever been here but a Raot. You will soon die. You have offended God!" screamed an old man, in a sudden outburst of temper. He bent his knees and curved his spine, protruding his head towards me. He shook his fists in my face, waved them about in the air, opened and tightly clenched them, digging his nails furiously into his palms. Instead of contracting the scalp of his forehead, the old Raot raised his eyebrows and turned his polished forehead into a succession of deep wrinkles, stretching in a straight line across almost from ear to ear, and showing only a dark dimple over his nose. His nostrils, flat and broad to begin with, became widely expanded and raised so as to cause two deep lines to diverge from the nose along his cheeks. His mouth was open and a peculiar vacillation of the lower lip demonstrated plainly that its owner had but little command over speech and articulation. His eyes, which may have been brown originally, were discoloured, probably through the abuse of excessive animal powers, to the possession of which the formation of his skull strongly testified, but they assumed extraordinary brilliancy as his fury increased. He opened them wide, apparently with an effort, and showed the entire circle of his iris. The pupils were dilated, notwithstanding that the light upon his face was strong at the time.

Following his example, some of the rest displayed their discontent in a similar fashion, but others, among whom I especially noticed two youths with sad languishing faces, drooping large eyes, and luxuriant growth of black hair, stood apathetically apart, with head reclining towards the right shoulder, their features perfectly composed, and supporting their chins on their hands. Even if they had overcome their stupor, they did certainly not betray it, and appeared perfectly emotionless as far as their countenances were concerned.

HEAD OF YOUNG MAN

One fellow with an extraordinary head, a mixture it seemed of a Mongolian and a Negroid type, was the first to calm himself of those who were so madly excited. With piercing though unsteady eyes, and with nervous twitching movements, he scrutinised my face more closely than the others, and seemed to reassure them all that I had not come to hurt them. He made signs to the rest to desist from their threats, and then, squatting down himself, invited me to follow his example, by sitting on my heels. When the storm had subsided and they had all sat down, I drew out of my pocket some coins and gave one to each of them, with the exception of one man on whom I thought I might study the passion of jealousy in its most primitive form. I watched the man closely, and soon saw him draw apart from the others and become sulky. The others were by now comparatively calm. They seemed predisposed towards sadness, and I could with difficulty extract from any of them more than a very faint sort of a smile. They turned and twisted the coins in their hands, and compared them among one another, jabbering and apparently content. The jealous man kept his head turned away from them determinedly, pretending not to see what was going on, and, resting his chin on his hand, he began to sing a weird, melancholy, guttural song, assuming an air of contempt, especially when the others chaffed him. Having allowed him to suffer enough, I gave him two coins instead of one, and with them the satisfaction of the last grin.

I then tried to photograph them, but my camera was looked upon with suspicion, and as plate after plate was exposed in portraying single individuals or groups, they shuddered at each "click" of the spring.

"The gods will be angry with you for doing *that*," said a Raot, pointing at the camera, "unless you give us a large white coin."

I took advantage of this, and promised them as best I could through my guide "two large coins" if they would take me to their huts, some few hundred yards below the lofty eyrie in the cliff, but I must for the sum be allowed not only to see but to touch and have explained to me anything I liked.

They consented, and we began our descent of the

precipitous track leading to their habitations, a track fit really only for monkeys. Several women and children, who had come up attracted by the sight of strangers, joined with the men in giving us a helping hand, and in fact, I believe there cannot have been a single paw in the company that did not

TWO MEN SITTING DOWN WITH CHILDREN

at one time or other during the descent clutch some portion of my clothing in the friendliest spirit. Holding on to one another, we proceeded in a body, not always at a pleasant pace, down the dangerous cliff. Two or three times one of the natives or myself tripped and almost dragged the remainder of the party over the precipice, while the piercing yells and screams of the women seemed to echo back for miles around. I was not sorry when we at last reached the small huts by the river which made up their village.

The habitations were squalid beyond measure. Constructed with a rough frame of tree-branches, fortified by wooden posts and rafters, roofed over with a thatch of dried grass, the majority of them measured about ten feet. They were built against the hillside, a strong bi-forked pole in the centre of the structure supporting the roof, and were usually divided into two sections, so as to give shelter each of them to two families. They contained no furniture, and but few utensils of the most primitive make. There were circular wooden bowls scooped out in the past by means of sharp-edged stones, and more recently by cheap blades, which were of Indian manufacture. For such cultivation as they were capable of these people used primitive earth rakes, and they also possessed coarse mallets, sticks, and net bags in which they kept their stores. Their staple food in former days was river fish, flesh of wild animals, and roots of certain trees; but they now eat grain also, and, like all savages, they have a craving for liquor. The interior of Raot habitations was so primitive and lacking of furniture, that it hardly requires to be described, and the odours that emanated from these huts are also better left to the imagination of the reader.

A YOUNG MAN

Entering one of the dwellings, I found squatted round a fire of wood some women and men, the women wearing silver bangles and glass bead necklaces, the men very little more than string earrings. Only one of the men had on as much as a diminutive loin-cloth, and the women had scanty dresses of Indian manufacture, obtained in Askote.

Scanning their features carefully, it struck me that in their facial lines many points could be traced which would make one feel inclined to attribute to them a remote Mongolian origin, modified largely by the climate, the nature of the country, and probably by intermarriage. In the scale of standard human races the Raots stood extremely low, as can be judged from the accompanying photographs. The women, as will be seen, had abnormally small skulls with low foreheads, and although they looked devoid even of a glint of reason, they were actually fairly intelligent. They had high cheek-bones; long, flattish noses, broad and rounded as in the Mongolian type. The chin was in most instances round, very receding, though the lips were in their normal position, thin, and very tightly closed with up-turned corners to the mouth. The lower jaw was extremely short and narrow, whereas the upper one seemed quite out of proportion to the size of the skull. Their ears were large, outstanding, and unmodelled, capable of catching sounds at great distances.

The men had better heads than the women, underdeveloped yet comparatively well balanced. They had higher and broader foreheads, similar though shorter noses, chins not quite so receding, the whole lower jaw extraordinarily narrow, but the upper lip, as with the women, huge and out of all proportion.

Undoubtedly the Raots are not a pure race, and even among the few I came across variations so considerable occurred as to puzzle one in tracing their origin. They invariably possess luxuriant coal-black hair, which never attains more than a moderate length. It is not coarse in texture, but is usually so dirty that it appears coarser than it really is. They have very little hair on their bodies except in the armpits, and their moustaches and beards hardly deserve the name.

The men generally part the crop on their head in the middle, so that it flows on either side of the skull, just covering the ears, and I found the same strange custom that I observed years ago among the Ainu of Yezo of shaving a lozenge-shaped portion of the scalp in the centre of the forehead directly above the nose. The women, using their fingers as a comb, draw their hair to the back of the head and tie it in a knot.

The bodies of the better specimens I saw were slight and agile, with no superfluous fat or flesh. Supple to a degree, yet solid and muscular, with well-proportioned limbs and a skin of a rich tinge between bronze and terra-cotta colour, these savages, dirty and unclothed as they were, certainly appealed to the artistic side of my temperament, particularly on account of their very majestic deportment. I noticed their regular breathing, which they usually did through the nose, keeping their mouths tightly closed, and also one very curious peculiarity about their feet, viz., the length of the second toe, protruding considerably beyond the others, and giving them no doubt the power of using their toes almost as we should our fingers. The palms of their hands were almost without lines, the finger-nails flat, and their thumbs stumpy with the last phalanx curiously short.

If the Raots to-day have adopted some articles of clothing and ornament, besides altering their diet to a certain extent, it is due entirely to the Rajiwar of Askote, who, taking a great interest in the tribes he rules over, provides them in a patriarchal way with all sorts of necessaries of life. Very few Raots have of late years visited Askote, as they are of a retiring nature and seem contented with their primitive abodes in the forests of Chipula, which they claim as their own. Their only occupations are fishing and hunting, and they are said to have a predilection for the flesh of the larger Himahlyan monkey, although from my own observation I should have said that they would eat almost anything they could get. It has generally been assumed that the Raot women are kept in strict seclusion and hidden from strangers, and I cannot better prove the absurdity of this than by reproducing in these pages one of several photographs of the Raot women, for which they posed at my request without the slightest objection from the men. They are generally believed to be chaste, and my photographs prove, I think, that whatever charm they may possess for the Raot men, their peculiar beauty offers but little temptation to others.

They are rapidly diminishing in numbers, chiefly no doubt on account of constant intermarriage. I was assured that the women are not sterile, but that there is enormous mortality among the young children. They bury their dead, and for several days afterwards offer food and water to the spirit of the departed.

I was unable to ascertain what their marriage ceremonies were like, or if they had any to speak of, but it appeared that there was a considerable family feeling among couples living maritally together. They are superstitious and hold in curious awe the spirits of the mountains, the sun, the moon, fire, water, and wind. Whether this amounts to a definite form of worship I cannot say: I certainly saw no signs of the offering of prayers or sacrifices.

The Raots claim to be the descendants of kings, and they refuse allegiance to any one. They will neither salute you nor bow to you.

"It is for other people to salute us. Our blood is the blood of kings, and though for choice we have for centuries retired to the jungle, we are none the less the sons of kings."

After a while, and when I had spent some considerable time among them, these royal savages seemed uncomfortable and apprehensive. I had turned over, examined, drawn or photographed every household article I had seen, had measured every one, male and female, who consented to be measured, and paid them the stipulated money. As I was about to leave, the grey-haired man approached me again.

"You have seen the home of the Raots. You are the first stranger who has done so, and you will suffer much. The gods are very angry with you."

"Yes," rejoined another savage, pointing at the ravine, "whoever treads along that track and is not a Raot will be afflicted by a great calamity."

"*Kush paruani, Sahib*" ("Never mind, sir"), interrupted the guide, "they are only barbarians, they know no better. I have myself never been here, so I suppose I shall also come in for my share."

"You too will suffer," said the old Raot, with self-assurance.

The Raots stood round me silently as I packed up the camera, and I felt that they looked upon me as a man whose fate was settled. They did not acknowledge my farewell, and, had I been in the least superstitious, might have made me thoroughly uncomfortable with their solemn, stolid gravity.

But it all came back to me with horrible intensity later on, when I was suffering the agonies of hell, and when I seemed to re-live in every moment the experiences of my whole former life.

RAOT WOMEN OF THE FOREST

CHAPTER V

A pilgrim from Mansarowar Lake—The spirits of the mountains—A safeguard against them—Tibetan encampments—The Rajiwar—A waterfall—Watermills.

THE RAJIWAR OF ASKOTE, HIS BROTHER AND SON

HAVING returned to Askote from my excursion, I saw while going round the town with Jagat Sing, in a low stone shed by the side of the palace, the tall gaunt figure of a man emerging from a cloud of smoke.

"Who is that?" I inquired of my companion.

"Oh, that is a fakir returning from a pilgrimage to the sacred lake of Mansarowar in Tibet. Many of these fanatics pass through here during the summer on their religious journeys."

My curiosity drew me towards the weird individual. He was over six feet in height, and his slim body had been covered with ashes, giving the dark skin a tinge of ghastly grey. I asked him to come out into the light. His masses of long hair had been plaited into small tresses which were wound round his head in the fashion of a turban—the "*Tatta.*" The hair, too, had been whitened, while the long thin beard had been dyed bright red. His eyes were sunken and, apparently to add to the ghastly and decidedly repulsive effect, his forehead and cheeks were plastered with a thick white paint. He seemed half stupefied, and had very little to say for himself. As can be seen by the illustration, he was scantily clothed, but he wore the *Kamarjuri* or fakir's chain about his loins, and he had a bead bracelet round his arm above the elbow. His waist was encircled with a belt of wooden beads, and a necklace of plaited hair ornamented his neck. He spent his days rolling himself in ashes and enduring self-imposed bodily privations, with a view to attain a state of sanctification.

Rumours had reached me of some curious superstitions prevalent among these mountain folk.

"Tell me," I said to Jagat Sing, "are there 'spirits of the mountains' in these ranges? And do the people really believe in them?"

"Yes, sir," replied the young fellow, "there certainly are a number of them, and they are often very troublesome, especially to certain people. They are seldon known, however, to kill any one."

"Then they are not quite so bad as some human beings," I replied.

"Well, sir, they are very bad. They seize sleeping people by the throat with claws like iron, sitting on the chests of their victims."

"Does not that sound more like an attack of indigestion?"

"No, sir. The ghosts of the mountains are the spirits of

people that have not gone to heaven. They are to be found in swarms at night in the forest. The people are terrified of them. They haunt the mountain-tops and slopes, and they can assume the semblance of a cat, a mouse, or any other animal; in fact they are said to frequently change their

FAKIR RETURNING FROM MANSAROWAR

appearance. Where no man can tread, among rocks and precipices, or in the thick jungle, the spirits seek their retreat, but often they abandon their haunts to seek for men. The person who becomes possessed generally remains in a semi-conscious condition and ejaculates mad cries and unintelligible words. There are men who profess to know charms to draw them out. Some remedies are for that purpose commonly used by the natives with more or less success. A grass called *Bichna* (nettles) has the faculty of frightening the spirits away when applied on the body of the sufferer, but the most effective remedy is to make pretence to beat with a red-hot iron the person possessed. The spirits seem to fear that more than anything else."

"Do the spirits ever speak?" I inquired, interested in the curious superstitions of these hill men.

"No, sir, not often, nor usually directly, but they do it through people who are possessed by them. It is they who tell many strange tales of the spirits. One curious point about them is that they only seize people who are afraid of them. If defied they vanish."

"Do the natives adopt any special method to protect themselves from these mountain demons?"

"Fire is the only sure protection. Any one sleeping near a fire is safe, and as long as there is a flame blazing the spirits keep away."

"Do you know any one who has seen them?"

"Yes. A chaprassi called Joga tells of having been compelled to travel at night through a forest: he heard a voice calling him by name. Terrified, he stopped, and for some moments his voice failed him. At last, trembling all over, he replied, and instantly a swarm of spirits appeared and challenged him to do them harm. Joga ran for his life and the demons vanished. Spirits have been known to throw stones at passers-by."

"Have you ever seen a spirit, Jagat Sing?"

"Only once. I was returning to the palace late in the evening when up the steep road I perceived a woman's figure. It was a beautiful moonlight night. I walked up, and as I passed, the face of the strange being appeared black, inhuman and ghastly. I staggered when I saw the weird apparition approach, my blood ran cold with fear. I struck a mighty blow with my stick, but behold! the cane whirled through the air and hit nothing. Instantly the ghost vanished."

"I wish, Jagat Sing, that you could show me some of these spirits; I would give anything to make a sketch of them."

"You cannot always see them when you want, sir, but they are always to be avoided. They are evil spirits and can do nothing but harm."

Leaving Askote (4600 feet) by the winding road through a dense forest, I crossed by a suspension bridge the Gori River at Gargia (2450 feet). The track was along the low and unpleasantly hot valley of the Kali River, a raging stream flowing with indescribable rapidity in the opposite direction to that in which I was travelling. It formed the boundary line between Nepal and Kumaon. Huts and patches of cultivation were to be seen on the Nepalese side, whereas on our side we came upon deserted and roofless winter dwellings of Shokas (usually but not correctly called Botiyas) and Tibetans, who migrate to these warmer regions to graze their sheep during the colder months of the year. The Shoka summer residences are at greater elevations, mostly along the highways to Tibet and nearer the Tibetan boundary. On arriving at the Kutzia Daramsalla, a messenger brought me the news that the Rajiwar, whom I had missed seeing at Askote, was now here for the purpose of making offerings to certain deities. He would call upon me at 3 P.M., so, having some time to spare, I went to bathe in the deliciously cold though, as I found, dangerously rapid stream. Swimming was out of the question, and even an immersion bath was attended with a certain amount of risk. The current caused me to lose my footing, and I soon found myself washed with great force against some rocks thirty or forty yards down stream. I came out of the water *minus* a few patches of skin on my knees and shins, and while drying myself in the sun, received a deputation of the *Patan* (head village man) and other natives, conveying with their most respectful salaams gifts of milk, *kielas* (bananas), *kakri* (gigantic cucumbers), and nuts. These hill fellows impressed me as being of a far superior standard to the Hindoos of the plains. They were lightly yet strongly built, and showed evidence of both character and dignity. With their fair complexion and luxuriant black hair and moustache they resembled Spaniards or Southern Italians. They lacked entirely the affected manner and falseness of speech and demeanour, so common among the natives who are constantly in contact with Europeans.

Below the Daramsalla, near the water-side, was a large Tibetan encampment of some twenty or thirty tents which had all originally been white, but were now black with smoke. In these were men, women, and children, with all their paraphernalia; and the first thing that attracted my eye in each tent was the quantity of shiny brass bowls strewn upon the ground, the entire energy of the tent-owners seemingly being spent in keeping these utensils clean and bright, to the utter neglect of their other property. Walls of sheep-loads were erected either inside the tent or directly outside, covered in the latter case with cloths in order to protect them from the rain.

Punctually at 3 P.M. the Rajiwar arrived, carried in a *dandy*, and followed by his brother, who sat in a mountain dandy. The Rajiwar's son and heir rode a splendid grey pony. I went to assist the old Rajiwar to alight, as for some years he had been paralysed. We shook hands heartily, and

I led him into the Daramsalla (2875 feet), where in default of furniture we all sat on packing-cases. His refined, well-cut features, his attractive manner, and the soft, dignified voice in which he spoke clearly indicated a man of superior blood and uncommon ability. His modesty and simplicity were delightful.

"I hope that your health is good and that you have not

THE RAJIWAR AND HIS BROTHER IN DANDIES.

suffered too much on your journey. I was grieved not to be in Askote to receive you. Are your dear parents alive? Have you any brothers and sisters? Are you married? I would much like to visit England. It must be a wonderful country, and so much do I admire it that I have given my nephews a British education, and one of them is now serving the Maharanee (Queen) Victoria as Political Peshkar."

I answered his questions as best I could with the aid of a Hindustani dictionary, expressive gestures, and quick sketches. He spoke of many of our latest inventions with marked interest and intelligence.

He seemed greatly struck with my scientific instruments, but he and his people were more particularly attracted by my rifles, revolvers, and other weapons, especially the 256· Mannlicher, sighted to 1000 yards.

The Rajiwar pressed me to return with him to Askote, where he offered to give me tiger, bear, and leopard shooting. Tempting as the invitation was, I could not accept it, for my plans would lead me in the opposite direction. His visit lasted for more than three hours; and I was pleased to feel that we parted great friends.

On the road to Dharchula, along the low-lying valley, the heat was unbearable, although the sun was near the horizon. We came upon a waterfall falling from a great height over a series of umbrella-like stalactites covered with moss. The last rays of the sun shone on the dropping water, brilliant and sparkling as a shower of diamonds. Several small rainbows added to the beauty of the scene. I rested some time in this cool and beautiful retreat. There were birds singing and monkeys playing among the trees. Farther on, where the river bends, there are two large caves hollowed in the rock; the smoke-blackened ceilings prove that these are used as camping grounds by travelling Shokas and Hunyas (Tibetans). Large black-faced, white-bearded monkeys swarmed everywhere, frankly and gladly mischievous. They throw or roll stones down upon the passers-by, often causing accidents, the track being rather narrow and sheer above the river.

Previous to arriving at the spot where the Tsuagar flows into the Kali River one meets with many Tibetan, Humli and Rongba encampments.

I camped at Kalika (3205 feet) by the side of a gigantic tree with boughs spreading well over the road, the chaprassis and men erecting a comfortable *chöpper* of mats, foliage, and branches.

I was anxious to get through the hot valley with the greatest possible speed, so, notwithstanding that we had halted very late at night, I roused my men at 3 A.M. and again set forth on the march. Here and there along the road we passed deserted winter dwellings of Shokas, nearly all with broken thatched roofs. Some, however, were roofed with slate, the distinctive mark of residence of the Darma Shokas.

The primitive Shoka water-mills were curious. By a very ingenious contrivance the water of a stream propelled a heavy cylindrical stone revolving on the top of another. The grain fell slowly from a magazine above into a hole pierced in the centre of the upper wheel, and finding its way through a channel between the two cylinders, was ground into fine flour.

Dharchula (3550 feet) the largest Shoka winter settlement, is situated on a fine stretch of flat land some hundred feet above the river ; the village consists of twelve long rows of roofless houses very similar in size and shape. Four larger buildings at the extreme limit of the settlement attract notice. One of these is a Daramsalla. The others, two high stone buildings, are a school, hospital and dispensary belonging to the Methodist Episcopal Mission and under the careful supervision of Miss Sheldon, M.D., Miss Brown, and that wonderful pioneer, Dr. H. Wilson. A bungalow of the same mission is built higher up on the hillside.

Between the two spots where from Nepal the Lachu and the Shakta join the Kali, was Dubart (3700 feet), and from thence one gradually rose to 4120 feet at the Relegar River, also a tributary of the larger stream. Having crossed the Rankuti River I ascended still higher by zigzag walking, slowly leaving behind me range after range of mountains beyond the valley of the river ; while on the Nepal side, beyond the three nearer ranges, snow peaks of great height and beauty stood out against the sky-line. The highest point on the road was 5450 feet, after which we descended to 5275 feet at Khela Daramsalla, which we did not reach till late at night.

Near Khela on the top of a high mountain stood a tall quadrangular rock not unlike a tower. The natives say that a mere touch causes it to shake and revolve, but this belief is not general, for others deny that it ever moves. I could not spare the time to go and test the facts, nor could I obtain reliable information from any one who had had actual experience. So far as I could see with the aid of my telescope, the rock seemed to be standing firmly on a very solid base. To my regret also, I was unable to visit the curious hot sulphur springs on the Darma Ganga, and the strange cave in which much animal life is lost owing to the noxious gases rising from the ground. I gathered from various reports that this cave or grotto is packed with skeletons of birds and quadrupeds who have unknowingly entered this chamber of death.

CHAPTER VI

Highways and trade routes—The Darma route—The Dholi River—A rough track connecting two valleys—Glaciers—Three ranges and their peaks—Altitudes—*Darma*, *Johar*, and the *Painkhanda* Parganas—The highest peak in the British Empire—Natural boundaries.

THERE are two principal highways from Khela to Hundes: one by the valley of the Dholi or Darma River, the other along the Kali River and over the Lippu Pass.

The trade route *viâ* Darma is less frequented than the one by the Lippu, but it is nevertheless of considerable importance, inasmuch as a certain portion of the trade of South-west Tibet with India is carried on through the medium of the Darma Shokas. It consists mainly of borax, salt, wool, skins, cloth, and utensils, in exchange for which the Tibetans take silver, wheat, rice, *satoo*, *ghur*, lump candied sugar, pepper, beads of all kinds, and articles of Indian manufacture. For a mountain track, and considering the altitudes to which it rises, the Darma way is comparatively good and safe, notwithstanding that in following upwards the course of the Dholi River the narrow path in many places overhangs deep ravines and precipices. There are many Shoka villages and settlements on the banks of the stream, the most important ones being the Nyu, Sobala, Sela, Nagling (9520 feet), Bahling (10,230 feet), Sona and Tuktung (10,630 feet), Dansu and Yansu, where there is a bridge. On the north-east bank is Goa, facing Dakar, and farther up, at an elevation of 10,400 feet, the Lissar, a rapid tributary with muddy water.

DARMA SHOKAS AND TIBETANS

The Dholi springs from a series of comparatively small glaciers north-east of a range forming a branch of the higher Himahlyan chain, and extending in a south-easterly direction as far as the point where the two streams meet. It receives, on its precipitous descent, many small snow-fed tributaries, those from the Katz snowfields and the Nui glacier being the most important. Its way lies in a tortuous channel amidst rocks and ravines, first tending towards the South-East, then due South, and last South-West down to the point where it is joined by the Lissar, coming from the North-West along a line almost parallel on the opposite watershed of the range.

Tyang, Sipu (11,400 feet), and Marcha (10,890 feet), are the three most important Shoka villages on the Lissar.

From Marcha there is a track connecting the valleys of the Lissar and Gori. You ascend the high mountain range west of the Lissar by skirting the northern edge of the Nipchung Kang glacier and keeping south of the Kharsa glacier, and, on a route that is unpopular on account of its constant difficulties and perils, you pass, as you descend in a westerly direction, the Tertcha glacier. South of the Shun Kalpa glacier you reach first Ralem and then Sumdu, which is situated on a tributary of the Gori River, itself a tributary of the Kali. The rugged, barren chain of mountains separating the Gori from the Lissar extends in a general direction from S.S.E. to N.N.E. up to the Ralfo glacier, and there turns in a curve North-West among a succession of perpetual snowfields and glaciers. The glaciers to the North-East and East of the range outnumber those on the West, but there is one of importance called in its different sections the Kala Baland, the Shun Kalpa, and the Tertcha. There are, along the fifteen most northerly miles of the range, south of the point where it joins the Himahlyan chain, other glaciers of considerable size and importance, but I was not able to ascertain their names, excepting that of the *Lissar seva,* the most northern of all, forming the source of the Lissar. The inter-Lissar-Gori range is of considerable geographical importance, not only because it forms the boundary between the two parts of Bhot called Darma and

Lithographed by F. A. Brockhaus, Leipzig (Germany).

OF THE HIMAHLYAS. SHOWING NANDA DEVI AND TRISUL PEAKS.

Johar, but also because of the magnificent peaks reaching in the Bambadhura an elevation of 20,760 feet, and in a higher unnamed peak, South-East of it, 21,470 feet. There are also the two Kharsa peaks, the one North-West of the glacier bearing its name being 19,650 feet, the one South-West of it slightly over 20,900 feet, and S.S.W. one peak 21,360 feet, another 21,520 feet, and farther still, North of the Telkot glacier, the highest of all, 22,660 feet. In a South-East direction there are peaks 20,700 feet, 20,783 feet, and 21,114 feet high. At the point where the ridge turns South the elevations become lower, the two highest being 19,923 feet and 19,814 feet, the latter situated at the point where a smaller range branches off to the South-East, the principal range running South for the next eleven or twelve miles, with no very remarkable elevations. In the side range there are peaks of 18,280 feet, 17,062 feet, 14,960 feet, 14,960 feet respectively.

In Lat. 29° 59′ 10″ N. and Long. 80° 31′ 45″ E. the range again separates into two secondary ridges, one extending South-East, the other South-West, and in turn both these are again subdivided into minor hill ridges, along which no summits are found surpassing 13,000 feet, except the Basili, 13,244 feet.

The Bungadhura Mountain (9037 feet), in close proximity to Khela, terminates the South-Easterly division of the range, separating the Pargana of Darma from that of Askote. The actual boundary line, however, does not follow the higher mountain range as far as the Kali River, but swerves to the south along the ridge overlooking the valley of the River Relegar. These mountains are called the Mangthil.

There is west of the above ridge a second and even more important chain, running out parallel to it from the backbone of the Himahlyan great mountain system. This second ridge contains the highest mountain in the British Empire, Nanda Devi (25,660 feet) with its second peak (24,380 feet), also Trisul (23,406 feet), East Trisul (22,360 feet), and Nanda Kot (22,530 feet). This range and its ramifications divide the valleys of the Gori River (the Pargana of Johar) from the most Western portion of Bhot, the Painkhanda Pargana.

The well-known Milam and Pindari glaciers are one on the Eastern, the other on the South-West side of this range. The Milam highway to Tibet, frequented by the Johari traders, traverses over the Kungribingri Pass (18,300 feet), and the Uttadhura (17,590 feet) directly S.S.W. of it into Hundes.

The Pargana Painkhanda, a region equally Alpine, similarly covered with vast stretches of perpetual snow and extensive glaciers, is in the North-East corner of Garwhal, bordering on Tibet, and along the Dhauli River; intersecting it, another trade route finds its way into Western Tibet by the Niti Pass. Leaving the course of the Dhauli at Jelam (10,100 feet), this track proceeds almost due east, rising to an altitude of 16,600 feet on the Niti, in Lat. 30° 57′ 59″ N. and Long. 79° 55′ 3″ E., which is, from all accounts, a very easy pass, and quite free from snow during the summer months. The people of the Painkhanda Pargana use this pass as well as the other passes of Malla Shilanch and Tumzun, besides the Shorhoti, visited by H. R. Strachey some years ago, over which, however, only a small portion of the trade with Hundes is carried, for it is considered the most dangerous of the three. The cold and turbid waters of the Dhauli, swollen by dozens of equally foaming and muddy tributaries, become ultimately the sacred waters of the Ganges.

The three Alpine Parganas, viz., the Painkhanda, Johar, and Darma (Darma, Chaudas, and Bias) are inhabited by races closely allied and akin to those of Tibet proper. The region is collectively named Bhot, although that designation is more particularly applied by the natives of India to that portion of the country which includes Darma, Bias, and Chaudas, and which has for natural boundaries the Kali River to the South-East, separating it from Nepal and the great Himahlyan chain to the North-East, extending from the Lissar Peak in a general direction of about 115°.

A ramification leaving the main range at the Darma Pass stretches across from N.N.W. to S.S.E., separating the above-mentioned Darma Ganga from the Kuti River, along which I eventually travelled on my way to Tibet. The main elevations found on this ridge are 18,510 feet on the Darma Pass; north-east of the Rama glacier a peak 20,760 feet; the Gurma Mountain 20,320 feet; and others south of them as high as 20,380 feet, 20,330 feet, 20,260 feet. East of the latter summit is one 20,455 feet.

CHAPTER VII

The word *Bhot* and its meaning—Tibetan influence—Tibetan abuses—The ever-helpful Chanden Sing—The first Shoka village—Chanden Sing in disgrace—Weaving-loom—Fabrics—All's well that ends well!

THE name *Bhot*, pronounced Bod, Pote, Tüpöt, or Taipöt, by which this inter-Alpine region is called, means Tibet. In fact *Tibet* is probably merely a corruption of *Tüpöt*. These lofty "pattis" of Darma, Bias, and Chaudas nominally form part of the British Empire, our geographical boundary with Nari Khorsum or Hundes (Great Tibet), being the main Himahlyan chain forming the watershed between the two countries. In spite of this actual territorial right, I found at the time of my visit in 1897 that it was impossible not to agree with the natives in asserting that British prestige and protection in those regions were mere myths; that Tibetan influence alone was dominant and prevailing, and Tibetan law enforced and feared. The natives invariably showed abject obsequiousness and servile submission to Tibetans, being at the same time compelled to display actual disrespect to British officials. They were driven to bring the greater number of civil and criminal cases before Tibetan magistrates in preference to having them tried in a British court.

The Tibetans, in fact, openly claimed possession of the "pattis" bordering on Nari Khorsum; and the more obviously to impress our natives with their influence as superior to British, they came over to hibernate on our side, and made themselves quite at home in the warmer valleys and in the larger bazaars. They brought their families with them, and drove before them thousands and thousands of sheep to graze on our pasture-lands; they gradually destroyed our forests in Bias to supply South-Western Tibet with fuel for the summer months. For this they not only paid nothing, but our native subjects had to convey the timber over the high passes without remuneration. Necessarily such unprincipled task-masters did not draw the line at extorting from our natives under any pretence money, food, clothes, and everything else they could possibly levy. Some were known to travel yearly as far south as Lucknow, Calcutta, and Bombay.

So much for the gentleness of the Tibetans—a hermit nation living in a closed country!

Chanden Sing, ever anxious to be polite and helpful, would not hear of my carrying my own sketch and note books as had always been my custom, but insisted on doing so himself.

"*Hum pagal neh!*" ("I am no fool!") said he with an expression of wounded feelings. "I will take great care of them."

We started up the steep road, having first descended to the level of the River Dholi, 800 feet lower than Khela, crossing by a wooden bridge. The zigzag up the mountain-side seemed endless. Here and there a cool spring of crystal water quenched our thirst, welcome indeed on that tedious ascent in the broiling sun. Six miles above Khela we had risen to 7120 feet, and from this point the incline became less trying. Still we rose to 7450 feet two miles farther on, where under the shade of some magnificent old trees, at Pungo, I halted for lunch. We had entered the first inhabited village of the Shokas, usually but erroneously

SHOKA WEAVERS

called Botiyas, and were now in that part of their country called Chaudas.

A pleasant surprise awaited me. A smart-looking lad in European clothes came boldly forward, and, stretching out his hand, shook mine for some considerable time in a jovial and friendly fashion.

"I am a Christian," said he.

"I should say that you were by they way you shake hands."

"Yes, sir," he proceeded. "I have prepared for you some milk, some *chapatis* (native bread), and some nuts. Please accept them."

"Thank you," I said. "You do not seem to be a bad Christian. What is your name?"

"Master G. B. Walter, sir. I teach in the school."

A crowd of Shokas had collected. Their first shyness having worn off, they proved to be polite and kind. The *naïve* nature and graceful manner of the Shoka girls struck me particularly on this my first introduction to them. Much less shy than the men, they came forward, and joked and laughed as if they had known me all their lives. I wished to sketch two or three of the more attractive.

"Where is my book, Chanden Sing?" I inquired of my bearer.

"*Hazur hum mallum neh!*" ("I do not know, sir!") was his melancholy answer as he searched his empty pockets.

"Ah! you villain! Is that the care you take of my notes and sketches? What have you done with them?"

"Oh Sahib, I drank some water at the Dholi River. I had the book then in my hand. I must have left it on a stone when I stooped to drink water from the stream," the wretched man explained.

It is hardly necessary to say that Chanden Sing was promptly despatched to the spot he had named, with strict orders not to appear before me again without the book. I spent two or three pleasant hours in having the primitive Shoka weaving-looms, the processes of spinning and cloth manufacture, explained to me. As can be seen from the illustration on p. 48, the weaving looms of the Shokas are in every way similar to those used by the Tibetans proper, and are quite simple in construction. The warp is kept at great tension, and the cloth-beam on which the woven tissue is rolled rests on the woman's lap during the process of weaving. There are no treadles in the Shoka loom, by which the two sets of warp threads are alternately raised or depressed between each time that the transverse thread is passed, and all work is done by hand. The transverse thread is beaten firmly home by means of a heavy prismatic piece of wood. The material used in weaving is yak or sheep's wool, either in its natural colour or dyed in the primary colours of red and blue and yellow, and one secondary only, green. Blue and red are used in the greater and equal proportion; then green. Yellow is very parsimoniously used. The thread is well twisted and is subjected to no preparation before spinning, leaving thus a certain greasiness in the closely-woven material that renders it waterproof.

Shoka women are very adept at this ancient art: they use several sets of heddles, and patiently sit out of doors day after day weaving most intricate and artistic patterns. These coloured tissues, if we except the simpler ones with blue ground and lines for women's garments, are usually very narrow (about seven inches in width), whereas the less elaborate ones, such as the white material of which men's clothes are made, average sixteen inches.

The patterns in these many-coloured materials are woven from memory, and do not contain curves or circles, but are entirely composed of lines and angles, combinations of small lozenges and squares separated by long tri-coloured parallel lines, forming, so far as weaving is concerned, the main Shoka ideas of decoration and ornament. The fabrics are extraordinarily strong. The narrow coloured cloth of better quality is used mostly for making bags in which money and food are carried; the coarser kind for the double sheep-loads.

The more talented of the Shoka young women show much ingenuity in carpet or rather rug making. They have copied the idea from old Chinese rugs which have found their way here *viâ* Lhassa, and though upon close examination it is true they differ considerably in quality and manufacture, they are pleasing enough to the eye. These rugs are woven upon coarse thread matting, the coloured material being let in vertically. A soft surface is obtained not unlike in general appearance to that of Persian carpets, but not quite so pleasant to the touch. These small rectangular rugs are offered in the house of Shoka gentlemen to guests to sit on, and are also used to render the Tibetan saddles less uncomfortable.

As time went on I became very anxious as to the missing book, for it contained all my notes of the journey. The thought of its being deposited on a rock washed by a rapid stream into which it might easily slip and be carried away kept me in a state of suspense. At last a staggering figure approached; it was Chanden Sing waving the book triumphantly in the air. He had run the distance of many miles down to the river and back so quickly that when he reached me he was utterly exhausted. He handed me the book, and once more we started, followed by Walter and the whole community, down the steep incline to the river. At this place some of the Shokas seized my hands and placed them on their foreheads, at the same time making deep bows. Others embraced my feet, while the women folks bade me the usual Hindustani "*Acha giao*" ("Go well").

After some time had been wasted, or at least spent, in receiving these odd salutations, I persuaded them to retrace their steps, and they left me.

CHAPTER VIII

Prayer by wind-power—Photography under difficulties—A night of misery—Drying up—Two lady missionaries—Their valuable work—An interesting dinner party—An "eccentric" man's tea party.

SHRINE AND FLYING PRAYERS

To reach Shosha I had to climb a further three miles, which proved almost as steep as the previous ascent to Pungo.

A curious custom of praying by wind - power, probably borrowed from the Tibetans, prevails among the Shokas. The Tibetans, with a more intense religion than the Shokas, use for this purpose not only the wind but even water to propel their praying machines. Let me explain these simple mechanical contrivances for prayers. One or more rags or pieces of cloth, usually white, but on occasions red or blue, are fastened and hung by one end to a string stretched across a road, a pass, or a path. On crossing a pass for the first time Shokas invariably cut a strip of cloth and place it so that it will flap in the breeze. Also when materials for a new dress are purchased or manufactured, it is customary for them to tear off a narrow strip of the stuff and make a flying prayer of it. As long as there is motion in it there is prayer, so that the natives tie them very fast to sticks, poles, or branches of trees; and certain shrubs and trees in weird romantic spots on the mountains are covered with these religious signs. Moreover, on the top of nearly every Shoka dwelling a vast number of similar little flags can be seen, as well as near their shrines and at the outer gates of a village.

I put up at the Titela Daramsalla, one mile above Shosha village. The weather had been threatening for several days, and a steady downpour came upon us during the evening. Work had been accumulating daily. I decided to develop the large number of plates I had taken on my journey, a job hateful beyond measure when you are on the move. Having duly unpacked all the developing dishes and prepared the different solutions, I set to work to make the shelter completely dark. The next important item required was water, and of this there was plenty in that wretched shanty! I had just developed half-a-dozen negatives, and was delighted at the excellent results, when, in consequence of the storm having grown more violent, the rain began dripping on my head through the leaky roof of the Daramsalla. To move all the trays of developers, baths, and fixing solution would have been a nuisance; besides, I was too interested in my work to be put out by such small trifles, so

I patiently stood this new discomfort. I shifted my position continually, merely with the result that the rain dripped alternately on my back, my legs, or my shoulders, according to my position. It fell in torrents, and the roof over me was so leaky that I might as well have been out in the open. I was sitting in a pool of water and could not lay my hands upon anything that was not drenched. Fortunately my boxes and cases were water-tight, or all the instruments and plates would have been damaged.

Annoying as it was, I had to give up work. The best thing to do was to go to sleep. Easier said than done. My bedding and blanket were soaked. The attempts to lie under a waterproof sheet failed, for I felt suffocated, so I passed the cover to my servant, who, rolling himself in it, was soon in the arms of Morpheus. Tired and disgusted, I crouched myself up and eventually fell asleep. I woke up in the morning with a biting pain in my toes. I had been lying face downwards, and had involuntarily stretched my legs during the night. I discovered to my horror that one foot rested in the developing bath and the other in the fixing solution, which I had forgotten to empty out of the large celluloid trays.

The morning was spent in drying up things in the sun, including our clothes, while we, clad in a "*doti*" (large loin-cloth as used by the natives of India), squatted down in the warmth in order to restore our saturated skins to their natural condition.

I was in the meantime interviewed by many Shokas, applying for medicines, and wishing to sell their native wares.

A pretty girl, from whom I bought a curious set of neck hangings made of musk-deer teeth, wished to be cured of the *goître*, a complaint too common, alas ! on these hills. Then a child was brought with a nasty tumour in a state of suppuration inside his left ear. Others wished to be cured of pains in the stomach and liver, which are very general among them owing to their abuse of liquor.

Upon hearing that two lady missionaries lived a mile and a half farther on, at Sirka, I gave myself the pleasure of calling upon them. They possessed a nice bungalow at an elevation of 8900 feet above sea level, by the side of which was another structure for the accommodation of converts and servants. Lower on the hillside they had built a dispensary and hospital.

I was received with the utmost courtesy by Miss Sheldon, M.D., and Miss Brown, of the Methodist Episcopal Mission. I have in my lifetime met with many missionaries of all creeds in nearly every part of the globe, but never has it been my luck before to meet two such charming, open-minded, and really hard-working ladies as the two who now so kindly received me.

WRINKLED SHOKA

"Come right in, Mr. Landor," said Miss Sheldon with her delightful American accent, and she shook hands with me in a good, hearty fashion.

The natives had praised to me the charity and helpfulness of this lady. I found this more than justified. By night or day she would never refuse help to the sick, and her deeds of kindness which became known to me are far too numerous to detail in these pages

Perhaps her most valuable quality is her perfect tact—a quality I have found none too common among missionaries. Her patience, her kindly manner towards the Shokas, her good heart, the wonderful cures she wrought among the sick, were items of which these honest mountaineers had everlasting praises to sing. A Shoka was telling me that it was not an uncommon thing for Miss Sheldon to give away all her own food supplies, and even the clothes from her back—courting for herself discomfort, yet happy in her good work.

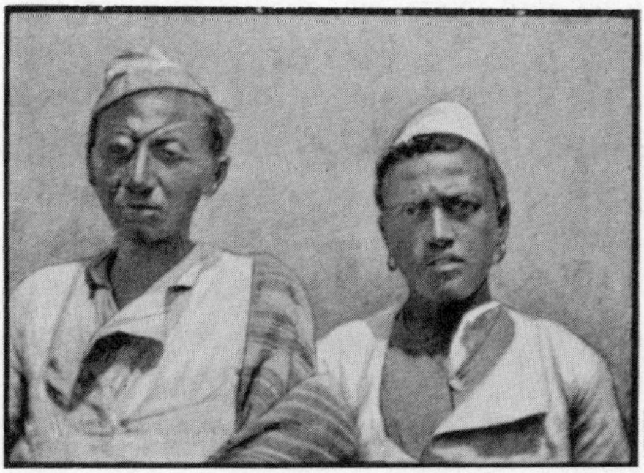

LAL SING TOKUDAR AND HIS BROTHER

With it was combined a charming modesty. No word about herself or her actions ever passed her lips. A pioneer in these parts, she evidently must have encountered much difficulty in the beginning. At present her good influence over the Shokas is very considerable. The same can be said of Miss Brown, who was in every way a worthy comrade of Miss Sheldon.

They have both in a comparatively short time become fully acquainted with the Shoka language, and can converse in it as fluently as in English, this fact alone endearing them greatly to the natives.

They were kind enough to ask me to dinner. "It is

Sunday," said Miss Sheldon, "and we shall have all our Christians dining with us. You will not mind, I am sure."

I assured her that nothing would interest me more.

I arrived punctually at the hour appointed, and on the verandah of the bungalow were laid some nice clean mats upon which we all sat cross-legged in native fashion. We three Europeans were provided with knife and fork, but all the natives helped themselves with their fingers, which they used with much dexterity. There were among the converts some Hindoos, some Shokas, some Humlis, and a Tibetan woman. All counted, I suppose they were about twenty, and it would be impossible to find a better behaved set of Christians anywhere. They ate heartily and only spoke when they were spoken to.

"I doubt whether I have ever dined with so many good Christians," said I jokingly to Miss Sheldon. "It is delightful."

"They would much like to hear some of the experiences of your travels if you would be kind enough to tell them. That is to say, if you are not too tired and do not mind."

Interpreted by Miss Brown, I related some of my adventures in the country of the Ainu. Rarely have I had such an interested audience. When the story ended they all salaamed me, and an old veteran Gourkha, one of the converts, took my hand and shook it warmly.

"You must not mind, Mr. Landor: you see, we treat our Christians like ourselves,"* quickly interrupted Miss Sheldon.

"Oh no, I do not mind," I replied. "On the contrary, I am glad to see it done."

I took my leave and asked the ladies to come to tea with

* N.B.—Anglo-Indians very rarely condescend to shake hands with the natives.

HOUSE OF A WEALTHY SHOKA

me the next day. The afternoon came and they arrived, when to my horror it flashed across my mind that I had neither cups, nor saucers, nor spoons. I had some tea, but I had no idea in which box it was, and to save my life I could not lay my hands upon it. This caused a frank and delightful remark on the part of Miss Sheldon to Miss Brown.

"Does not Mr. Landor remind you of 'that other' eccentric gentleman that came through here last year?"

The moment she had uttered the words Miss Sheldon saw what she had said, and we all laughed heartily.

"You know, Mr. Landor," put in Miss Brown, "we half foresaw that you would not be provided with these articles of luxury, and we brought our own cups and saucers."

The news was a great relief to me.

"Well now, let me persuade you to take some delicious chocolate instead of tea."

"Very good, we would prefer it. We have not had chocolate for a long time."

A solid block of chocolate was produced weighing twenty-eight pounds, and Chanden Sing set to chip off bits with a stone—a primitive but effective method. In the meantime the kettle was boiling, while my two visitors made themselves as comfortable as was possible under the circumstances on pack-saddle cases.

The tea party went off well, for the ladies, evidently suspecting the "eccentricity" of their host, had come provided not only with cups and saucers, but with spoons, cake, bread, butter, and biscuits!

CHAPTER IX

Discouraging reports—A steep ascent—How I came to deserve the name of "monkey"—Hard at work—Promoted in rank—Collapse in a gale of wind—Time and labour lost.

THE weather again became rainy and cold. The reports that I received of the state of the roads farther up were not encouraging.

"The track is impassable," said an old Shoka who had just arrived from Garbyang. "The Lippu Pass by which you wish to enter Tibet is still closed, and there is much snow on it still. Then the Jong Pen of Taklakot in Tibet, having been left unpunished for his last years' attack on Lieutenant Gaussen, has now a strong guard of three hundred men to prevent foreigners entering the country. The *Dakus* (brigands) infesting the region of the Mansarowar Lake seem to be more numerous this year than ever."

I shall come in for a lively time, I thought to myself.

My next camp was at Shankula, 7450 feet above the sea level. It was reached by going over a delightfully cool track, not unlike a shady path through a picturesque park, among tall cedars of Lebanon, beeches and maples, with here and there a stream or spring of water, and hundreds of black-faced, white-bearded monkeys playing and leaping from tree to tree.

I encamped by the river. The day was glorious. In front of me, north-east by east, stood, gigantic and majestic, some high snowy peaks. The valley was narrow, and the remainder of the snowy range of mountains was hidden from sight. What a lovely subject for a picture! I was tempted to halt and get out my paint-box and sketch-book; and abandoning my lunch, which was being cooked, I climbed to the summit of a high peak in order to obtain a more extensive view. The ascent, first on slippery grass, then over slaty rocks, was by no means easy, nor devoid of a certain amount of danger; but so keen was I to get to the top that I reached the summit very quickly, leaving halfway down the mountain slope the two men who had followed me. In places near the top there were rocks to climb that stood almost perpendicular, and it was necessary to use hands as well as feet. It was not unlike climbing up a rough wall. I was nevertheless well repaid for my trouble. The view from that high point of vantage was magnificent, and I confess that I felt almost too ambitious when, having unslung my paint-box, I attempted to reproduce on paper the scene before me.

"I am a fool," said I to myself, "to try and paint that! What painter could do those mountains justice?"

I dashed off the picture as usual very hastily, but never was a rash venture rewarded with poorer result, and those eternal giants remained unpainted.

Disconsolate, I made my way down. It was more difficult even than the climb up. A false step, a slip, and it might have cost my life, especially along the steep precipice, where I had to cling to anything projecting in the wall-like rock. I had gone four thousand feet higher than the camp, reaching an elevation of 11,450 feet above sea level.

It was this performance, watched anxiously from my camp

down below, as well as by the army of men belonging to the Deputy Commissioner of Almora, who was also here encamped, that won me the name among the natives of "Chota Sahib," the "Langur," the "small sir," the "monkey," a name of which I have been proud ever since.

Some seventy-three miles from Pithoragarh the Shankula River enters the Kali, the course of the Shankula being roughly from N.N.W. to S.S.E.

The track once crossed, the Shankula stream tends towards the South-East and with a gentle incline rises to 8570 feet at Gibti, where I encamped somewhat above the Gala Daramsalla. I had gone through forests of maple, beech, oak and rhododendrons, with a thick undergrowth of scrub and bamboo.

The Kali River, about two thousand feet down below my camp, marks the boundary between Nepal and Kumaon. From this high point the foaming stream can be seen for miles, winding between thickly wooded hills and mountains like a silver ribbon on a dark reposeful background.

The march from my last camp was a very short one, so I had the greater part of the day left for work. Previously I had usually halted in Daramsallas (stone-walled shelters), and in default of these my men put up for me a neatly-made "Chahna"* or "chöpper," a hut of mats and branches of trees, in the construction of which the Paharis are wonderfully dexterous. I had also my small "mountain tent," a *tente d'abri*, quite comfortable enough for ordinary requirements.

It seems, however, that this style of travelling is not considered *comme il faut* by the officials of India. It is the number and size of one's tents, according to these authorities,

* *Chahna*—Pahari. *Chöpper*, Dehsi—Hindustani.

that make one a greater or a smaller gentleman ! I had put up my tent—three feet high, seven feet long, and four feet wide—by the side of the two double-leaf eighty pound tents of the Deputy Commissioner, but this official and his companions were far from pleased with this act of familiarity. For a

THE TENT

double-tented sahib to be seen in company of another sahib whose bijou tent rose from the ground hardly up to one's waist, was *infra dig* and a serious threat to the prestige of the British in India. I was therefore politely requested to move from my cosy quarters to a more dignified abode lent me by the one-eyed Lal Sing, a Tokudar* and brother of the Patwari.†

* *Tokudar*—Head-village man. † *Patwari*—Accountant for a Pargana.

Being thus promoted in everybody's estimation except my own, I wrote and copied out my first article for *The Daily Mail,* and, having done this, I dined and spent a pleasant evening with Mr. G.

The night was stormy; the wind shook my tent. I went to sleep wrapped in my solitary camel-hair blanket. Some hours later a sharp knock on my head woke me. It was the centre pole of the tent that had moved out of its sockets and had fallen on me. This was followed by a rushing noise of canvas, and I found myself in a moment uncovered and gazing at the stars.

There were white things flying about in the air, and, to my horror, I discovered the leaves of my *Daily Mail* article scattered in the wind.

I jumped up, but of the ten or twelve foolscap leaves on very thin paper, I only managed to recover two or three. The others soared gracefully to and fro in the air, and I suppose settled eventually in the Kali. This meant recopying the article next day, a tedious job when you are burning to get on.

The sun rose. The camp began to wake up. All were shivering with cold. I took my usual cold bath surrounded by a half-frozen crowd of astonished onlookers, wrapped up in their thick woollen blankets, crouching round me with their chins on their knees.

The tent was recovered after a while, and soon all was ready to start.

CHAPTER X

The *Nerpani*, or "waterless track"—Exaggerated accounts—A long shot—The rescue of two coolies—Picturesque Nature—An involuntary shower-bath—The *Chai* Pass.

THE NERPANI ROAD

THE renowned *Nerpani*, or *Nerpania*, "waterless track," begins at Gibti. Very few travellers have been on this road, and by the accounts brought back many people have been prevented from imitating their example.

Personally I found the track far better than I anticipated. I have been on worse mountain roads among less precipitous cliffs. From what I had heard it seemed as if the greater part of the road for several miles was supported on crow-bars fixed in the rock, but such is not the case. Here and there, however, are spots where tracks have to be trodden upon overhanging precipices; and where the perpendicular cliff did not allow of a road to be cut except at great expense, crowbars have been more or less firmly planted horizontally in the rock, and a narrow path made over them with large slabs of stone. The drop from the path to the river is often from eighteen hundred to two thousand feet, and the path is in many places no wider than six inches. But to any sure-footed traveller that would not constitute a real danger. The road is tedious, for the Nerpania cliff along which it has been constructed is subdivided into three smaller cliffs, separated in turn one from the other by ravines. It is thus troublesome to climb up and down some thousands of feet, each time along interminable and badly put together flights of steps, only to descend again on the other side. Some of the descents, especially the last to Gulamla, are precipitous, but with no nails in one's shoes and no stick in one's hand, there is really very little danger for people accustomed to mountaineering.

These are the main elevations on the road: Gibti, 8650 feet, 6750 feet, 7600 feet, 6700 feet, 7100 feet, 6600 feet from Gulamla. At bearings magnetic 350°, going close to the river-bed through a gorge, one obtains a fine view of a huge gneiss peak towering on the left side of the *Neganza* or *Nejangar* Mountain. This peculiar rock, shaped like a fortress, goes by the name of the Ladjekut Peak and rises where the Nejangar River meets the Kali. Here we pitched our tents.

Towards sunset there was much agitation in camp over the appearance of wild goats on the other side of the Kali River in Nepal.

"Your rifle, Sahib, your rifle!" shouted a chorus of impatient natives. "Quick, quick, your rifle!"

I seized my Mannlicher and followed the excited gang to a place some hundred yards away, where a large boisterous crowd had collected to watch the game.

"Where are they?" said I, as I could not see anything.

"There, there!" they all screamed at the top of their voices, pointing to the summit of the opposite cliff over four hundred yards distant.

"Oh, that is too far."

"No, no, Sahib, please shoot," they all implored.

I put up the Lyman back-sight to four hundred yards, took aim and fired. Down came rolling from rock to rock the poor wild goat, amid the frantic excitement of the crowd around me. It rolled down until it came to the shrub and vegetation, where its progress became slower. It fell on the small trees and, bending them by its weight, it would drop a few seconds later on to a lower one. The trepidation on our side was intense. At last the graceful body struck across a bigger tree and swung on it for some minutes. The oscillation slowly ceased, and tree and goat became motionless. There our prey stuck fast.

Hatchets were immediately produced, and two tall trees hurriedly cut and felled. A bridge was being spanned to cross the dangerous cold and swift waters of the Kali. A tree was thrown across, and its point just about reached a high rock on the other side. Then, amidst a dead silence, a coolie balanced himself over it. He had nearly reached the opposite bank when there was a crash. The tree broke, and the man was in the water, frightened and screaming pitifully, clutching a branch with convulsive fingers.

Another coolie went to his rescue, but the tree being now swung by the current, he also was pitched into the water. It was only after a terrible moment of suspense that our men had the common sense to draw the tree back towards the shore. One and all joined in a supreme effort, and the two men were eventually saved.

Our way to the next camp was first through a high narrow gorge. A beautiful waterfall on terraces faced us. From 6700 feet, the road ascended to 7650 feet, then on flights of steps and in places over crowbars the weary traveller descended to 7000 feet, where at Malpa the road was for a

THE NERPANI ROAD

space nearly level. The Malpa River, running from North to South, was crossed. On the Nepal side across the Kali the vegetation was luxuriant, while on the Kumaon side it was sparse and bare. Farther on another beautiful waterfall.

The track now rose on a steep incline to 8120 feet among huge rocks and boulders. What with the gigantic snow-peaks, the pretty waterfalls, the weird character

Lithographed by F. A. Brockhaus, Leipzig (Germany).

THE NERPANI TRACK.

of the country traversed, one got so interested in one's surroundings that one forgot all about any difficulty of climbing. From barren hills and rocks the track suddenly became clayish and sandy, and in a series of zigzags well

THE NERPANI ROAD

shaded by *Tchuk*, *Utish*, and *Ritch* trees, with a thick undergrowth of scrub wood and stunted vegetation, we found ourselves down as low as 6750 feet, ascending immediately after in a very short distance to 8100 feet to Camp Lahmari.

In olden times the path went over the highest part of the cliff, and it took a good walker the whole day to reach from one spring of water to the next, hence the name of "waterless."

Here practically ended the *Nerpani* (waterless track), and an involuntary shower-bath soon awaited the passer-by,

THE CHAI-LEK PASS

drenching him to the skin, unless he was provided with waterproof and umbrella. The spray descended from a great height for a length of some thirty or forty yards, the road being very narrow and very slippery, so that progress was particularly slow. The name of the waterfall was *Takti*.

The track, if not more level, was nevertheless better after this to the sore-footed walker. It was less rocky and devoid of the tiresome flights of steps.

On leaving Lahmari we immediately had a steep rise to 9600 feet. Then a drop of 400 feet, and we found ourselves on the Buddi River, a tributary of the Kali. Just above the bridge was a magnificent waterfall, by the left side of which we found a kind of grotto hollowed out under a rock. The Shokas and Tibetans used it as a camping ground.

A NARROW GORGE BETWEEN TWO MOUNTAINS

To our right, high up on the cliffside, was the picturesque village of Buddi (9300 feet), with its two- and three-storeyed houses. Below and over it in long zig-zags could be seen the track ascending to the top of *Chai-Lek,* or *Tcheto* Pass as the Shokas call it. At bearings magnetic 170° we had the towering Namjun peak, so high that I was told it could be seen even from Almora and Ranikhet.

Then as we proceeded up the steep clayish track, I could not, on looking back, help admiring the magnificent Kali valley with its gigantic cliffs and gorges surmounted by lofty snow peaks. On the *Chai* Pass my two aneroids registered an altitude of 11,190 feet. I was now on a small flat tableland. Darcy Bura, the richest Shoka trader from Buddi, had erected here a bargain-house for the purchase and exchange of borax, salt, wool, and other articles from Tibet. On the left side of the road a large cave in the rock had been walled and partly roofed over for the use of wife-seekers from the villages of Buddi and Garbyang. These houses were called *Rambangs,* and were an old institution among the Shokas, of which I shall have occasion to speak at length later on. As everywhere else, a few high poles with flying prayers and a bell had been placed near the pass.

CHAPTER XI

A series of misfortunes—Tibetan atrocities on British subjects—Tibetan exactions—Revolting cruelty to one of her Majesty's subjects—Assault on a British officer—A smart British Envoy.

MY arrival at Garbyang was watched by hundreds of men, women, and children, all squatting on the edge of the flat mud roofs of their habitations, while a few dozen people followed me respectfully to my camping ground beyond the village. A large tent had been put up for me by Pundit Gobaria's brother, who had been informed of my coming by Anti Ram Sah, my banker at Almora. Mr. G., Deputy Commissioner, arrived later.

I was very anxious to make immediate arrangements to enter Tibet, but all my efforts to obtain reliable followers were of little avail.

I heard to my regret, a day or two later, that the plan of my journey, which with so much trouble and care I had kept secret, had been divulged to the Tibetan authorities. Misfortunes never come singly! Against my will I had been advised to pay a certain sum at Almora, in exchange for which I received a letter of credit on Pundit Gobaria, a rich trader of Garbyang, who was to pay me the amount in silver. Unluckily, Gobaria was still absent in Nepal, and no one else could cash a cheque for the amount I wanted,

This was tiresome—all the more so as I had counted on the money. I immediately sent a runner to Almora to have the sum in silver sent at once. This involved much publicity and considerable risk.

THE GATES OF GARBYANG

Also delay was inevitable. All the passes were closed and fresh snow was falling daily. It was just possible with much difficulty for a man to cross the Lippu Pass, but no baggage could be taken through. I made up my mind to remain a few days in Garbyang, and took this opportunity to have a large Tibetan tent manufactured to shelter my future followers—if ever I could find any—and it might help me, I calculated, to become friendly with the natives, among whom I hoped to find some willing followers.

Doctor H. Wilson, of the Methodist Evangelical Mission, went to much trouble in trying to get together men for me, but though his influence was and is considerable in Bias and Chaudas, his efforts were not crowned with success. The Shokas know well how terribly cruel the Tibetans are. They have suffered at their hands more than once, and even of recent years the Government of India has had reported by its own officers cases of horrible tortures inflicted by the Tibetan authorities on British subjects captured by them on our side of the frontier. Some of the atrocities committed by the Lamas on British subjects are revolting, and it is a matter of great regret and indignation to the Englishmen who visit these regions to think that the weakness of our officials in Kumaon has allowed and is allowing such proceedings still to go on. So incapable are they, in fact, that the Jong Pen of Taklakot in Tibet sends over, "with the sanction of the Government of India," his yearly emissaries to collect Land Revenue* from British subjects living on British soil. The Shokas have to pay this tribute, and do so out of fear—in addition to other taxes and trade dues iniquitously exacted by the Tibetans.

On the slightest pretext the Tibetans arrest, torture mercilessly, fine, and confiscate property of, British subjects on British territory.

At the time of my visit there could be seen, in Garbyang and other villages, British subjects (Shokas) who had been mutilated by the Tibetan authorities.

Even Dr. H. Wilson, who had erected a dispensary at

* The sums are now collected by the Political Peskhar and handed over in Garbyang to the Tibetans.

Gungi (one march beyond Garbyang), was lately threatened with confiscation—and worse perhaps—if he did not immediately comply with the exactions of the Tibetans. He declined to do so and reported the matter to the Government, relying on a good rifle in the house and his many servants. His determination not to be intimidated seems to have given him temporary security, for the Tibetans are as cowardly, when they think themselves matched, as they are cruel.

Let me quote one example of cruelty which occurred as late as 1896. A Shoka trader, undeniably a British subject, had gone over the border, as is customary with them during the summer, to dispose of his merchandise on the Tibetan market. He and another Shoka, also a British subject, had a quarrel. Aware that the first Shoka was wealthy, the Tibetan authorities took this pretext to arrest him and impose upon him an exorbitant fine, besides the additional punishment of two hundred lashes to be administered to him by order of the Jong Pen. The Shoka remonstrated on the plea that he had done no harm, and that being a British subject they had no right to so punish him. The Jong Pen saw his orders executed, and further commanded his men to cut off the wretched prisoner's hands. He was made over to two soldiers entrusted with the carrying out of the sentence. They led him away to the place of punishment. The Shoka was of a powerful build and possessed courage. Though half dead and covered with wounds, he overcame his guardians and escaped. The alarm was instantly given and a large party of horsemen sent to capture him. They caught him up, and when at close range fired on him and wounded him in the knee, smashing the kneecap.

GARBYANG

He was surrounded, pounced upon, beaten mercilessly, and last but not least, all his fingers were one by one crushed into pulp between two heavy stones. In this condition he was dragged before the Lamas, only to be decapitated! Mr. Sturt, an able and just officer, who was then Deputy Commissioner at Almora, became acquainted with these facts, and, having fully ascertained their accuracy, reported them to the Government, strongly advising immediate action against the Tibetans for this and other cruelties that were constantly taking place on our frontier. Though it was undeniably proved that the victim was a British subject, the Government of India took no steps in the matter.

MATAN SING CHAPRASSI

The same year, 1896, Lieutenant Gaussen, who on a shooting trip tried to enter Tibet by the Lippu Pass, was surrounded by Tibetan soldiers, and he and his servants were seriously ill-treated. The British officer received a nasty wound on his forehead, and one of his servants, who behaved heroically, was so cruelly handled that to-day, two years later, I hear he is still an invalid.

NARENGHIRI CHAPRASSI

Mr. J. Larkin, Deputy Collector at Almora, was then despatched to the frontier. No better man could have been sent. Firm, just, and painstaking, he became popular and much respected among the Shokas. He listened to their troubles and sufferings; he administered justice wherever possible. He refused audience to no one, and during his flying visit became well acquainted with the country, the people, and all that went on. The poor Shokas felt much relieved, thinking that at last the Tibetan abuses would be put an end to. They were not mistaken, at least for a time. The Jong Pen of Taklakot was called upon to answer for his many misdeeds. He refused an interview. Mr. Larkin, sent word across the border that he would have no trifling and that he must come, upon which the Jong Pen, with his officers and Lamas, crossed the snowy Lippu Pass. Trembling with fear and bending low to the ground, the Tibetans, with abject servility, entered the tent of our British envoy. The account of the interview, which I received in full from a Shōka gentleman who was present as interpreter, is amusing and curious, showing the mutability and hypocrisy of the Tibetans. In the long run, and being well acquainted with the cowardice of his visitors, Mr. Larkin not only obtained redress on every point but gave the Jong Pen and his officers a severe harangue. The result of the interview was that the collection of the Land Revenue should be put a stop to, and that Tibetan law should no more be administered on our side of the frontier.

Mr. Larkin's visit to Bhot was cut short by urgent orders to return immediately to Almora.

The following year (the year of my visit, 1897), Mr. G., Deputy Commissioner, undid much that the previous officer had accomplished. The Jong Pen, when summoned, declined to come, and sent over deputies in his place. The upshot of it is, that Land Revenue is again paid by the Shokas to the Tibetan tax-collectors through the Peshar.

I have mentioned these facts as representative of many, and to show how it came that the natives, who had never had any protection from our Government, were disinclined, notwithstanding the temptations I offered them, to brave the dangers of Tibet. I, who later on suffered so much through being betrayed by Shokas, am the first to forgive and not to blame them. Though nominally our subjects, their actual rulers are the Tibetans, and we do nothing to protect them against the exactions and tortures of the intruders. Why then should we expect them to be faithful to us? The Shokas are not treacherous by nature, but they are compelled to be deceitful to protect their lives and their homes. Properly treated, these honest, gentle, good-natured mountaineers would assuredly become loyal and trustworthy subjects of her Majesty

CHAPTER XII

Tibetan threats—My birthday—Ravenous dogs—A big dinner—Shoka hospitality.

THE HOUSE WHERE I STAYED AT GARBYANG

THE Jong Pen of Taklakot, on hearing of my proposed visit, sent threats that he would confiscate the land of any man who came in my employ, besides menaces of "flogging" and subsequent "beheading" of myself and any one caught with me. Personally I paid little attention to these intimidations.

Consulting the calendar one day—a thing I did with great regularity in these regions—I made out that it was the first of June, and I then remembered that the following day would be my birthday. Feasts were scarce in these high altitudes, and the prospect before me was that they would in the near future be even scarcer. It therefore occurred to me that I could not better while away a day at least of this weary waiting than by treating myself to a real big feast.

SHOKA HOUSE WITH STRANGE LADDER

Chanden Sing was despatched round the village to summon up to my tent all the local Bunyas (tradespeople). Rice, flour, eight pounds of butter (*ghi*), a large quantity of lump sugar, pepper, salt, and a fat sheep were purchased. The latter was forthwith beheaded, skinned, and dressed in the approved fashion by the faithful Chanden Sing, who was indeed a jack of all trades.

Unfortunately, I am a careless house or rather tent keeper, and I entrusted my chaprassis with the job of stowing away the provisions, for which purpose a recess under the native low bedstead served to perfection, holding as it did the different-sized vessels, with the *bachri* (sheep) in pieces, and the rice, flour, butter, etc.

While this was being done, I worked away hard at writing, and getting interested, continued at it till an early hour of the morning; I got tired at last, and, wrapping myself up in my blanket, I soon went to sleep next to a heap of stones piled up by the cautious Chanden Sing.

"Sahib," had been his warning, "there are many hungry dogs about. If they come, here are a few missiles ready for them!" and he pointed at the ammunition.

"All right; good-night."

The wisdom of this was soon apparent, for I had not slept long when I was aroused by the hollow sound of lip-smacking, apparently arising from more than one mouth, accompanied by the movement of the stretched canvas bed on which I was lying. Jumping to my feet, I alighted upon a living mass of unwelcome guests; but before I even realised what had been going on, they had scampered away, the brutes! carrying between their tightly-closed jaws a last mouthful of my dainties.

The ammunition at my disposal was quickly used up—a poor revenge, even when I heard the yell of a dog I happened to hit in the dark. On striking a match, I found the large brass bowls emptied, the rice and flour scattered all over the tent, and the sheep practically vanished.

I determined not to be done out of this piece of indulgence, which now seemed desirable beyond words, although I crawled back into my blanket, and found for a while oblivion in sleep. I was no sooner up in the morning than I planned a new banquet. But in the nick of time, Mr. G., who had gone a march farther, returned with his escort of policemen, *moonshees*, pundits, and chaprassis.

SHOKA HOUSES

"Never mind, Landor," said he kindly, when I had told him of my trouble, "you come and dine with me. These chaps shall get you up a special dinner in their own way."

My stores were put under tribute, instead of the native Bunyas, and we had a very excellent meal indeed. We had Bovril soup and Irish stew, roast mutton, potted tongue, roast chicken, gigantic swan eggs poached on anchovy toast, jam omelette, chow-chow preserves, ginger biscuits, boiled rhubarb, and what not else—remembered by me with desperate longing, in the near future when any of these dainties would have been like manna from heaven. I must not forget, by the way, an excellent plum cake of no small dimensions, crammed full of raisins and candy, which I had brought from Mrs. G. at Almora to her husband, and to which we did, with blessings for her, the fullest justice.

Thanks to Mr. G. and also to the fortunate coincidence of receiving a batch of letters from parents and friends, which reached me on that day by runner from Khela, I do not think that I could have spent a happier birthday anywhere, and I knew well enough that these were to be the last moments of contentment—an end to the fleshpots of Egypt. After this I should be cut off from civilisation, from comfort even in its primitive form; and to emphasise this fact, it happened that on the very morning following my birthday, Mr. G. left and continued his journey to Almora.

The weather was cold and rain fell in torrents, the thermometer being never above 52° during the warmest hours of the day. My soaked tent stood in a regular pool of water, notwithstanding the double trenches round it, and several Shoka gentlemen had before asked me to abandon it and live in a house. They were all most anxious to extend to me hospitality, which I, not wishing to trouble them, and in order at all hazards to be entirely free and unhampered in my actions, courteously but firmly declined. Nevertheless, quite a deputation arrived on June 4, renewing their request; but I was determined to have my way. In vain! They would not see a Sahib under cold canvas while they themselves had comfortable homes. They held a consultation. Unexpectedly, and notwithstanding my remonstrances, my loads were suddenly seized and carried triumphantly on the backs of a long row of powerful Shokas towards the village. I had to follow *nolens volens*, and from that day on I grew through constant contact daily more convinced of the genuine friendliness and kindheartedness of these people.

To prevent my coming back, they even pulled down the tent, and, wet as it was, carried it away. Zeheram and Jaimal, two leading Shokas, held my hands and patted me on the back as they led me with every sign of courtesy to my new dwelling.

This turned out to be a fine two-storeyed building with nicely carved wooden door and windows coloured red and green. So great was the anxiety and fear of these good people that I should turn back at this juncture, that some twenty outstretched hands seized me by the arms, while others pushed me from behind up a flight of ten or twelve steps into the house, where I found myself the guest of my good friend Zeheram. I was given the front of the first floor, consisting of two large clean rooms, with a very fair native bedstead, a table and two or more *moras* (round cane stools covered with skin); and I had no sooner realised that I must stay than presents of sweets, preserved fruit, dried dates, and tea were brought for my acceptance—tea made in the Tibetan fashion with butter and salt in it.

Even if at first I had had slight apprehensions at the expression of such very unusual hospitality, these were soon dispelled, and I was proud to be assured by my host that I was the first Englishman (or for that, European or American) who had been allowed to enter the living part of a Shoka house and partake of food in a Shoka dwelling. The opportunity was too good to be lost, and I was sorely tempted to tarry among them, so as really to get an insight into their mode of living, their customs and manners.

CHAPTER XIII

Shoka hospitality—How I obtained much information—On a reconnoitring trip—A terrible slide.

THEY are indeed Nature's gentlemen, these worthy Shokas, and as such they did all in their power to make my stay among them pleasant. It was a contest between them as to who should entertain me first, and who should be the next. Invitations to breakfast and dinner literally poured in ; and those convenient "sick headaches," "colds," and "previous engagements," so opportune in more conventional parts, were of no avail here. No card—no friendly note bade one to come and be merry. They generally arrived *en masse* to fetch me. Pulling and pushing played a not unimportant part in their urging, and to decline was thus out of the question. Indeed I must confess there was but little inclination to decline on my part. When you arrived, your host spread out fine mats and rugs, of Tibetan and ancient Chinese manufacture, and often of great value. In front of a raised seat were displayed in shiny brass bowls the various viands and delicacies which constituted the meal. There was rice always ; there was curried mutton, milk and curd with sugar ; then *chapatis* made in Hindustani fashion and *Shale,* a kind of sweet pancake made of flour, *ghi* (butter), sugar or honey, also *Parsad,* a thick paste of honey, burnt sugar, butter and flour, all well cooked together—a dainty morsel even for a jaded palate.

I was invariably made to sit on the raised seat, which I did cross-legged, while the crowd squatted respectfully on the floor round the room, forming a semicircle with me in the centre. I generally ate with my fingers in their own manner, a courtesy they particularly appreciated, and

SHOKA CHILD BEING SMEARED WITH BUTTER

although I must have seemed awkward to them at first, I soon acquired a sort of dexterity in manipulating hot food—meat and vegetables, for instance—with my hand. The trick is not very difficult, but it requires practice. You gather up your five fingers downwards in the dish, seizing a mouthful, and with a rapid circular twist of the hand you collect as much sauce as you can round the morsel you have caught. With a still more rapid movement, and before anything has time to drip between your fingers, you half drop and half throw it into your mouth.

I soon found that I could, during these cordial repasts, enlivened as they were by moderate libations of *chökti* and *syrap* (wine and spirit distilled from wheat), acquire considerable knowledge of anthropological and ethnological interest, and gather also much valuable information about Tibet and its people. They became, in fact, in the few days I spent among them, confiding to such a degree, and looked upon me so much as one of themselves, that I soon obtained the run of the whole place. They came to confide their grievances and troubles; they related to me their legends and folk-lore. They sang to me their weird songs and taught me their dances. They brought me to their marriages and strange funerals; they took me to their sick men, women, and children, or conveyed them to me for cure. Thus, to my delight, and with such unique chances, my observations of a pathological, physiological, and anatomical character became more interesting to me day by day, and I have attempted to describe in a later chapter some of the things I was able to note.

After lingering in Garbyang for several days, I paid off my two chaprassis, Matan Sing and Narenghiri, and they returned to Almora.

On June 6 I started on a journey towards the frontier, with a view to reconnoitre.

Crossing into Nepal territory below Chongur village, and following upwards the right bank of the Kali River in a direction of 320° (bearings magnetic) I reached Kanwa, a Shoka village on a high cliff-like plateau under which meet the three rivers Kali, Taki, and Kuti. The Kali turns suddenly to 37° (bearings magnetic), while the

Kuti River keeps a general direction of 325° (bearings magnetic).

Having crossed again into Kumaon, I struck camp at Gungi. Before entering the village, I passed Dr. Wilson's dispensary, not then completed. In the village the houses were decorated with long poles joined by strings, from which hung and flew gaily in the breeze hundreds of wind prayers. The dwellings were mostly of the ancient, pure Shoka architecture, and not so fine or so clean as those in Garbyang. The place was picturesque, clear-cut against the curious background of the dome-like mountain, the Nabi Shankom, a peak of uncommon beauty with its grey and reddish striped strata. Near it on another mountain is the Gungi Shankom, a gigantic quadrangular rock of a warm yellow and reddish colour, not unlike a huge tower. When I reached its foot, the sun was casting his last dying rays on it, and the picture was so magical that I was tempted to sketch it. As I sat there, the shadow of the coming night rose higher and higher on the mountain-side, tinting it violet blue, and above it the Gungi Shankom stood resplendent

THE MASTER OF A HIGH SCHOOL
ALTITUDE 10,940 FEET

in all its glory like a tower of fire—till night descended covering the mountain first, and little by little the Gungi Shankom itself. I shall not easily forget this sight.

I slept under my little *tente d'abri* and found it delightfully cosy and warm.

GUNGI SHANKOM

At 10 A.M. the next day I raised camp. The elevation here was 10,940 feet. Interesting was the *Chiram*, a collection of tombs, five in number, made of slabs of white stone with poles placed vertically upon them, and from the summit of which hung flying prayers. The Kuti River to my left was wide and rapid. On the opposite bank the village of Ronkan (11,100 feet) made a pretty *vis-à-vis* to the Nabi village on our side of the stream, at the same elevation, and directly under the lee of the Nabi Shankom.

As I rose gradually along the river course the vegetation grew sparse, and in front of me there remained nothing but barren rocks and high snowy peaks. The spot where, from opposite sides, the Gunkan River and the Nail River throw themselves into the Kuti River is most picturesque. There are on the water's edge a few pine-trees, but above there is nothing but wilderness—rock and ice and snow.

I soon came upon much snow, and places where the track along the mountain-side was undiscoverable. Walking was tiresome enough on the loose shingle and shale, but it

ZAZZELA MOUNT, NEAR GUNGI

became worse when I actually had to cut each step into the frozen snow. The work was tedious to a degree, and the progress slow. After a while I noticed a series of lofty snow tunnels over the raging stream, which is earlier in the season covered entirely by a vault of ice and snow. The higher I got the harder and more slippery grew the snow. The soles of my shoes having become soaked and frozen made walking very difficult. At 12,000 feet, being about

INVOLUNTARY TOBOGGANING

three hundred feet above the stream, I had to cross a particularly extensive snowfield, hard frozen and rising at a very steep angle. Some of my coolies had gone ahead, the others were behind. Notwithstanding the track cut by those ahead, it was necessary to re-cut each step with one's own feet, so as to prevent slipping. This was best done by hammering several times into the white sheet with the point of one's shoe until a cavity was made deep enough to contain the foot and to support one upright. It ought to be done carefully each time, but I fear I had not the patience for that. I thought I had found a quicker method, and by raising my knee high, I struck the snow with my heel, leaving my foot planted until the other one had by the same process cut the next step.

CHIRAM

It was in giving one of these vigorous thumps that I hit a spot where, under a thin coating of snow, was hard ice. My foot, failing in its grip, slipped, and the impulse caused me to lose my balance. I slid down the steep incline at a terrific pace, accompanied in my involuntary tobogganing over ice and snow by the screams of my horror-stricken coolies. I realised that in another moment I should be pitched into the stream, which would have meant being carried under the long tunnel of ice to meet certain death beneath it. In those few seconds I found time to speculate even as to whether those stones by the water's edge would stop me, or whether the impetus must fling me past them into the river. I attempted to get a grip in the snow with my frozen fingers, to stem myself with my heels, but with no success, when I saw ahead of me a large stone rising above the snow. With desperate tension of every nerve and muscle, I knew as I approached it, with the foaming water yonder, that it was my only hope. I consciously straightened my legs for the contact. The bump was tremendous, and seemed to shatter every bone in my body. But it stopped me, and I was saved only a few feet from the water's edge—miraculously, although fearfully bruised, with no bones broken.

My fingers were cut by the ice and bleeding; my clothes were torn. When I was able to stand, I signalled to the frightened and wailing coolies above to go on, and I myself proceeded along the watercourse until I found a spot from which I could regain the upper track.

SHOKA CHILD SMEARED WITH BUTTER WHICH IS LEFT TO BE ABSORBED IN THE SUN

CHAPTER XIV

A palaver—To see is to believe—Dangers and perils on the snow and ice—*Thar* and *Ghural*—Stalking—A tiring climb to 16,000 feet—The collapse of a snow bridge.

AT Kuti I halted and summoned the leading natives to my tent.

Would it be possible, I asked them, to get over the Lumpiya Pass or the still higher Mangshan ? The first is a rarely frequented pass on the way to Gyanema, the other a high and most difficult pass by which it is possible, though not easy, to reach the Rakstal Lake by the jungle without going near a Tibetan settlement or encampment.

"No," was the decided answer from all the Shokas. "The snow is now too deep. Fresh snow falls daily. For another fortnight at least no human being can get across. To attempt it will mean losing one's life. At their best during one month in summer, those two passes are arduous and dangerous. Now it would be mere folly to attempt their ascent."

With my distressingly sceptical nature I believe little that I do not see. I started next morning to observe for myself. My bearings were roughly North-West. Seeing me determined, several of the Kutial Shokas changed their mind and volunteered to follow me. They were of considerable help in many dangerous places. Here and there a few paces of narrow track were uncovered, otherwise we went long distances on frozen snow, over precipices down which it was almost fatal to look.

The lucky hairbreadth escape of the previous day con-

KUTI

tributed to make me lose confidence, not in myself, but in that white emblem of purity and innocence, in reality the most treacherous substance in creation. I soon found that wherever there was snow there was trouble. In spots where the snow was particularly hard frozen we dared not attempt to walk on the steep slippery surface, and we had to descend to the river, which was here bridged over completely with ice and snow. Crossing, we would attempt progress on the other side, and having proceeded with difficulty for a few hundred yards, had to retrace our steps and try the first bank again. We thus crossed and recrossed the Kuti River more than half-a-dozen times, each crossing being preceded

OLD SHOKA WOMAN SMOKING

by a precipitous descent and immediately followed by a steep ascent. The cracks in the ice by the water-side were constant and perilous, and we did not risk remaining near them longer than was necessary. In six or seven hours we had walked a distance of less than four miles. Leaving the Kuti River and following due North the course of a tributary, the Kambelshio, we crossed over to its farther bank and pitched our tents at an altitude of 13,420 feet.

There remained a few hours of daylight when we arrived, and I employed them by going after *Thar* or *Tehr* and *Ghural* (Himahlyan chamois) a couple of miles farther. I rose to 15,000 feet on a needle-like peak towering over the spot where, in a narrow picturesque gorge, the Tongzu pangti enters the Kuti River. The sources of the Tongzu pangti are about a thousand feet higher than the spot where it meets the Kuti River, and the stream has its birth from the melting snows, descending precipitously and in a very short distance into the larger river.

The rocks are here furred with saltpetre, and it is said to be a favourite spot for Thar.*

I enjoyed my trip so much that, rising with the sun, I started on the following morning to repeat my experience. Moreover, I wanted to climb to some high point wherefrom I could make certain whether it was possible to proceed immediately across the Himahlyan range, or whether it was advisable to wait patiently until the snow had to some extent disappeared. I walked four miles from camp, reaching an altitude of 16,000 feet. The ascent was rather tiring. Having wounded a Thar, I went after it up

* The *Gural* is the Himahlyan chamois found at even comparatively low elevations. They are generally seen in herds, with the exception of the oldest males, which are usually met with alone. It is not uncommon to see as many as eight or ten together, especially during their feeding time, shortly after sunrise and an hour or two before sunset.

Tehr or Thar (male) and Jahral (female) is the true and proper wild goat of the higher Himahlyan range. It is rarely found lower than 7000 feet and often as high as 15,000 feet above sea level. Those found at lower elevations do not possess quite such a luxuriant growth of hair, nor, I am told, are their curved horns quite so long. They climb about precipices and dangerous spots with the greatest ease.

SNOW BRIDGES OVER THE KUTI RIVER

a fatiguing snow-field at a speed too great to be comfortable at such a very high elevation. When I reached the top, I was out of breath and the Thar too far off for a second shot.

The view this high point commanded was stupendous. For miles and miles—and it seemed hundreds of miles—snow, snow, nothing but snow! There stood Jolinkan Mount rising above 19,000 feet. On either side of the Kuti River were peaks as high as 20,000 feet and more. Here and there the white sheet that covered the surrounding country seemed almost greenish. Those spots were glaciers, and I saw many of them, feeding as they do the numerous streams flowing into the Kuti River. I returned to camp for lunch. It was useless to proceed and even more useless remaining still. I gave orders to raise the camp, and at 2 P.M. we were under way back to Kuti.

The day had been an unusually warm one, and the surface of the snow, so hard the previous day, was now soft and watery. Several of the snow bridges had already disappeared.

I had descended to the river preceded by some of my coolies. Two of them just in front of me were crossing over the stream on a thick and broad archway of ice. I was waiting for them to be safely across. When the men had nearly reached the other side they noticed a peculiar vibration underfoot. Scrambling away as best they could, they gave the alarm.

I drew back hastily. In the nick of time! for with a deafening roar like magnified thunder echoed from cliff to cliff, down went the bridge. The huge pieces of ice, only a moment before forming part of the vault, were now swept away by the furious stream and thrown with tremendous force against the next bridge, which quivered under the terrible clash.

Three days' marching over the same route brought me back to Garbyang.

CHANDEN SING AND THE DAKU ROLLING UP MY BEDDING

CHAPTER XV

An earthquake—Curious notions of the natives—A Shoka tailor and his ways—The arrival of silver cash—Two rocks in the Kali—Arrogance of a Tibetan spy.

ON hearing that Dr. Wilson was now in Garbyang I went to call upon him. Squatted on soft Chinese and Tibetan mats and rugs, we were enjoying cup after cup of tea and devouring *chapatis*, when suddenly the whole building began to shake and rumble in the queerest manner, upsetting teapot and milk and sending the *chapatis* roaming to and fro all over the room.

Leaving Dr. Wilson to save our precious beverage, I pulled out watch and compass to notice duration and direction of the shock. It was undulatory, very violent, and oscillating from S.S.W. to N.N.E. The duration was exactly four minutes two seconds. The earthquake began at 5.20 P.M. and ended at 5h. 24m. 2s.

"It strikes me that it would have been wise to have gone out of the house," said I. "It is a wonder the building did not collapse. My cup is full of mud and débris from the ceiling." *

"I have saved the tea for you!" said the Doctor, trium-

* The ceilings of Shoka houses are plastered with mud.

phantly lifting in his muscular hands the teapot, which he had carefully nursed. He had soon discovered my devotion to the yellow liquid.

We were quietly going on with our refreshment when a band of excited Shokas broke into the room.

"Sahib! Sahib! where has it gone?" cried they in a

A WELL-ATTENDED SCHOOL

chorus, stretching their hands towards me and then folding them in sign of prayer. "Sahib! tell us where it has gone!"

"What?" rejoined I, amused at their suspense.

"Did you not feel the earth shake and quiver?" exclaimed the astounded visitors.

"Oh yes, but that is nothing."

"Oh no, Sahib! That is the precursory notice of some great calamity. The 'spirit' under the earth is waking up and is shaking its back."

"I would rather it shook its back than mine," said I jokingly.

"Or mine," added the Doctor lightly, much to the astonishment of our awestricken callers.

"Which way did it go?" repeated the impatient Shokas.

I pointed towards the N.N.E. and they gave a sigh of satisfaction. It must have proceeded to the other side of the Himahlyas.

It appears, according to the primitive notions of the Shokas, that inside the earth lives in a torpid condition an evil spirit in the shape of a gigantic reptile. The rumbling preceding an earthquake is, to the Shoka mind, nothing else than the heavy breathing of the monster previous to waking, whereas the actual shock is caused by the brute stretching its limbs. When fully awake the serpent-like demon darts and forces its way in one direction, compelling the earth to quake all along its subterranean passage, often causing by so violent a procedure great damage to property and loss of life, not to speak of the fear and terror which it strikes in man and beast, should the capricious spirit by chance make a return journey to the spot below the earth's crust directly underfoot. It is curious and interesting, in analysing these crude notions, to find that, independently of the cause attributed to its origin, the Shokas are aware of the fact that an earthquake "travels" in a certain direction. Moreover, common symptoms of the approach of a violent earthquake, such as depression and heaviness in the atmosphere, which they attribute to a feverish state of the giant reptile, are readily recognised by them.

On my return to civilisation some months later I discovered that on the same day a violent shock was felt all over India, causing considerable damage, especially in Calcutta.

I had on first arriving in Garbyang ordered a tent, and

the tailor who was entrusted with its manufacture had, after several days' intoxication, completed it. It was on the Tibetan pattern, with picturesque ornaments in blue. He had also been making me some Nepalese clothes, and these really turned out quite a success, no small wonder considering the way he went to work. I had given him cloth and lining, which he took away with him, but he never troubled to take my measure ! He simply assured me that the suit would be ready on the following day. This was of course not the case, and on the next afternoon and for six consecutive days he placed himself in a state of hopeless intoxication under my window, singing, and making comical salaams each time I, after the custom of the country, threw something at him to induce him to go away. On the seventh day I caught him and shook him by the ears, explaining that if the clothes were not ready before nightfall, I would, in default of other tailors, sew them myself.

"I have a drop too much in me," confessed the amusing rascal. "I will go to sleep now. When I wake in the afternoon I shall be sober and will finish my work. Do not be angry, Sahib. If only you drank yourself, Sahib, you would know how lovely it is to be drunk." His philosophy did not agree with mine. But I felt sure that I had so far impressed him, that he knew he must risk some personal violence if he delayed much longer. Sure enough, late in the evening he came with his work.

"How they will fit I do not dare to guess," I remarked to Dr. Wilson, "considering the condition the man has been in while making them, and taking into account that he never measured me nor tried them on. After all, Nepalese clothes should be tight-fitting all over."

Wonderful as it may seem, the clothes fitted like a glove.

Clearly, that man was a genius. Anyhow he was intemperate enough to have been one.

* * * * *

One day I had gone for a walk along the deserted road from the village. I was about a mile and a half from the inhabited part, when three men, who had been fast approaching, stood with blunt swords in front of me. They waved their blades clumsily and shouted at the top of their voices in an excited manner: "*Rupiya! Rupiya!*" ("Rupees! Rupees!") Without thinking of the money that I had sent for and expected to receive, I took their attitude as a threatening demand for the cash I might have on me. They were really grotesque in their gesticulations, and I brusquely pushed by them and continued my constitutional. When they saw me depart, they scurried away hastily towards Garbyang, and I gave the occurrence no further thought. On my return to the village, however, some hours later, a crowd of Shokas came up to me announcing that my money had arrived, and that the scared messengers, not daring to come near me a second time, had gone to Dr. Wilson's house. There I found a *peon* and two *chaprassis*, the three men I had met on the road. They had brought a sum of eighteen hundred rupees in silver, nearly all in two-anna and four-anna pieces (sixteen annas to a rupee), which I had sent for from my banker, Anti Ram Sah, at Almora, and which it had taken three men to carry, owing to its weight.

After an easy explanation with these three very peaceful highwaymen, the silver was conveyed to my room, and the greater part of the night had to be spent in counting the diminutive coins and packing them up in rolls of ten rupees each.

* * * * *

Just below Garbyang in the Kali River were, among a mass of others, two large rocks in the centre of the stream. These two rocks were constantly watched by the Shokas. The Kali, though named after a small spring below its real source, is, like most of its tributaries, mainly fed by melting snows. The greater quantity of water descends from the Jolinkan, the Lumpiya, the Mangshan, the Lippu, and the Tinker passes. The first four are in Kumaon, the last in Nepal. It stands to reason that the warmer the weather the greater is the quantity of snow melting on the passes, and therefore the higher the level of the river. When the two rocks are altogether under water all the passes are known to be open.*

MY BANKER AND AGENT

During the time I was in Garbyang I never had the luck to see this, but the level of the river was daily rising, and the time of tiresome expectation was certainly relieved by many amusing, and a few awkward incidents.

Having once been informed of my plans, the Jong Pen of Taklakot in Tibet was kept fully acquainted with my movements. His spies went daily backwards and forwards with details about me. This my friends confided to me regularly.

* N.B. The Lippu Pass, the lowest of all, may be crossed, with difficulty, nearly all the year round.

One of these emissaries, a stalwart Tibetan, more daring than the rest, actually had the impudence to enter my room, and to address me in a boisterous tone of voice. At first I treated him kindly, but he became more and more arrogant, and

THE VALLEY OF GARBYANG

informed me, before several frightened Shokas to whom he was showing off, that the British soil I was standing on was Tibetan property. The British, he said, were usurpers and only there on sufferance. He declared that the English were cowards and afraid of the Tibetans, even if they oppressed the Shokas.

This remark was too much for me, and it might anyhow have been unwise to allow it to pass unchallenged. Throwing myself on him, I grabbed him by his pigtail and landed in his face a number of blows straight from the shoulder. When I let him go, he threw himself down crying, and implored my pardon. Once and for all to disillusion the Tibetan on one or two points, I made him lick my shoes clean with his tongue, in the presence of the assembled Shokas. This done, he tried to scamper away, but I caught him once more by his pigtail, and kicked him down the front steps which he had dared to come up unasked.

Chanden Sing happened to be basking in the sun at the foot, and seeing the hated foreigner make so contemptible an exit, leapt on him like a cat. He had heard me say, "Ye admi bura crab!" ("That man is very bad.") That was enough for him, and before the Tibetan had regained his feet, my bearer covered his angular features with a perfect shower of blows. In the excitement of the moment, Chanden Sing, thinking himself quite the hero, began even to shy huge stones at his terror-stricken victim, and at last, getting hold of his pigtail, to drag him round the yard—until I interfered and stopped the sport.

CHAPTER XVI

The *Rambang*—Shcka music—Love-songs—Doleful singing—Abrupt ending—Solos—Smoking—When marriage is contem-plated—The *Delang*—Adultery—Punishment.

MOTEMA, A SHOKA BEAUTY

ONE Shoka institution, surprising in a primitive people, but nevertheless, to my way of thinking, eminently sensible and advantageous, is the Rambang, a meeting-place or club where girls and young men come together at night, for the sake of better acquaintance, prior to entering into matrimony. Each village possesses one or more institutions of this kind, and they are indiscriminately patronised by all well-to-do people, who recognise the institution as a sound basis on which marriage can be arranged. The Rambang houses are either in the village itself, or half way between one village and the next, the young women of one village thus entering into amicable relations with the young men of the other and *vice versâ.* I visited many of these in company with Shokas, and found them very interesting. Round a big fire in the centre of the room men and women sat in couples, spinning wool and chatting merrily, for everything appeared decorous and cheerful. With the small hours of the morning, they

ON THE WAY TO THE RAMBANG

seemed to become more sentimental, and began singing songs without instrumental accompaniment, the rise and fall of the voices sounding weird and haunting to a degree. The Shoka men and women possess soft, musical voices, and the sounds which they utter are not simply a series of notes emitted through the throat, but, as it were, the vibration of impressions coming from the heart, and transmitted by means of their voices to others. Eastern in its character, the Shoka music is pleasing to the Western ear, not because it possesses quick progressions, flourishes, or any elaborate technicalities, but because it conveys the impression of reality and feeling. The responsive duets, sung by a young man and answered by a girl, pleased me most. All their songs are plaintive, and contain modulations of the voice so mysteriously charming in effect, and so good in tone, that they really affect one profoundly. They only sing when the mood takes them; never with a view to please others, but always simply to give vent to their emotions. Their love-songs generally open with a sentimental recitative, and then change into actual singing, with frequent modulations from one key into another. The time is irregular, and though certain rhythmical peculiarities recur constantly, yet each performer gives to what he sings so strong a personality of execution as to make it almost an individual composition. Any one hearing Shokas sing for the first time would imagine that each singer was improvising as he went along, but on closer comparison it will be found that musical phrases, certain favourite passages and modulations in the voice, constantly recur not only in each song, but in all songs. They seem all of them based on the same doleful tune, probably a very ancient one, and only the different time in which it is given, and the eccentricities of the singer, give it a separate and special character. One characteristic of Shoka songs—as of so many other Oriental tunes—is that they have no rounded ending, and this, to my ears, rather spoiled them. A similar abrupt break is a feature of their dances and their drum-beating. The song suddenly stops in the middle of the air with a curious grating sound of the voice, and I could not obtain any entirely satisfactory explanation of this : the only answer given me was that the singer could not go on for ever, and that as long as he stopped it did not matter how he did it. Further, they considered an abrupt ending most suitable to music (or dancing), as it immediately brought you back to your normal state, should your mind have been carried away. One pleasant feature was that their songs were never sung in a loud tone of voice, nor did they aim at notes too high or too low for their voices, but kept themselves well within their compass.

SHOKA EARRING

SHOKA EARRING

The only difference between solos given by men, and those sung by women, was that the former showed more plaintiveness and sentimentality, and greater mutability of thought, whereas the latter were more uniform, more lively, and less imaginative in their representation of feelings. The words of the love-songs, nearly always *impromptu*, can hardly be set down in these pages. From our standard of morality, and away from their own special surroundings, they might seem almost lewd, while in their place they certainly did not impress me as offensive. When singing, the Shokas usually raise the end of their white shawl or dress, and hold it by the side of the head.

Smoking was general, each couple sharing the same pipe. A few burning sticks of pine stuck in the rough wall formed the only illumination, save the fire in the centre of the room slowly burning out. Signs of sleepiness became evident as morning came, and soon they all retired in couples, and went to sleep in their clothes on a soft layer of straw and grass. There they slept peacefully in a row, and I retraced my steps to my diggings amidst a deafening barking of pariah-dogs. At these gatherings every Shoka girl regularly meets with young men, and while she entertains the idea of selecting among them a suitable partner for life, she also does a considerable quantity of work with her spinning-wheel. Eventually, when a couple consider marriage advisable, the young man, dressed in his best clothes, proceeds to the house of his intended father-in-law, carrying with him a pot of *chökti* (wine), dried fruit, *ghur* (sweet paste), *miseri* (sugar-candy), and grilled grain. If the bridegroom is considered a suitable match, the parents of the girl receive the young man with due consideration, and partake heartily of the food and drink proffered by him. The marriage is there and then arranged, the bridegroom further disbursing to the father a sum of not less than five rupees and not more than one hundred. This is the etiquette of good Shoka society, and of all people who can afford it, the payment being called "milk-money," or money equivalent to the sum

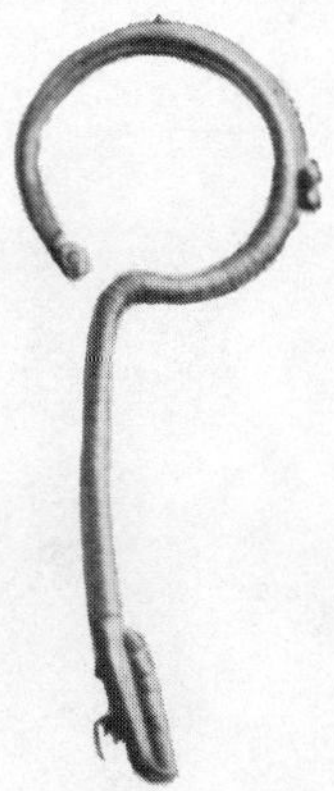

SILVER EARRING OF TIBETAN ORIGIN, WITH CORAL BEADS

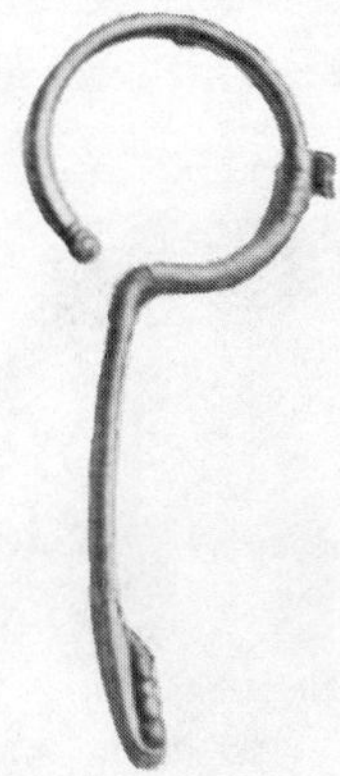

SILVER EARRING OF TIBETAN ORIGIN, WITH CORAL BEADS

spent by the girl's relations in bringing her up. The marriage ceremony is simple enough. A cake called *Delang* is baked, of which the friends of the two families partake. If either the bridegroom or bride refuses to eat a share of the cake, the marriage is broken off ; if they both eat some of the cake, and later any dissension arises between them, all those

SHOKA WOMAN WEAVING

who assisted at the function are called as witnesses that the marriage took place. Often even this primitive ceremony of eating cake is dispensed with, and Shoka marriages begin and continue as happy and faithful unions, without any special form of service or rite to solemnise the tie.

They not only visit adultery on the guilty man himself by beating him, but the men proceed *en masse* to the house of his parents and denude it of all furniture, stores of grain, and merchandise. They confiscate the sheep, goats, yaks, and all their valuable saddles and loads, and present the whole proceeds to the man whose wife has been seduced—a recompense for the shame suffered. Frequently the unfortunate and innocent relations of the evil-doer are bound and even beaten to death by the villagers. These severe measures are resorted to in order to maintain a high standard of morality and honour, and there is little doubt that, primitive as these methods may seem, the good results obtained more than justify them. There are very few illegitimate births, with the exception of occasional Rambang children, and their arrival is a matter of such disgrace that they cannot be looked upon as seriously discrediting the social value of the Rambang.

RAMBANG GIRLS WITH ORNAMENTS

CHAPTER XVII

FUNERAL RITES

Departure of the soul—Cremation—Amusement of the dead man's soul—The lay figure—Feasting—Doleful dance—Transmigration of the soul—Expensive ceremonies—Offerings before the lay figure—Dancing and contortions—Martial dances—Solo dances—The animal to be sacrificed and the lay figure—Chasing the animal from the village—Tearing out its heart—The yak driven over a precipice—Head shaving—A sacred cave.

THE Shokas ascribe death to the departure of the soul from the body, and to this notion is due the curious reverence they show for the spirit or memory of their dead. I witnessed a funeral ceremony quaint enough to deserve record.

A man had died a painful death, the result of an accident. His friends were immediately sent for, and the corpse, having been smeared with butter (*ghi*), was dressed in his best clothes. They bent his body double before the rigor set in, and placed him on a hurriedly constructed wooden hearse. He was covered with a blue-and-gold embroidered cloth, and a white one over it. At sunrise, the funeral procession left the house for the place of cremation. First came a row of ten women, their heads covered with a long strip of white cotton cloth, one end of which was tied to the hearse. Among these were the near relations of the deceased, including his wife and daughters, crying and wailing the words, "*Oh bajo! Oh bajo!*" (Oh father! oh father!), the rest of them sobbing and making great show of grief. The

WEEPING WOMEN UNDER WHITE CLOTH

deceased having been somewhat of a favourite in Garbyang, the villagers turned out in force to render him this last tribute, and they took their place in the procession as it slowly wound down the cliff towards the river. The hearse was carried by two men, and each male Shoka following bore a log or bundle of firewood. We reached the Kali. The body was temporarily laid on the bank of the stream, while all the men, with heads uncovered, collected large stones and pieces of wood. With the stones a circular crematory oven, five feet high, six feet in diameter, with an opening on the side facing the wind, was erected by the waterside. The wife and daughters of the departed, with their hoods turned inside

SHOKA FUNERAL PILE

out and with covered faces, squatted down meanwhile by the hearse, moaning and keeping a small fire alight. When all preparations were made, the oven being heaped up with logs of wood, the body was untied from the stretcher and lifted by two intimates of the departed on to the funeral pile. All valuables were removed, his gold earrings, his silver locket and bracelets; and a large knife was used for some purpose or other which I could not quite see, except in slitting the lobes of the corpse's ears to remove his earrings more quickly. Branches of pine-tree were deposited on the body, and a large pot of butter was set by its side. A brass bowl of *chökti* (wine) was poured on the head, and then, in profound silence, fire was set to the pile.

A few white puffs showed that it had caught fire, and then a dense column of black smoke rose from it, filling the atmosphere with a sickening smell of singed hair and burning flesh. The wind blew the smoke towards me, and I was enveloped in it for some moments, during which I could see nothing of what was going on, and I felt my eyes smart and my nostrils fill with the smoke and the stench. Gradually a tall flame, over twenty feet high, leaked out, consuming the body and showing me, as the atmosphere cleared, the Shokas down by the river washing their hands and faces to cleanse themselves of what they look upon as unclean, the contact with a corpse. Retracing their steps to the village, the women cried and moaned, carrying back to the house the clothes of the deceased and his brass bowls.

Reaching home, it was incumbent on them to provide lavishly for the amusement of the dead man's soul. A lay figure crudely constructed of straw and sticks was attired by them in the clothes of the departed, and covered over with Indian fabrics embroidered in gold and red and blue, and a turban was stuck on the head, with a *panache* made of a branch of fir-tree. The *Kalihé* was at the side of the image. When the fire was extinguished, a visit was paid to the cremation spot by the relatives of the deceased, and such pieces of bone as the knee-joints, elbows, and the larger vertebræ of the spine, usually left undestroyed by the flames, were collected and deposited inside the clothes of the image.

Wheat, rice, and flour were purchased in large quantities and cooked to provide food for the multitude of friends who remained the guests of the family during the whole time of the funeral. A sheep a day is usually killed and eaten on such occasions, and cask after cask of *chökti* (wine), *zahn* (a liquor distilled from barley, rice and wheat), and *anag* (from fermented grain of various kinds) are emptied by the mourning crowd. The women folk of the dead man mourned round the effigy, resting their heads on it, crying and imploring the beloved one to return to life. Other rows of women, with their hoods turned inside out in sign of mourning, danced gracefully in circles round the dressed-up figure, left the house by one door in the basement, described an arc in the open, and returned by another door, while men were dancing a doleful dance outside the house. Beating of drums went on the whole day—languid and sad at moments ; excited, violent and rowdy at others, according to the mood of the musicians and the quantity of liquor consumed by them. On each day of these proceedings, which lasted for three or four days, rice, baked wheat, and wine were placed before the effigy, until, when it was assumed that the soul of the dead had had a sufficiently amusing time, arrangements were made for its transmigration from the lay figure into a live sheep or yak. If the deceased is a man, the animal chosen to represent him is a male ; if a woman, a female ; but no ceremony of this sort follows the cremation of children under ten or twelve. In the case of the old man whose funeral I witnessed, a sheep was chosen, instead of the time-hallowed yak, the procuring of which from Tibet used to be a very costly business. The use of a sheep for these sacrifices is quite a recent innovation, brought into fashion by the greatest Shoka trader in

DANCE IN FRONT OF DECEASED MAN'S HOUSE

Garbyang, called Gobaria, whose intention it was to put down the unnecessary waste of these ceremonies; but many pious Shokas, I was assured, are not satisfied with so small an offering as a single sheep, and slaughter two or even more on these occasions.

After several days' dancing and gorging indoors, a crowd

WOMEN DUSTING AND CARESSING THE LAY FIGURE

collects, to the sound of the drums, outside the habitation. The lay figure is from the room transported either directly outside the dwelling or to some picturesque spot in the woods. This is generally on the fourth day. Bowls with food are placed in front of it, and the dancing is begun, to a curious sentimental strain, with a graceful series of contortions, by girls and women waving large pieces of white material. The legs keep time with the arms, and each leg is alternately bent at the knee until it nearly touches the ground. The head is inclined to the right or left, and thrown backwards or forwards according to the beating of the drum. The circular motion in the dancing begins first very slowly, and the speed then increases by degrees,

WOMEN DANCING ROUND THE LAY FIGURE

abruptly ending in odd and suggestive postures. During the intervals of dancing the relatives go round and round the lay figure, dusting and fanning it with their white cloths.

In the afternoon the men join the performance, and though their dancing has practically the same characteristics and motions as the women's dance, it is usually so much more violent that it almost partakes of the character of a war-dance. They hold in their right hands a sword, in the left a circular shield, and some of the younger men show great skill in the rapid manipulation of their blades, twirling them round their heads and behind their backs. There are solos, duets and trios, in which the drummer or drummers

THE GOAT WITH SOUL OF DECEASED BEING FED

take part, and when the dancing is collective, they head the procession, contorting their bodies and beating their drums with a stick on one side and the palm of the hand on the other.

The whole crowd is constantly regaled by the family with corn baked with sugar, roasted Indian corn, rice, sweets *ghur* and *miseri*, when the lay figure is supposed to have had its fill. While the mob eat, the ladies of the house return to the effigy with quick beating of the drums, and again double themselves up in solemn lengthy curtsies. Perhaps the most interesting, because the most accomplished, were the solo male dancers, each performer displaying

GOAT, WITH SOUL AND CLOTHES OF DECEASED

his own particular genius. The drummer beats his drum whimsically—fast and slow alternately, with no rule—just as it pleases his fancy, and the dancer always keeps time with him in all his frenzies and eccentricities, so that his movements are sometimes so slow as to be barely noticeable, and at others so rapid that his arms and legs can no longer be distinguished. I happened to witness no less than six funerals simultaneously in Garbyang, and a collective war-

MARTIAL DANCE ROUND LAY FIGURE

dance of as many as three hundred men. It went on during a whole day and the greater part of the following night, torches and a big bonfire burning.

Eventually, amidst firing of guns, howls, yells and deafen-

SENDING THE GOAT AWAY FROM THE VILLAGE

ing hissing of the assembled crowd, the animal to be sacrificed is dragged before the lay figure. Long coloured ribbons are tied round its horns, and the ends left hanging by the side of its head. Sandal-wood is burnt under the beast's nostrils, which is supposed to induce the soul of the departed to enter and establish itself in the animal. The clothes, the turban, the shield, the jewellery, are torn from the figure's back and piled on to the goat, which is now the impersonation of the deceased. It is fed until it can hold no more, wine and liquor being poured down its throat, and large dishes of all possible delicacies being placed before it. The women relatives devote to it their tenderest affection, and shed tears over it in the conviction that it holds the spirit of their lost protector. Stuffed with food, and stupefied by the alcohol, the beast submits, emotionless and immovable, to the wild caresses, prayers, and salaams showered on it. Again the hissing, whistling and yelling begin, and a rush is made for the animal, which is seized by the horns, the neck, the tail, wherever it can be caught hold of, and dragged, pushed, beaten, and at last chased out of the village, but not until after the clothes, shield, sword, turban, and ornaments have been torn from its back. It is eventually handed over to the Hunyas or Jumlis or Humlis, who on these occasions benefit by the simplicity and superstition of the Shokas, and who throw it down, rip the body open, and pull out the heart, or twist it in the inside with a jerk that kills instantly. This method applies to sheep or goat.

When a yak is sacrificed, very much the same rites take place up to the moment when the lay figure is deprived of its clothing and the yak invested with it. It is similarly beaten and dragged about, and left on the top of some mountain, the crowd calling after it, "Go! go! We have feasted, fêted and fed you. We have done all in our power for your welfare. We cannot do more! Go now!" With this the yak, with the soul that has been driven into it, is left to its own devices, and as soon as the Shokas have departed, is driven by the Tibetans over a precipice, it being against their faith to draw blood from a yak. In the fatal leap the animal is smashed to pieces, and the Tibetans, collecting the remains, gorge themselves with the prized meat of their cherished yak.

As a mark of reverence the Shoka men remove their caps

TEARING OUT THE HEART OF THE GOAT

not only while following the corpse to cremation, but also during the feasting, the male relatives themselves even shaving their heads; and this practice is occasionally extended to the whole male community in the case of a particularly respected villager dying. The women remove their jewellery, and, as already noted, turn their hoods inside out.

YAK DRIVEN OVER PRECIPICE

When all is over, some restitution of his property is made to the dead, and odd articles, such as brass bowls or a gun or a shield or sword, are placed in a sacred cave, which none dare desecrate by entering to remove anything. These caves are high up on the mountain-sides, and are said to be full of sacred offerings, which have accumulated there in the centuries.

I expressed the wish to see the cave on the mountain side above Garbyang, but the natives politely asked me not to do so, as the visit of a stranger to this sacred spot might bring misfortune on the Shoka living community. Therefore I abstained from going rather than cause unpleasantness.

CHAPTER XVIII

Touching Shoka farewell—Feelings curiously expressed—Sobs and tears—The start—A funereal procession—Distressed father and mother—Kachi and Dola the worse for drink—Anxious moments—The bridge destroyed.

KACHI AND HIS RELATIONS

THE day of my departure came. It was after dark. Outside my dwelling a crowd of Shokas had assembled. I bade farewell to my host Zeheram and to his wife and children, who with tears in their eyes wished me God-speed.

"Salaam, sahib, salaam!" repeated Zeheram, sobbing and bringing his hand respectfully to his forehead. "You know, sahib, that a horse goes to a horse, a tiger to a tiger, a yak to a yak, and a man to a man. A man's house is another man's house, no matter whether the colour of our skin differs or not. Therefore I thank Heaven that you have accepted shelter under my humble roof. You must have been uncomfortable, for all you sahibs are rich and accustomed to luxury. I am only a trader and a cultivator. I am poor, but I possess a heart. You, unlike other sahibs,

THE PATAN SUMMONING MY COOLIES FROM THE ROOF OF HIS HOUSE

have always spoken kindly to me and to all of us Shokas. We feel that you are our brother. You have given us presents, but we needed them not. The only present we wish for is that, when you reach the end of your perilous journey, you will send us a message that you are well. We will all pray day and night for you. Our hearts are sore at your leaving us."

This from the rough old boy, whom I had got really to like, was touching, and I told him I hoped I might some day be able to repay him for his kindness. When I descended the steps there was quite a crowd in the yard. Every one wished to bid me farewell. The men took my right hand in both theirs and brought it up to their foreheads, muttering words of grief at my leaving. The women gently caressed my face and bade me "*Niku tza*" ("Go well," "Farewell"). These are the Shoka fashions of taking leave of friends who are departing for distant lands.

Led by the hand by a really grieving company, I moved towards the narrow, steep descent to the Chongur bridge, cut into the slope of the high cliffs of clay. On the way I called at Kachi's house, but he had gone ahead. A more mournful procession could not be imagined. The faint rays of a new moon gave an added melancholy to the scene, and that peculiarly impressive sound of sad steps, if I may thus express the pathetic cadence of people's gait when afflicted, made me feel as if I were attending my own funeral. I begged them to return to their homes, and one after the other they came to embrace my feet and to hold my fingers. Then, hiding their faces in the palms of their hands, they one by one made their way up the grey track cut into the lofty cliff, and like phantoms, gradually becoming smaller and smaller, vanished in the distance. Still some twenty or thirty insisted on escorting me down to the stream. Farther on I came upon the excited figure of an old woman tearing her hair and crying pitifully. She threw herself at my feet, imploring me to take care of her son. It was Kachi's distressed mother. I comforted her as best I could, and also the desolate father (good old Junia), who was there with tears streaming down his cheeks, to bid me an affectionate farewell.

"Where is your son?"

"You will find him a little farther down, sahib."

I did—together with four other people lying on the ground all in a heap. One of them who tried to stand up, called out: "Kachi, get up, here is the sahib," and then collapsed again on the top of the others. Neither Kachi nor the others gave any sign of life, and when I spoke to them I discovered that they were in a state of hopeless intoxication, arm-in-arm as they had fallen and slept.

By the side of Kachi was Dola, his uncle, supposed to be employed by me in the quadruple capacity of interpreter, carrier, Kachi's valet, and cook, in which latter art, after Shoka fashion, he was quite an adept, his fame having spread all over Bias. He was, therefore, a treasure not lightly to be abandoned, and yet, now that I wanted to act quickly and decisively, I had to weigh whether I should proceed with two of the most important characters in my play disabled. Should I, hampered by these semi-corpses, be able to pass unseen the watchful Tibetan guard at the Chongur bridge, only a few hundred yards farther on? I decided to try. Seizing one on each side under their arm-pits, I supported them and kept them erect. It was no easy job, and I felt our speed increase at every step as I moved with my staggering mates down the steep and slippery track. We reached the bottom of the hill at a breakneck rate, and as the track was narrow along the water's edge, it was a wonder that we did not all three of us land in the river. As it was, in coming suddenly to a stop, my two men utterly collapsed again, and I was so exhausted that I had to sit down and rest.

Kachi Ram had a lucid interval. He gazed round and saw me for the first time that night.

"Sahib!" he exclaimed, with long pauses between each word, "I am drunk!"

"That is quite true," said I.

"We Shokas have this bad habit," he continued. "I had to drink *chökti* with all my relations and friends prior to leaving for this long journey. They would have been offended if I had not divided with each a cup of wine. I now see everything go round. Please put my head into cold water. Oh! the moon is jumping about, and is now under my feet!"

I complied with his request, and gave both his head and Dola's a good ducking in the freezing Kali River.

This had the unfortunate effect of sending them to sleep so soundly that I thought they would never wake again. Some of the sober Shokas offered to carry the two helpless men on their backs. We were wasting valuable time and the sky was getting clouded. When the moon had disappeared behind the high mountain, I went ahead to reconnoitre. All was darkness but for the glimmer of a brilliant star here and there in the sky. I crawled to the bridge and listened. Not a sound, not a light on the opposite bank. All was silence, that dead silence of nature and human life asleep. I stopped on the bridge. This structure spans the river, a huge boulder in the centre of the stream serving as a pillar, and forms, in fact, two separate bridges joined on the opposite sides of this central boulder. I walked cautiously across the first portion, stood to listen again on the rock dividing the foaming waters, and tried to penetrate the obscurity. There was not a soul to be seen, nor a sound to be heard. I went over the rock and proceeded towards the second half of the bridge, when I found to my horror that this second half of the bridge had been cut down. The entire section had collapsed, and with the exception of a long beam still swinging to and fro with one end in the turbid stream, and a plank or two, the whole material had been washed away.

I returned to my men.

"We must continue our way on this side of the river," I whispered to them. "The Tibetans have destroyed the bridge."

THE CHONGUR BRIDGE PREVIOUS TO BEING DESTROYED

"The track is traced," they replied, "but it is impassable at night."

"Never mind; we must go. Come." And I headed the silent procession.

We went about a mile. Yet another dilemma. Kachi and Dola were still fast asleep. The others, tired and worn out with the fatigue of carrying them, wished to turn back. The sky was now clouded all over and rain was coming on.

I felt that it was useless to persist. Having seen the two drunken creatures laid flat under a shed, and well covered with blankets, I therefore returned to Garbyang, with the intention of making a fresh start shortly before sunrise, when the drunkards would probably be fit to walk by themselves, and found shelter under the ever hospitable roof of Dr. Wilson.

CHAPTER XIX

A dangerous track—Perilous passage—A curious bridge over a precipice—Pathetic Shoka custom—Small misadventures—A grand reception—Tea for all tastes.

AT 4 A.M., before the sun rose, I made a fresh and hurried start. I proceeded quickly to the spot where I had left the two drunken men. They had gone ahead.

Indeed the track was a bad and dangerous one, overhanging precipices, and hardly wide enough to give standing room upon it. We came to a spot where the narrow path stopped. There was before us a perpendicular rock descending straight as a wall to the Kali River. The corrosive action of dripping water and melting snow, of which last there seemed to be a thick layer higher above on the summit of the cliff, had worn the face of the rock quite smooth. The distance across this vertical wall-like ravine was not more than forty or fifty feet. On the other side of it the narrow track began again.

Owing to this and other dangerous places, this route is but very seldom used by the natives or by any one else. The road generally taken is on the opposite side of the Kali River, in Nepal territory. Nevertheless, a few Shokas possess bits of land on this bank of the stream, and it was by them that, in order to surmount the obstacle before which I now stood, the following expedient was devised in former years.

By letting down a man from above with ropes they succeeded in making two rows of small hollows in the rock, along two parallel horizontal lines, the higher of which was about six feet or so above the lower. The holes were dug at intervals of three or four feet along each line, the upper ones to be caught on by one's hands, the lower ones to support one's feet, and none of the cavities are deeper than a few inches.

The transit seemed dangerous at any time, and impossible just then, because the drizzling rain which had set in had wetted the rock and made it as slippery as glass, but I realised that the thing had to be risked, and at any cost. With an affected air of assurance, I therefore took off my boots and went ahead.

I could not look about me, for I clung with my body to the wall, feeling my way with my toes and fingers. The cavities were, as a matter of fact, so shallow that progress was slow and troublesome. When the toes of the right limb seemed firmly planted in a receptacle, the right arm was made to slide along the rock until the fingers had obtained a firm grip in the cavity directly above the one in which the toes were. Then the entire body had to be shifted from left to right, bringing the left foot and hand close to the right extremities and suspending one's weight on the former, so as to render the right foot and arm ready to make the next move forward, and so on, till I reached the other side and alighted upon the narrow track, which was itself only five or six inches wide. Chanden Sing having tied his shoes and mine over his shoulders, proceeded barefooted on the same hazardous enterprise. With none of the excitement of personal danger, the moments of apprehension while he groped his way with toes and fingers, half paralysed with cold and fear, were to me worse even than those of my own passage. But he too got across safe and sound, and after that the rest was comparatively easy.

It was necessary now to look out for signs of the two men, Kachi and Dola, who had preceded us. I was glad to find a little farther on fresh footmarks, undoubtedly those of the two Shokas. The track still ascended and descended nearly all along precipitous cliffs, and was everywhere dangerously narrow, with here and there bits on shaky crow-bars. At one spot the rugged formation of the cliff forced one suddenly to ascend to its very top and cross (on all-fours) a rude kind of bridge made of branches of trees spanned not horizontally, but at an angle of sixty degrees over a precipice of several hundred feet. I found a white thread of wool laid over this primitive structure, in accordance with the custom of the Shokas at the death of relatives or friends away from their native village. The soul is supposed to migrate during the dark hours of the night and to return to the birthplace of the deceased, these white threads showing the way at dangerous places on the road.

Having lost the track more than once, we found ourselves down at the edge of the Kali and compelled to climb up some three hundred feet over sand and rolling stones to regain the path.

We arrived at last at Nabi. There I found my loads safe an dsound, having got here by the better track on the Nepalese side previously to the Chongur bridge being destroyed by the Tibetans, also Kachi and Dola, who had got over and recovered from their drink. To make up, perhaps, for their

A PERILOUS PASSAGE

past misbehaviour, and probably to make me overlook or forget it, they seemed to have induced the natives to welcome me with particular cordiality. I was invited by them, with much show of hospitality, to spend the night in the village.

I was led with some ceremony to a primitive sort of ladder with very roughly carved steps, and shoved, with help from above and below, on to a flat mud roof. Here a tent had been pitched, the floor of which was covered with mats and rugs for me to rest on. I no sooner laid myself down than a string of men, women and children arrived, carrying bowls with a particularly sumptuous meal of rice, *dhal*, meat, *balab* (or boiled buckwheat leaves), curd, milk, broiled corn with sugar, *chapatis*, *shale*, sweets, native wine and liquor.

During the meal, tea was served in all sorts of fashions. There was Chinese tea and Indian tea, tea boiled with sugar and tea without it, tea with milk, and tea with butter and salt in it, pale tea and dark tea, sweet tea and bitter tea—in fact, tea until I—devoted as I am to it—wished that no tea-leaf had ever been picked and stewed in boiling water.

CHAPTER XX

Dr. Wilson joins my expedition for a few marches—What misdeeds a photographic camera can do—Weighing, dividing, and packing provisions—Two extra men wanted—The last friendly faces.

I WAS examining a young woman who had badly injured and partly fractured a central vertebra of the spine, when Dr. Wilson turned up and gave the poor wretch the little relief possible in her condition, for which she had hoped in vain from me. He was welcome to me for many reasons besides the pleasure of being in his company. He had offered to join my expedition for a few marches into Tibet, and I was glad indeed to have him with me. We pushed on as soon as possible over the road between Nabi and Kuti, which I have already described. Our journey was quite uneventful, and the snow-bridges and snow-fields, so troublesome when I had first taken this road, had melted and altogether disappeared. Even at Nabi little happened. But I must just mention the following incident as illustrative of the curious suspicion and dislike I found everywhere of the photographic apparatus I carried with me.

I was on the point of leaving the place when a handsome

Tibetan woman, whom I had not previously noticed, accosted me with hysterical sobs—inarticulate, but conveying a very clear impression of suffering.

"You have killed my child, and now you will kill my husband," she complained, when she was able to talk; and I then discovered that I had on my previous visit to Nabi

THE PHOTOGRAPH THAT CAUSED THE CHILD'S DEATH

taken a snapshot at a child perched on the top of a very heavy load that happened to be carried on the woman's back through my camp, and that when she complained I had appeased her, in the usual way, with a coin. She had conveyed her load to Kuti, and had slipped, on her way back, with her child—at a spot not far from where I had had my slide—but, less fortunate than myself, had rolled right into the foaming stream. She managed to cling to the rock and was eventually saved, but the infant was washed from rock to rock by the current, and disappeared under a snow tunnel.

"Oh, sahib!" cried the woman, "if you had not before we started looked at us through *the eyes* (the twin lenses) of your *black box* (the photographic camera), I should not have lost my baby."

"And how about your husband?"

"Oh, you will kill him too."

"But I don't know your husband. Anyhow, I promise not to look at him with these eyes."

"It is not that, sahib, but he is coming with you to Tibet. He is carrying one of your loads. You will all be killed."

She pointed him out to me—one of the strongest among the men I had, and the most anxious to accompany me. He was too good to lose, and I was certainly unwilling to renounce my claim to him on account of his good woman's tears. So I consoled her as best I could; promised to take good care of him, and under no circumstances to photograph him.

At Kuti, Dr. Wilson and I were busy for several hours weighing, dividing and packing in equal loads the provisions I had purchased: fourteen *munds* in all (1120 lbs.) of flour, rice, red sugar (*ghur*), salt, red pepper (32 lbs.), *dhal*, *miseri* (lump sugar), *ghi* (butter), and a large quantity of *satoo* (oatmeal), and broiled corn. There were, in addition, the preserved and tinned provisions which I had brought with me from London.

To give my carriers no cause for complaint, I allowed them to choose their own shoes, blankets, &c., and I did all in my power to humour them, because the loads threatened to be excessively heavy. In fact, I found that, even after dispensing with everything but what was absolutely essential, there was still ample to carry for at least two strong men. Every available Shoka had joined the party, and no inducement that I could offer brought me more volunteers. I was very unwilling to delay, and I was on the point of subdividing among the men I already had the two extra loads, when two stray shepherds turned up, half famished and naked, with long unkempt heads of hair, and only a coral necklace and a silver bangle by way of clothing. I quickly secured them, and although one was really only a boy, I decided to trust to luck and take Dr. Wilson's assurance that he looked tough enough and would be useful.

This brought my little force up to thirty strong, and now I was ready to start.

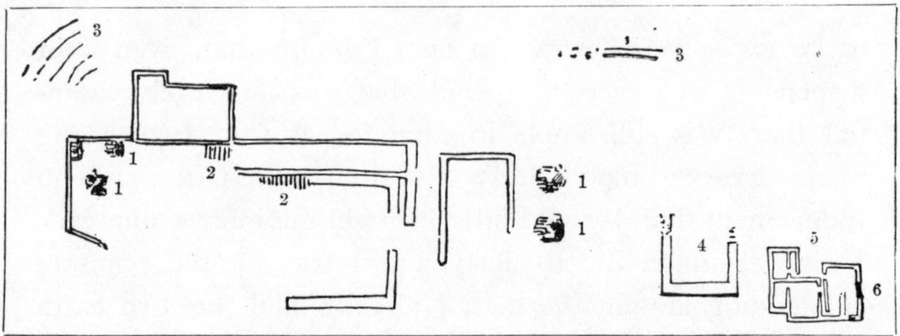

PLAN OF KUTI CASTLE

1. PILES OF STONES — 2. STEPS
3. OUTER WALL — 4. TOWER
5. BLACKSMITH'S HOUSE — 6. WINDOWS

CHAPTER XXI

The Kuti Castle—Under way—Our first disaster—A cheerful and a sulky coolie—Mansing—A brigand—A strange medley of followers—A character—Tailoring—Fields of stones—Troublesome rivers—The Jolinkan or Lebung Pass—Sense of humour—Pleased with small comforts.

BEFORE leaving Kuti, I went to see the curious and ancient castle perched on a small hill about three hundred yards south of the village. It is now in ruins, with the exception of a quadrangular tower called by the natives the Kuti Ker, but the foundations of the whole structure can still be plainly seen. I made a plan, which is here reproduced, as it may be of archæological interest. The natives could give me no information regarding it, except that it was once a king's palace strongly fortified. A small house of several rooms by the side of the tower is said to have been the blacksmith's shop in which the arrowheads and swords for the king's soldiers were made. The tower is four yards square at its base, and built of stone. Judging by its shape and construction, and the curious windows, I am inclined to

THE KUTI CASTLE

attribute this castle to Tibetan workmanship, for identical towers are seen in Tibet, even at Taklakot. The windows, or rather slits, on each floor of the tower were six inches square ; those in the blacksmith's house were considerably larger. There were outer walls for the defence of the fort at places where the castle would have been most accessible. Quantities of stones piled up in heaps probably served as ammunition for the defenders of the fortress in centuries gone by.

When I returned to camp all was ready, and after endless trouble with some of my men, who were already uncertain as to whether they would accompany me on my journey or not, I eventually got under way in the afternoon. The Kuti village is the highest in Bias, being situated at an elevation of 12,920 feet.

The track was now comparatively free from snow and ice except here and there, where we had to cross extensive slopes covered with snow. On one of these we had our first disaster. A coolie fell who carried in his hand a large pot containing butter. He fortunately did not slide far down, but we had the bitter disappointment of seeing our precious pot roll into the water and disappear for ever. We camped at an elevation of 13,050 feet. Late in the evening, as my men were collecting wood to keep up a huge fire round which we sat, my two coolies, who had remained at Kuti with instructions to follow, arrived with their respective loads. They were two strange characters. The one with a coral necklace was mournful and sulky, the other lively and talkative. They professed to be by caste Rajiputs.

"You see," exclaimed the cheerful coolie, "I am small, but I fear nothing. When we cross into Tibet I shall go ahead with a pointed stick and clear all the Tibetans away. I am not afraid of them. I am ready to fight the whole world."

Knowing the value of this sort of talk on the part of natives, I shut him up and sent him away to fetch wood. The sulky fellow interested me more. He seldom uttered a word, and when he did he never spoke pleasantly; he was apparently immersed in deep thought, from which it seemed a great effort to draw his mind away. He looked painfully ill. Motionless and speechless, he would stare at a fixed point as if in a trance.

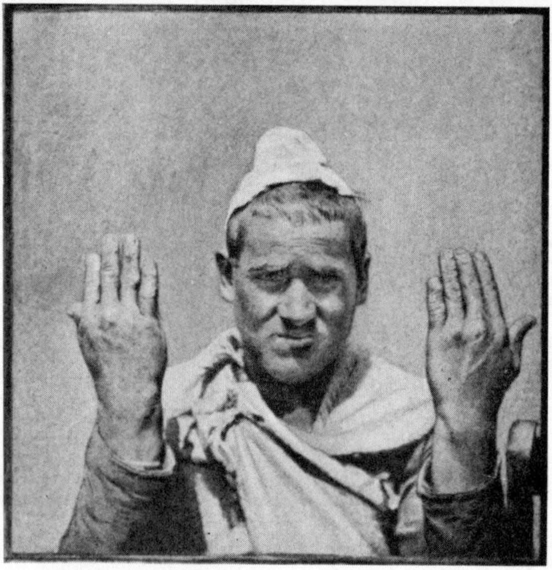

MANSING THE LEPER SHOWING HIS HANDS

His features were peculiarly refined and regular, but his skin had that ghastly shiny whitish tinge so peculiar to lepers. I waited for an opportunity to examine his hands, on which he sat to keep them warm. It is there, in the contracted or dropping off fingers, that one finds the first certain symptoms of that most terrible of all diseases, leprosy. I asked the man to come and sit nearer the blazing fire. He came and stretched out his open palms towards the flickering flame.

Alas! my suspicions were but too correct. His fingers, distorted and contracted, with the skin sore at the joints, were sad and certain proof. I examined his feet and found the same symptoms there also.

"What is your name?" I inquired of him.

"Mansing," he said drily, becoming immediately again absorbed in one of his reveries.

The crackling fire was dying down, when a stalwart Tibetan suddenly appeared bent low under the heavy weight of a huge tree-trunk which he was carrying on his back. He approached and threw the wood on the fire.

Here was another character! As strong as an ox, this servant of mine had queer antecedents. He was at one time a well-known bandit in the neighbourhood of Lhassa. He was said to have taken many lives, and, finding his own in danger in his country, had come to settle on our side of the border, marrying different wives, whom he constantly beat and in turn banished from under his roof. It was owing to his latest family squabble that he came into my employ; his abnormal strength, valuable for carrying loads, was to me his only recommendation. In camp he went by the name of *Daku*, "the brigand."

In looking round to inspect my other followers, with whom I had hardly yet got acquainted, I was amused and interested at the strange medley of creatures forming my band. There were Humlis and Jumlis with their luxuriant black hair tied into small tresses and a top-knot over the head, like the Coreans. There were Tibetans, Shokas of Bias, Rongbas, Nepalese, Rajiputs and Totolas, also a Brahmin, two native Christians and a Johari. Then Dr. Wilson. What a collection! What a chaos of languages and dialects!

An amusing feature of this odd crowd was that each

particular caste looked down upon all the others. This from the very beginning occasioned separation during meal-time, and the camp was lively with as many burning fires in as many sheltered spots as there were castes of men following me. I was glad of this, as it seemed a sort of guarantee that they would never all join together to conspire against me.

Poor Mansing, the leper, was shivering with cold. He had been unable to purchase himself a blanket and shoes at Kuti. He had spent the money in tobacco instead. Dr. Wilson and I took pity upon him. The long evening was still before us, so I got out the cloth I had purchased at Kuti, and with scissors and needle we began to cut and sew a new set of garments for the poor wretch. The Doctor did the cutting and I the sewing. I cannot boast that a professional tailor would not have turned out a better fit, but for all general purposes the newly-made clothes answered well enough. There was only one inconvenience in the single-breasted jacket. I had no buttons, and was therefore compelled to sew the coat on the man himself. It thus remained a fixture, and not only looked all right, but —which was our chief object—kept him warm.

We left camp at 5.30 the following morning. High mountains rose on either side of us, and we followed the Kuti River flowing here from West to East. At an elevation of 13,980 feet we crossed the Bitroguare River. On the other side of the Kuti River were high perpendicular cliffs of a vividly red-coloured rock with blue horizontal stratifications, and towering over them a succession of very pointed peaks.

The action of ice on the rock was noticeable everywhere. As we went farther we came upon extensive fields of stones and boulders brought down from the higher peaks by the ice, and in some places we found actual *moraines*. To our left stood a gigantic wall of stone like a natural impregnable fortress. Travelling in a direction of 320° (b.m.), and at elevations of 13,900 feet, 14,200 feet, 14,300 feet, we waded through three tributaries of the Kuti; then we came to a foaming, rapid and deep river which we had great difficulty in crossing. It was getting towards the middle of the day, and the stream, fed by the snows melting under the hot sun, was rising from moment to moment. Two of my coolies whom I first sent in reached the middle, where the water came up to their chins. They lost their footing and were temporarily helpless, and in some danger of being swamped, the loads which they carried on their heads being partly spoiled when we succeeded in recovering them. The other men got frightened by the time they were ready to cross. The river had risen so high that it was impossible to get to the other side except by swimming, and this was out of the question, on account of the loads. We therefore had to follow the stream upwards for about a mile, when fortunately we found a somewhat dangerous, yet passable, snow bridge, over which the remainder of my men and goods effected a crossing in safety. We returned to our course on the Kuti, still passing between high, rugged mountains along an undulating plain averaging about 400 yards wide. Though at comparatively high elevations, there were large patches of brightly coloured flowers—red, violet, white and vivid yellow—which gave to the landscape a picturesque and constantly changing effect.

On reaching a small pass, 14,750 feet, the path branched to Darma by the Jolinkan towards bearings 260°, and over the Lebung Pass. It is really only a goat track, exceedingly difficult and fatiguing, except in the month of August, when there is only a small quantity of snow, and it leads to the Dholi River about half a mile south of Khumling.

The Jolinkan River, rising from the snow field to the East of the Lebung or Jolinkan Pass, had now to be crossed.

THE JOLINKAN OR LEBUNG PASS

The stalwart dacoit, ever ready to make himself useful, conveyed his load across, and lifting me like a feather on to his back, saved me from plunging higher than my waist into the bitterly cold water, whereas he was covered up to his neck. The course of the Kuti turns now to 330° (b.m.). Going up and down small barren hills, round the foot of high mountains, we attained an altitude of 15,000 feet. Here, to the left of the track, and eighty feet above it, is a small and beautiful lake 500 yards long and 400 wide. Its waters, in which the high snowy peaks round it are reflected as in a silver mirror, find an outlet in a short but most precipitous river flowing with tremendous force into the Kuti. Soon after leaving this lake we came upon another small sheet of water, near which were thirteen peculiar piles or columns of stones, each one having been erected by the first Tibetan or Shoka who crossed the pass during the summer. A similar erection could also be seen perched on a large rock jutting out from the water of the larger lake. Though the sun was fast going down behind the mountains to the west, we pressed on, trying to make as much headway as we could towards the perpetual snows. We still travelled over undulating ground, and the marching was not heavy or difficult, save for the freezingly cold and very rapid streams we had to wade through. It was all we could do to get warm again after having been immersed in one, and before we had ceased shivering we had to wade through the next, and yet the next, so that one's chilliness increased, and the constant discomfort of cold became very trying. Much discontent prevailed among my carriers over the very long march, as their feet were numbed with cold. They nearly mutinied when I would not let them stop at a camp they had selected, but ordered them to proceed farther. A mile and a half from the point they had favoured, we overlooked a large, flat basin of stones and gravel, about half a mile wide and three-quarters of a mile long, which had the appearance of having formerly been a lake. It was surrounded by high snowy peaks, and its bed lay at an altitude of 15,400 feet. It seemed as if the immense quantity of stones and pebbles carried by the river feeding it had raised its bed until it had caused the water to flow into the Kuti. When I saw it, the river formed an extensive delta with as many as twelve arms, joining again within the basin into one single stream before throwing itself into the Kuti. Naturally we selected the wider expanse of water to ford, assuming that it would be shallower than the narrow ones. Once more that day I took off my lower garments and entered the cold water. It came direct from the snows, and its temperature was slightly above freezing-point. The sun had gone down, and there was a piercing wind. My feet, as I went in and out of the numerous branches of the stream, became so cold that I could hardly stand for the stinging pain; moreover, treading on sharp-edged stones under the water and knocking my frozen toes against them was at first very painful, but after a time they got so frozen that, though at each step the soles of my feet and toes were cut and bruised, I suffered no actual pain until after crossing five or six arms of the delta. Unable to balance myself any longer, I struggled as best I could out of the water and rubbed my feet violently, until slowly, and with intense pain, they came back to life.

It is curious how a little sense of humour helps on such occasions. To an onlooker not suffering as we were, the sight of our party crossing that dreadful delta would have been curious. The expression of disgust on all my men's faces, not to speak of my own, could not but have caused merriment. We carried our footgear on our shoulders; we struggled, stumbled, and splashed in the greenish water, and now one, then another, fell helpless through frost-bite on some island or other, until we were all disabled, and still only half-way through. In spite of our condition, worn out as we were, the soles and sides of our feet badly cut and bleeding, my men, so sulky at having been firmly baulked in their wishes, became quite good-natured and amusing when I chaffed them over their present troubles, and they saw that I was in the same plight. After endless rubbing, we restored a certain amount of circulation to our lower limbs, and proceeded to cross the next six arms of the delta. When, after an hour or longer of suffering, we were at last able to put on our footgear, we felt the happiness which comes from the knowledge of difficulties overcome. Never can I forget the great joy arising from what may seem a small comfort—a warm pair of socks! As I write these lines I live over again the particular pleasure of gently drawing them on, and it is impressed for ever on my mind as a fitting reward for the hardships I had put up with.

We pitched our tents in a sheltered narrow valley to the North-West of the large basin. Altitude, 15,400 feet. Thermometer: Minimum, 24°, Maximum, 51°.

CHAPTER XXII

Want of fuel—Cooking under difficulty—Mansing lost and found—Saved from summary justice—Tibetan visitors—We purchase sheep—The snow-line—Cold streams—The petrified *chapati* and human hand.

ONE of the main drawbacks of travelling at these great altitudes was the want of vegetable fuel. There was not a tree, not a shrub to be seen near our camp. Nature wore her most desolate and barren look. Failing wood, my men dispersed to collect and bring in the dry dung of yak, pony and sheep to serve as fuel. Kindling this was no easy matter, box after box of matches was quickly used, and our collective lung power severely drawn upon in fanning the unwilling sparks into a flame only a few inches high. Upon this meagre fire we attempted to cook our food and boil our water (a trying process at such an altitude), keeping our own circulation fairly normal by constantly required efforts. The cuisine that night was not of the usual excellence, and did but little credit to the cook. We had to eat everything half-cooked, or, to be accurate, almost altogether uncooked. The night was a bitterly cold one, with a heavy fall of snow. When we rose in the morning it lay quite two feet deep around us, and the glare was painful to the eyes. I mustered my men. Mansing was missing. He had not

CAMPING IN SNOW

arrived the previous night, and there was no sign of the man I had sent in search of him. I was anxious not only from my personal interest in his load (the fellow carried a load of flour, salt, pepper, and five pounds of butter), but I was afraid that the poor leper might himself have been washed away in one of the dangerous streams. Even if this fear were groundless, he must, I felt, have suffered terribly from the cold with no shelter and no fire. Bijesing, who had gone in search of him, had eaten some food before starting, and had taken blankets with him in case he could not return to camp during the night.

It was long after sunrise when, with the aid of my telescope, I discovered the two men coming towards us. They arrived an hour or so later. Mansing had been found sound asleep, several miles back, lying by the side of the empty butter-pot, the contents of which he had devoured. The discovery of this misdeed caused the greatest indignation in camp, for fatty matter and butter were much cherished by the natives, as being warmth-producing, when going over these cold passes. He was nearly the victim of summary justice at the hands of my angry men, and it was only with trouble that I rescued him from their clutches. To prevent a recurrence of the offence, I ordered the culprit to carry in future a heavy load of photographic plates and instruments, which I thought would not prove quite so appetising.

Before starting I took my usual bath in the cold stream and rubbed myself all over with snow. I found this very invigorating, and when the reaction came I experienced a delightful glow of warmth, notwithstanding the thin clothes I was wearing.

While we were camping, a flock of some six hundred

sheep appeared, and with them some Tibetans. As I had put up my Tibetan tent, they had made for it, expecting to find some of their own countrymen, and their embarrassment was amusing when they found themselves face to face with Dr. Wilson and myself. Hurriedly removing their fur caps, they laid them upon the ground and made a comical jerky curtsey, as if their heads and knees moved by means of a spring. They put out their tongues full length and kept them so until I made signs that they could draw them back, as I wanted them to answer some questions. This unexpected meeting with us frightened them greatly; they were trembling all over with fear, and after getting as much information out of them as they seemed to possess, I took advantage of the opportunity to buy some of their fattest sheep. When the money was paid there was a further display of furred tongues, and more grand salaams ere they departed, while all hands on our side were busy trying to prevent our newly purchased animals from rejoining the flock moving away from us. On our next march these animals proved a great trouble, and we had to drag them the greater part of the way. Kachi, who had been entrusted with a very recalcitrant and strong beast, which I had specially promised my men for their dinner if they made a long march that day, found himself discomfited when he saw that the sheep had freed its head from the cord with which he was dragging it, and was cantering away full speed in the opposite direction. Now, it is well known that at considerable altitudes running is a very painful operation for human beings, the rarified air making the effect of such exertion almost suffocating. Yet Kachi, having overcome his first surprise, was soon chasing the escaped beast, and, urged by the cheers and shouts of my other men, who seemed much concerned over this new calamity, he succeeded, after an exciting chase, in capturing it by its tail, a feat easier to describe than to accomplish, for Tibetan sheep have very short stumpy tails. Kachi fell to the ground exhausted, but he held fast with both hands to his capture, and eventually the animal was secured with ropes. This was the sort of minor trouble with which we had to contend at almost every turn during our journey, and although it may appear trivial, it was exasperating enough at the time.

On fairly undulating ground we gradually rose to a pass 15,580 feet high; then traversing a wide flat land, we followed the Kuti River with its high snowy mountains to the West and East. The snow-line was at 16,000 feet; the snow below this level melts daily, except in a few shaded places. Red and white flowers were still to be seen, though not in such quantities as lower down, and I saw enamoured couples of small black and white butterflies.*

After a while there was yet another bitterly cold stream to ford; two small lakes to skirt; three more deep rivers to wade, with cold water from the snows up to our chests, and then we had to make the best way we could through a large field of rocks and stones showing strong indications of iron, my compasses being at once affected, and becoming for a time quite unreliable owing to the deviation. A curious flat circular stone, resting on the top of others, was pointed out to me as a wonder; the accepted legend of the Shokas being that, centuries ago, one of their countrymen halted by the side of this rock, and having baked a *chapati*, laid it upon

* N.B.—This same kind of butterfly I found at even greater elevations in Tibet.

the rock, proceeding to make others, when to his great astonishment, on raising his hand to take his first *chapati*, he found it had turned into solid stone, and had furthermore assumed gigantic proportions. A few feet farther on I was pointed out another wonder, a great human hand (as the

THE SNOW-LINE AT 16,000 FEET

Tibetans and Shokas call it), which is supposed to have belonged to the maker of the *chapati*. Not being satisfied with his first experience, he laid his hand on the rock, and there it remained, petrified, and in this case also, increasing tenfold in size. I could see, with some stretch of the imagination, a certain resemblance to an enormous human hand, but the thing required more faith than observation.

Mile after mile we marched over sharp stones, wading through a second troublesome delta of eight arms fully a mile in width, across a flat basin of pointed pebbles and stones, until at last, to our great delight, we came to smooth grass land, a soothing comfort to one's torn feet.

Here the Kuti River ran through a large basin, not dissimilar to the one near which we had camped the night before, having also the appearance of lake formation with high perpendicular rocks on the left, which gave one the impression of a vast wall—a rugged and forbidding barrier. Proceeding N.W. the basin became wider and the Kuti River turned to the N.W., while the Mangshan River, descending from the East, joined the first stream in the centre of the basin. In crossing the numerous branches of the two rivers we again experienced, with almost accentuated discomfort, the trials and weariness of the preceding day. The water was colder than ever, our feet were by this time in a dreadful condition, cut and bleeding, because it was constantly necessary to walk barefooted. Aching and benumbed we stumbled on, in and out of water, always, it seemed, encountering sharp small stones. For us there could be no turning back however ; the pain had to be borne before the march was finished, and we won our camping-ground at last under the lee of the high chain of mountains to the North of us, and on the northern bank of the Mangshan River. Directly in front stood the final obstacle, the stupendous backbone of the Himahlyas ; once past this I should be on that high Tibetan plateau so accurately and picturesquely called " the roof of the world."

CHAPTER XXIII

The scouts return—A small exploring party—The Mangshan glacier.

FROM Kuti I had despatched a sturdy Shoka, named Nattoo, to ascertain whether it was possible to cross the chain over the high Mangshan Pass, as in this case I should be enabled to get many marches into Tibet by the jungle without fear of being detected. I should thus get behind the force of soldiers which I was informed the Jong Pen of Taklakot had concentrated at the Lippu Pass to prevent my entering the country, and before they could have time to discover my whereabouts I should be too far ahead for them to find me. Nattoo arrived in camp almost simultaneously with ourselves and had a long tale of woe to relate. He had been half way up the mountain. The snow was deep and there were huge and treacherous cracks in the ice. As he was on his way up, an avalanche had fallen, and it was merely by the skin of his teeth that he had escaped with his life. This was to him an evil omen, and he had turned back without reaching the summit of the pass. He seemed scared and worn out, and declared that it was impossible for us to proceed that way. Unfortunately the thrilling account of the Kutial's misfortunes had a depressing effect on my men. What with the intense cold, the fatigue of carrying heavy loads at high elevations over such rough country, and the fearful rivers which they dreaded, and so many of which we had crossed, my carriers became absolutely demoralised at the thought of new hardships ahead, all the more when I assured them that I did not believe Nattoo, and that I should go and see for myself.

It was 4.30 in the afternoon, and therefore some time before sunset. There would be moonlight. I had on that day marched eight miles,* and though the soles of my feet were cut and sore I was not really tired. Our camp was at an elevation of 16,150 feet, a pretty respectable altitude considering that the highest mountain in Europe is only 15,781 feet. Dr. Wilson insisted on accompanying me to the top, and Kachi Ram and a Rongba coolie volunteered to come as well. Bijesing, the Johari, got on his feet after some persuasion, and that completed our little exploration party. Chanden Sing, who was really the only man I could trust, was left in charge of the camp, with strict orders to punish severely any one who might attempt to turn back during my absence.

We set out almost immediately after reaching camp, following up stream the course of the Mangshan River, which is boxed in between high cliffs, those south of it running in a direction of 100° (b.m.), those to the north converging to 130°; the two ranges eventually meeting in the glacier at the foot of Mangshan, about three miles E.-E.S.E. of our camp. There was no track, and the walking was extremely difficult and troublesome, over large slippery stones, between which one's feet constantly slipped

* It must be remembered that at high elevations the exertion of walking eight miles would be equivalent to that of marching about twice the distance at much lower altitudes.

and got jammed, straining and injuring one's ankles. Little trusting my followers, who seemed on the verge of mutiny, I did not care to leave behind in camp the heavy load of silver rupees (R. 800) sewn in my coat, which, by the way, I always carried on my person, as well as my rifle, two compasses (prismatic and luminous), two aneroids, one half-chronometer, and another watch and some thirty cartridges. The combined weight of these articles was considerable,* and I felt it especially during the first days of my march. On this particular afternoon it was almost too much for my strength. However, one gets accustomed to most things, and after a while I felt comparatively little discomfort in marching under it. I persisted in thus weighting myself simply to be on the safe side, so as to be always prepared in case my men revolted or abandoned me.

We proceeded up and down the series of hillocks and in and out of the innumerable channels that the melting snow and ice had, with the aid of centuries, cut deep into the mass of rolling stones. At the point where the two ranges met there stood before us the magnificent pale green ice-terraces of the Mangshan glacier, surmounted by extensive snowfields winding their way to the summit of the mountain range. Clouds enveloped the higher peaks. The clear Alpine ice showed vertical streaks, especially in the lower part of the glacier, where it was granulated to a certain extent. The base, the sides and top being covered with a thick coat of fresh snow, and my time being very limited, I was unable to make careful investigations to ascertain the recent movement and oscillations of this glacier. Judging by the nature of the stony tracts we had passed over, and also by the mounds, similar to those of

* See Appendix. Letter by Dr. H. Wilson.

THE MANGSHAN GLACIER

a terminal moraine, which increased as we approached the glacier and its snow-covered fringe, I concluded that the glacier must have retreated considerably. The rocks and stones, as I have already mentioned, were shiny and slippery, which I attributed to the friction of the ice, and where the ice had extended over gravel, this was greatly disturbed, and scarred by innumerable channels, due, no doubt, to the mighty force of the moving ice besides the constant action of melting snows during the summer. The slopes of the mountains on the north showed no indication of having been disturbed, but the range on the southern side had all the appearance of having been cut and excavated by the ice. Probably the large basins which I had crossed on my way from Kuti, and even the last one, facing our camp, were after all reservoirs formed by ancient moraines with alluvial deposits.

CHAPTER XXIV

Snow and troublesome *débris*—The doctor's sufferings—Kachi disabled—Further trials—A weird apparition—Delirium—All safe—The descent.

THE Mangshan River rises from this glacier, but we left the glacier (17,800 feet) to the right, and, turning sharply northwards, began our ascent towards the pass. To gaze upon the incline before us was alone sufficient to deter one from attempting to climb it, had one a choice; in addition to this, the snow we struggled over was so soft and deep that we sank into it up to our waists. Occasionally the snow alternated with patches of loose *débris* and rotten rock, on which we were no better off; in fact, the fatigue of progressing over them was simply overpowering. Having climbed up half-a-dozen steps among the loose cutting stones, we felt ourselves sliding back to almost our original point of departure, followed by a small avalanche of shifting material that only stopped when it got to the foot of the mountain.

At 19,000 feet we were for a considerable distance on soft snow, covering an ice-field with deep crevasses and cracks in it. We had to feel our way with great caution, particularly as there was only the light of the moon to depend upon.

Fortunately, as we rose higher, there were no more crevasses, but I began to feel a curious exhaustion that I had never experienced before. At sunset the thermometer which Kachi carried for me had descended forty degrees within a few minutes, and the sudden change in the temperature seemed to affect us all more or less; but we went on, with the exception of Bijesing, who was seized with mountain sickness so violently that he was unable to proceed. The doctor, too, a man of powerful build, was suffering considerably. His legs, he said, had become like lead, and each seemed to weigh a ton. The effort of lifting, or even moving, them required all his energy. Although he was terribly blown and gasping for breath, yet he would not give in, and he struggled on bravely until we reached an altitude of 20,500 feet. Here he was seized with such exhaustion and pain that he was unable to proceed. Kachi Ram, the Rongba and I went ahead, but we also were suffering, Kachi complaining of violent beating in his temples and loud buzzing in his ears. He also gasped and staggered dangerously, threatening to collapse at any moment. At 21,000 feet he fell flat on the snow. He was instantly asleep, breathing heavily and snoring raspingly. His hands and feet were icy cold, and I rubbed them. But what caused me more anxiety than anything was the irregular beating and throbbing of his heart. I wrapped him up in his blanket and my waterproof, and, having seen to his general comfort, I shouted to the doctor, telling him what had happened, and that I was going to push on as much higher as I could stand, the Rongba being now the only one of the party who was able to keep up.

A thick mist came on and enveloped us, which considerably added to our trials. Our efforts to get on after we left Kachi at 21,000 feet were desperate, our lungs in convulsion as if about to burst, our pulses hastened, our hearts throbbing (mine being ordinarily very regular) as if they would beat themselves out of our bodies. Exhausted and seized by irresistible drowsiness, the Rongba and I nevertheless at last reached the top. It was a satisfaction to have got there, to have reached such an altitude, although I had long realised the impossibility of getting my men over by this way. It served me also to ascertain the amount of snow on the other side of the range, which, when the fog lifted somewhat, I found to be greater on the northern slope than on the southern. Although almost fainting with fatigue, I registered my observations. The altitude was 22,000 feet, the hour 11 P.M., and there was a strong, cutting North-East wind. I had stupidly forgotten to take my thermometer out of Kachi's pocket when I left him, and was unable to register the temperature, but the cold was intense. The stars were extraordinarily brilliant and the moon shone bright for a while over the panorama around me, and though it was a view of utter desolation, it had nevertheless a curious indescribable fascination. Below me, to the south, were mountainous masses buried in snow, and to the South-West and North-East were peaks even higher than the one on which I stood. To the north stretched the immense, dreary Tibetan plateau with undulations and intricate hill ranges, beyond which a high mountain range with snow peaks could just be perceived in the distance. I could see very little snow near by, except on the northern slope of the range I was standing on, and on the hill-tops which dotted the plateau.

I had barely taken it in, barely realised the wonder of

nature asleep when the mist again rose before me and I saw a gigantic phantom rising out of it. It stood in the centre of a luminous circle, a tall, dark figure in the folds of an enormous veil of mist. The effect was overwhelming, and it was only after some moments that I realised that the spectre wore my features, was a liquid presentation of my own proportions colossally enlarged; that I stood in the centre of a lunar rainbow, and that I was gazing on the reflection of myself in the mist. As I moved my arms, my body, or my head, the ghost-like figure moved, and I felt myself irresistibly changing my postures—oddly and nervously at first—then, with an awakening sense of the ridiculous in my actions—so as to make my image change and do as I did. I felt like a child placed for the first time in front of a mirror.

The coloured plate given in this book represents a solar spectre with circular rainbow which I saw later on at a comparatively low altitude; the lunar effect differed from this in that the colours of the rainbow were but faintly distinguishable.

The Rongba had fallen exhausted, and I felt so faint with the awful pressure on my lungs, that, despite all my efforts to resist it, I collapsed on the snow. The coolie and I, shivering pitifully, shared the same blanket for additional warmth. Both of us were seized with irresistible drowsiness, as if we had taken a strong narcotic. I fought hard against it, for I well knew that if my eyelids once closed they would almost certainly remain so for ever. I called to the Rongba. He was fast asleep. I summoned up my last atom of vitality to keep my eyes open. The wind blew hard and biting, with a hissing noise. How that hiss still sounds in my ears! It seemed like the whisper of death. The Rongba, crouched with teeth chattering, was moaning, and his sudden shudders bespoke great pain. It seemed only common charity to let him have the blanket, which was in any case too small for both, so I wrapped it tightly round his head and body. He was doubled up with his chin on his knees. This small exertion was quite sufficient to make me lose the tug-of-war in which I was pulling against nature. Just like the subject who, under hypnotic influence, feels his own will and power suddenly going from him, so I felt the entire hopelessness of further struggle against the supernatural forces I was contending with. Falling backwards on the snow, I made a last desperate effort to gaze at the glittering stars . . . my sight became dim and obscured. . . .

For how long this semi-consciousness lasted, I do not know. "God! how ghastly! Doctor! Kachi!" I tried to articulate. My voice seemed choked in my throat. Was what I saw before me real? The two men, as if frozen to death by the side of each other, seemed lying on that vast white sheet of snow, motionless as statues of ice. In my dream I attempted to raise them. They were quite rigid. I knelt beside them, calling them and frantically striving to bring them back to consciousness and life. Bewildered, I turned round to look for Bijesing, and, as I did so, all sense of vitality seemed to freeze within me. I saw myself enclosed in a quickly contracting tomb of transparent ice. It was easy to realise that I too would shortly be nothing but a solid block of ice, like my companions. My legs, my arms were already congealed. Horror-stricken as I was at the approach of such a hopeless, ghastly death, my sensations were accompanied by a languor and lassitude indescribable but far from unpleasant. To some

Lithographed by F. A. Brockhaus, Leipzig (Germany).

THE SPECTRE AND CIRCULAR RAIN BOW.

extent thought or wonderment was still alive. Should I dwindle painlessly away, preferring rest and peace to effort, or should I make a last struggle to save myself? The ice seemed to close in more and more every moment. I was choking.

I tried to scream! to force myself through the suffocating

"I ROUSED THE RONGBA"

weight on me! I gave a violent plunge, and then everything had vanished. The frozen Kachi, the doctor, the transparent tomb! Nothingness!

At last I was able to open my eyes, which ached as if needles had been stuck into them. It was snowing hard. I had temporarily lost the use of my legs and fingers. They were frozen. So violent was the shock of realising how very near death I had really been, that in waking up from the ghastly nightmare I became acutely alive to the full importance of instantly making my way down to a lower level. I was already covered with a layer of snow, and I suppose it was the frigid pressure on my forehead that caused the dream. It is, however, probable that, had it not been for the hideous vision that shook my nerves free of paralysing torpor, I should never have awakened from that spell-bound silence.

I sat up with difficulty, and by rubbing and beating them, slowly regained the use of my lower limbs. I roused the Rongba, rubbed him, and shook him till he was able to move. We began our descent.

No doubt the satisfaction of going up high mountains is very great; but can it be compared to that of coming down?

Descending was dangerous but not wearisome. The incline being extremely steep, we took gigantic strides on the snow, and when we came to patches of *débris*, we slid ten or fifteen feet each step amidst a deafening roar from the huge mass of loose stones set in motion by our descent.

"Hark!" I said to the Rongba, "what is that?"

We waited till all was silence, and with hands up to our ears listened attentively. It was still snowing.

"*Ao, ao, ao! Jaldi ao! Tumka hatte?* Come, come, come quickly! Where are you?" cried a faint distressed voice from far down below.

We quickened our pace; having hardly any control over our legs, our descent was precipitous. The snow-fall ceased and we became enveloped in a thick mist which pierced into our very bones.

Guided by the anxious cries of the doctor, whose voice

we recognised, we continued our breakneck journey downward. The cries got more and more distinct, and at last, to my great joy, we came face to face with Wilson, who, thank Heaven, was alive but almost helpless, as he said his legs were still like lead, and it was all he could do to move them.

Owing to his anxiety about us, he had been shouting for a long time, and getting no answer, he became very uneasy, all the more so as he found he could in no way come to our help. He had quite given us up for lost.

We looked for and found Kachi. He had slept like a top, curled up in his warm blanket and my overcoat, and was now quite refreshed, so all united again, we continued our race downwards, exchanging our experiences and sensations. We had no very serious mishaps, and life and strength gradually came back to us again when we descended to lower elevations. The ascent from the glacier at the bottom of the mountain to the summit occupied four and a half hours; the precipitous descent, without counting stoppages, only the ninth part of that time.

Over the same trying stony valley we reached camp during the early hours of the morning. The distance from camp to the altitude reached and back was over ten miles; therefore, during the twenty-four hours I had altogether gone eighteen miles (quite a record at such great altitudes). I may here also remark that, since breakfast at six o'clock the previous morning, I had taken no food of any kind, thus making an interval of twenty-three hours between one meal and the next. The anxiety of my men in camp was intense. They had lost all hope of seeing us again, and they were quite reassured when I told them that we would proceed later in the morning by the Lumpiya Pass, which was believed to be far easier.

In no time they had lighted a fire of dung, and after having had (at five o'clock in the morning) a handsome feed of rice, *chapatis*, extract of meat, and strengthening emergency food, we felt we were entitled to a well-deserved rest.

CHAPTER XXV

The sources of the Kuti River—The Lumpiya glacier—The summit of the range—Bird's-eye view of Tibet—Rubso frozen almost to death—The Lumpiya Pass—Two coolies in distress.

At 9 A.M. we were ready again to start. The thermometer registered 40° inside the tent, and the minimum temperature outside during the night had been 14°. We followed the Kuti River at the foot of the mountain range, travelling in a direction of 298° (b.m). On rounding a prominent headland, where the Kuti River flows through a narrow passage, we saw facing us on a mound, fourteen stone pillars and pyramids with white stones on them and the customary flying prayers of cloth. It is from this point that the ascent to the Lumpiya Pass begins.

There are two sources of the Kuti Yangti, joining in a large basin; one comes from two extensive glaciers to the S.W., the other from a glacier directly under the Lumpiya Pass. The river at the junction of the two sources is not more than six yards across. Our route gradually ascended, going N.W. first, then swinging away to N.E. until we attained an elevation of 17,350 feet on a flat basin covered with deep snow. So far we had proceeded with no very great trouble or fatigue, but matters suddenly altered for the worse.

Each coolie in the long silent row at the head of which I marched, sank in the snow up to his knees, often up to his waist. They formed, undoubtedly, a picturesque sight in this lonely region, the only bit of life in the picture, the white frozen sheet of snow throwing into strong contrast their faces wrapped tightly round with white turbans. Some wore fur caps with ear flaps; all had long sheep-skin coats and high boots of skins; many used snow spectacles; and as this procession, silent and grave, with loads on their backs, struggled higher and higher with piteous panting, you speculated apprehensively as to how many of them would ever return. Moving cautiously to avoid the many treacherous cracks, I made my way ahead with considerable trouble to a spot six hundred feet higher, where I halted for a while on a rocky island fairly clear of snow. As coolie after coolie arrived, breathing convulsively, he dropped his load and sat quietly by the side of it. There was not a grumble, not a word of reproach for the hard work they were made to endure. Sleet was falling, and the wet and cold increased the discomfort. There was now a very steep pull before us. To the left, we had a glacier beginning in a precipitous fall of ice, about one hundred feet in height. Like the Mangshan glacier, it was in horizontal ribbon-like strata of beautifully clear ice, showing no dirt bands. Perpendicular stripes of a darker greenish colour could be observed arising from the unequal degrees of compactness of the ice; the strata showed almost horizontal, with no curvatures nor depressions in any part of them. The top, the base and the sides of the glacier were in this case also buried in deep snow.

The doctor and I went ahead. In our anxiety to reach

ASCENDING THE LUMPIYA PASS

the summit, unable to discern the track, now covered by several feet of snow, we mistook our bearings, and with great fatigue climbed up an extremely steep incline. Here we were on a patch of the troublesome loose *débris*, on which we struggled for over half an hour until we reached the top of the range, 18,750 feet, considerably higher than the pass itself. Four men had come with us, the others, to whom we signalled, bearing more to the west by another dangerous track skirting the glacier.

The wind from the N.E. was piercing and the cold terrible. Under the lee of a large rock we found temporary shelter, and through my telescope scanned the Tibetan plateau spread out before us. From this high eyrie we obtained a superb bird's-eye view. Huge masses of snow covered the Tibetan side of the Himahlyas, as well as the lower range of mountains immediately in front of us, running almost parallel to our range. Two thousand feet below, between these two ranges, flowed, in a wide barren valley, a river which is afterwards called the Darma Yankti or Lumpiya Yankti. In the distance, a flat plateau, rising some eight hundred feet above the river, and resembling a gigantic embankment of a railway line, could be seen extending for many miles; and far away to the north, a chain of high blue mountains capped with snow, undoubtedly the Kangri chain with the Kelas peaks.

A painful incident had unfortunately happened to one of my followers: poor Rubso, a Christian convert, had fallen exhausted from cold and fatigue. He had been seized with cramp, and was lying in a semi-conscious state, his teeth chattering and his features distorted and livid; his eyes were sunken and lifeless, and he showed signs of complete collapse. We hastily carried him under the shelter of a rock and rubbed him vigorously, in the hope of restoring his circulation. After more than half an hour of the greatest anxiety and exertion, to our intense relief he partially recovered, and was able to proceed slowly with our help.

Having climbed the wrong path, we now had to descend to the pass, six hundred feet lower. We made our way along dangerous rocks and *débris*. I was just clinging with my half-frozen fingers to a prominent rock, striving to get on the other side, when screams of distress from below struck my ears. Notwithstanding the unsafe position I was in, I could not help turning my head to see what had happened. On the steep incline of snow two coolies with their respective loads were sliding, at incredible speed. They eventually reached the basin, where the angle of the descent being suddenly altered, it caused them to revolve several times on their own axes, the different bags, &c., forming their loads, flying about and being scattered in every direction. I gave a sigh of relief when I saw the men getting up. One coolie picked up one after the other the goods that had been entrusted to him, tied them together, got them on his back, and began the difficult ascent a second time. The other was crying and moaning, so that we could plainly hear him from our elevation. He seemed giddy. After a moment or two he staggered, fell back and lay as if dead. Hastening over the slippery rocks, and then down precipitously on the loose *débris*, I gained the pass, 18,150 feet. Two reluctant men were immediately despatched to the relief of the coolie in distress. They first carried his load up, then him. After some time he, too, got over the severe shock and fright, and though he was rather shattered and aching all over, I succeeded in persuading the man that nothing was the matter with him.

THE LUMPIYA GLACIER AND PASS

We then hurried down the steep declivity on the Tibetan side, to get away quickly from the bitterly cold, windy pass. Describing a wide arc of a circle, and then making straight down across several long snow-beds, we at last reached the river level and pitched our tents on snow at an altitude of 16,900 feet. There was no wood, no yak or pony dung, no lichens, no moss, and therefore nothing with which we could make a fire. It seemed hard upon my men that, after such a toilsome day, they should be compelled to go to sleep without having had a good meal. They believe—and they are right—that eating cold food at such high elevations, with such low temperature, leads to certain death. They preferred, therefore, to remain without food altogether. Night came, and with it the wind blowing in gusts, and piling the grit and snow around our tents. During the nocturnal hours, with the hurricane raging, we had to turn out of our flapping canvases several times to make the loose pegs firmer. Fastening all the frozen ropes was very cold work. At 2 A.M. the thermometer was down to 12°. At 9 A.M. in the sun, it went up to 26°, and inside the tent at the same hour we had a temperature as high as 32°—freezing-point.

CHAPTER XXVI

Mysterious footprints—Brigand or spy?—Passes and tracks—Intense cold—No fuel—A high flat plateau—Fuel at last!—Two spies in disguise—What they took us for.

In a hurricane of grit and drenching rain we packed up our traps as best we could and again started on our way. I was slightly in advance when, to my surprise, I noticed, some two hundred yards only from camp, a double line of recent footmarks on the snow. Those coming towards us were somewhat indistinct and nearly covered with grit, those going in the opposite direction seemed quite recent. After carefully examining these footprints, I felt pretty certain that they had been made by a Tibetan. Where the footprints stopped, marks in the snow showed that the man had at different points laid himself flat on the ground. No doubt we had been spied upon and watched. My own men had shown many signs of terror ever since we had crossed to this side of the Himahlyas, and were now all anxiously stooping low over these prints and speculating on their origin. Their excitement and fear were strange to watch. Some surmised that the man must be a *Daku*, a brigand, and that in the evening we should be attacked by the whole band; others maintained that the spy could only be a Sepoy sent by the Gyanema officers to watch our movements. In any case, this incident was held to be an evil omen, and during our march in a N.W. direction along the bank of the river we continually saw the trail. The wildest speculations and imaginations were rife. To the left of us we passed the valleys leading south to the Neway Pass; then a second to the Kats, 230° (b.m.). The bearings were taken from the mouth of the river descending from it, a tributary of the Darma Yangti.

Six miles from our last camp, at bearings 340°, was the Luway Pass.

We were travelling on flat or slightly undulating barren ground. We waded across another cold river with water up to our waists, and my men became so exhausted that one mile farther we had to halt at 16,650 feet.

The cold was intense, and again we had no fuel of any kind. A furious wind was blowing, with snow falling heavily in the evening. My carriers, half starved, ate a little *satoo*, a kind of oatmeal, but Chanden Sing, a Rajiput, could not, without breaking his caste, eat his food without undressing. It was two days since he had had his last meal, but rather than infringe the rules of his religion, or take off his clothes in such frigid regions, he preferred to curl up in his blanket and go to sleep fasting.

The doctor left the warmth and comfort of blankets to go and talk with the men, and get their views about weather prospects and the chances of our route. I preferred the comfort of such warmth as I could get in our tent, where the temperature was 28° Fahr., or four degrees below freezing. The snow was lying a foot deep, and it was still falling heavily. The carriers were all attempting to sleep, huddled as close as possible to each other for warmth; they refused to move, saying they would rather die, and we found it convenient to believe them, and get what warmth and sleep we could under blankets in the tent.

Two or three hours later the weather cleared. The coolies, half starved, came to complain that they were again unable to find fuel to cook their food, and that they would leave me. The position of affairs was critical. I immediately took my telescope and clambered to the top of a small hillock. It was curious to note what unbounded faith the coolies had in this glass. It was evident that they believed in a childlike fashion that I could see through mountains with it. I came down with the reassuring news that one day's march further would bring us to a fine supply of fuel.

They cheerfully hastened to pack up the loads, and set forth with unusual energy in the direction I had pointed out. We followed a parallel line to the high flat plateau on the other side of the stream, the slopes of which, in relation to the plain we were standing on, were at an obtuse angle of about 115°. The snow-covered plateau extended from S.W. to N.E. Beyond it to the N. could be seen some high snowy peaks, in all probability the lofty summits S.E. of Gartok. At the point where the Luway joins the other three rivers there is a direct way to the summit of the tableland, along which it continues across the Himahlyas by the Luway Pass. To our right we were flanked by high rugged mountains, with an occasional precipitous torrent. Six hours' brisk marching took us to a sheltered nook, where a few lichens and shrubs were growing. If we had suddenly descended into the Black Forest of Germany, or

SPIED

the Yosemite Valley, with their gigantic century old trees, our delight could not have been greater. As it was, the highest of these shrubs stood no higher than six or seven inches from the ground, while the diameter of the largest piece of wood we collected was smaller than that of an ordinary pencil. With feverish activity all hands went to work to root up these plants for fuel.

When night came, the same number of hands were busy cooking and transferring with alarming celerity such steaming food as was available from the different fires to the mouths of the famished coolies. Happiness reigned in camp, and all recent hardships were forgotten.

A fresh surprise was awaiting us when we rose. Two Tibetans disguised as beggars had come to our camp. They professed to be suffering from cold and starvation. I gave orders that they should be properly fed and kindly treated. On being cross-examined they confessed that they were spies sent by the officer at Gyanema to ascertain whether a sahib had crossed the frontier, and whether we had seen anything of him.

We had so many things to attend to in the morning, and it was so cold, that washing had really become a nuisance, and I for my part gave it up, at least *pro tem.* We were sunburnt, and we wore turbans and snow-glasses, so the Tibetans departed under the impression that our party consisted of a Hindoo doctor, his brother, and a caravan of servants (none of whom had seen a sahib coming), and that we were now on a pilgrimage to the sacred Mansarowar Lake and Kelas Mount.

Before the men we treated this as a great joke, but, all the same, Wilson and I anxiously consulted as to our immediate plans. Should we make a rapid march during the night over the mountain range to our right, and strike east by the jungle, or should we face the Gyanema leader and his soldiers ?

We decided to meet them rather than go out of our way, and I gave orders to raise camp immediately.

CHAPTER XXVII

Lama Chokden—A Tibetan guard—The sacred Kelas—Reverence of my men for the Sacred Mountain—Trying hard to keep friends with the gods—*Obos*—Water flowing to us.

WE altered our course from N. to N.E., rising to 16,600 feet, and leaving the high tableland to the west. We arrived at Lama Chokden (or Chorten), a pass protected by a Tibetan guard, who quickly turned out, matchlocks in hand, as we approached. They seemed a miserable lot, and not only offered no resistance, but actually begged for money and food. They complained of ill-treatment by their superiors, stating that they received no pay, and even food was only occasionally sent to them at this outpost. Their tunics were in rags ; each man carried a sword stuck in front through the girdle. Here, too, we had more inquiries about the young sahib, as messengers on horseback had been sent post-haste from Taklakot to warn the Gyanema officer not to let him penetrate into Hundes* by the Lumpiya Pass, should he attempt it. Their description of my supposed appearance was very amusing, and when they said that if the sahib came they would have to cut his head off, I felt so touched by their good-natured

* Hundes = Tibet.

confidence that I wanted to distribute a few rupees among them.

"Do not give them anything, sir," said Kachi and the doctor. "These fellows are hand and glove with the bands of dacoits; the latter will soon be told that we have money, and we shall run great risk of being attacked at night."

I insisted on giving them a present.

"No, sir," cried Kachi, distressed; "do not do it, or it will bring us no end of trouble and misfortune. If you give them four annas, that will be ample."

Accordingly the officer in command had this large sum deposited in the outstretched palm of his hand, and to show his satisfaction, he pulled out his tongue to its full length, waving both his hands at me for some minutes, and bowing clumsily at the same time. His fur cap had been previously removed and thrown on the ground. This was indeed a grand salaam, a ceremonious acknowledgment of a gift of something less than fourpence!

While the doctor remained in conversation with him, I happened to witness a very beautiful sight. To the north the clouds had dispersed, and the snow-capped sacred Kelas Mount stood majestic before us. In appearance not unlike the graceful roof of a temple, Kelas towers over the long white-capped range, contrasting in beautiful blending of tints with the warm sienna colour of the lower elevations. Kelas is some two thousand feet higher than the other peaks of the Gangir chain, with strongly defined ledges and terraces marking its stratifications, and covered with horizontal layers of snow standing out in brilliant colour against the dark ice-worn rock. The Tibetans, the Nepalese, the Shokas, the Humlis, Jumlis and Hindoos, all have a strong veneration for this mountain, which is believed by them to be the

MY MEN SALAAMING KELAS AT LAMA CHOKDEN

abode of all the good gods, especially of the god Siva. In fact, the ledge round its base is said by the Hindoos to be the mark of the ropes used by the devil (Rakas) to pull down the throne of Siva.

My men, with heads uncovered, their faces turned towards the sacred peak, were muttering prayers. With joined hands, which they slowly raised as high as the forehead, they prayed fervently, and then went down on their knees, with heads bent low to the ground. My brigand follower, who was standing close by me, hurriedly whispered that I should join in this act of prayer.

"You must keep friends with the gods," said the bandit; "misfortune will attend you if you do not salaam to Kelas; that is the home of a good god!" and he pointed to the peak with the most devout air of conviction.

To please him I saluted the mountain with the utmost deference, and, taking my cue from the others, placed a white stone on one of the hundreds of *Chokdens* or *Obos* (stone pillars) erected by devotees at this spot. These *Obos*, or rough pyramids of stones, are found on the tracks traversing all high passes, near lakes, in fact, everywhere, but rarely in such quantities as at Lama Chokden. The hill in front, and at the back of the guard-house, was literally covered with these structures. Each passer-by deposits a stone on one of them—a white stone if possible—and this is supposed to bring him good fortune, or if he has a wish he desires accomplished, such a contribution will enhance the chances of its fulfilment.

The guard-house itself was of rough stone, mean and desolate, and in any country but Tibet would not be considered fit accommodation for pigs.

After going a mile or so farther, as the sun was fast

disappearing, we searched for a suitable spot to pitch our tents. There was no sign of any water, only the stony bed of a dried rivulet. We were discussing the situation, when a faint sound as of rushing water struck our ears. It grew louder and louder, and then we saw coming towards us a stream of limpid molten snow, gradually advancing over the bed of stones. Evidently the snow of the mountains had taken all day to melt, and the water was only now reaching this spot. My dacoit was in a great state of excitement.

"Water flowing to you, sahib!" he exclaimed, with his arms outstretched. "You will have great luck! Look! Look! You want water for your camp, and a stream comes to you! Heaven blesses you. You must dip your fingers into the water as soon as it comes up to you, and throw some drops over your shoulders. Then will fortune attend you on your journey."

I readily fell in with this Tibetan superstition, and we all dipped our fingers, and sprinkled the water behind our backs. Wilson, however, who took the matter quite seriously, said it was all nonsense, and would not give in to such "childish fancy."

Good fortune would have meant much to me, but in the days to come this simple rite proved to have been futile! Certainly no good fairy watched over my steps, and often the thought of this ceremony came back to me with bitterness.

CHAPTER XXVIII

An extensive valley—Kiang, or wild horse—Their strange ways—The Gyanema fort—Apprehension at our appearance—A parley—"Cut off our heads!"—Revolt and murder contemplated—Hypocritical ways of Tibetan officials—Help summoned from everywhere—Preparing for war.

In front of our camp was a great stretch of flat alluvial land, which had been, to all appearance, at some remote time the bed of a large lake about ten miles long and fourteen wide. With my telescope I could see plainly to 40° (b.m.), at the foot of a small hill, the camping-ground of Karko. There were many tents, and my men seemed much reassured when by their shape and colour we made them out to be those of the Joharis from Milam, who come over at this place to trade with the Hunyas.* To E.N.E. we had a valley extending for many miles between two high ranges, and to the W. and N.W. were hills between us and the Darma Yangti, flowing there in a N.N.E. direction. Beyond Karko to the North, a stretch of water, the Gyanema Lake, showed brilliantly, and beyond it some comparatively low hill ranges. In the distance, more snowy peaks were visible.

On leaving camp we traversed the plain for six miles in a N.E. direction, and then, on a course of 80° (b.m.),

* Hunyas = Tibetans.

turned into a smaller valley well enclosed by hills, following it for a distance of three or four miles. This formed, as it were, an arm of the other large valley.

During our march we saw many large herds of *Kiang* (wild horse). These animals came quite close to us. They resembled zebras in shape and movement of body, but in colour they were mostly light brown. The natives regarded their near proximity as extremely dangerous; for their apparent tameness is often deceptive, enabling them to draw quite close to the unwary traveller, and then with a sudden dash seize him by the stomach, inflicting a horrible wound with their powerful jaws. Their graceful and coquettish ways were most taking; we occasionally threw stones at them to keep them at a safe distance, but after cantering prettily away, they would follow us again and come within a few yards. I succeeded in taking some very good negatives, which unfortunately were afterwards destroyed by the Tibetan authorities. I still have, however, some of the sketches I made of them. We climbed over another hill range, and descended on the other side into a grassy stretch of flat land, in the Northern portion of which was a sheet of water. On a hill South of the lake stood the Gyanema Khar or fort, a primitive tower-like structure of stones, with a tent pitched over it to answer the purpose of roof, supporting a flagstaff, on which flew two dirty white rags. They were not the colours of Hundes, but only wind prayers. Lower down, at the foot of the hill, were two or three large black tents and a small shed of stones. Hundreds of black, white, and brown yaks were grazing on the green patches of grass.

The appearance of our party evidently created some apprehension, for we had hardly shown ourselves on the summit of the col when from the fort a gong began to sound loudly, filling the air with its unmelodious metallic notes. A shot was fired. Soldiers with their matchlocks were seen running here and there. They pulled down one of the black tents and hastily conveyed it inside the fort, the greater part of the garrison also seeking shelter within the walls with the *empressement* almost of a stampede. When, after some little time, they convinced themselves that we had no evil intentions, some of the Tibetan officers, followed by their men, came trembling to meet us. The doctor, unarmed, went ahead to talk with them, whereas my bearer and I remained with the coolies for the double purpose of protecting our baggage in case of a treacherous attack, and of preventing my panic-stricken carriers from abandoning their loads and escaping. But matters looked peaceful enough. Rugs were spread on the grass, and eventually we all sat down. An hour's trying parley with the Tibetan officers, during which time the same things were repeated over and over again, led to nothing. They said they could on no account allow any one from India, whether native or sahib, to proceed, and we must go back. We on our side stated that we were doing no harm. We were pilgrims to the sacred Lake of Mansarowar, only a few miles farther. We had gone to much expense and trouble. How could we now turn back when so near our goal? We would not go back, and trusted they would allow us to proceed.

We treated them courteously and kindly, and probably mistaking this for fear they promptly took advantage of it, especially the Magbun * or chief officer in charge of the Gyanema fort. His marked humility, of which at first he had made so much display, suddenly turned into arrogance.

* *Magpun* or *Magbun* = General-in-Chief.

"You will have to cut off my head," said he with a vicious countenance, "or rather I will cut off yours before I let you go another step."

"Cut off my head?" cried I, jumping on my feet and shoving a cartridge into my rifle.

"Cut off my head?" repeated my bearer, pointing with his Martini-Henry at the official.

"Cut off our heads?" queried angrily the Brahmin and the two Christian servants of Dr. Wilson, handling a Winchester and a couple of Gourkha *kukris* (large knives).

"No, no, no, no! Salaam, salaam, salaam!" poured forth the Magbun with the celerity of speech only possessed by a panic-stricken man. "Salaam, salaam," repeated he again, bowing down to the ground, tongue out, and depositing his hat at our feet in a disgustingly servile manner. "Let us talk like friends!"

The Magbun's men, no braver than their master, shifted their positions in a nonchalant manner so as to be screened by their superiors in case of our firing, and on second thoughts, judging even such a precaution to ensure them but scanty safety, they one after the other got up, walked steadily away for half-a-dozen steps, to show it was not fear that made them leave, and then took to their heels.

The Magbun and the other officers who remained became more and more meek. We spoke and argued in a friendly manner for two long hours, but with no appreciable results. The Magbun could not decide of his own accord. He would consult with his officers, and he could give us an answer no sooner than the next morning. In the meantime he would provide for our general comfort and ensure our safety, if we would encamp near his tent. This, of course,

I well knew to be an expedient to gain time, so as to send for soldiers to Barca, north of the Rakstal Lake, as well as to all the neighbouring camps. I frankly told him my suspicions, but added that I wished to deal fairly with the Tibetan authorities before resorting to force. I reminded the Magbun again, and made him plainly understand, that we were merely peaceful travellers, and had not come to fight; that I was paying tenfold for anything I purchased from him or his men, and was glad to do so; but at the same time, let the hand beware that dared touch or twist a single hair of any one belonging to my party! The Magbun declared that he understood perfectly. He swore friendship, and as friends he begged us to stop over the night near his camp. By the Sun and Kunju Sum (Trinity) he gave a solemn oath that we should in no way be harmed. He took humble leave of us and retired.

The doctor and I had been sitting in front, next were Chanden Sing, the Brahmin, and the two Christians. The carriers were behind. When the Magbun had gone I turned round to look at them. Behold, what a sight! They one and all were crying miserably, each man hiding his face in his hands. Kachi had tears streaming down his cheeks, Dola was sobbing, while the Daku and the other Tibetan in my employ, who had for the occasion assumed a disguise, were concealing themselves behind their loads. Serious though the situation was, I could not help laughing at the demoralisation of my men. We pitched our tents, and I had been sitting a while inside one, registering my observations and writing up my diary, when Kachi crept in, apparently in great distress. He seemed so upset that he could hardly speak.

"Master!" he whispered. "Master! The Tibetans have

sent a man to your coolies threatening them that they must betray you or die. They must abandon you during the night, and if you attempt to retain them, they must kill you."

At the same time that this agent had been sent to conspire with my coolies, other envoys of the Magbun brought huge masses of dry dung to make our fires, conveying to me his renewed declarations of friendship. Notwithstanding this, soldiers were despatched in every direction to call for help. I saw them start: one went towards Kardam and Taklakot; a second proceeded in the direction of Barca, and a third galloped to the West.

My carriers were evidently preparing a *coup-de-main* as I watched them through an opening in the tent. They were busily engaged separating their blankets and clothes from my loads, dividing the provisions among themselves, and throwing aside my goods. I went out to them, patiently made them repack the things, and cautioned them that I would shoot any one who attempted to revolt or desert.

While the doctor and I sat down to a hearty meal, which rumours in camp said would be our last, Chanden Sing was entrusted with the preparations for war on our side. He cleaned the rifles with much care, and got the ammunition ready, for he was longing to fight. The Brahmin, on whose faithfulness we could also rely, remained cool and collected through the whole affair. He was a philosopher, and never worried over anything. He took no active part in preparing for our defence, for he feared not death. God alone could kill him, he argued, and all the matchlocks in the country together could not send a bullet through him unless God wished it. And if it were the God's decree that he should die, what could be the use of rebelling against it? The two converts, like good Christians, were more practical, and lost no time in grinding the huge blades of their *kukris* to the sharpness of razors.

When darkness came a guard was placed, at a little distance off, all round our camp. It seemed likely that a rush on our tent with the help of my treacherous carriers was contemplated, should an opportunity occur. One of us kept watch outside all through the night, and those inside lay down in their clothes, with loaded rifles by them. I can't say that either Dr. Wilson or I felt particularly uneasy, for the Tibetan soldiers with their clumsy matchlocks, long spears, and jewelled swords and daggers, inspired us more with admiration for their picturesque appearance than with fear.

CHAPTER XXIX

Arrival of a high official—The Barca Tarjum—A tedious palaver—The Tarjum's anxiety—Permission to proceed—A traitor—Entreated to retrace our steps—Thirty armed horsemen—A pretty speech.

Quite early the next morning we were roused by the distant sound of tinkling horse-bells. On looking out of the tent, I saw a long row of pack-ponies heavily laden, escorted by a number of mounted soldiers with matchlocks and spears. It was evident that some high official was coming. This advance detachment consisted of his subalterns and his baggage. They took a long sweep far away from our tent and dismounted by the Gyanema fort. Other soldiers and messengers were constantly arriving in groups from all directions. The leader of one party, with a considerable escort of soldiers, was received with profuse salaams and I concluded that he must be an important personage.

After some time a message was sent to us that this new comer, the Barca Tarjum, practically a potentate equal in rank to a king under a protectorate, wished to have the honour of seeing us. We replied that we were having our breakfast and that we would send for him when we wished to speak to him. Our experience had taught us that it was advisable to treat Tibetan officials as inferiors, as they

THE ARRIVAL OF REINFORCEMENTS

were then more subdued, and easier to deal with. At eleven we despatched a messenger to the fort to say we should be pleased to receive the Tarjum. He came immediately with a large following, a picturesque figure dressed in a long coat of green silk of Chinese shape, with large sleeves turned up, showing his arms up to the elbow; he had a cap similar to those worn by Chinese officials, and was shod with heavy long black boots, with large nails under the soles. His long, pale, angular face was remarkable in many ways; it was interestingly stolid, and though somewhat effeminate, had rather fine features; unmistakable signs of depravity indicated his low class of mind and morals. Long hair fell in loose curls down to his shoulders, and hanging from his left ear was an earring of large dimensions, with malachite ornaments and a pendant. In his nervous fingers he held a small roll of Tibetan material, which he used with both hands as a handkerchief to blow his nose inconsequently every time that he was at a loss to answer a question. The Tarjum and his men were profuse in their bows, and there was, as usual, a great display of tongues. These were, I noticed, of an unhealthy whitish colour, caused throughout Tibet by excessive tea-drinking, a practice which ruins the digestion, and furs their tongues.

We had rugs placed outside our principal tent, and the doctor and I sat on one, asking the Tarjum to sit on the one facing us. His followers squatted around him. It is a well-known fact that in Tibet, if you are a "somebody," or if you wish people to recognise your importance, you must have an umbrella spread over your head. Fortunately, the ever-prudent doctor had two in his possession; which two of our men held over our respective heads. The

Tarjum himself was shaded by a parasol of colossal dimensions, held in position by his secretary.

In spite of the extravagant terms of friendship which fell from the Tarjum's lips, I was convinced, by close observation of the man's face, that his words were insincere and that it would be unsafe to trust him. He never looked us straight in the face; his eyes were fixed on the ground all the time, and he spoke in a despicably affected manner. I did not like the man from the very first, and, friend or no friend, I kept my loaded rifle on my lap.

After endless ponderous speeches, clumsy compliments, and tender inquiries after all relations they could possibly think of; after tiring parabolic sentences with fine sounds but no meaning; after repeated blowing of the nose and loud coughing, which always came on opportunely when we asked whether they had yet come to a conclusion as to what we should be allowed to do, at last, when my patience was nearly exhausted, our negotiations of the previous day were reopened. We argued for hours. We asked to be allowed to go on. They were still uncertain whether they would let us or not. To simplify matters, and hasten their decision before other reinforcements arrived, the doctor applied for permission to let only eight of us proceed to Mansarowar. He (the doctor) himself would remain at Gyanema with the remainder of the party as a guarantee of good faith. But even this offer they rejected, not directly, but with hypocritical excuses and delays, for they thought we would not find our way, and that if we did, we should find it very rough, and the climate too severe; that the brigands might attack us, and so on, and so on. All this was very tiresome, and there were signs even of a nasty side to their attitude. I decided to know what I was about.

THE BARCA TARJUM AND HIS OFFICERS

Still holding the rifle cocked at safety on my lap, I turned the muzzle of it towards the Tarjum, and purposely let my hand slide down to the trigger. He became uncomfortable and his face showed signs of wild terror. His eyes, until now fixed upon the ground, became first unsteady, and then settled fixedly, and with a look of distress, on the muzzle of my rifle. At the same time he tried to dodge the aim right or left by moving his head, but I made the weapon follow all his movements. The Tarjum's servants fully shared their master's fear. Without doubt the poor fellow was in agony ; his tone of voice, a moment before boisterous and aggressive, now dwindled into the humblest intonations imaginable. With much meekness he expressed himself ready to please us in every way.

" I see that you are good people," said he in a faint whisper, accompanied by a deep bow. " I cannot give, as I would like to do, my official sanction to your journey forward, but you can go if you wish. I cannot say more. Eight of you can proceed to the sacred Mansarowar Lake. The others will remain here."

Before giving his final decision he said that he would prefer to have another consultation with his officers.

We accorded this readily.

The Tarjum then presented the doctor with a roll of Tibetan cloth.

I had bathed as usual in the morning, and my Turkish towel was spread outside the tent to dry. The Tarjum, who showed great interest in all our things, took a particular fancy to its knotty fabric. He sent for his child to see this wonderful material, and when he arrived the towel was placed on the youth's back as if it were a shawl. I at once offered it to him as a present if he would accept it. There were no bounds to his delight, and our relations, somewhat strained a few minutes earlier, became now of the friendliest character. We invited the party inside our tent, and they examined everything with curiosity, asking endlesss questions. They were now quite jovial and pleasant, and even occasionally amusing. Tibetans have a craving for alcohol at all times and they soon asked me if I had any to give them; there was nothing they would like more. As I never carry any when travelling, I could not offer them any recognised drink, but not wishing to disappoint them, I produced a bottle of methylated spirits (which I used for my hypsometrical apparatus). This they readily drank, apparently appreciating its throat-burning qualities, and asked for more. The Tarjum complained of an ailment from which he had suffered for some time, and the doctor was able to give him a suitable remedy, and all the other officers received small presents when they departed.

In the afternoon a messenger came from the Barca Tarjum. He had good news for us. The Tarjum wished us to understand that "as we had been so kind to him and his followers, he regarded us as his personal friends; and as we were so anxious to visit the Mansarowar Lake and the great Kelas Mount, and had already experienced many difficulties and great expense in coming so far, he agreed to eight of our party proceeding to the sacred spots. It was impossible for him to give an official consent, but he repeated again that we could go if we wished."

This news naturally delighted me. Once at Kelas, I felt sure I could easily find some means of going farther.

On the same evening, a traitor in our camp sneaked from under the tent in which my men were sleeping, and paid a visit to the Tarjum. There is no doubt that he told him I was not the doctor's brother, nor a Hindoo pilgrim. He disclosed that I was a sahib, and that I was on my way to Lhassa. From what I heard afterwards, it seemed that the Tarjum did not quite believe his informant; but fresh doubts arising in his mind, he sent a message during the night, entreating us to return the way we came.

"If there is really a sahib in your party, whom you have kept concealed from me, and I let you go on, my head will be cut off by the Lhassa people. You are now my friends, and you will not allow this."

"Tell the Tarjum," I replied to the messenger, "that he is my friend, and I will treat him as a friend."

In the morning, we found thirty horsemen fully armed posted some hundred yards from our tent. To proceed with the demoralised crowd under me, and be followed by this company, would certainly prove disastrous and I felt again that some ruse was a necessity.

Much to the astonishment and terror of the armed force and their superiors, the doctor, Chanden Sing and I, rifles in hand, walked firmly towards the contingent of sepoys. After us came the trembling coolies. The Magbun and the Tarjum's officers could hardly believe their eyes. The soldiers quickly dismounted, and laid their arms down to show that they had no intention of fighting. We passed them without any notice. The Magbun ran after me. He begged me to stop one moment. Dola was summoned to interpret his elaborate speech. A pair of prettily embroidered cloth-boots were produced from the loose folds of the official's coat, and he offered them with the following words:

"Though your face is sunburnt and black, and your eyes are sore (they were not, as a matter of fact, but I wore snow-spectacles), your features tell me that you are of a good family, therefore, you must be a high officer in your country. Your noble feelings also show that you would not have us punished for your sake, and now our hearts are glad to see you retrace your steps. Let me offer you these boots, so that your feet may not get sore on the long and difficult journey back to your native land."

It was neatly put, though the mode of reasoning was peculiar. It was not to my interest to disillusionise the Tibetan as to my purpose, so I accepted the boots. The Magbun and his guard salaamed to the ground.

Without further parleying, we left the Magbun, and retracing our steps, proceeded in a W.S.W. direction as though we had decided to turn back, and leave the country.

CHAPTER XXX

Spying our movements—Disguised sepoys—A gloomy look-out — Troublesome followers — Another march back — An amusing incident.

WE reached the summit of the hill and crossed to the other side. My men went on down the slope, but I remained, screened by a large stone, to observe with my telescope the folks at Gyanema. No sooner had my last man disappeared on the other side of the pass, than the cavalrymen jumped into their saddles and, raising clouds of dust, galloped after us. This was what I had expected. I hastened to rejoin my men. When down in the plain, I again took my telescope, and watched the skyline of the hill we had just descended. Some thirty heads could be seen peeping over the rocks from among the boulders. The soldiers had evidently dismounted, and were spying our movements. I felt annoyed that they did not openly follow us, if they so wished, instead of watching us from a distance, so I sighted my rifle to eight hundred yards, lay down flat, and took aim at a figure I could see more plainly than the others.

The doctor snatched the rifle from my shoulder.

"You must not shoot," said he, with his usual calmness; "you might kill somebody."

"I only wish to teach these cowards a lesson."

"That is all very well. But every man in Tibet is so cowardly that the lesson would have to be constantly repeated," answered Wilson with his perpetual wisdom.

I slung my rifle over my shoulder and made up my mind to start some other time on the cyclopean task I had then so nearly begun.

When we had covered a mile or so of the plain, our phantomlike escort crossed the pass, and came full gallop down the hill. I gave orders to my men to halt, seeing which, the soldiers also came to a dead stop. I watched them through the telescope. They seemed to be holding a discussion. At last five men rode full speed northwards, probably to guard the track in that direction. Three men remained where they were, and the remainder, as if seized by panic, galloped frantically up the hill again, and disappeared over the summit.

We resumed our march. The three horsemen followed a course one mile south of ours, close against the foot of the hills, and lying low upon their ponies' heads, they probably imagined that they were passing us unperceived. Seeing that our bearings were for our old camp at Lama Chokden, they left our line and rode ahead of us.

When in the evening we reached Lama Chokden, two shepherds came to greet us. Then another appeared.

"Our sheep are far away," said they. "We are hungry. We are poor. Can we stop near your camp and pick up the food that you will throw away?"

"Certainly," I replied. "But mind you do not pick up anything else."

These simple folk, thinking I should not know them, had left their ponies at the Lama Chokden guard-house, and, disguised as shepherds, they were now trying to ingratiate themselves with us, with the object of discovering our movements and plans. They were, of course, no other than the three sepoys from Gyanema.

At each step in our retreat towards the Himahlyas my heart became heavier and my spirits more depressed. I was full of stratagems, but to think out plans and to carry them into effect were two different things.

How many times had not my schemes been upset? How often had I not had to begin afresh when all seemed ready and in perfect working order?—that, too, when I had plenty of good material at my disposal to work upon. Now things had changed altogether for the worse. My chances of success, notwithstanding my incessant struggle, were getting smaller and smaller every day. I could not but feel that there must be an end eventually to the capability and endurance of my followers and myself. It is hard enough to start on a difficult task, but when you are well started, and have already overcome many difficulties, to have to come back and begin again is more than galling.

The outlook was dark and gloomy; I stood face to face with apparent failure, and uncertain of the loyalty of my own men.

At this camp, for instance, the Daku (brigand), who had changed his disguise several times since coming in contact with the Tibetans, announced his immediate departure. The doctor, with his usual kindness, had already entreated him to remain, but without avail. We well knew that in this region, infested by dacoits, this man was only leaving us to recommence his late marauding habits. He would, in all probability, join some band, and without much doubt we might soon expect a visit during the darkest hours of the night. The Daku knew that I carried a large sum of money, and during the last two days his behaviour had been more than strange. Had he come across some of his mates? or had he heard from the sepoys that they were in the neighbourhood?

The Daku had a bundle of his blankets strapped on his back in readiness for immediate departure. My men, distressed at this new danger, came to report it to me. I immediately sent for him. Speaking bluntly, and keeping his eyes fixed on the ground, he said: "I am going, sahib."

"Where?" I inquired.

"I have friends near here, and I am going to them."

"Very good, go," I replied, calmly taking up my rifle.

His load was off his shoulder in less time than it takes to describe the event. He resumed his work as usual. One or two other riotous coolies were brought back to reason by similar menaces.

I heard later that a band of brigands attacked a party near the frontier only two days after this occurred.

Another march back! How painful it was to me! Yet it was advisable. We went a few miles and encamped on the bank of a rapid stream, the Shirlangdu. From this point, with some difficulty and danger, it would be possible to climb over the mountain range during the night, and attempt to elude the spies and watchmen, by crossing the jungle to Mansarowar. I made up my mind to attempt this. It seemed to add to the risk to have so large a following as my thirty men, so I decided that only four or five should accompany me. Going alone was impracticable, because of the difficulty of carrying sufficient food, or I would have by far preferred it. Nevertheless, if the worst came to the worst, I resolved to attempt this latter mode of travelling, and rely on the chance of obtaining food from Tibetans.

All the loads were made ready. Articles of clothing and comfort, niceties in the way of food, and extras in the way of medicines, were left behind to make room for my scientific instruments.

Each pound in weight more that I dedicated to science meant a pound less food to take us to Lhassa. Everything that was not of absolute necessity had to be left.

Two Tibetan spies came to camp in the afternoon, in the disguise, as usual, of beggars. They asked for food, and exacted it. Their manner was unbearably insulting. This was a little too much for us, and Bijesing the Johari, and Rubso the Christian cook, were the first to enter into an open fight with them! They punched and kicked them, driving them down a steep ravine leading to a river, then, assisted by other men in camp, showered stones upon them. The unfortunate intruders, unable to wade quickly across the rapid stream, received as fine a reception as they deserved.

This little skirmish amused the camp, but many of the Shokas and Hunyas in my service were still scared out of their wits. It was quite sufficient for them to see a Tibetan to crumble into nothing.

CHAPTER XXXI

An attempt that failed—A resolution—A smart Shoka lad—The plucky Chanden Sing proposes to accompany me—Mansing the leper becomes my servant's servant.

THE hour fixed for my flight was 9 P.M. Five men had been induced to follow me by the offer of a handsome reward.

At the hour appointed no single one of them had put in an appearance. I went in search of them. One man had purposely injured his feet and was disabled, another pretended to be dying, the others positively refused to come. They were shivering with fright and cold.

"Kill us, sahib, if you like," they implored of me, "but we will not follow you."

At 3 A.M. all attempts to get even one man to carry a load had proved futile. I had to abandon the idea of starting.

My prospects became more gloomy than ever. Another march back towards the cold and dreary pass by which I had entered Tibet!

"You are depressed, Mr. Landor," remarked the doctor.

I admitted the fact. Every step backwards was to me like a stab in the heart. I had wished to push on at all costs, and it was only in consideration of my good and kind friend, the doctor, that I had reluctantly refrained from making my way by force. My blood was boiling. I felt feverish. The cowardice of my men made them absolutely contemptible, and I could not bear to see them even.

Immersed in my thoughts, I walked quickly on, and the rugged way seemed short and easy. I found a suitable spot for our next camp. Here before me, and on every side, stood high snowy mountains ; there, in front, towered that same Lumpiya Pass by which I had crossed into Tibet with such high hopes. I detested the sight of it on the present occasion; its snowy slopes seemed to mock at my failure.

Whether it is that storms invariably come when one is depressed, or whether one gets depressed when storms are coming, I am not here prepared to say, but the fact remains that, before we had time to pitch our tents, the wind, which had been high all through the afternoon, increased tenfold. The clouds above were wild and threatening, and snow soon fell in feathery flakes.

"What are you going to do ?" inquired the doctor of me. "I think you had better return to Garbyang, get fresh men, and make another start."

"No, doctor. I will die rather than continue this backward march. There will be a far better chance if I go alone, and I have resolved to start to-night, for I am convinced that I shall find my way over the range."

"No, no, it is impossible, Mr. Landor," cried the doctor, with tears in his eyes. "That must mean death to any one attempting it."

I told him that I was quite determined.

The poor doctor was dumbfounded. He knew that it

was useless to try to dissuade me. I went into the tent to rearrange and reduce my baggage, making a load small enough to carry on my back, in addition to the daily kit and instruments.

Whilst I was making preparations for my journey, Kachi Ram entered the tent. He looked frightened and perplexed.

"What are you doing, sir?" inquired he hurriedly. "The doctor says you are going to leave alone to-night, cross the mountain range, and go to Lhassa by yourself."

"Yes, that is true."

"Oh, sir! The perils and dangers are too great, you cannot go."

"I know, but I am going to try."

"Oh, sir! Then I will come with you."

"No, Kachi. You will suffer too much. Go back to your father and mother now that you have the opportunity."

"No, sir; where you go, I will go. Small men never suffer. If they do it does not matter. Only great men's sufferings are worth noticing. If you suffer, I will suffer. I will come."

Kachi's philosophy touched me. I ascertained beyond doubt that he meant what he said, and then decided to take him.

This was a piece of luck. Kachi Ram had five bosom friends among the young Shoka coolies. They were all friends of the Rambang, and in the evenings in camp they often used to join and sing weird songs in honour of the fair maids of their hearts, whom they had left on the other side of the Himahlyas.

Kachi hurried away in a state of feverish excitement. He was back in a few minutes.

"How many coolies will you take, sir?"

"None will come."

"Oh, I will get them. Will five do?"

"Yes," I murmured incredulously.

My scepticism sustained a shock when Kachi returned, buoyant, saying in his peculiar English:

"Five Shokas come, sir. Then you, sir, I, sir, five coolies, sir, start night-time, what clock?"

"By Jove, Kachi," I could not help exclaiming, "you are a smart lad."

"'Smart,' sir?" inquired he sharply, hearing a new word. He was most anxious to learn English, and he had a mania for spelling. "'Smart!' What is meaning? How spell?"

"S-m-a-r-t. It means 'quick, intelligent.'"

"Smart," he repeated solemnly, as he wrote the newly-acquired word in a book which I had given him for the purpose. Kachi was undoubtedly, in spite of some small faults, a great character. He was a most intelligent, sharp, well-meaning fellow. His never failing good humour, and his earnest desire to learn and to be useful, were quite refreshing.

My luck seemed to have turned indeed. A few minutes later my bearer, quite unaware that any one would accompany me, entered the tent, and exclaimed in a disgusted manner:

"*Shoka crab, sahib! Hunya log bura crab. Hazur hum, do admi jaldi Lhasa giao.*" ("The Shokas are bad. The Hunyas are very bad. Your honour and I, we two alone, will go quickly by ourselves to Lhassa.")

Here was another plucky and useful man anxious to come. He professed to have no fear of death. He was the type of man I wanted. How true the poor fellow's protestations were I learned at a later date !

Chanden Sing was a man of strong sporting proclivities. His happiness was complete when he could fire his rifle at something, though he was never known to hit the mark. He had been severely reprimanded and punished by me only a few days before for wasting several cartridges on *kiang* (wild horse) three miles distant. Ordinary work, however, such as doing his own cooking, or keeping my things tidy, was distasteful to him, and was invariably passed on to others.

Mansing the leper, being unfortunately of the same caste as Chanden Sing, became my servant's servant. The two Hindoos constantly quarrelled and fought, but at heart they were the best of friends. The bearer, by means of promises, mingled at intervals with blows, eventually succeeded in inducing his *protégé* to join in our new plan, and face with us the unknown dangers ahead.

CHAPTER XXXII

"Devil's Camp"—A fierce snowstorm—Abandoning our tents—Dangers and perils in prospect—Collecting the mer—One load too many!—Another man wanted and found—A propitious night—Good-bye to Wilson—The escape—Brigands.

By eight o'clock in the evening I had collected all the men who had promised to follow me. They comprised my bearer, Kachi and six coolies.

We named this camp "Devil's Camp," for diabolical indeed was the wind that shook our tents, not to speak of the snow blown into our shelters by the raging storm. During the night the wind grew in fury. Neither wood, dung, nor lichen for fuel was to be found. Our tents were pitched at 16,900 feet above sea-level, and to ascend to the summit of the range would mean a further climb of two thousand feet. In such weather the difficulties of the ascent were increased tenfold, though for evading the vigilance of the Tibetan watchmen, who spied upon our movements, we could have no better chance than a dirty night like this. I arranged with the doctor that he was to take back to Garbyang all the baggage I had discarded and the men who had declined to follow me. He must display all our tents until late in the afternoon of the next day, so as to let the Tibetans suppose that we were all under them, and give me time to make a long forced march before they could get on our track. Hard as it would be for us going forward, we would take no tent except the small *tente d'abri*, weighing about four pounds. We should anyhow be unable to pitch one for several days, for fear of being detected by the Tibetans, who would be soon seen abroad in search of us. We should have to march long distances at night, keeping mostly on the summit of the range, instead of proceeding, like other travellers, along the valleys, and we must get what little sleep we could during the day, when we could hide in some secluded spot. The thought of seeing a fire had to be abandoned for an indefinite period, because, even in the remote contingency of our finding fuel at the great altitudes where we should have to camp, every one knows that a fire and a column of smoke can be seen at a very great distance, both by day and night. We pondered and discussed all these matters before we made a start, and, moreover, we were fully aware that, if the Tibetans could once lay their hands upon us, our numbers were too small to offer a stout resistance, and we might well give ourselves up for lost. In fact, taking things all round, I rather doubted whether the lives of my few followers and my own were worth more than a song from the moment of our leaving "Devils' Camp."

With this full knowledge of what we were undertaking, we may have been foolish in starting at all, but lack of determination cannot in fairness be credited as one of our faults.

The thoughtful doctor had brought with him from our last camp a few lichens, with which he was now attempting to light a fire, to cook me some *chapatis* before leaving. Alas! four hours' hard work, and an equal number of boxes of matches, failed to produce the semblance of a flame.

At midnight I sent Chanden Sing and Kachi to collect the men. Two came trembling into the tent; the others could not be roused. I went myself and took them, one by one, to their loads. They were all crying like children. It was then that I discovered that in the haste and confusion I had made one load too many. Here was a dilemma! Everything was ready and propitious for our flight, and a delay at this juncture was fatal. At any cost, I must have another man.

The moans and groans in the coolies' tent, when I went in search of one, were pitiful. You would have thought that they were all going to die within a few minutes, and that they were now in their last agonies, all because of the terror of being picked out to follow me.

At last, after endless trouble, threats and promises, Bijesing the Johari was persuaded to come. But the load was too heavy for him; he would only carry half. To save trouble, I agreed I would carry the other half myself in addition to my own load.

We put out our hurricane lantern, and at 2 P.M., when the gale was raging at its height, driving the grit and snow like spikes into our faces; when the wind and cold seemed to penetrate with biting force to the marrow of our bones, when, as it seemed, all the gods were giving vent to their anger by putting every obstacle in our way, a handful of silent men, half frozen and staggering, left the camp to face the blizzard. I ordered my men to keep close together, and we made immediately for the mountain side, taking care to avoid the places where we supposed the Tibetan spies were posted.

We could not have selected a more suitable night for our escape. It was so dark that we could only see a few inches in front of our noses. The doctor, silent and with a swelling heart, accompanied me for a couple of hundred yards. I urged him to return to the tent. He stopped to grasp my hand, and in a broken voice the good man bade me farewell and God-speed.

"The dangers of your journey," whispered Wilson, "are so great and so numerous that God alone can guide you through. When I think of the cold, hunger and hardships you will have to endure, I can but tremble for you."

"Good-bye, doctor," said I, deeply moved.

"Good-bye," he repeated, "good——" and his voice failed him.

Two or three steps and the darkness separated us, but his touching words of farewell rang and echoed in my ears, as with sadness I remembered the loyalty and cheerful kindness of this good friend. The journey towards Lhassa had recommenced in grim earnest. In a short while our ears, fingers, and toes were almost frozen, and the fast driving snow beat mercilessly against our faces, making our eyes ache. We proceeded like so many blind people, speechless and exhausted, rising slowly higher on the mountain range, and feeling our way with our feet. As we reached greater altitudes it grew still colder, and the wind became more piercing. Every few minutes we were compelled to halt and sit close together in order to keep warm and get breath, as the air was so rarefied that we could barely proceed under our heavy loads.

We heard a whistle, and sounds like distant voices. My men collected round me, whispered, "*Dakus, dakus!*" ("Brigands, brigands!"), and then threw themselves flat on

"AT NIGHT I LED MY MEN UP THE MOUNTAIN IN A FIERCE SNOW STORM"

the snow. I loaded my rifle and went ahead, but it was vain to hope to pierce the obscurity. I listened. Yet another shrill whistle!

My Shokas were terrified. The sound seemed to come from straight in front of us. We slightly altered our course, winning our way upward slowly and steadily, until we found at sunrise we were near the mountain top. It was still snowing hard. One final effort brought us to the plateau on the summit.

Here we felt comparatively safe. Thoroughly exhausted, we deposited our burdens on the snow, and laid ourselves down in a row close to one another to keep ourselves warm, piling on the top of us all the blankets available.

CHAPTER XXXIII

S.E. wind—Hungry and half frozen—Lakes at 18,960 feet above sea-level—Cold food at high altitudes—Buried in snow—Mansing's sufferings—Fuel at last.

AT 1 P.M. we woke up, drenched to the skin, the sun having thawed the thick coating of snow over us. This camp was at 18,000 feet. The wind from the S.E. cut like a knife, and we suffered from it, not only on this occasion, but every day during the whole time we were in Tibet. It begins to blow with great fierceness and regularity at one o'clock in the afternoon, and it is only at about eight in the evening that it sometimes abates and gradually ceases. Frequently, however, the wind, instead of dropping at this time, increases in violence, blowing with terrible vehemence during the whole night. As we were making ready to start again, with limbs cramped and stiff, the sky once more became suddenly covered with heavy grey clouds, and fresh snow fell. There was no possibility of making a fire, so we started hungry and half-frozen, following a course of 70° (b.m.). We waded up to our waists through a freezingly cold stream, and climbing steadily higher and higher for six miles, we at last reached another and loftier plateau to the N.E. of the one where we had camped in the morning. The altitude was 18,960 feet, and we were surprised to find four lakes of considerable size close to one another on this high tableland. The sun, breaking for a moment through the clouds, shone on the snow-covered tops of the surrounding mountains, silvering the water of the lakes, and making a beautiful and spectacular picture, wild and fascinating in effect.

Hunger and exhaustion prevented full appreciation of the scene ; nothing could stand in the way of quickly finding a suitable place to rest our weak and jaded bodies, under the shelter of the higher hills round the plateau, or in some depression in the ground. I was anxious to push across the plateau, and descend on the N.E. side to some lower altitude where we should more probably find fuel, but my men, half-starved and fagged, could go no farther. Their wet loads were considerably heavier than usual, they panted terribly owing to the great altitude, and no sooner had we come to a partially sheltered spot between the larger lake and its most eastern neighbouring sheet of water, than they all collapsed and were unable to proceed. I was much concerned about them, as they refused to take any cold food, saying it would cause their death. I was really at a loss to see how they could recover sufficient strength for the next day's marching. Eventually, by personally pledging them that they would not die, I persuaded them to eat a little *sato* and *ghur*. Unfortunately, no sooner had they eaten some of it mixed with cold water, than nearly all were seized with violent pains in their stomachs, from which they suffered for the greater part of the night.

There is no doubt that experience had taught them that eating cold food at great altitudes is more dangerous than eating no food at all, and I regretted my ill-timed, if kindly meant advice. One is apt to judge other people by oneself, and personally I never felt any difference, whether my food was cold or hot.

Soon after sunset the cold was intense. It was still snowing hard, and our wet garments and blankets were now freezing. I lighted a small spirit lamp, round which we all sat close together, and covered over with our frozen wraps. I even attempted to cook on the flame some concentrated broth, but, owing to the high altitude, the water was a long time losing its chill, apart from boiling, and when it was just getting tepid the flame went out, and I could afford no more spirits of wine to light it again: so the cooking had to be abandoned, and as the night grew colder and colder, we huddled together under our respective blankets in a vain attempt to sleep. We had made a protecting wall with our baggage, and my men covered their heads and everything with their blankets; but I never could adopt their style of sleeping, as it seemed to suffocate me. I always slept with my head uncovered, for not only was it more comfortable, but I wished to be on the alert should we at any time be surprised by Tibetans. My men moaned, groaned, and chattered their teeth convulsively during the night. I woke many times with a bad pain in my ears from frostbite; my eyes, too, suffered as the eyelashes became covered with icicles. Every time I tried to open them there was an uncomfortable feeling as if the eyelashes were being torn off, for the slit of the eye became fast frozen directly the lids were closed.

At last the morning came! The night had seemed endless. When I tried to raise the blanket in order to sit up, it seemed of an extraordinary weight and stiffness. No wonder! It was frozen hard, and as rigid as cardboard,

BURIED IN SNOW

covered over with a foot of snow. The thermometer during the night had gone down to 24°. I called my men. They were hard to wake, and they, too, were buried in snow.

"*Uta, uta, uta!*" ("Get up, get up, get up!") I called, shaking one by one, and brushing off as much snow as I could.

"*Baroff bahut!*" ("There is much snow!") remarked one as he put his nose outside his blanket, and rubbed his eyes, smarting from the white glare around us. "Salaam, sahib," added he, as, having overcome his first surprise, he perceived me, and he waved his hand gracefully up to his forehead.

The others behaved in a similar manner. Kachi was, as usual, the last one to wake.

"O, Kachi," I shouted, "get up!"

"*O, bahiyoh!*" ("O, father!") yawned he, stretching his arms. Half asleep, half awake, he looked round as if in a trance, muttering incoherent words.

"Good morning, sir. Oh, much snow. Oh look, sir, two kiangs there! What is 'kiang' in English?"

"Wild horse."

"'Wild' you spell w-i-l-d?"

"Yes."

Here the note-book was produced from under his pillow, and the word registered in it.

Odd creatures these Shokas! The average European, half-starved and frozen, would hardly give much thought to exact spelling.

Poor Mansing the leper suffered terribly. He groaned through the whole night. I had given him one of my wrappers, but his circulation seemed suspended. His face was grey and cadaverous, with deep lines drawn by suffering, and his feet were so frozen that for some time he could not stand.

Again the Shokas would eat nothing, for snow was still falling. We started towards the N.E. After a mile of flat we began a steep descent over unpleasant loose *débris* and sharp rocks. The progress was rapid, but very painful. Scouring the country below with my telescope, I perceived shrubs and lichens far down in the valley to the N.E. and also a tent and some sheep. This was unfortunate, for we had to alter our course in order not to be seen. We again climbed up to the top of the plateau and rounded unperceived the mountain summit, striking a more Easterly route. Towards sunset we began our descent from the latter point, and we crossed the river with no great difficulty. Having selected a nicely sheltered depression in the ground, we pitched my little *tente d'abri* there, by the side of a pond of melted snow. With natural eagerness, we all set out collecting lichens and shrubs for our fires, and each man carried into camp several loads of the drier fuel. In a moment there were three big fires blazing, and not only were we able to cook a specially abundant dinner and drown our past troubles in a bucketful of boiling tea, but we also managed to dry our clothes and blankets. The relief of this warmth was wonderful, and in our comparative happiness we forgot the hardships and sufferings we had so far encountered. With the exception of a handful of *sato*, this was the first solid meal we had had for forty-eight hours. In those two days we had travelled twenty miles, each of us carrying a weight averaging considerably over sixty pounds.

We were at 16,500 feet, which seemed quite a low elevation

after our colder and loftier camping-grounds. The reaction was quite pleasant, and for myself I contemplated our future plans and possibilities with better hope. The outlook had changed from our deepest depression to a condition of comparative cheerfulness and content.

CHAPTER XXXIV

Dacoits—No nonsense allowed—A much-frequented region—A plateau—The Gyanema-Taklakot track—A dangerous spot—Soldiers waiting for us—Burying our baggage—Out of provisions—A fall into the Gakkon River—A bright idea—Nettles our only diet.

IN front of us, to the N.E., was a high mountain, then farther towards the East, a narrow valley between two hill ranges, while at 238° (b.m.) a river passed through a picturesque gorge in the direction of the Mangshan Mountain.

It was necessary for me to proceed along the valley to the east, as we should thus save ourselves much trouble, time and exertion, though there would be some risk of our meeting Tibetans, especially bands of dacoits, with whom this part of Nari Khorsum* is infested. We had, therefore, to proceed cautiously, especially as my Shokas seemed no less timid and afraid of these folks. We had hardly gone half a mile over the undulating country, and I had stopped behind my men to take some observations with my prismatic compass, when my carriers suddenly threw themselves flat on the ground and began to retreat, crawling on hands and knees.

"*Dakus, Dakus!*" ("Brigands, brigands!") they whispered, as I got near them.

* Nari Khorsum—name of that province.

It was too late. We had been seen, and a number of dacoits, armed with matchlocks and swords, came rapidly towards us. It has always been my experience that, in such cases, the worst thing to do is to run away, for nothing encourages a man more than to see that his opponent is afraid of him. I therefore loaded my Mannlicher, and my bearer did likewise with the Martini-Henry. I gave orders to the Shokas to squat down by their respective loads and

SHEEP CARRYING LOAD

not stir an inch. We two strolled towards the fast approaching band, now less than a hundred yards distant. I shouted to them to stop, and Chanden Sing signalled that they must go back ; but they took no notice of our warnings, and came on all the faster towards us. Undoubtedly they thought that we were only Shoka traders, and looked, from experience, to find an easy prey. Making ready to rush us as soon as they got near enough, they separated with the obvious intention of taking us on all sides.

"*Dushu! Dushu!*" ("Go back!") I cried angrily at them, raising my rifle to my shoulder and taking a steady aim at the leader. Chanden Sing followed suit with one of the others, and this seemed to have a salutary effect on them, for they immediately made a comical salaam and took to their heels, Chanden Sing and I pursuing them for some distance so as to get them well out of our way. Having occupied a prominent position on a small mound, we discovered that a short way off they had a number of mates and some three thousand sheep, presumably their last loot. We signalled that they must get away from our course, and eventually, driving their booty before them, they scurried off in the direction I indicated. When they were well clear of us, and my Shokas, who thought their last hour had come, had partly recovered from their fright, we proceeded on our journey, entering the narrow valley between the two hill ranges. That we were now in a much-frequented region could be plainly seen from the numerous encamping-grounds alongside the stream. But our success of the morning had raised our spirits, and we stepped out cheerily, keeping to the left bank. A steepish climb brought us to a plateau at an altitude of 16,400 feet, from which we obtained a fine view of the snow range running from East to West from the Mangshan Mountain to the Lippu Pass, and beyond to the N.E. the four lofty peaks of Nimo Nangil, 25,360 feet, 22,200 feet, 22,850 feet, 22,670 feet. The highest peaks were at 84°, 92°, 117° (b.m.). This plateau sloped gently, and was broken by many deep crevasses, conveying the water-flow down into the Gakkon River.

On the lower portion of this plateau, and then along the course of the river, a track ran from Gyanema to Taklakot *viâ* Kardam and Dogmar, and another seldom-frequented

DACOITS WITH A BOOTY OF SHEEP

track to Mangshan, S.S.W. of this place. The edge of the plateau was 15,800 feet above sea-level, and the river 550 feet lower.

This was for us a very dangerous spot, since, no doubt, by this time the Tibetans must be aware that I had escaped and was well on my way into their country. I knew that soldiers and spies must be guarding all the tracks and searching for us. This thoroughfare, being more frequented than the others, was all the more insecure, and we had to display great caution in order to avoid detection. In Tibet, I may here note, the atmosphere is so clear that moving objects can be plainly seen at exceptionally long distances. I scoured the country with my telescope, but I could see no one, so we went on. However, my men considered it safer to descend into one of the numerous creeks, where we should be less exposed, but we had hardly reached the border of it when we heard noises rising from the valley below.

Crawling on our stomachs, my bearer and I peeped over the edge of the plateau. Some five hundred feet below was a Tibetan encampment, with a number of yaks and ponies grazing. Unnoticed, I watched them for some time. There were several soldiers, most probably posted there on the look-out for me. With my glass I recognised some of the Gyanema men. We deemed it advisable to find a spot where we could hide until night came. Then, making a detour, we descended to the river, 15,250 feet, scrambled across in the dark, and made our way up a narrow gorge between high cliffs until we came to a well-hidden spot, where I called a halt. Followed by my men, I climbed up from rock to rock on the cliff to our left, and found a small natural platform, sheltered by a huge boulder projecting over it. This seemed a safe enough spot for us to stop. We dared not put up a tent, and we took the precaution of burying all our baggage in case of a surprise during the night. Unhampered, we should at any moment be able to hide ourselves away from our pursuers or run before them, and we could always come back afterwards for our things if an opportunity offered itself.

And now, just as everything seemed to be running smoothly, I made a terrible discovery. At this stage of the journey, when it was important for me to move very rapidly, I found that we were out of provisions. This was indeed an unpleasant surprise, for before leaving the larger body of my expedition I had given orders to my men to take food for ten days. The doctor, who had been deputed to see to this, had assured me that the loads contained quite enough to last us over that length of time, and now for some unaccountable reason we had only sufficient food for one meagre meal. Moreover, I discovered that we had only a few grains of salt left.

"What have you done with it?" I inquired angrily, as it immediately flashed across my mind that there had been foul play among my carriers. I had ordered each man to take half seer (1 lb.) of salt.

"Yes, sahib, but we forgot to take it," said the men in a chorus.

After the terrible hardships and fatigue we had gone through, and the anxiety and difficulty of carrying on my surveying, photography, sketching, writing, collecting, &c., under conditions of unusual discomfort and risk, it was, indeed, a hard blow to me to see all my plans thus unexpectedly frustrated, for we were still three or four days' journey from Mansarowar, where I relied on getting fresh supplies. Having come thus far, should I be compelled now to go back or give in, and be captured by the Tibetan soldiers whom I had so successfully evaded ? Though not usually much affected by physical pain, I unfortunately suffer greatly under any mental stress. I felt quite ill and depressed, and, to add bodily discomfort to my moral sufferings, came the fact that I had slipped, while jumping in semi-darkness from stone to stone across the Gakkon River, and had fallen flat into about four feet of water. The wind was very high at the time, and the thermometer down to 26°, so that, sitting in my wet clothes to discuss our present situation with my men, I suddenly became so cold, shivery and exhausted, that I thought I was about to collapse altogether. My usual good spirits, which had done much towards carrying me so far, seemed extinguished ; my strength failed me entirely, and a high fever set in, increasing in violence so fast that, notwithstanding my desperate struggle not to give in, I became almost delirious. With my teeth chattering and my temperature at its highest, I saw all my troubles assume an exaggerated form, and failure seemed inevitable. The more I ransacked my brain the more hopeless seemed our position, until, when I was almost in despair, an expedient suddenly flashed across my mind ; an idea more adapted for romance perhaps than real life, yet not, I hoped, impossible to be carried into execution. Four of my men should go disguised, two as traders and two as beggars, into the Takla* fort, and purchase food from my enemies. We remaining in camp would, in the meantime, keep well hidden until they returned. I spoke to my followers, and after some easily conceivable reluctance, four Shokas undertook to perform the daring duty. Discovery

* Takla-khar or Taklakot = *Takla* fort.

would mean to them the loss of their heads, probably preceded by cruel tortures of all kinds; so, though they eventually betrayed me, I cannot help giving them credit for the pluck and fidelity they displayed in the present emergency.

During the night my men were extremely good to me. We did not sleep for fear of being surprised by the Tibetan soldiers, and we passed hour after hour listening to Shoka stories of brigands and Tibetan tortures, terrible enough not only to keep us awake, but to make every hair on our heads stand on end. Early in the morning, when it grew light, we gathered a quantity of nettles, which were to be found in profusion at this camp, and having boiled them in different fashions, we made of them a hearty if not an appetising meal. They did not seem very unpalatable at the time, only it was unfortunate that we had no more salt, for that would have added to the digestibility of our prickly diet. We supplied the deficiency by mixing with them a double quantity of pepper, and it was a relief to know that, while nettles existed near our camp, we should at least not die of starvation.

CHAPTER XXXV

All that remained of my men's provisions—The plan to enter the fort—Appearance of yaks—A band of brigands—Erecting fortifications—Changes in the temperature—Soldiers in search of us!

THE food supply for my men was now reduced in all to four pounds of flour, two pounds of rice, and two pounds of *sato*. This we gave to the four men who were to attempt to enter Taklakot, for their road would be long and fatiguing. For us, there were plenty of nettles to fall back upon.

I carefully instructed the four Shokas how to enter the Tibetan fort one by one in their disguises, and purchase, in small quantities at a time, the provisions we required. When a sufficient amount was obtained to make a load, a man should immediately start towards our camp, and the others were to follow separately for a few marches, when at a given spot, they would all four meet again and return to us. It was exciting work to prepare the different disguises and arrange for everything, and at last, after repeated good-byes and words of encouragement, the four messengers left on their perilous errand. All seemed very quiet round us, so quiet that I unburied my sextant and artificial horizon, and was taking observations for longitude as well as for latitude (by double altitudes, as the angle was too great to be measured at noon), when, to our dismay, a herd consisting of over a hundred yaks appeared on the pass, North of our camp, and slowly advanced towards us. Were we discovered? Were the Tarjum's men coming, preceded by their animals? No time was to be lost; instruments and blankets were quickly cleared away and hidden, and then, crawling up towards the animals, who had stopped on perceiving us, we threw stones at them in order to drive them down the next creek. As luck would have it, we were just in time to do this, for from our hiding-place on the summit of the pass we could see, on the other side, a number of Tibetans following the yaks we had driven away. They passed only a couple of hundred yards below us, evidently quite unconscious of our presence. They were singing, and apparently looking for somebody's tracks, for they often stooped to examine the ground. Later in the afternoon I went to reconnoitre down the Gyanema road, and in the hope of watching, unseen, the Tibetans who passed on their way to and from Taklakot. I saw no soldiers, but a strong band of Jogpas (brigands), driving before them thousands of sheep and yaks, was an interesting sight. They all rode ponies, and seemed to obey their leader very smartly, when in a hoarse voice, and never ceasing to turn his prayer-wheel, he muttered orders. They went briskly along in fine style, women as well as men riding their ponies astride. The men had matchlocks and swords, and each pony carried, besides its rider, bags of food slung behind the saddle. I watched the long procession from behind some rocks, and felt somewhat relieved when the last horsemen, who passed only some twenty yards from me, rode away with the rest of the caravan. I retraced my steps, and judging that this camp was not quite so safe as I had at first supposed, I proceeded, with the aid of my men, to erect a rough entrenchment and wall round our platform, along the rock under which we lived. These bulwarks answered the double purpose of sheltering us from the sight of the Tibetans and of acting as fortifications in case of a night attack. All our things were buried a little way above our camp.

Another long dreary day had elapsed. We had used our last grain of salt; and yet another day on nettles alone; and a third day and a fourth, on the same diet! How sick we got of nettles! The days seemed endless as, lying flat on a peak above our camp, I remained hour after hour scanning with my telescope the long plateau above the Gakkon River in search of our returning messengers. Every time I perceived men in the distance my heart leaped, but on focussing them with my glass they turned out to be Jogpas (bandits), or Dogpas (nomad tribes of smugglers), or travelling Humlis or Jumlis, on their way to Gyanema and Gartok. And how many times did we not listen and then anxiously peep through the fissures in our fortifications when some unusual noise struck our ears! As time went on, and they did not put in an appearance, we began to entertain doubts as to their safety, or would they betray us and never return? Or, as was more likely, had they been caught by the Jong Pen (the master of the fort), and been imprisoned and tortured?

My bearer, who was somewhat of a *bon vivant*, declined to eat any more food, as he said it was better not to eat at all than to eat the same thing constantly. He swore he could fast for ten days, and he made up for want of food by sleeping.

My fortified abode was comfortable enough during the morning, when the sun shone on it, though often it got so warm that we had to abandon it in the middle of the day, when the thermometer registered as much as 120°, 122°, and even 124°. From 1 P.M. till 10 at night a bitter wind blew from the S.E., and seemed to get right into our bones ; so cold was it that the temperature suddenly dropped down to 60°, and even lower, the moment the sun disappeared behind the mountains, and continued to fall as low as 40°, 34° and 32° ; the minimum during the night. One night we had a terrible gale and a snowstorm. Such was the force of the wind, that our wall was blown down upon us as we slept in its shelter, and the hours we had dedicated to rest had to be spent in repairing the damage done. On the following morning we were gathering nettles for our meal, when we heard the distant tinkling of fast approaching horse-bells. We quickly put out the fires, hid our things, and hastened behind our entrenchment. I seized my rifle ; Chanden Sing loaded the Martini. A Shoka, who was too far off to reach our fortified abode in time, screened himself behind some rocks. In the nick of time ! Half-a-dozen sepoys with matchlocks, to which were attached red flags, slung over their shoulders, were cantering gaily up the hillside only a few yards in front of us. They were undoubtedly searching for me, judging by the way they looked in every direction, but fortunately they never turned towards the castle walls that concealed us. They were expecting, I presumed, to see a large European tent in one of the valleys, and never even dreamt that we should be where we were. We covered them well with our rifles, but we had no occasion to fire. They rode on, and the sound of their horse-bells grew fainter and fainter as they

BEHIND OUR BULWARKS

disappeared behind the pass. To be sure, these horsemen could only be soldiers despatched by the Tarjum to guard this track. They were now probably on their way back to him, satisfied that the sahib was not to be found in that part of the country.

CHAPTER XXXVI

"Terror Camp"—Two more messengers leave camp—A tribe of Dogpas—A strange sahib—Our messengers return from Taklakot—The account and adventures of their mission—In great distress—Two fakirs who suffered through me—Five hundred rupees offered for my head—The Shokas want to abandon me—A plot—How it failed.

We named this spot "Terror Camp," for many and horrible were the experiences that befell us here. Another weary day dragged slowly to its close, and there was still no sign of the messengers' return. Two men volunteered to go into Kardam, a settlement some miles off, and try to obtain food from the Tibetans. One of them had a friend at this place, and he thought he could get from him sufficient provisions to enable us to go on a few days longer.

They started, disguised as pilgrims, a disguise not difficult to assume, for their clothes were falling to pieces owing to the rough marching we had done of late. They were away the whole day, and only returned late at night, having an amusing tale to tell. Meeting a tribe of Dogpas, they had boldly entered their camp, asking to purchase food. Unfortunately the Dogpas had not sufficient for themselves, and could not spare any. Incidentally my men were informed that *Lando Plenki*—the name the Tibetans had given me—had taken a large army of men into Tibet, and that great excitement prevailed at Taklakot as well as at other places, owing to the fact that the sahib had the extraordinary power of making himself invisible when the Tibetan soldiers were in his vicinity. He had been reported as having been seen in many places in Tibet: soldiers had been despatched in all directions to capture him. His tracks had several times been discovered and followed, and yet he could never be found. Messengers had been hastily sent out from Taklakot to Lhassa (sixteen days' journey), and to Gartok, a great bazaar in West Tibet, asking for soldiers to assist in the capture of this strange invader, who was also said to have the power of walking on the water when crossing the rivers, and of flying over mountains when he chose. When I recalled our struggles and sufferings in climbing over the mountains, and in crossing the streams on our journey, this account of myself given by the Tibetans, and now repeated to me, struck me as almost cruelly ironical. Anyhow, I was pleased that the Tibetans credited me with such supernatural powers, for it could hardly fail to be an advantage in keeping them from getting to too close quarters with us.

Three more days had to be spent in a state of painful uncertainty and anxiety regarding the fate of our messengers to Taklakot. On the night of the 3rd we had retired to our fortress in despair, fearing that they had been captured and probably beheaded. It was 10 P.M., and we were worn out and ready to turn in; our fire down below at the bottom of the creek was slowly dying out, and nature around us was still and silent, when I suddenly heard sounds of approaching steps. We listened, peeping through the fissures in our wall. Were these Tibetans trying to surprise us in our sleep, or could they be our men returning at last ?

We closely watched the gorge from which the sounds came, faint sounds of voices and of footsteps. Silent as we were, there were not wanting signs of the nervous excitement of my men. At last four staggering figures crawled cautiously into camp, and we could not even then discern in the dim light whether these were our messengers or not.

"*Kuan hai ?*" ("Who is there ?") I shouted.

"Dola !" replied a voice, and instantly we gave them a joyful and hearty greeting. But our happiness was not to last long. The men did not respond. They seemed quite exhausted, and apparently terrified. I asked them to explain the cause of their distress, but, sobbing and embracing my feet, they showed great disinclination to tell me. Grave, indeed, was the news they brought, presaging much trouble in store.

"Your days are numbered, sahib," at last cried Dola. "It is impossible for you to get out of this country alive . . . they will kill you, and the Jong Pen of Taklakot says that he must have your head at all costs."

"Do not look so far ahead, Dola," I replied, trying to calm him, "but tell me first how you reached Taklakot."

"Oh, sahib, we followed your plan. We suffered much on the road, as the marches were long and severe, and we had very little food. We walked day and night for two days, keeping away from the track, and hiding whenever we saw any one. When we got near the Tibetan fort, we saw at the foot of the hill a few tents of the Tinker and Chongur Shokas from Nepal. None of the Biassi or Chaudassi

Shokas had been allowed to enter Tibet owing to the Jong Pen's anger with them regarding his claims for land revenue. There was a guard day and night at the river, and a sharp look-out was kept to stop and arrest anybody entering the country. Two fakirs, who were on a pilgrimage to the sacred Mansarowar, unaware of the danger, had crossed over the Lippu Pass, and had proceeded down to Taklakot, where they were immediately seized and accused of being you, sahib, in disguise. As the Tibetans were not quite certain as to which of the two was the real sahib, they severely punished both, beating them almost to death. What became of them afterwards we were unable to learn. Anyhow, the Tibetans subsequently found out that you had entered Tibet by another pass, and soldiers have been sent in every direction to look for you.

"No sooner did we appear at Taklakot," sobbed Dola, "than we were pounced upon, knocked about, and arrested. They cross-examined us closely. We professed to be Johari traders, who had run short of food, and had made for Taklakot to buy provisions. They beat us and treated us badly, until your friend Zeniram, the head village man of Chongur (in Nepal), came to our rescue and gave thirty rupees surety for us. We were then allowed to remain in his tent, guarded by Tibetan soldiers. We secretly purchased from him and packed the provisions, and at night Zeniram succeeded in decoying the soldiers that were guarding us into his tent, and gave them *chökti* to drink until they became intoxicated. One by one we four succeeded in escaping with our loads. For three nights we marched steadily back, concealing ourselves during the day for the sake of safety. Now we have returned to you, sahib."

Dola paused for a minute or two.

"Sahib," he continued, "we were told in Taklakot that over a thousand soldiers are searching for you everywhere, and more are expected from Lhassa and Sigatz,* whither the Jong Pen has hastily sent messengers. They fear you, sahib, but they have orders from Lhassa to capture you at all costs. They say that you can make yourself invisible when you like, and exorcisms are made and prayers offered daily, so that in future you may be seen and arrested. Once caught, they will have no pity on you, and you will be beheaded, for the Jong Pen is angry with you owing to the defiant messages you sent him from Garbyang. He has given orders to the soldiers to bring you back dead or alive, and whoever brings your head will receive a reward of 500 rupees."

"I had no idea that my head was so valuable," I could not help exclaiming. "I shall take great care of it in the future."

As a matter of fact 500 rupees in Tibet represents a fortune, and the man possessing it is a very rich man.

But my men were not in a laughing mood and they looked upon the whole affair as very serious.

I gave a handsome backshish to the four men who had brought the provisions, but that did not prevent all the Shokas declaring that the danger was so great that they must leave me there and then. Appeals are useless on such occasions, and so I simply stated that I should shoot any man attempting to leave camp. Having now provisions for ten days, I informed them that we must at once push on.

Sulky and grumbling they left our fortified corner and went below to the creek. They said they preferred

* Sigatz, usually called "Shigatze" by English people.

sleeping down there. I suspected them, however, and I sat up watching them and listening instead of sleeping. My bearer rolled himself up in his blanket and, as usual, was soon asleep. The Shokas lighted a fire, sat round it, and with their heads close together, held an excited council in semi-whispers. In the heated discussion some spoke louder than they imagined, and the night being particularly still and the place well adapted for carrying sound, I overheard words which put me on the alert, for I soon convinced myself that they were arranging to sell my head . . . yes . . . and to divide the money.

The men got closer together, and spoke so faintly, that I could hear no more. Then they each in turn placed one hand above the other along a stick, until the end of it was reached ; each man then passed it to his neighbour, who went through the same form ; a complicated manner of drawing lots, common among the Shokas. Eventually the man selected by fate drew from a load a large Gourkha *kukri*, and removed its scabbard. A strange, almost fantastic impresssion remains on my mind of the moment when the men, with their faces lighted by the small flame of the flickering fire, all looked up towards my eyrie. The culminating point of their treachery had come, and their countenances seemed ghastly and distorted, as seen from the fissure in the wall behind which I knelt. They listened to hear if we were asleep. Then all but one rolled themselves in their blankets, completely covering their heads and bodies. The one figure I could now see sat up by the fire for some time, as if absorbed in thought. Every now and then he turned his head up towards my fortress, and listened. At last he got up, and with his feet smothered the fire. It was a lovely night, and as soon as the reddish flame was put out the stars shone again like diamonds in the small patch of deep blue sky visible above my head.

I rested the barrel of my rifle on the wall, my eyes being fixed on the black figure down below. I watched as, stooping low, it crawled step by step the few yards up to my abode, pausing to listen each time that a rolling stone caused a noise. It was now only two or three yards away, and seemed to hesitate. Drawing back, and ready to spring up, I kept my eyes fixed on the top of the wall. I waited some time, but the man was in no hurry, and I grew impatient.

I slowly got up, rifle in hand, and as I raised my head above the wall I found myself face to face with the man on the other side. I lost no time in placing the muzzle of my Mannlicher close to his face, and the perplexed Shoka, dropping his *kukri*, went down on his knees to implore my pardon. After giving him a good pounding with the butt of my rifle, I sent him about his business. The man lacked the qualities of a murderer, but I felt I had better see that no other disturbance took place during the night. It is true that two men attempted to crawl out of camp and desert, but I discovered this and stopped them in time. At last the sun rose, and the night ended with all its troubles and anxieties.

CHAPTER XXXVII

A Tibetan guard's encampment—Nattoo volunteers to be a guide—Treachery and punishment of the Shokas—All ways forward barred to me—Evading the soldiers by another perilous march at night—Mansing again lost—A marvellous phenomenon—Sufferings of my men—Severe cold.

On my last scouting journey up the hill above the camp, I had espied, by the aid of my telescope, the encampment of a guard of Tibetans, about three miles north of us, and I informed my followers of this fact.

In the morning, when we again dug up the main part of our baggage and made ready to start, one of the men, the Kutial Nattoo, came forward and professed to be able to guide us directly to the Mansarowar Lake. He seemed very anxious to undertake this task, saying that there would be no chance of detection by the route he knew, and consequently we might march during the daytime.

We started up the creek, led by this man, and I was astonished at the willingness with which the Shokas agreed to proceed. In a little time I felt convinced that he was deliberately taking us to the spot I most wished to avoid. On my remonstrating and stopping further progress in that direction, the Shokas mutinied and, depositing their loads, tried to escape, but my bearer quickly barred their way ahead in the narrow creek and I prevented their escape from the opposite side, so they had to surrender. Painful as it was to me, I had to severely punish them all, and while I took care that no one should bolt, Chanden Sing took special pleasure in knocking them about until they were brought back to their senses. On being closely cross-examined, they openly confessed that they had made a plot to hand me over to the Tibetan guard, in order to escape the horrors of torture by the Tibetans. This last act of treachery, coming after what had happened during the night, and from the very men whom I had just been more than lenient towards, was too much for me, and I used a stick, which Chanden Sing handed me, very freely on their backs and legs, Nattoo the Kutial receiving the largest share of blows, because he was undoubtedly the head of the conspiracy.

On climbing to a point of vantage, I now further discovered that, besides the guard we had to the north of us, both east and west our way was barred by Tibetan soldiers, and although it was not possible to get on during the day without being seen, I absolutely refused to go back south. I held a palaver with my men, who were apparently resigned, and they agreed to accompany me as far as the Maium Pass (on the road to Lhassa), which we reckoned to be some fifteen or eighteen marches. They further agreed to endeavour to obtain yaks and food for me, and I was then to dismiss them. From the summit of the hill I had climbed, I had taken careful bearings, and when night came, aided by my luminous compass, I led my men high up along the mountain range at an average elevation of 1500 feet above the Gyanema-Taklakot track.

The night was dark and stormy, and we encountered

much difficulty in our journey forward owing to the slippery ground, alternated with the ever troublesome loose *débris* and shifting rocks. We could not see far ahead, and though we well knew from the angle of the slope that we were travelling along a precipice, we could not distinguish anything under us except a peculiarly luminous streak far, far down below—undoubtedly the river.

I could not explain this luminosity of the water, which did not seem to come from reflection of the light of stars or the moon, because the sky was very cloudy at the time. Moreover, the river had a curious greenish tint quite peculiar to itself, and closely resembling the light produced by electricity. In the more dangerous spots we had to proceed for long distances on all-fours, and even then we felt hardly safe, for we could hear the rattling of the stones rolling down the steep slope, and by this sound we could judge that we were proceeding over a precipice of extraordinary height. So difficult and painful was the walking, that it took us four hours to go about three miles; and we felt so exhausted, that from time to time we had to lie down and rest, shivering with cold, and our hands bleeding from cuts caused by the sharp stones. I mustered my men. Poor Mansing the leper was missing. When we last saw him he was moaning under his load, and he constantly stumbled and fell. Two men were sent in search, but after an hour's absence they failed to discover him. The faithful Chanden Sing and the Shoka Dola were then despatched, as I would not abandon the poor wretch if by any means he could be saved. After another hour of anxiety, the two returned, bringing the unfortunate coolie with them. The poor fellow's hands and feet were badly cut, and the pain in the latter was so great that he could not stand erect. He had fallen fainting from exhaustion, and it was by a mere stroke of luck that in the darkness Chanden Sing stumbled against his senseless body. Apart from his life, his loss would have been a very serious matter for me, as he carried my bedding and photographic cameras.

Sleet and rain commenced to fall, and the cold was intense. We continued to climb steadily, Chanden Sing and I helping the poor leper along. The march soon became less difficult, as we were following a depression formed by the action of melting snows, and were sheltered from the piercing wind which had been hitherto driving the sleet hard into our faces. We slowly covered some three miles more, and during that time the storm passed away, leaving the atmosphere beautifully clear. When we reached the pass (over 17,000 feet), a curious optical phenomenon astonished us all. The larger stars and planets, of a dazzling brilliancy such as I had never in my life seen before, seemed to swing to and fro in the sky with rapid and sudden jerks, describing short arcs of a circle, and returning each time to their normal position. The effect was so weird, that the first thing that struck me was that something had gone wrong with my vision, but my companions saw the same phenomenon : another curious thing was that the stars nearer the horizon disappeared and reappeared behind the mountain range. The oscillations of the heavenly bodies nearer the horizon were less rapid, but the angle of the arc described measured almost double that traced by the stars directly above our heads. The oscillations of these, however, were very much more rapid, especially at certain moments, when the star itself could no more be discerned, and a continuous line of light appeared on the deep blue background of the sky. This strange optical illusion, which began soon after the storm had entirely cleared away, lasted some time; then the vibrations gradually became less violent, and stars and planets eventually resumed their normal steadiness, and shone with great brilliancy and beauty. We crossed the pass, and halted directly on the northern side of it, for my men's feet were in such a condition that they could bear the pain no longer. The minimum temperature was but 12°, and as we had no tent there was only a blanket between us and heaven. When we woke in the morning, we found the thermometer had risen to 30°, but we were enveloped in a thick mist which chilled us to our very marrow. I had icicles hanging down my moustache, eyelashes and hair, and my cheeks and nose were covered with a thin layer of ice caused by the respiration settling and congealing on my face.

CHAPTER XXXVIII

Night marching—The Lafan and Mafan Lakes—Tize, the sacred Kelas—Rhubarb—Butterflies—A hermit Lama—More Dacoits—Surrounded by them—Routed.

DURING our night marches, up and down mountain ranges of considerable height, we naturally had adventures and escapes far too numerous to relate here in exact detail, and I shall not give a full description of each march on account of the unavoidable monotony of such a narrative. In constant storms of grit and snow we crossed range after range, travelling during the night and hiding by day, camping at very great altitudes and undergoing considerable privations. I steered my men towards the Rakstal* Lake, and one day, having risen to 17,550 feet, we obtained a magnificent view of the two great sheets of water, the Lafan-cho and Mafan-cho, or Rakstal and Mansarowar Lakes, by which latter names they are more commonly known to non-Tibetans.

To the N. of the lakes stood the magnificent Tize, the sacred Kelas mountain, overtopping by some two thousand feet all the other snowy peaks of the Gangri chain, which extended roughly from N.W. to S.E. From this spot we could see more distinctly than from Lama Chokden the

* *Rakastal*—Devil's Lake, also very frequently pronounced Rakstal.

band round the base of the mountain, which, according to legend, was formed by the rope of the Rakas (devil) trying to tear down this throne of the gods.

Tize, the great sacred peak, is of fascinating interest, owing to its peculiar shape. It resembles, as I have said, the giant roof of a temple, but to my mind it lacks the gracefulness of

OUR FIRST VIEW OF RAKASTAL

sweeping curves such as are found in Fujiama of Japan, the most artistically beautiful mountain I have ever seen. Tize is angular, uncomfortably angular, if I may be allowed the expression, and although its height, the vivid colour of its base, and the masses of snow that cover its slopes, give it a peculiar attraction, it nevertheless struck me as being intensely unpicturesque, at least from the point from which I saw it, and from which the whole of it was visible.

When clouds were round it, toning down and modifying its shape, Tize appeared at its best from the painter's point of view. Under these conditions, I have thought it very beautiful, especially at sunrise, with one side tinted red and

RAKASTAL AND

yellow, and its rocky mass standing majestic against a background of shiny gold. With my telescope I could plainly distinguish, especially on the E. side, the defile along which the worshippers make the circuit at the base of the mountain, though I was told that some pilgrims actually march round it on the snowy ledge directly over the base, and just above the darker band of rock described before. On the S.W. side can be seen, on the top of a lower peak, a gigantic Obo.

MANSAROWAR LAKES

The peregrination round Tize usually takes three days, though some accomplish it in two days, and under favourable circumstances it has even been done in one day. It is usual for the pilgrims to say certain prayers and make sacrifices as they proceed, and the more fanatical perform the journey serpentwise, lying flat on the ground; others, again, do it on their hands and knees, and others walking backwards.

Tize, or Kelas, has an elevation of 21,830 feet, and Nandiphu, W. of it, 10,440 feet, while N.W. of the sacred mountain are visible other summits 20,460 feet, 19,970 feet, and 20,280 feet. Animal life seemed to abound, for while I was sketching the panorama before me, a snow leopard bounded gracefully past us. I had a shot or two at *thar*, and we saw any number of *kiang*. We found rhubarb, which seemed to be thriving, at so high an elevation as 17,000 feet, and quantities of yellow flowers in the same locality and at the same elevation; and at 19,000 feet I netted two couples of small white and black butterflies. They seemed to have great difficulty in flying, and hardly rose more than two or three inches off the ground, flapping their wings irregularly; they seldom flew more than a few feet, and then remained motionless for long periods before they attempted to fly again. I had come across the same kind of butterfly at lower altitudes, 18,600 feet and 17,000 feet, and I invariably found them in couples.

On nearing the lakes, the atmosphere seemed saturated with moisture, for no sooner had the sun gone down than there was a heavy dew, which soaked our blankets and clothes. We were at 16,550 feet in a narrow marshy creek in which we had descended *à pic* from the last mountain range. From the summit of the range we had seen many columns of smoke rising from the neighbourhood of the Rakas Lake, and we judged that again we must proceed with great caution.

We cooked our food, and in the middle of the night, for greater safety, we shifted our camp on the summit of the plateau in a North-Easterly direction, and continued our journey in the morning, high above the magnificent blue sheet of the Devil's Lake with its pretty islands.

"Sahib, do you see that island?" exclaimed the Kutial, pointing at a barren rock that emerged from the lake. "On it," he continued, "lives a hermit Lama, a saintly man. He has been there alone for many years, and he is held in great veneration by the Tibetans. He exists almost entirely on fish, and occasional swan's eggs, and only in winter, when the lake is frozen, is communication established with the shore, and supplies of *tsamba* are brought to him, for they have no boats in Rakastal, nor any way of constructing rafts, owing to the absence of wood. The hermit sleeps in a cave, but generally comes out in the open to pray to Buddha." During the following night, when everything was still, a slight breeze blowing from the North brought to us, faint and indistinct, the broken howls of the hermit.

"What is that?" I asked of the Shokas.

"It is the hermit speaking to God. Every night he climbs to the summit of the rock, and from there addresses his prayers to Buddha the Great."

"How is he clothed?" I inquired.

"In skins."

Late in the afternoon we had an amusing incident. We came to a creek in which were a number of men and women, hundreds of yaks and sheep, and some thirty ponies.

The Shokas became alarmed, and immediately pronounced the folks to be brigands. I maintained that they were not, and as Kachi expounded the theory that the only way to distinguish Dakus from honest beings was to hear them talk (the Dakus he declared usually shout at the top of their voices when conversing, and use language far from select, while well-to-do Tibetans speak gently and with refinement), I thought the only thing to do was to go and address the people, when by the tone of voice we should find out what they were. This, however, did not suit my Shokas, and we were placed in rather a curious position, for to proceed we must either pass by the Tibetan encampment, or we must march southwards round a mountain, which would involve considerable trouble, fatigue, and waste of time. We waited till night came, watching, unseen, the Tibetans below us. As is customary with them, they retired at sundown to their tents. Leaving my men behind, I crawled into their camp during the night and peeped into one of the tents. The men were squatting on the ground, round a fire in the centre, upon which steamed two vessels with stewing tea. One old man, with strongly-marked Mongolian features, accentuated by the heavy shadows which were cast by the light of the fire above his angular cheek-bones and prominent and wrinkled brow, was busily revolving his prayer-wheel from left to right, repeating in a mechanical way the usual *Omne mani padme hun*, words which come from the Sanscrit, and refer to the reincarnation of Buddha from a lotus flower, meaning literally, "O God, the gem emerging from a lotus flower." Two or three other men, whose faces I could not well see, as they were stooping very low, were busy counting money and examining several articles of Indian manufacture, which undoubtedly had been seized from Shokas. It was fortunate that they had no dogs in this camp, for I, having discovered our best way to pass them unperceived, went back to my men and led them, in the middle of the night, through the camp itself. We proceeded for a mile or so beyond the encampment, and having selected a well-sheltered spot where we could rest without fear of discovery, we laid down our loads and tried to get a few hours' sleep. Waking at sunrise we were startled to find ourselves surrounded by a band of dacoits. They were our friends of the previous night, who, having followed our tracks, and mistaking us for Shoka traders, had now come for a little festive looting. On drawing near they were given a somewhat warm reception, and their instant retreat was more speedy than dignified.

CHAPTER XXXIX

Spied and followed by robbers—Jogpas' hospitality—Hares—Tibetan charms resisted—Attempt to snatch Chanden Sing's rifle out of his hands—The ridge between Rakas and Mansarowar Lakes.

WE wended our way along a narrow valley towards the shore of the Devil's Lake, halting to cook our food about half a mile from the water's edge, and I took this opportunity to make observations for longitude and altitude with hypsometrical apparatus. Water boiled at 185° with temperature of atmosphere at 64°.

I had just repacked my instruments, and was lying flat in the sun, some distance away from my men, when I thought I saw something move. Jumping up, I beheld a stalwart Tibetan stealing along the ground only a few yards away from me, with the object no doubt of taking possession of my rifle before I had time to discover him. Unfortunately for him, he was not quick enough, and all that he gained for his attempt was a good pounding with the butt of my Mannlicher. He was one of the Dakus we had seen in the morning, and no doubt they had followed and spied upon us all along. Having got over his first surprise, the dacoit, with an amusing air of assumed innocence, requested us to go and spend the night in his tent with him and his mates. They would treat us right royally, he said. Being, however, well acquainted with the hospitality of dacoits, we declined the invitation. The brigand went away somewhat shaken and disappointed, and we continued our journey along the water-edge

A DACOIT

of the Devil's Lake (Rakas-tal), where hundreds of hares sprang from under our feet, several of which I killed with my rifle, using bullet cartridges. There were signs all along that at some previous epoch the level of the lake must have been much higher than it is at present.

Marching during the day we encountered many Tibetans, some of whom were Dogpas, others Jogpas. When they saw us approaching they generally bolted, driving their sheep or yaks in front of them. Nevertheless, we came upon two Tibetan women, very dirty, and their faces smeared with black ointment to prevent the skin from cracking in the high wind. They were dressed in long sheepskin garments, worn out and filthy, and their coiffures were so unwashed that they emitted a sickening odour. I ordered them not to come too near us, for although these females had no claims whatever to beauty—and, as far as I could see they possessed no other charm—one being old and toothless, the other with a skin like a lizard, they actually tried to decoy us to their tents, possibly with the object of getting us robbed by their men. My men seemed little attracted by the comical speeches and gestures with which they sought to beguile us, and I pushed on so as to be rid of this uncanny pack as soon as possible.

Four Tibetans, who attempted to snatch Chanden Sing's rifle out of his hand, received from him a battering that they were unlikely soon to forget, and after this we were fortunately left alone for the remainder of the day. In the evening, Chanden Sing fired at a black wolf which came close to camp, and I discovered, about one hundred feet above lake-level, imbedded in the mountain side, a stratum of gigantic fossils, which, owing to their size and weight, I regretted to be unable to dig out and carry away.

Feeling almost certain that we were being spied upon all the time by the numerous Jogpas we had met, we attempted to dodge them by pretending to encamp before sunset.

However, we only lighted a fine fire, and then after dark escaped, walking and stumbling for several miles, until we found a spot high on the hillside where we considered ourselves safe. Snow fell heavily during the night, and, as usual, we woke up with icicles hanging from our moustaches, eyelashes and hair, notwithstanding which we really were quite happy and well.

It was my good fortune to make quite sure from many points that, as can be seen from the illustration reproduced in these pages, the ridge between the Rakas and Mansarowar Lakes is continuous, and no communication between the two lakes exists. With the exception of a small depression about half-way across, the ridge has an average height of 1000 feet all along, a fact which ought in itself to dispose of the theory that the two lakes are one. I also further ascertained from the natives that there is no communication whatever between them, though the depression in the ridge makes it probable that at a very remote period some connection existed. The lowest point in this depression is over 300 feet above the level of the lake.

CHAPTER XL

More robbers—The friends of Tibetan authorities—A snapshot—A meek lot—Prepossessing female and her curious ways—The purchase of two yaks.

JUST before leaving the shores of the Rakstal I had a great slice of luck. It happened thus. We had been detected by another band of dacoits who were trying their hardest to overtake us. I had been spying them with my telescope as they rode in our direction. They were driving some twenty yaks in front of them at an unusually fast pace. The dacoits rode ponies. We were about a mile and a half ahead of them now, and close to the edge of the Devil's Lake. We saw them coming down the hillside at a breakneck speed straight in our direction. It was evident that they were after us. My men became terror-stricken when I gave the order to halt.

The band of dacoits approached and left the yaks in charge of two women. When they galloped in a line towards us, my men, with the exception of Chanden Sing and Mansing, were paralysed with fright.

They were now a hundred yards off. With loaded rifle in one hand, and my camera in the other, I advanced to meet them, knowing that, with their old-fashioned match-

THE BANDITS LAID DOWN THEIR ARMS

locks, it takes them a considerable time to light the fuse and fire a shot. Moreover, it is almost an impossibility for them to fire on horseback, their weapons being heavy and cumbersome.

I focussed them in my twin lens photographic apparatus, and waited till I had them well in the field. I snapped the shot when they were only thirty yards away, vaulting over their ponies in the act of dismounting. The camera, having done its work, was quickly deposited on the ground, and the rifle shouldered. I shouted to them to put down their weapons, and to give force to my request I aimed at them with my Mannlicher.

A meeker lot of brigands I do not believe could be found, though people of that kind are often brave when it is easy for them to be courageous. Their match-locks were unslung from their shoulders with remarkable quickness and flung to the ground, and their jewelled swords were laid by the side of their firearms. They went down on their knees, and taking off their caps with both hands, put out their tongues in sign of salute and submission, and I could not help taking another snap-shot at them in that attitude, which was comical, to say the least of it.

My bearer, who had been left to look after the baggage, had placed Mansing in charge, and was now by my side with the Martini-Henry, when one of the women, riding astride, arrived on the scene. She was evidently furious at the cowardice of her men, and I liked her for that. She jumped off her steed, ejaculated words at the top of her voice, shaking her fists at the men still kneeling before me, and at last, foaming with rage, spat on them. While thus haranguing the band of highwaymen, she had an annoying way of pointing at my baggage, but her speech seemed to have little effect on the submissive crowd.

I, therefore, went up to her, patted her on the back, and gave her a rupee to hold her tongue. She grabbed the coin and rubbed it on her skin coat to make the silver shine. She instantly became calm, and rubbing the coin until it was quite bright, she raised her fiery eyes, staring into mine, and pulled out her tongue to express her thanks.

Kachi and Dola, who knew Tibetan well, were now summoned to address the filibusters for me, and these two Shokas were in such trepidation that they could hardly walk, much less speak. After a while, however, seeing how well I had these supposed terrific rangers under control, they were at last able to translate.

"I want them to sell me some yaks and some ponies," I said. "I will pay handsomely for them."

"They say they cannot. The Tarjum will cut their heads off if he comes to know it. They will only sell one or two yaks."

"Very good. How much do they want?"

"Two hundred silver rupees. But," added Dola, "sahib, do not give them more than forty. That is a great deal more than they are worth. A good yak costs from ten to sixteen rupees."

After some three or four hours' bargaining, during which time the bandits descended gradually from two hundred rupees to forty and I rose from twenty to that figure, we at last agreed, amidst the greatest excitement on both sides, that their two best yaks should become my property. I then, becoming quite friendly, purchased pack-saddles from them, and sundry other curiosities. They gave me tea even and *tsamba*. The fiery woman only had still a peculiar way of keeping her eyes fixed on my baggage, and her longing for my property seemed to increase when she saw me paying for the yaks. If she kept one eye on my goods, I kept both there; and I took good care that my rifle was never out of my hand, and that no one ever came too near me from behind.

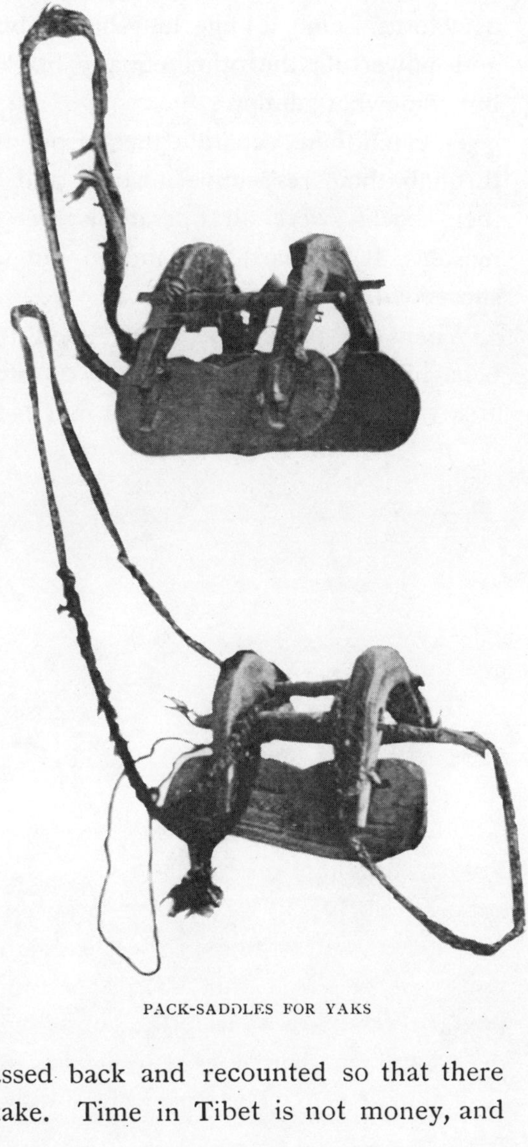

PACK-SADDLES FOR YAKS

We counted the money down, some fifty rupees, including all purchases. Each coin was passed round and sounded by each of our sellers, and when the entire sum was handed over the coins were passed back and recounted so that there should be no mistake. Time in Tibet is not money, and my readers must not be surprised when I tell them that counting, recounting and sounding the small amount took two more hours. The two yaks were eventually handed over to us. One, a huge long-haired black animal, restless and powerful; the other equally black, strong and hairy, but somewhat gentler.

To catch them, separate them from the herd, pass ropes through their respective nostrils, and tie pack-saddles on their backs, were all operations we as novices had to master. It was hard work indeed, but we struggled till we succeeded.

When we parted we were good friends, the bandits behaving admirably, and I made up my mind that I would at any time rather trust a bandit in Tibet than an official.

CHAPTER XLI

Tibetan coats, hats, and boots—Why a Tibetan prefers to leave half the chest and one arm bare—Ornamentations—Manner and speech—Ignorance and superstition—Way of eating—Jogpa women and children—Head-dress.

IN a way, I was sorry when my interview with the Jogpas came to an end, for, although they were undoubtedly brigands, they were certainly interesting. Their original and curious dress and manner of conversation, their unusual but eminently suitable mode of eating, and their jovial freedom of demeanour, were really quite refreshing. Their dress was quite representative of Tibet, for the men wore a great variety of coats and hats, probably owing to the facility with which they obtained them, and no two individuals were dressed alike, though certain leading characteristics of dress were conserved in each case. One man wore a gaudy coat trimmed with leopard skin, another had a long grey woollen robe like a dressing-gown, taken up at the waist by a kamarband, and a third was garbed in a loose raiment of sheepskin, with the wool inside. Yet a fourth was arrayed in a deep red tunic fastened by a belt of leather with silver ornamentations inlaid in wrought-iron to hold a needle-case, tinder-pouch and steel, with a bead hanging from the leather thong, and a pretty dagger with sheath of ebony, steel, and filigree silver, besides other articles, such as a bullet-pouch and bag. In their kamarbands or belts, the Jogpas, in common with the majority of Tibetan men, wear a sword in front, and whether the coat is long or short, it is invariably loose and made to bulge at the waist in order that it may contain a store of eating

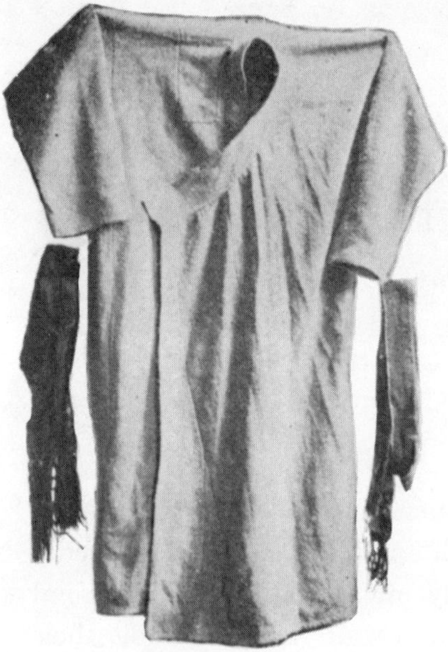

WHITE WOOLLEN COAT AND SASHES

and drinking bowls, the "*pu-kus,*" snuff-box, and sundry bags of money, and *tsamba* and bricks of tea ! It is owing to this custom that most Tibetan men, when seen at first, impress one as being very stout, whereas, as a matter of fact, they are somewhat slight in figure. Tibetans leave one arm and part of the chest bare, letting the sleeve hang loose. The reason for this practice, which seems to have puzzled many people, is that in Tibet the days are very hot

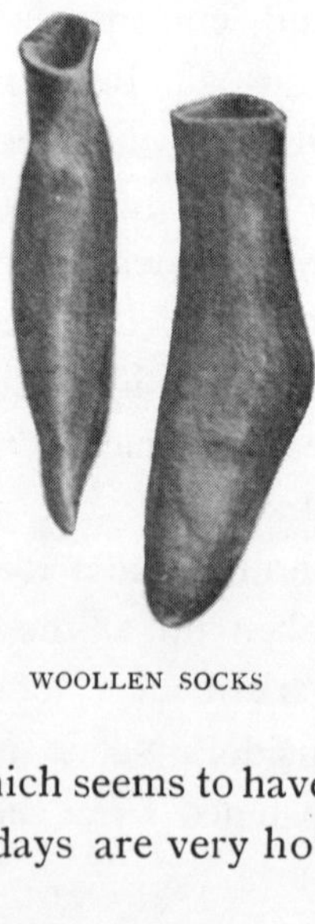

WOOLLEN SOCKS

and the nights cold (the drop in the thermometer in S.W. Tibet being at times as much as 80° and even 100°), and as the Tibetans always sleep in their clothes, the garments that protect their bodies from being frozen at night are found too heavy and warm in the hot sun, and therefore this simple expedient is adopted. When sitting down, both arms are drawn from the sleeves and the chest and back are left bare; but when on foot, one arm, usually the left, is slipped in, to prevent the coat and its heavy contents from falling off.

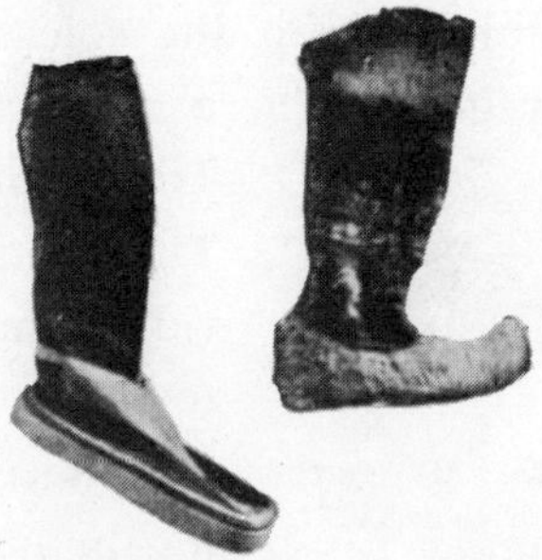

MAN'S BOOT, MADE AT SIGATZ   SNOW BOOT

I have no hesitation in pronouncing the Tibetan boots, from a practical point of view of utility, as the best in the world. They have all the advantages a boot should possess, especially those with flat soles of thick twisted cord. The upper part, being made of red and green felt, keeps the foot warm without preventing ventilation, and plenty of spreading room is left for the toes when walking. The felt gaiter, reaching to just below the knee, holds the soft sole of the boot flat under the foot, giving absolutely free action to the ankle. The most salient and sensible point in the Tibetan footgear, however, is that the foot, all but the top part, is

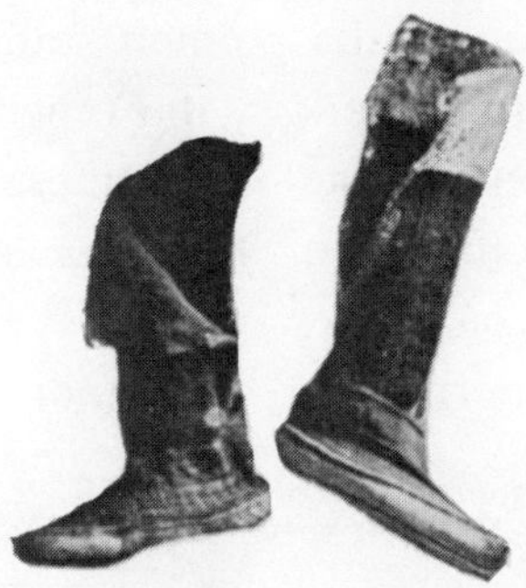

WOMAN'S BOOT   BOOT MADE IN LHASSA

encased in the thick sole, thus preventing the jamming of toes between stones when walking, for instance, on *débris*, and also doing away with the accumulation of snow and mud between the sole and boot, so inconvenient in our footgear. There are many varieties and makes of boots in Tibet, but the principle is always the same. The boots are always home-made, each individual making his own, except in large towns, where footgear can be purchased, and necessarily the quality is then not up to the same high standard. The difference in Tibetan boots is mainly in the quality or texture of the soles; for instance, the Lhassa boots have finer, softer, and more elastic soles than those made in Sigatz (usually written Shigatze), which are quite hard and stiff, and supposed to wear out much sooner than the more pliable ones of the sacred city. Then there are some with leather soles, made specially for wet or snowy regions, and these when greased over are quite waterproof. Two kinds of these are in use, one with pointed and curled toes for cutting one's way into the snow, the other of the usual shape. Men and women alike wear these boots. The principal Lamas and officials of Tibet have adopted the Chinese-pattern boots of leather, with heavy leather or wooden soles and enormous nails under them.

HAT, AS WORN BY OFFICIALS

The Tibetans have innumerable varieties of headgear. The most peculiar of all, worn chiefly by soldiers and dacoits, is one in the form of a section of a cone with large rim, made entirely of twisted cord like that used for the soles of the boots, and with a hole at the top for ventilation. The conical part being too small to fit the head, it is held upon the skull by means of two strings tied under the chin. There are also conical brown and grey felt ones, not unlike filters used in chemical laboratories, and these, when of the better quality, are frequently ornamented with gold, blue, or red embroidery of Chinese manufacture. An impressive headgear was worn by the medicine man attached to the band of robbers I had interviewed. It resembled at first sight an exaggerated jockey's cap of red silk, but closer examination showed that it consisted of two long strips of red silk, well stretched on a light frame of bamboo, set at an angle of about 90°. This hat was held on the head by means of a band round the back of the head, and it projected some fifteen inches over the forehead. In addition to these there are of course common cloth or fur caps with ear-flaps; and it is not uncommon to see, in Tibet, soldiers wearing a silk kamarband bound tightly round the head, turban-fashion, with one end left hanging down over the ear. The commoner Tibetan, however, is not fond of covering his head, and though he often has one or more caps stowed away in the loose folds of his coat, he seldom wears one on his head under ordinary circumstances. This does not apply to officials, who are never seen without a circular cap of Chinese shape, surmounted by a top-knot. All men, except the Lamas, who shave their heads clean, wear a pigtail, short and shaggy at times, or long and ornamented with a piece of cloth, in which it is sewn, and passed through rings of ivory, bone, glass, metal, or coral. Ornaments of silver, such as perforated coins, are much used in adorning the men's pigtails, and coral and malachite ornaments are also common in Tibet for the same purpose, and are much valued by the natives. Men wear, passed through the lobe of the ear, an earring with malachite ornamentations, and often with an additional long pendant. It is usually of brass or silver, and occasionally of gold. More common than the solitary earring is the brass or silver charm-box, frequently containing a likeness of Buddha, which nearly every Tibetan carries slung round his neck. Tibetans are, as a rule, excessively superstitious and fond of charms of every sort. Their superstitions are, of course, the result of ignorance, and so are most of their other bad qualities. Except among the higher officials and the Lamas, education can hardly be said to exist in Tibet, the population being kept in the most obscure ignorance. Few can read, and none can write, and the Lamas take very good care that only those shall learn who are likely to be of use. Honesty and honour are two qualities almost unknown in any class or condition in Tibet, and as for truthfulness, all travellers in the country can testify to the practical impossibility of obtaining it from a Tibetan. Cruelty is innate in them, and vice and crime are everywhere rampant.

That the Jogpas had good digestions was evident from the way they ate when, having concluded the sale of the yaks, they squatted down to a hearty meal of *tsamba, chura,* and tea. They took from their coats their wooden and metal *pu-kus,* and quickly filled them with *tsamba;* pouring over it some steaming tea made as usual with butter and salt in a churn, they stirred it round and round the bowl with their dirty fingers until a paste was formed, which they rolled into a ball and ate, the same operation being repeated over and over again until their appetite was satisfied. Each time, before refilling, the bowl was licked clean by rotating the *pu-ku* round and round the tongue. Feeling the heat of the sun, after their meal both men and women removed their garments above the waist, showing ornaments of gold, silver and copper encircling their necks.

The women-folk of the dacoits, though far from beautiful, possessed a certain charm, arising from their curious wildness. Unlike those of the generality of Tibetan women, their teeth were very good, and their complexion was not specially dark, the black ointment with which their cheeks, noses, and foreheads were smeared making them appear darker than they really were, and being decidedly unbecoming. All of them had regular features, and their eyes and mouths were full of expression. Their hair had been plaited into numberless little tresses, brought up and fastened in a graceful curve over the head, kept firm by a red turban, which was arranged to show another row of little tresses on the forehead, the ends being joined in succession to one another. They wore large earrings of gold inlaid with malachite, and were in manner so unaffected that they disregarded even the most primitive conventions.

The children were talkative, and had the bearing of adults. They wore swords in their belts, even at the early age of eight or ten years. In a basket that had been carried by one of the yaks I saw an infant only a few months old. I caressed it, to the horror of his superstitious mother, who snatched the child away and washed and rubbed the poor little fellow's face until the skin was sore, declaring that children die who are touched by strangers.

The men were just as bad in this, and when I purchased some rice from them they would not let me handle it till it had become my property. They objected each time that

I stretched out my arm to touch the bag of rice, and showed me eventually a handful of rice at a considerable distance, to let me judge of its quality. I had to purchase only the handful at first. Having assured myself that it was all right, I then purchased the remainder.

CHAPTER XLII

A Daku's strange ideas—The ridge between the two lakes—Black tents—Confronting the two lakes—A chain of high peaks—Gombas—Change in the weather.

WE had marched on the same afternoon about half a mile in the direction of Mansarowar, when we were overtaken by one of the Dakus, whom we had left a short time before. He rode towards us, apparently in a great state of excitement. Having dismounted, he drew his sword and began chasing one of my yaks. This seemed so strange a proceeding that we were at a loss to understand his intentions, but as he screamed to us that he meant no harm we let him go on. He eventually overtook one recalcitrant yak, and, after a struggle with the unfortunate beast, he flung his arms round its neck and rested his head between its horns. I was anything but pleased with these antics, fearing that this effusion was only a dodge to cut the beast's throat. Much to my astonishment, I found that the young Jogpa had seized a tuft of the yak's hair with his teeth and was trying to tear it off, while the unfortunate beast was making desperate efforts to shake off its persecutor. The hair eventually gave way, and with a mouthful of it hanging from both sides of his tightly closed lips the Jogpa now let go of the animal's head, and, brandishing his sword, made a dash for its tail.

I seized the man by his pigtail, while he in his turn clung to the tail of the frightened yak, which bolting, dragged us after it at an unpleasant pace.

The Jogpa, in our mad flight, cut off a long lock of the

A BLACK YAK

yak's silky hair, and having secured this, appeared to be quite satisfied, let go and sheathed his sword. He concealed the stolen locks in his coat, and then made profound obeisances to us, putting out his tongue as usual and declaring that unless that precaution is taken when parting with a beast, bad luck is sure to come to you. This closed the incident: the Jogpa rode away perfectly happy, and we continued our march across the stony plain until we reached the ridge which extends across it and divides the two sheets of water. We climbed up to the top, rising to 16,450 feet, and to make certain that the ridge really extended right across, I made an expedition about half-way across, finding the northern part somewhat lower than the southern, still rising several hundred feet above the level of the lakes. This expedition incurred some loss of time, and when night came we were still on the ridge.

From our camping-ground we saw fifteen black tents on the hillside, and to the E. on the lake shore there was a large Gomba or Lamasery, with a temple and a number of mud houses. I estimated the distance between ourselves and the Gomba at only eight miles, a cheering fact, because I hoped to get fresh provisions there to enable us to proceed more rapidly on our journey. We were now quite out of reach of the Gyanema sepoys, as well as of the Barca Tarjum and the Taklakot Jong Pen, and if we could only obtain a sufficient quantity of food during the night, and proceed by the jungle early the next day, there would be little danger of our being overtaken. The Shokas were, of course, again shaking with fright at the idea of entering a Tibetan settlement, but I told them very firmly that we must reach Tucker Gomba and village that night.

We had below us the two great lakes, and before I left this magnificent panorama, I could not help taking a last long look at the marvellous scene. The Devil's Lake, with its broken, precipitous shores, its rocky islands and outstretching peninsulas, was far more enchanting to me than the sacred lake at its side, in which, according to tradition, dwell Mahadeva (pronounced Mahadeve) and all the other good gods. Although the water is equally blue and limpid ; although each lake has for background the same magnificent Gangri chain, Mansarowar, the creation of Brahma, from whom it takes its name, is not nearly so weirdly fascinating as its neighbour. Mansarowar has no ravines rising precipitously from its waters, in which their vivid colouring would be reflected as in a mirror ; it is almost a perfect oval, without indentations. There is a stony, slanting plain some two miles wide between the water's edge and the hills surrounding it, except along the ridge separating it from the Rakstal, where its shore is slightly more rugged and precipitous.

Directly south of the lake is a chain of high peaks covered with snow, from which several streams descend. From where we stood we could see evident signs, as in the case of the Rakstal, that the level of the lake must at one time have been at least thirty feet higher than it is at present, and the slanting bed of small rounded and smooth stones, which extends from one-and-a-half to two miles beyond the water-line, is evidence enough that the water must once have been up to that point ; I believe that it is still gradually receding.

Round the lake there are several tumbling-down sheds in charge of Lamas, but only one important Gomba (monastery) and temple are to be found—viz., at Tucker village.

I was told that a small Gomba and *serai* in charge of Lamas stands to the N.W. of the lake, but I cannot vouch for the accuracy of the statement, as I did not visit it myself, and the information I received from Tibetans regarding its position and importance was conflicting.

As the nature of the country suddenly altered between the Devil's Lake and Mansarowar, so, too, the weather and the temperature greatly changed. Over the Rakstal we invariably saw a lovely blue sky, whereas over Mansarowar heavy black clouds always lowered, and rain fell incessantly. From time to time the wind blew off the rain for a few minutes, and lovely effects of light played on the water, but fresh clouds, with violent bursts of thunder, soon made the scene again gloomy and depressing.

It was much warmer on the Mansarowar side of the ridge than on the other, and, probably owing to dampness, the air seemed quite thick to breathe, instead of being crisp and light, as it was along the shores of the Devil's Lake. Indeed, when I recall the Mansarowar, I cannot help thinking that it is the home, not only of the gods, but also of all the storms.

CHAPTER XLIII

The Langa Tsangpo—A terrific storm—Drenched to the skin—Heavy marching—Against the gods—Difficulty in finding the Lamasery and village—A bark!—Arrival at last—Gentle tapping—Under a roof.

WE descended some two miles to the plain, and crossed a rapid delta of the Langa Tsangpo or Langa River; then another, a mile farther. As these rivers came directly from the snows, the water was very cold, and often three or four feet deep, owing to the thawing of the snow and ice during the day.

No sooner had we reached the shores of the Mansarowar, than the heavy clouds which had been hanging over our heads poured forth such a torrent of rain, that in a moment we were drenched to the skin. We were marching very fast, as all our heavy loads were now on the two yaks, but night was well advanced, and the darkness was such that we could only see a few inches in front of us. We were actually walking in an inch or two of water, and a fierce S.E. wind drove the rain and hail so hard into our faces and hands as to cause us considerable pain. We were frozen in our wet garments, and our teeth were chattering, though we walked quickly, keeping close together. From time to time a bright flash of lightning shone on the lake, followed

MY TWO YAKS

by a terrific crash of thunder, and by what we could see during those few seconds of light we tried to steer our way towards Tucker village and Gomba.

The rivers, swollen by the rain, were extremely difficult to cross, and the water seemed to flow so rapidly on the inclined bed, that it was all we could do to keep on our feet. So wet were we that we did not even take the trouble to remove our shoes or garments, and we splashed through, clothes and all. Three times we went into the freezing water above our waists, and then we marched for apparently endless miles on the pebbly and stony incline. We could not see where we were going, and the storm seemed to grow worse every moment: we stumbled on amidst large stones and boulders, and fell over one another on slippery rocks. Farther on, we sank up to our knees in mud, and each time that we lifted a foot it seemed to be of lead. It was a downpour such as I had seldom before experienced.

"Are you quite sure, Kachi, that this lake is the home of the gods?" I inquired of Kachi. "Why, even on the Devil's Lake we had better weather than this."

"Yes, sir," replied Kachi. "But you make the gods angry, and that is why they send thunder, hail and rain to stop your progress. You are going on against the gods, sir."

"Never mind, Kachi. It cannot pour for ever."

At midnight we had no idea of our position, still we pushed on.

"Have we passed the Gomba? Have we not yet reached it?" were the questions we asked each other. It seemed to me that, at the rate we were going, we ought by now to be very near the place, and yet after another hour's tramp we had not struck it. I was under the belief that we had gone about nine miles, and I expressed the opinion that we had passed it, but the Shokas insisted that we had not, so we again proceeded.

We had hardly gone five hundred yards, when we heard a faint, distant, and most welcome dog's bark. It came from the N.W., and we surmised that it must come from Tucker. We had steered too far south of the place, which accounted for our missing it in the darkness.

Guided by the yelping, we hastily directed our steps towards the settlements. The dog's solitary howl was at once supplemented by fifty more angry barks, and though we knew by the sound that we were approaching the village, it was so dark and stormy that we could not find the place. Only when we found ourselves close to the mud huts could we be certain that we had at last arrived.

It was now between 2 and 3 A.M. The rain still came down in torrents, and, alas! there was no sign of any of the inhabitants being willing to give us shelter. It was quite out of the question to pitch our little *tente d'abri*, for our things were already wringing wet.

The noise we made tapping outside a door was determined, so much so that the door itself nearly gave way. This was a shelter-house, a *serai* for pilgrims, and as we claimed to be pilgrims, we had, by the laws of the country, a right to admission. The Kutial Nattoo, who had once before reached this lake by a different route, led us to this house.

"You are dacoits," said a hoarse voice from inside; "or you would not come at this hour."

"No, we are not," we entreated. "Please open. We are well-to-do people. We will harm no one, and pay for all."

"*Middu, Middu!*" ("Cannot be, no.") "You are dacoits. I will not open."

To show that we were not what they imagined, faithful Chanden Sing and Dola tapped again so gently at the door that the bolt gave way. The next moment ten strangers were squatting down round a warm fire drying their shrivelled-up, soaked skins by the flame of dried tamarisk and dung. The landlord, a doctor by the way, was re-assured when he saw that we had no evil intentions, and found some silver coins in the palm of his hand. Yet he said he would rather that we slept somewhere else : there was a capital empty hut next door.

On our agreeing to this, he conducted us to the place, and there we spent the remainder of the night, or rather the early morning.

CHAPTER XLIV

The interior of a *serai*—Vermin—Fish, local jewellery, and pottery for sale—Favourite shapes and patterns—How pottery is made.

OUR abode was a one-storeyed house built of stones and mud with a flat roof. There were two rooms, the first lighted by the door, the second and larger having a square aperture in the ceiling for the triple purpose of ventilation, lighting and outlet for the smoke of the fire, which burnt directly underneath in the centre of the room. The beams and rafters supporting the roof had been brought over from the other side of the Himahlyas, as no wood is to be found in Western Tibet.

This *serai* was in charge of a young, half-demented lama, who was most profuse in salutations, and who remained open-mouthed, gazing at us for a considerable time. He was polite and attentive in helping to dry our things in the morning, and, whenever we asked for anything, he ran out of the *serai* in frantic fits of merriment, always bringing in what we required.

The heavy storm during the night had flooded our room, and there was only one corner slightly drier than the rest of the floor, where we all slept huddled together. These *serais*

Lithographed by F. A. Brockhaus, Leipzig (Germany).

A TIBETAN FORTUNE TELLER.

have no claim to cleanliness, and on this occasion all the minor animal life that inhabited the floor had, with a view to avoiding the water, retreated to the higher portion of the room, which we also had selected, so that one more trial was added to all our other miseries, for we were half devoured by a variety of "insects." This, indeed, was a dreadful pest, and one from which we suffered indescribable agonies, not only on this occasion but whenever we halted near Tibetan camps. When we rose in the morning the room was full of Tibetan men, women and children, who seemed very good-natured and friendly.

SILVER LHASSA COINS

"*Tanga chick!*" (a silver coin equivalent to half a rupee) cried an old woman, who stuck a dried fish under my nose, professing volubly that it had been caught in Mansarowar, and that it would make its possessor the happiest of mortals. Others unrolled, from pieces of red cloth, jewellery

COPPER COINS

EARRINGS WORN BY MEN

in the form of brooches, rings, and earrings of brass or silver, inlaid with malachite.

"*Gurmoh sum!*" (three rupees), "*Diu, diu, diu*" ("Yes, yes, yes"), "*Karuga ni!*" (two two-anna pieces), "*Gieutcheke!*" (a four-anna piece), and so on, all talking at the same time, in their anxiety to dispose of their goods.

The jewellery was of local manufacture, and in some cases the pieces of malachite were firmly set, but usually a kind of paste is used for holding the stones, and consequently, pretty as the jewels are, they soon break.

SILVER CHARM

The earrings are usually better made than the brooches, but the most interesting of all, because simpler and more characteristic, are the flat silver charms, such as the one I give in the illustration, ornamented with a primitive design. This particular one, which is now in my possession is of great antiquity, the edges being much worn down. It has the lotus pattern in the centre and leaf ornamentations filled in with lines radiating from a parent stem. Concentric circles occupy the inner square, which also contains circular dots in sets of threes and contiguous semicircles. Triangles filled in with parallel lines are a favourite form of ornamentation in Tibetan work, and, perhaps, most popular of all in the mind of the Tibetan artist is the square or the lozenge outline, with a special inclination towards purely geometrical patterns, a tradition probably inherited from their Mongol ancestors.

GOLD AND MALACHITE BROOCH

The most interesting objects to me at Tucker were the

specimens of pottery made by the natives, which is manufactured from clay of fine quality, although it is not properly beaten previous to being worked into vases, jugs, &c. Moulds are used to fashion the bases of the larger vessels and the inner part is shaped by the hand; a rough turning-machine simplifies the finishing of the upper part of the vase, leaving it comparatively smooth. Two handles with rough line ornamentations are added to the larger vessels, but one suffices for the jars with longer neck and small aperture.

The two patterns reproduced in the illustration are those more commonly adopted; the colour is a light greyish terra-cotta, left fairly smooth and unvarnished. They are well burnt, in primitive furnaces, the Lamas showing much skill in the manufacture of these vessels, which find a ready market among the pilgrims to the sacred lake. The tools used in fashioning the vessels are extremely simple; a piece of flat stone, and two or three wands of wood, beyond which the Tucker potter does not really require more than his fingers and his nails to accomplish his work.

MANSAROWAR POTTERY

CHAPTER XLV

Friendly Lamas—Chanden Sing and Mansing purified—Mansing's sarcasm—Pilgrims to Mansarowar and their privileges——For luck !—Outside the Gomba.

SEVERAL Lamas came to visit me in the morning, and professed to be pleased to see us ; in fact they asked me to go and pay them a visit in the Lamasery and temple. They said there was much sickness in the village, and as they believed me to be a Hindoo doctor, they wished I could do something to relieve their sufferings. I promised to do all I could, and was very glad to have this unique chance of visiting a Lamasery, and of studying the cases that would be brought before me. I carried my rifle in my hand even during this friendly visit to the Lamas.

When I came out of our stuffy, dark room, preceded and followed by a crowd of inquisitive natives, I had a good look round this strange village. After the storm of the night, we did not have the beautiful blue sky that might have been expected, but over us hung threatening clouds, while the waters of the sacred lake, softly moved by the wind, made a gentle lapping sound on the beach. Chanden Sing and Mansing, the two Hindoos, divested of all their clothing except a *doti*, were squatting near the edge of the lake, having their heads shaved clean by Bijesing the Johari. I must confess that I was somewhat annoyed when I saw them using my best razor for the purpose, but I repressed my anger on remembering that, according to their religion, the fact of being at Mansarowar absolved them from all sins. My two servants, with heads turned towards Kelas Mount, seemed excited, and were praying so fervently that I stood to watch them. They washed themselves repeatedly in the water of the lake, and at last plunged into it. On coming out shivering, they each took out of their clothes a silver rupee, and flung it into the lake as an offering to the God Mahadeva. Then, with hairless faces and heads, they dressed and came to pay their salaams to me, professing to be now happy and pure.

"Siva, the greatest of all gods, lives in the waters of Mansarowar," exclaimed my bearer in a poetic mood. "I have bathed in its waters, and of its waters I have drunk. I have salaamed the great Kelas, the sight of which alone can absolve all sins of humanity; I shall now go to heaven."

"I shall be satisfied if we get as far as Lhassa," grumbled the sceptical Mansing, out of ear-reach of the Tibetans.

Chanden Sing, who was well versed in religious matters, explained that only Hindoo pilgrims who had lost both parents shaved their heads on visiting Mansarowar, as a sacrifice to Siva, and if they were of a high caste, on their return to their native land after the pilgrimage, it was customary to entertain all the Brahmins of the town to a banquet. A man who had bathed in Mansarowar was held in great respect by everybody, and commanded the admiration and envy of the entire world.

The Mansarowar Lake is about forty-six miles round, and those pilgrims who wish to attain a greater state of sanctity make a *kora* or circuit on foot, along the water-line. The journey occupies from four to seven days, according to circumstances, and one trip round will absolve the pilgrim from ordinary sins ; twice the circuit clears the conscience of any murder ; and three times will make honest and good a person who has killed his or her father, mother, brother or sister. There are fanatics who make the tour on their knees, others accomplish the distance lying down flat at each step on their faces like the pilgrims to Kelas.

According to legend, Mansarowar was created by Brahma, and he who shall bathe in its waters will share the paradise of Mahadeva ! No matter what crimes he may have previously committed, a dip in the holy lake is sufficient to purge the soul as well as the body ! To please my men, therefore, and perhaps bring myself some luck, I too hurled a couple of coins into the water.

The purifying ablutions being over, I ordered Chanden Sing to take his rifle and follow me into the Gomba, as the Lamas were so polite that I feared treachery on their part.

The large square building, with its walls painted red and its flattish dome of gilt copper, rose by the waterside, and was both picturesque and handsome in its severe simplicity.

There came sounds from inside of deep, hoarse voices muttering prayers, the tinkling of bells and clanging of cymbals. From time to time a drum was beaten, giving a hollow sound, and an occasional and sudden touch upon a gong caused the air to vibrate until the notes in a gradual diminuendo were carried away over the holy lake.

CHAPTER XLVI

Entering the Lamasery—The Lama's dwelling—Novices—Were we in a trap?—Images—Oblations—Urghin—The holy water, the veil of friendship, and absolution—Musical instruments, books, &c.—God and the Trinity—Heaven and hell—A mystery.

AFTER Chanden Sing and I had entered into the Lamasery, the large door, which had been pushed wide open, was immediately closed. We were in a spacious courtyard, three sides of which had two tiers of galleries supported by columns. This was the *Lhaprang*, or Lama's house, and directly in front of me was the *Lha Kang*, or temple, the floor of which was raised some five feet above the level of the ground, with a very large door leading into it. At this entrance were, one on either side, recesses in which, by the side of a big drum, squatted two Lamas with books of prayers before them, a praying-wheel and a rosary in their hands, the beads of which they shifted after every prayer. At our appearance the monks ceased their prayers and beat the drums in an excited manner. From what I could judge, there was a commotion in the Gomba. Lamas, old and young, rushed to and fro out of their rooms, while a number of Chibbis or novices—boys between the ages of twelve and twenty—lined the banisters of the upper verandah with expressions of evident suspense and curiosity depicted on their faces. No doubt the Lamas had prepared a trap for us. I warned Chanden Sing to be on the alert, and set him on guard at the entrance of the temple, while I, depositing a few silver coins on the drum

ENTRANCE TO THE TUCKER TEMPLE

of the Lama to my right, took off my shoes in sign of respect and—much to the amazement of the monks—quietly entered the house of worship. Partly astonished at the sight of the silver, and more so at my want of caution, the Lamas, of whom there was a good number in the court-yard, remained motionless and mute. The high Lama, or Father Superior of the monastery, at last came forward, stooping low and placing one thumb above the other and putting his tongue out to show his superlative approval of my visit to the many images representing deities or sanctified Buddhist heroes which were grouped along the walls of the temple. The largest of these were about five feet high, the others about three feet. Some were carved out of wood, their drapery and ornaments being fairly artistic in arrangement and execution, while others were fashioned in gilt metal. There were a number in a sitting posture and some standing erect; and they all rested on ornamented pedestals or plainer bases painted blue, red, white and yellow. Many wore the ancient Chinese double-winged cap, as used to this day by Corean officials, and were placed in recesses in the wall decorated with stuffs, wood carvings, and rough paintings of images.

At the foot of these images was a long shelf, on which, in bright brass vessels of all sizes, were oblations of *tsamba*, dried fruit, *chura*, wheat and rice offered through the Lamas by the devotees to the different saints. Some of the ears of barley were ornamented with imitation leaves of *murr* (butter), coloured red, blue and yellow.

The ceiling of the temple was draped in red woollen cloth similar to that of the clothes worn by the Lamas themselves, and from it hung hundreds of strips of silk, wool and cotton of all imaginable colours. The roof was supported by columns of wood forming a quadrangle in the centre of the temple and joined by a balustrade, compelling the worshippers to make a circuit from left to right in order to pass before the several images. In a shrine in the central part of the wall facing the entrance was *Urghin* or *Kunjuk-chick*, "God alone," and in front of it on a kind of altar covered with a carpet a collection of donations far more abundant than those offered to the other images.

The Lama, pointing at it, told me that it was a good God, and so I salaamed it and deposited a small offering in a handy collection-box, which seemed to please the Lama greatly, for he at once fetched a holy water amphora, hung with long veils of friendship and love, and poured some scented liquid on the palms of my hands. Then, producing a strip of veil, he wetted it with the scent and presented it to me. The majority of pilgrims generally go round the inside of the temple on their knees, but, notwithstanding that, to avoid offending prejudices, I generally follow the principle of doing in Rome as the Romans do, I could not here afford the chance of placing myself at such a disadvantage in case of a surprise. The high Lama explained the different images and threw handfuls of rice over them as he called them by their respective names, all of which I tried hard to remember, but, alas! before I could get back to the *serai* and scribble down their appellations, they had all escaped my memory. A separate entrance led from the living part of the monastery into the temple.

Lights, burning in brass bowls, their wicks being fed with melted butter, were scattered on the floor in the central quadrangle, and near them lay oblong books of prayers printed on the smooth yellow Tibetan paper made from a fibrous bark. Near these books were small drums and cymbals. One double drum, I noticed, was made from reversed sections of human skulls, and my attention was also attracted by some peculiar headgear worn by the Lamas during their services and ceremonies. On these occasions they not only accompany their chanting and prayers with the beating of drums and clashing of cymbals, but they at the same time make a noise on cane flutes, tinkle hand-bells, and sound a large gong. The noise of these instruments is at times so great that the prayers themselves are quite inaudible. Unfortunately, I failed to see any of the awe-inspiring masks which are used by Lamas in their eccentric and mystic dances, during which, when the Lamas spend the whole day in the temple, they consume much tea with butter and salt in it, which is brought to them in cups by Lamas of an inferior order, acting as servants. They pass hour after hour in their temples apparently absolutely absorbed in praying to the God above all gods, the incarnation of all the saints together united in a trinity, the *Kunjuk-Sum*.

Kunjuk-Sum, translated literally, means "the three deities," and some take it to refer to the elements, air, water and fire, which in the Tibetan mind are symbols of speech, charity and force and life. One great point in Buddhism, as every-one knows, is the advocation of love and respect to one's father and mother and the prohibition against injuring one's neighbours in any way. According to the precepts contained in some eight hundred volumes called the Kajars, the Tibetans believe in a heaven (the Deva Tsembo) free from all anxieties of human existence, full of love and joy, and ruled over by a god of infinite goodness, helped by countless disciples called the *Chanchubs*, who spend their existence in performing charitable deeds among living creatures. With a number of intermediate places of happiness and punishment they even believe in a hell, where the souls of sinners are tormented by fire and ice.

"God sees and knows everything, and He is everywhere," exclaimed the Lama, "but we cannot see Him. Only the *Chanchubs* can see and speak to Him."

"What are the evil qualities to be mostly avoided ? I inquired of the high Lama, who spoke a little Hindustani.

"Luxury, pride and envy," he replied.

"Do you ever expect to become a saint ?" I asked him.

"Yes, I hope so, but it takes five hundred transmigrations of an uncontaminated soul before one can be one."

Then, as if waking to a sudden thought, he seized my hand impulsively and spread my fingers open. Having done this, he muttered two or three words of surprise. His face became serious, even solemn, and he treated me with strange obsequiousness. Rushing out of the temple, he went to inform the other Lamas of his discovery, whatever it was. They crowded round him, and from their words and gestures it was easy to see that they were bewildered.

When I left the company of the strange idols and came into the courtyard, every Lama wished to examine and touch my hand, and the sudden change in their behaviour was to me a source of great curiosity, until I learnt the real cause of it some weeks later.

CHAPTER XLVII

The Jong Pen's statements regarding me—Sects of Lamas—Lamaseries—Government allowance—Ignorance of the crowds—How Lamas are recruited—Lamas, novices, and menials—Dances and hypnotism—Infallibility—Celibacy and vice—Sculptors—Prayer-wheels and revolving instruments—Nunneries—Human bones for eating vessels and musical instruments—Blood-drinking.

BEFORE I left the monastery, the Lamas, who had now become more or less accustomed to me, asked me many questions regarding India and concerning medicine. These seemed to be subjects of great interest to them. They also questioned me as to whether I had heard that a young sahib had crossed over the frontier with a large army, which the Jong Pen of Taklakot had defeated, beheading the sahib and the principal members of the expedition.

I professed to be ignorant of these facts, and so I really was, though I naturally felt much amused at the casual way in which the Jong Pen of Taklakot had disposed of the bearskin before he had even caught the bear himself. The Lamas took me for a Hindoo doctor, owing to the colour of my face, which was sunburnt and had long remained unwashed, and they thought that I was on a pilgrimage of circumambulation round the Mansarowar Lake. They appeared anxious to know whether illnesses were cured by occult sciences in India, or by medicines only. I, who, on the other hand, was more interested in getting information than in giving it, turned the conversation on the Lamas themselves.

Of course I knew that there are sects of red, yellow, white and black Lamas, the red ones being the older and more numerous throughout the country; next to them come the yellow Lamas, the *Gelupkas*, equally powerful in political and religious matters, but not quite so numerous; and, lastly, the white Lamas and the black Lamas, the *Julinba*, who are the craftsmen in the monasteries, working at painting, printing, pottery and ornamentation, besides attending on the other Lamas and making themselves useful all round in the capacities of cooks, shepherds, water-carriers, writers, and last, but not least, executioners. The lamaseries are usually very rich, for the Tibetans are a deeply devout race, and the Lamas are not backward in learning how to extort money from the ignorant worshippers under pretences of all kinds. Besides attending to their religious functions, the Lamas are traders at large, carrying on a smart money-lending business, and charging a very high interest, which falls due every month. If this should remain unpaid, all the property of the borrower is confiscated, and if this prove insufficient to repay the loan the debtor himself becomes a slave to the monastery. It is evident, from the well-fed countenances of the Lamas, that, notwithstanding their occasional bodily privations, they as a rule do not allow themselves to suffer in any way, and no doubt can be entertained as to their leading a smooth and comfortable existence of comparative luxury —a condition which frequently degenerates into vice and depravity.

TUCKER VILLAGE AND GOMBA

The larger lamaseries receive a yearly Government allowance, and considerable sums are collected from the oblations of the faithful, while other moneys are obtained by all sorts of devices which, in any country less religious than Tibet, would be considered hardly honourable and often even altogether criminal. To any one acquainted with Tibet, it is a well-known fact that, except in the larger towns, nearly all people besides brigands and Lamas are absolutely poor, while the monks themselves and their agents live and prosper on the fat of the land. The masses are maintained in complete ignorance, and seldom is a layman found who can write or even read. Thus everything has to go through the Lamas' hands before it can be sanctioned.

The lamaseries and the Lamas, and the land and property belonging to them, are absolutely free from all taxes and dues, and each Lama or novice is supported for life by an allowance of *tsamba*, bricks of tea, and salt. They are recruited from all ranks, and whether honest folks or murderers, thieves or swindlers, all are eagerly welcomed on joining the brotherhood. One or two male members of each family in Tibet take monastic orders, and by these means the monks obtain a great hold over each house- or tent-hold. It is hardly an exaggeration to say that in Tibet half the male population are Lamas.

In each monastery are found Lamas, Chibbis, and a lower grade of ignorant and depraved Lamas, slaves, as it were, of the higher order. They dress, and have clean-shaven heads like their superiors, and do all the handiwork of the monastery; but they are mere servants, and take no direct, active part in the politics of the Lama Government. The Chibbis are novices. They enter the lamasery when very young, and remain students for many years. They are constantly under the teaching and supervision of the older ones, and confession is practised from inferior to superior. After undergoing, successfully, several examinations they become effective Lamas, which word translated means "high priest." These Chibbis take minor parts in the strange religious ceremonies in which the Lamas, disguised in skins and ghastly masks, sing and dance with extraordinary contortions to the accompaniment of weird music made by bells, horns, flutes, cymbals and drums.

Each large monastery has at its head a Grand Lama, not to be confounded with the Dalai Lama of Lhassa, who is believed, or rather supposed, to have an immortal soul transmigrating successively from one body into another.

The Lamas eat, drink and sleep together in the monastery, with the exception of the Grand Lama, who has a room to himself. For one moon in every twelve they observe a strict seclusion, which they devote to praying, and during which time they are not allowed to speak. They fast for twenty-four hours at a time, with only water and butter-tea, eating on fast-days sufficient food only to remain alive, and depriving themselves of everything else, including snuff and spitting, the two most common habits among Tibetan men.

The Lamas have great pretensions to infallibility, and on account of this they claim, and obtain, the veneration of the people, by whom they are supported, fed and clothed. I found them, as a rule, very intelligent, but inhuman, barbarously cruel and dishonourable, and this was not my own experience alone : I heard the same from the overridden natives, who wish for nothing better than a chance to shake off their yoke.

Availing themselves of the absolute ignorance in which they succeed in keeping the people, the Lamas practise to a great extent occult arts, by which they profess to cure illnesses, discover murders and thefts, stop rivers from flowing, and bring storms about at a moment's notice. Certain exorcisms, they say, drive away the evil spirits that cause disease. It is certain that the Lamas are adepts at hypnotic experiments, by which means they contrive to let the subjects under their influence see many things and objects that are not there in reality. To this power are due the frequent reports of apparitions of Buddha, seen generally by single individuals, and the visions of demons, the accounts of which alone terrify the simple-minded folk, and cause them to pay all their spare cash in donations to the monastery.

Mesmerism plays an important part in their weird dances, during which extraordinary contortions are performed, and strange positions assumed, the body of the dancer being eventually reduced to a cataleptic state, in which it remains for a great length of time.

The Lamas swear to celibacy when they enter a lamasery; but they do not always keep these vows, and they are besides addicted to the most disgusting of all vices in its very worst forms, which accounts for the repulsive appearance of far-gone depravity so common among the middle-aged Lamas.

All the larger lamaseries support one or more Lama sculptors, who travel all over the district, and go to the most inaccessible spots to carve on rocks, stones, or pieces of horn, the everlasting inscription, "*Omne mani padme hun*," which one sees all over the country. Unseen, I once succeeded, after much difficulty and discomfort, in carrying away two of these very heavy inscribed stones, which are still in my possession, and of which reproductions are here given.

Weird and picturesque places, such as the highest points on mountain passes, gigantic boulders, rocks near the sources of rivers, or any spot where a *mani* wall exists, are the places most generally selected by these artists to engrave

STONE WITH INSCRIPTION

the magic formula alluding to the reincarnation of Buddha from a lotus flower.

The famous prayer-wheels, those mechanical contrivances by which the Tibetans pray to their god by means of water, wind and hand-power, are also manufactured by Lama artists. The larger ones, moved by water, are constructed by the side of, or over, a stream, and the huge cylinders on which the entire Tibetan prayer-book is inscribed are revolved by the flowing water. The wheels moved by wind-power are similar to those used by the Shokas, which I have already described, but the Tibetans often have prayers printed on the slips of cloth. The smaller prayer-wheels, revolved by hand, are of two different kinds, and are made either of silver or copper. Those for home use are cylinders, about six inches high. Inside these revolve on pivots, on the principle of a spinning top, the rolls of prayers which, by means of a projecting knob above the machine, the worshipper sets in motion. The prayers can be seen revolving inside through a square opening in the cylinder. The more universal prayer-wheel in everyday use in Tibet is, however, of the pattern shown in the illustration. It is usually constructed of copper, sometimes of brass, and frequently entirely or partly of silver. The cylinder has two movable lids, between which the prayer-roll fits tightly. A handle with an iron rod is passed through the centre of the cylinder and roll, and is kept in its place by means of a knob. A ring, encircling the cylinder, attaches it to a short chain and weight; this serves, when started by a jerk of the hand, to give a rotatory movement, which must, according to rule, be from left to right, and which is kept up indefinitely, the words "*Omne mani padme hun*," or simply "*Mani, mani*," being repeated all the time.

The more ancient wheels have the prayers written by hand instead of printed, and are contained in a small black bag. Charms, such as rings of malachite, jade, bone, or silver, are often attached to the weight and chain by which the rotary movement is given to the wheel. These praying-machines are found in every Tibetan family, and nearly every Lama possesses one. They keep them jealously, and it is very difficult to get the real ones. I was particularly fortunate, and during my journey in Tibet I was able to purchase as many as twelve, two of which were extremely old.

Besides the rosary, which the Lamas always use in a similar way to the Roman Catholics, they have a brass instrument which they twist between the palms of their

PRAYER WHEELS—ANCIENT AND MODERN. SHOWING ROLLS OF PRAYERS TO GO INSIDE

hands while saying prayers, and this is used exclusively by Lamas. It is from 2½ to 3 inches in length, and is rounded so as to be easily held in the hollow of the two hands.

In Tibet, as in other Buddhist countries, there are nunneries besides lamaseries. The nuns, unattractive in themselves mostly, and looked down upon, shave their heads and practise witchcraft and magic, just as the Lamas do. In some of these nunneries strict *clausura* is enforced, but in most of them the Lamas are allowed free access, with the usual result, that the nuns become the concubines of the Lamas. Even apart from this, the women of the nunneries are quite as immoral as their brethren of the lamaseries, and at their best they are but a low type of humanity.

The Lamas who, at certain periods of the year, are allowed an unusual amount of freedom with women, are those who practise the art of making musical instruments and eating-vessels out of human bones. The skull is used for making drinking-cups, *tsamba* bowls, and single and double drums, and the humerus, femur, and tibia bones are turned into trumpets and pipes. These particular Lamas are said to relish human blood, which they drink out of the cups made from men's skulls.

STONE WITH INSCRIPTION

CHAPTER XLVIII

Illnesses and remedies—Curious theories about fever—Evil spirits—Blacksmith and dentist—Exorcisms—Surgical operations—Massage and cupping—Incurable illnesses—Deformities—Deafness—Fits and insanity—Melancholia—Suicides.

THE Lamas became quite communicative, enabling me, partly with the little Hindustani that I knew and partly with the Tibetan I had picked up, to enter into a conversation about illnesses and their remedies, certain as I was that they must have strange notions on the subject. I was not disappointed in this surmise, and from that conversation and my own observation on previous and subsequent occasions, I am able to give a few details of the methods of the Lamas in curing the more frequent ailments found in the country.

The Lamas explained to me that all diseases arose from fever, instead of fever being an accompaniment of most illnesses, and furthermore, that fever itself was but an evil spirit, which assumed different forms when it entered the body, and caused all sorts of complaints. The fever demon, they asserted, was a spirit, but there were yet other demons who were so good as to bring us riches and happiness. For instance, when a man after a dangerous illness visited a cave, waterfall or river-gorge which these demons were supposed to haunt, he might have a relapse and die, or he might be instantly cured and live happy ever afterwards. In the latter case, as would naturally be expected, the recipient of such inestimable privileges generally returned to pay a second visit to the kindly spirits who made his life worth living, "but," said the Lamas quite seriously, "when he goes a second time he will get blind or paralytic, as a punishment for his greediness."

"The evil spirits," continued a fat old Lama with crooked fingers, which he clenched and shook as he spoke, "are in the shape of human beings or like goats, dogs, sheep or ponies, and sometimes they assume the semblance of wild animals, such as bears and snow leopards."

I told the Lamas that I had remarked many cases of goître and also other abnormalities, such as hare-lip and webbed fingers and toes, as well as the very frequent occurrence of supernumerary fingers or toes. I asked them the reason for such cases, and they attributed them, with the exception of webbed fingers, to the mischievous work of demons before the child's birth; they could not, however, suggest a remedy for goître.

Inguinal and umbilical hernia are quite common, as I have on several occasions observed, and coarse belts are made according to the taste and ingenuity of the sufferer, but are of hardly any efficacy in preventing the increase of the swellings.

A common complaint, especially among the older women, was rheumatism, from which they seemed to suffer considerably. It affected their fingers and toes, and particularly the wrists and ankles, the joints swelling so as to render them quite stiff, the tendons contracting, swelling, and becoming prominent and hard in the palms of the hands.

Both before and after my conversation with the Lamas I had opportunities of ascertaining that the stomachs of the Tibetans are seldom in good working order. But how could they be when you consider the gallons of filthy tea which they drink daily, and the liquor to which they are so partial? This poisonous concoction is enough to destroy the gastric juices of an ostrich! The tongue, as I have mentioned already, is invariably thickly furred with a whitish coating, and Tibetans have often complained to me of tumours as well as of painful burnings in the stomach, the latter undoubtedly caused by ulcerations. It is to be regretted that, even in the high land of Tibet, the worst of all sexual diseases (called by the Tibetans *Boru*) has made vast numbers of victims, palpable traces of it showing themselves in eruptions, particularly on the forehead and on the ears, round the mouth and under the nostrils, on the arms and legs. In cases of very long standing, a peculiar whitish discoloration of the skin and gums was to be noticed, with abnormal contraction of the pupils. That such a disease is well rooted in the country we have proof enough in the foul teeth which the majority of Tibetans possess. In nearly all cases that I examined, the teeth were, even in young men, so loose, decayed and broken as to make me feel quite sorry for their owners, and during the whole time I was in Tibet —and I came in contact with several thousand people—I believe that I could almost count on my fingers the sets of teeth that appeared quite regular, healthy and strong. As a rule, too, the women had better teeth than the men. No doubt the admixture of bad blood in the Tibetan race contributes a great deal to the unevenness and malformation of their teeth, and if we add to this the fact that the corruption of the blood, even apart from disease, is very great owing to their peculiar laws of marriage, it is not surprising that the services of dentists are everywhere required. The teeth of Tibetans are generally of such a brittle nature that the dentist of Tibet—usually a Lama and a blacksmith as well—has devised an ingenious way of protecting them from further destruction by means of a silver cap encasing the broken tooth. I once saw a man with all his front teeth covered in this fashion, and as the dentist who had attended to him had constructed the small cases apparently with no regard to shape or comfort, but had made most of them end in a point for mastication's sake, the poor man had a ghastly appearance every time that he opened his mouth. The Tibetans are not very sensitive to physical pain, as I have had reason to judge on several occasions, when I have seen teeth extracted in the most primitive fashion, without a sound being emitted from the sufferer.

In South-Western Tibet the *Hunyas* (Tibetans) have the same strange notions on transmigration of evil spirits that are common to the Shokas. For instance, if a man falls ill, they maintain that the only remedy is to drive away the evil spirit which has entered his body. Now, according to Tibetan and Shoka ideas, evil spirits always enter a living body to satisfy their craving for blood: therefore, to please the spirit and decoy him away, if the illness be slight, a small animal such as a dog or a bird is brought and placed close by the patient; if the illness be grave, a sheep is produced and exorcisms are made in the following fashion. A bowl of water is whirled three or four times over the sick man's head, and then again over the animal selected, upon whose head it is poured. These circles, described with certain mystic words, have the power of drawing the spirit out of its first quarters and causing it to enter the brain of the second victim, upon whose skull the water is poured to prevent its returning back.

"Of course," said my informer with an air of great gravity, "if you can give the evil spirit a present in the shape of a living being that will satisfy him, he will depart quite happy." If the illness is slight, it means that the spirit is not much out of temper, and a small present is enough to satisfy him, but if the disease is serious, nothing less than a sheep or even a yak will be sufficient. As soon as the spirit has changed his temporary abode the animal is quickly dragged away to a crossing of four roads, and if there are no roads a cross is previously drawn on the ground, where a grave for the animal is dug, into which it is mercilessly thrown and buried alive. The spirit, unable to make a rapid escape, remains to suck the blood of his last victim, and in the meantime the sick man, deprived of the company of his ethereal and unwelcome guest, has time to make a speedy recovery. When a smaller animal is used, such as a dog or a bird, and when the patient complains of more than one ailment, the poor beast, having been conveyed to the crossing of four roads, is suddenly seized and brutally torn into four parts, which are flung in four different directions, the idea being that, wherever there may be spirits waiting for blood, they will get their share and depart happy. After their craving is satisfied, the evil spirits are not very particular whether the blood is human or not. In Shoka

BRANCH WITH THORNS TO PREVENT RETURN OF EVIL SPIRITS.

land especially, branches with thorns and small flying prayers are placed on each road to prevent their immediate return. These are said to be insuperable barriers to the evil spirits.

When a patient completely recovers, the Lamas naturally obtain money for the exorcisms which have expelled the illness, and they never fail to impress upon the people the extraordinary powers they possess over the much-dreaded demons.

The Tibetans are unsuccessful in surgery, first of all because they do not possess sufficient knowledge of human anatomy; secondly, because their fingers are wanting in suppleness and sensitiveness of touch; and lastly, because they are not able to manufacture instruments of sufficient sharpness to perform surgical operations with speed and cleanliness. In Tibet everybody is a surgeon, thus woe to the unfortunate who needs one. It is true that amputation is seldom performed; but if it should become necessary, and the operation is at all difficult, the patient invariably succumbs. The Tibetan surgeon does not know how to saw bones, and so merely severs the limb at the place where the fracture has occurred. The operation is performed with any knife or dagger that happens to be at hand, and is, therefore, attended with much pain, and frequently has disastrous results. The precaution is taken to tie up the broken limb above the fracture, but it is done in such a clumsy way that very often, owing to the bad quality of Tibetan blood, mortification sets in, and, as the Tibetans are at a loss what to do on such occasions, another victim goes to join the majority.

Considering the nomadic habits of the Tibetans and the rough life they lead, they are comparatively immune from very bad accidents. Occasionally there is a broken arm or leg which they manage to set roughly, if the fracture is not a compound one, by putting the bones back in their right position, and by tightly bandaging the limbs with rags, pieces of cloth and rope. Splinters are used when wood is obtainable. A powder made from a fungus growing on oak-trees in the Himahlyas is imported and used by the Tibetans near the frontier. A thick layer of it, when wet, is rubbed and left upon the broken limb, over which the bandaging is afterwards done. In a healthy person, a simple fracture of the leg, which by chance has been properly set, takes from twenty to thirty days to heal, after which the patient can begin moving about; and a broken arm does not require to be kept in a sling more than fifteen or twenty days. If these cures are somewhat more rapid than with our more civilised methods of bone-setting, it is merely due to the wholesome climate and the fact that the natives spend most of their days out in the open air and in the sun, undoubtedly the best cure for any complaint of that kind; but, of course, it is but seldom that the bones are joined properly, and they generally remain a deformity. More satisfactory results are obtained with cases of dislocations by pulling the bones into their right position.

In case of wounds the bleeding is arrested by the application of a wet rag tightly bound over the wound. In most cases of unbandaged wounds that came under my notice the process of healing was a very slow one, the great changes in the temperature between night and day often causing them to open of themselves. They made good headway towards recovery in the beginning, but the skin was very slow in joining and re-forming.

Burns are treated by smearing butter over them; and a

poultice of rhubarb is used to send down swellings of contusions as well as for the purpose of bringing boils, from which the Tibetans suffer much, to a speedy maturation.

Aconite is given for fever and rheumatism, and a rough kind of massage is used to allay pain in the muscles of limbs. It is generally done by the women, who, as far as I could judge, practised it with no real knowledge but merely contented themselves with violent rubbing and pinching and thumping until signs of relief appeared on the sufferer's face. Whether, however, these manifestations were due to actual soothing of pain, or to the prospect of the masseuse bringing her treatment to an end, I could never properly ascertain. Tibetan fingers are not well adapted for such work, being clumsy and, compared with those of other Asiatic races, quite stiff and hard.

Cupping is adopted with success. Three or four small incisions are made close to one another and a conical cupping-horn about seven inches long, having a tiny hole at its point, is applied over them. The operator then sucks through this small aperture until the horn is full of blood, when it is removed and the operation begun again. With poisoned wounds the sucking is done by applying the lips to the wound itself.

Bleeding is used as a remedy for bruises and swellings, and for internal pain, also for acute attacks of rheumatism and articular pains. If it is not sufficient, the branding cure is resorted to, and if this should also fail, then the tinder cones, to be described later on, come into play and, the seat of the pain being encircled with them, they are set alight. When even this remedy proves inefficacious, and the patient survives it, the illness is pronounced incurable!

Natural abnormalities and deformities are frequent

enough in Tibet, and some came under my notice in nearly every camp I entered. Deformities of the spine were common, such as displacement of the shoulder-blades; and I saw during my stay in Tibet many cases of actually humpbacked people. There were frequent cases, too, of crookedness of the legs, and clubfoot was not rare, while one constantly met with webbed fingers and supernumerary fingers and toes, as well as the absence of one or more of them. Malformations of the skull, such as the two sides being of marked unequal shape or an abnormal distance between the eye sockets, were the two most common deformities that came under my notice.

The ears of men of the better classes were much elongated artificially by the constant wearing of heavy earrings, which sometimes even tore the lobe of the ear.

The most frequent and curious of all was the extreme swelling of children's stomachs, caused by the umbilical cord not being properly tied at birth. The operation was generally performed by the mother and father of the newly-born or by some friend at hand. The infants had such enormous paunches that in some cases they were hardly able to stand; but, as they grew older, the swelling seemed to gradually abate and the body assumed its normal shape.

Deafness was common, but I never came across any dumb people, though I now and then encountered cases of painful stammering and other defects of articulation arising from malformation of the palate and tongue.

Occasionally, however, the difficulty of speech was caused by dementia, which seemed very common in Tibet, especially among the young men. Whether it was caused by cardiac affection subsequent to organic vices, as I suspected, or by other trouble, I could not say for certain, but presently I based my suspicions on certain facts which I happened to notice, besides the presence of symptoms indicating great nervous depression and strain, extreme weakness of the spine and oscillations of the hands when spread horizontally with the fingers and thumbs wide apart. This may in one way be accounted for by the difficulty that men have in obtaining wives, owing to the scarcity of women. Apoplectic and epileptic fits and convulsions were not of very frequent occurrence, but they seemed severe when they did occur. The fire cure was usually applied in order to drive away the spirits that were supposed to have entered the body, but, all the same, these fits at times resulted in temporary or occasionally permanent paralysis, and much derangement and disfiguration of the facial expression, particularly about the eyes and mouth. I had occasion to study three very good specimens of this kind at Tucker, at Tarbar, north of the Brahmaputra River, and at Tokchim.

Much to my regret I never came across any violent cases of insanity during my stay in the country, though many times I observed strange peculiarities among the men, and signs of mania, more particularly religious.

In women I several times noticed symptoms of melancholia, caused no doubt by abuse of sexual intercourse, owing to their strange laws of polyandry. I was told that occasionally it led to suicide by drowning or strangulation. However, I was never able to keep any of the suspicious cases under close observation for any length of time, and, as our arrival into Tibetan camps generally created some amount of fear and sensation, and we usually left before they could be quite at home with us, I never had a chance of studying the subject more closely.

CHAPTER XLIX

A Tibetan medicine-man—Lumbago, and a startling cure for it—Combustible fuses—Fire and butter—Prayers, agony, and distortions—Strange ideas on medicine.

STRANGE as the Tibetan remedies seemed to be, none came up, as far as interest went, to one I saw applied at a place called Kutzia. I had entered a camp of some twenty or thirty tents, when my attention was drawn to an excited crowd collected round an old man whose garments had been removed. He was tightly bound with ropes, and agony was depicted on his features. A tall, long-haired man with red coat and heavy boots knelt by the side of the sufferer and prayed fervently, twirling round a prayer-wheel which he held in his right hand.

My curiosity aroused, I approached the gathering, whereupon three or four Tibetans got up and signed to me to be off. I pretended not to understand, and, after a heated discussion, I was allowed to remain.

An operation was obviously being performed by a Tibetan medicine-man, and the suspense in the crowd round the sick man was considerable. The doctor was busy preparing combustible fuses, which he wrapped up carefully in silk paper. When cut in the centre they formed two cones, each with a little tail of twisted paper protruding beyond its summit. Having completed six or eight of these, the medicine - man made his patient, or rather his victim, assume a sitting posture. I inquired what ailed the sick man. From what they told me, and from an examination made on my own account, I was satisfied that the man was suffering from an attack of lumbago. The coming cure, however, interested me more than the illness itself, and the doctor, seeing how absorbed I was in the performance, asked me to sit by his side. First of all the man called for "fire," and a woman handed him a blazing brand from a fire near by. He swung it to and fro in the air, and pronounced certain exorcisms. Next the patient was subjected to a thorough examination, giving vent to a piercing yell each time that the long bony fingers of the physician touched his sides, whereupon the man of science, pointing to the spot, informed his open-mouthed audience that the pain was "there." Putting on a huge pair of spectacles, he rubbed with

A MEDICINE-MAN

the palm of his hand the umbilical region of the sufferer and then measured with folded thumb two inches on each side of, and slightly under, the umbilicus. To mark these distances he used the burning brand, applying it to the flesh at these points.

"*Murr, murr!*" ("Butter, butter!") he next called for, and butter was produced. Having rubbed a little on the burns, he placed upon each of them a separate cone, and pressed until it remained a fixture, the point upwards. Shifting the beads of a rosary, revolving the praying-wheel, and muttering prayers, the medicine-man now worked himself into a perfect frenzy. He stared at the sun, raising his voice from a faint whisper to a thundering baritone at its loudest, and his whole audience seemed so affected by the performance that they all shook and trembled and prayed in their terror. He now again nervously clutched the burning wood in one hand, and, blowing upon it with the full strength of his lungs, produced a flame. The excitement in the crowd became intense. Every one, head down to the ground, prayed fervently. The doctor waved the ignited wood three or four times in the air and then applied the flames to the paper tips of the combustible cones. Apparently saltpetre and sulphur had been mixed in the preparation of these. They burned fast, making a noise like the fuse of a rocket.

At this juncture the animation of the onlookers was not to be compared with the agitation of the patient, who began to feel the effects of this primitive remedy. The fire spluttered on his bare skin. The cure was doing its work. The wretched man's mouth foamed, and his eyes bulged out of their sockets. He moaned and groaned, making desperate efforts to unloose the bonds that kept his hands fast behind his back. Two stalwart men sprang forward and held him, while the medicine-man and all the women present, leaning over the prostrate form, blew with all their might upon what remained of the three smoking cones frizzling away into the flesh of the wretched victim.

The pain of which the man complained seemed to encircle his waist, wherefore the strange physician, having untied his patient's arms from behind, and retied them in front, began his measurements again, this time from the spinal column.

"*Chik, ni, sum!*" ("One, two, three!") he exclaimed, as he marked the three spots in the same fashion as before, smeared them over with butter, and affixed the cones. Here ensued a repetition of the previous excitement; prayers, agony, and distortions, but the patient was not thoroughly cured, and more cones were subsequently ignited on both his sides, in spite of his protests and my appeals on his behalf. The poor fellow soon had a regular circle of severe burns round his body.

Needless to say, when, two hours later, the operation was over, the sick man had become a dying man. With a view to obtaining a few hints on Tibetan medicine from this eminent physician—the Tibetans held him in great esteem—I sent him a small present and requested him to visit me. He was flattered and showed no desire to keep his methods a secret, but even pressed me to try some of his unique remedies.

According to him, fire would cure most illnesses; what fire could not cure, water would. He had, nevertheless, some small packets of variously coloured powders, for which he claimed extraordinary powers.

"I am afraid your patient will die," I remarked.

"He may," was the reply, "but it will be the fault of the patient, not the cure. Besides, what does it matter whether you die to-day or to-morrow?"

And with this unprofessional dictum he left me.

CHAPTER L

Tucker village—Chokdens—Houses—Flying prayers—Soldiers or robbers?—A stampede—Fresh provisions—Disappointment—Treachery—Shokas leave me—Observations—Five men, all counted!

WHEN I left the Gomba, having been salaamed to the ground by my new friends the Lamas, I walked about the village to examine all there was to be seen.

Along the water's edge stood a number of dilapidated Chokdens made of mud and stones, with a square base surmounted by a moulding, and an upper decoration in steps, topped by a cylindrical column. They were in a row at the east end of the village, and, as is well known, they are supposed to contain a piece of bone, cloth or metal, and books or parts of them, that had once belonged to a great man or a saint. Roughly drawn images are occasionally found in them. In rare cases, when cremation has been applied, the ashes are collected into a small earthenware urn, and deposited in one of the Chokdens. The ashes are usually made into a paste with clay, on which, when flattened like a medallion, a representation of Buddha is either stamped from a mould, or engraved by means of a pointed tool.

The interior of the houses at Tucker was no more

pleasing than the exterior. Each habitation had a walled courtyard, and the top of the wall, as well as the edge of the flat roof, was lined with masses of tamarisk for fuel. In the courtyard, sheep and goats were penned at night ; and the human beings who occupied the rooms were dirty beyond all description. There were hundreds of flying prayers over the monastery as well as over each house, and as the people stood on their roofs watching us, laughing and chatting, the place had quite a gay aspect.

While I was strolling about some fifty or sixty men appeared on the scene, armed with matchlocks and swords, and I looked upon them with suspicion, but Kachi reassured me, and said they were not soldiers, but a powerful band of robbers encamped about half a mile off, and on very friendly terms with the Lamas. As a precaution, I loaded my rifle, which was quite sufficient to occasion a stampede of the armed crowd, followed, in the panic, by all the other villagers that had collected round us. Like all Tibetans, they were a miserable lot, though powerfully built, and with plenty of bounce about them.

Early in the morning I had made inquiries about provisions, and had arranged for the purchase of two fat sheep and some 450 lbs. of food (flour, rice, *tsamba, ghur,* sugar, salt and butter), and several Tibetans stated that they could supply me with any quantity I required. Among others was a trader from Buddhi, Darcey Bura's brother, who promised to bring me within an hour a sufficient quantity of food to last us ten men twenty-five days. I noticed, when these men left, that two of my Shokas ran after them, and entered into an excited discussion with them. Some two or three hours later, the traders returned, swearing that not an ounce of food could be obtained in the place. The way in which these men could lie was indeed marvellous to study. I suspected treachery, and reprimanded my Shokas, threatening to punish them very severely if my suspicions proved to be well founded.

The Shokas, knowing themselves discovered, and partly

THE PANKU GOMBA

through fear of the Tibetans, were now again quite unreasonable and demoralised. It was no use keeping them by force and I decided to discharge them. From the moment I had entered the forbidden country I had been compelled to protect myself against them as much as against the Tibetans. I reflected, however, when I made up my mind to let them go, that these fellows had stood for my sake hardships and privations which few men could stand; and in paying them off I therefore rewarded them suitably, and they undertook to bring back safely across the frontier part of my baggage containing photographs, ethnological collections, &c. With infinite trouble I then managed to purchase enough provisions to last five men ten days.

The whole party accompanied me three-and-a-quarter miles farther, where, in sight of the tumble-down Panku Gomba, a mile to the West of us, we halted in order to make the necessary arrangements for our parting, unseen by the Tibetans. I took observations for latitude and longitude. The water of the hypsometrical apparatus boiled at 185° Fahr. fifty feet above the level of the lake, the temperature of the air being 76° and the hour 10 A.M.

We had a high snowy chain to the South of us, extending from 70° to 33° (b.m.), the direction of the range being approximately from South-West to North-East, starting at Nimo Namgil.

When everything was ready, the five Shokas, including Kachi and Dola, left me, swearing by the sun and all that they hold most sacred, that they would in no way betray me to the Tibetans, who so far had no suspicion as to who I was.

Bijesing the Johari and the Kutial Bura Nattoo agreed to accompany me as far as the Maium Pass, so that my party, including myself, now was reduced to only five.

END OF VOL. I.

Printed by BALLANTYNE, HANSON & Co.
London & Edinburgh

IN THE FORBIDDEN LAND

Lithographed by F. A. Brockhaus, Leipzig (Germany).

THE TOKCHIM TARJUM.

IN THE
FORBIDDEN LAND

AN ACCOUNT OF A JOURNEY IN TIBET
CAPTURE BY THE TIBETAN AUTHORITIES
IMPRISONMENT, TORTURE, AND
ULTIMATE RELEASE

BY

A. HENRY SAVAGE LANDOR

AUTHOR OF
"COREA, OR THE LAND OF THE MORNING CALM,"
"ALONE WITH THE HAIRY AINU," ETC.

ALSO VARIOUS OFFICIAL DOCUMENTS INCLUDING THE ENQUIRY
AND REPORT BY J. LARKIN, ESQ. APPOINTED
BY THE GOVERNMENT OF INDIA

WITH A MAP AND TWO HUNDRED AND FIFTY ILLUSTRATIONS

IN TWO VOLUMES
VOL. II

LONDON
WILLIAM HEINEMANN
1898

CONTENTS

CHAPTER LXV

CHAPTER LXVI

CHAPTER LXVII

CHAPTER LXVIII

CHAPTER LXIX

CHAPTER LXX

CHAPTER LXXI

CHAPTER LXXII

CHAPTER LXXXI

CHAPTER LXXXII

CHAPTER LXXXIII

CHAPTER LXXXIV

CHAPTER LXXXV

CHAPTER LXXXVI

CHAPTER LXXXVII

CHAPTER LXXXVIII

CHAPTER XCVII

CHAPTER XCVIII

APTER XCIX

CHAPTER C

LIST OF ILLUSTRATIONS

COLOURED PLATES

FULL-PAGE PLATES

TEXT ILLUSTRATIONS.

MAP

CHAPTER LI

The start with a further reduced party—A reconnaissance—Natural fortress—Black tents and animals—On the wrong tack—Slings and their use—A visit to a Tibetan camp—Mistaken for brigands—Bargaining and begging.

ALL was promising well when, with my reduced party, I started towards the N.E., first following for three-and-a-quarter miles a course of 49°,* skirting the lake, then ascending over the barren hill ranges in a direction of 90° for a distance of twelve miles. The journey was uneventful, and my four men seemed in the best of spirits. We descended to a plain where water and grass could be found, and having seen a camping-ground with a protecting wall, such as are usually put up by Tibetans at their halting-places, we made ourselves comfortable for the night, notwithstanding the high wind and a passing storm of hail and rain, which drenched us to the skin. The thermometer during the night went down to 34°.

At sunrise I started to make a reconnaissance from the top of a high hill wherefrom I could get a bird's-eye view of a great portion of the surrounding country. It was of the utmost importance for me to find out which would be the easiest way to get through the intricate succession of

* All bearings given are magnetic.

hills and mountains, and to discover the exact direction of a large river to the N. of us, throwing itself into the Mansarowar, the name of which no one could tell me. I started alone towards 352° 30′ (b.m.), and three-and-a-half miles' climb brought me to 16,480 feet on the summit of a hill, where I was able to ascertain and note down all that I wished to know. I returned to camp, and we went on towards 73° 30′, crossing over a pass 16,450 feet, and ultimately finding ourselves at the foot of a hill, the summit of which resembled a fortress, with flying-prayers flapping to and fro in the wind. At the foot of the hill were some twenty ponies grazing.

SLING

With the aid of my telescope I was able to make sure that what at first appeared to be a castle was nothing but a work of nature, and that apparently no one was concealed up there. The ponies, however, indicated the presence of men, and we had to move cautiously. In fact, rounding the next hill, we discerned in the grassy valley below a number of black tents, two hundred yaks, and about a thousand sheep. We kept well out of sight behind the hill, and making a long détour, we at last descended in an extensive valley, in which the river described a semicircle, washing the southern hill ranges, where it was joined by a tributary coming from the S.E. This tributary at first appeared to me larger than what I afterwards recognised to be the main stream, so that I followed its course for four miles (92° 30′ b.m.), till I found that it was taking me in a more southerly direction than I wished, and had to retrace my steps along a flattish plateau. Meeting two Tibetan women, I purchased, after endless trouble, a fat

A NATURAL CASTLE

sheep out of a flock they were driving before them. These two females carried rope slings in their hands, and the accuracy with which they could fling stones and hit the mark at very great distances was really marvellous. For the sake of a few annas they gave an exhibition of their skill, hitting any sheep you pointed at in their flock, even at distances of thirty and forty yards. I tried to obtain from these dangerous females a little information about the country, but they professed absolute ignorance.

"We are menials," they said, "and we know nothing. We know each sheep in our flock, and that is all, but our lord, of whom we are the slaves, knows all. He knows where the rivers come from, and the ways to all Gombas. He is a great king."

"And where does he live?" I inquired.

"There, two miles off, where that smoke rises to the sky."

The temptation was great to go and call on this "great king," who knew so many things, all the more so as we might probably persuade him to sell us provisions, which, as we had none too many, would be of great assistance to us. Anyhow the visit would be interesting, and I decided to risk it.

We steered towards the several columns of smoke that rose before us, and eventually we approached a large camp of black tents. Our appearance caused a good deal of commotion, and men and women rushed in and out of their tents in great excitement.

"*Jogpas, jogpas!*" ("Brigands! brigands!") somebody in their camp shouted, and in a moment their matchlocks were made ready, and the few men who had remained outside the tents drew their swords, holding them clumsily in their hands in a way hardly likely to terrify any one.

To be taken for brigands was a novel experience for us, and the warlike array was in strange contrast to the terrified expressions on the faces of those who stood there armed. In fact, when Chanden Sing and I walked forward and encouraged them to sheathe their steels and put their match-locks by, they readily followed our advice, and brought out rugs for us to sit upon. Having overcome their fright, they were now most anxious to be pleasant.

"*Kiula gunge gozai deva labodù!*" ("You have nice clothes!") I began the conversation, attempting flattery, to put the chieftain at his ease.

"*Lasso, leh!*" ("Yes, sir") answered the Tibetan, apparently astonished, and looking at his own attire with an air of comical pride.

His answer was sufficient to show me that the man considered me his superior, the affirmative in Tibetan to an equal or inferior being the mere word *lasso* without the *leh*.

WOMAN CARRYING CHILD IN BASKET

"*Kiula tuku taka zando?*" ("How many children have you?") I rejoined.

"*Ni.*" ("Two.")

"*Chuwen bogpe, tsamba, chon woni?*" ("Will you sell me flour or *tsamba?*")

"*Middù*—have not got any," he replied, making several quick semicircular movements with the upturned palm of his right hand.

This is a most characteristic action of the Tibetan, and nearly invariably accompanies the word "No," instead of a movement of the head, as with us.

"*Keran ga naddoung?*" ("Where are you going?") he asked me eagerly.

"*Nhgarang ne Koroun!*" ("I am a pilgrim!") "*Lungba quorghen neh jelghen.*" ("I go looking at sacred places.")

"*Gopria zaldo. Chakzal wortzié. Tsamba middù. Bogpe middù, guram middù, dié middù, kassur middù.*" ("I am very poor. Please hear me. I have no *tsamba*, no flour, no sweet paste, no rice, no dried fruit.")

This, of course, I knew to be untrue, so I calmly said that I would remain seated where I was until food was sold to me, and at the same time produced one or two silver coins, the display of which to the covetous eyes of the Tibetans was always the means of hastening the transaction of business. In small handfuls, after each of which the Tibetans swore that they had not another atom to sell, I managed, with somewhat of a trial to my patience, to purchase some twenty pounds of food. The moment the money was handed over they had a quarrel among themselves about it, and almost came to blows, greed and avarice being the most marked characteristic of the Tibetans. No Tibetan of any rank is ashamed to beg in the most abject manner for the smallest silver coin, and when he sells and is paid, he always implores for another coin, to be thrown into the bargain.

CHAPTER LII

What the men were like—Their timidity—Leather work—Metal work—Blades and swords—Filigree—Saddles and harness—Pack saddles.

THE men of the party were extremely picturesque, with hair flowing down their shoulders and long pigtails ornamented with pieces of red cloth, circles of ivory and silver coins. Nearly all had the stereotyped pattern coat, with ample sleeves hanging well over the hands, and pulled up at the waist to receive the paraphernalia of eating-bowls, snuff-box, &c., employed in daily life. Most of them were dressed in dark red, and all were armed with jewelled swords.

With flat, broad noses and slits of piercing eyes, high cheek-bones and skin giving out abundant oily excretions, most of the men stood at a respectful distance, scrutinising our faces and watching our movements apparently with much interest. I have hardly ever seen such cowardice and timidity as among these big, hulking fellows; to a European it scarcely seems conceivable. The mere raising of one's eyes was sufficient to make a man dash away frightened, and, with the exception of the chief, who pretended to be unafraid, notwithstanding that even he was trembling with fear, they one and all showed ridiculous nervousness when I approached them to examine their clothes or the ornaments they wore round their necks, the most prominent of which were the charm-boxes that dangled on their chests. The larger of these charm-boxes contained an image of Budda, the others were mere brass or silver cases with nothing in them.

TIBETAN YOUNG MAN

I was struck here, as well as in other camps, by the skill of the Tibetans in working leather, which they tan and prepare themselves, often giving to it a fine red or green colour. As a rule, however, the natural tint is preserved, especially when the leather is used for belts, bullet and powder-pouches, and flint-and-steel cases. The hair of the skins is removed by plucking and scraping, and preference is shown for skins of the yak, antelope, and kiang. The Tibetans are masters of the art of skinning, the hides being afterwards beaten, trodden upon and manipulated to be rendered soft. There were simple ornamentations stamped upon some of the leather articles, but in most instances either metal or leather ornaments of various colours were fastened on the belts

SWORDS

and pouches, iron clasps inlaid with silver or silver ones being the commonest.

These metals are found in the country, and the Tibetans smelt and cast the ore when sufficient fuel is obtainable for the purpose. Earthen crucibles are employed to liquefy the metals, and the castings are made in clay moulds. For the inlaid work, in which the Tibetans greatly excel, they use hammer and chisel. Inlaid ornamentation is frequently to be seen on the sheaths of Tibetan swords, the leaf pattern, varied scrolls and geometrical combinations being most commonly preferred. The process of hardening metals is still in its infancy, and Tibetan blades are of wrought-iron, and not of steel. They succeed, however, in bringing them to a wonderful degree of sharpness, although they entirely lack the elasticity of steel blades. Grooves to let in air, and thus make wounds incurable, are generally ground in the sides of the daggers, but the blades of the common swords are perfectly smooth and made to cut on one side only. As can be seen from the illustrations, these weapons are hardly adapted to meet the requirements of severe fighting, as they do not allow a firm grip, nor have they any guard for the hand. The sheaths and handles of some of the more valuable swords are made of solid silver inlaid with turquoises and coral beads, others of silver with gold ornamentations. At Lhassa and at Sigatz (Shigatze), silver filigree decorations are used on the best daggers; but nowhere else in Tibet is fine wire-making practised.

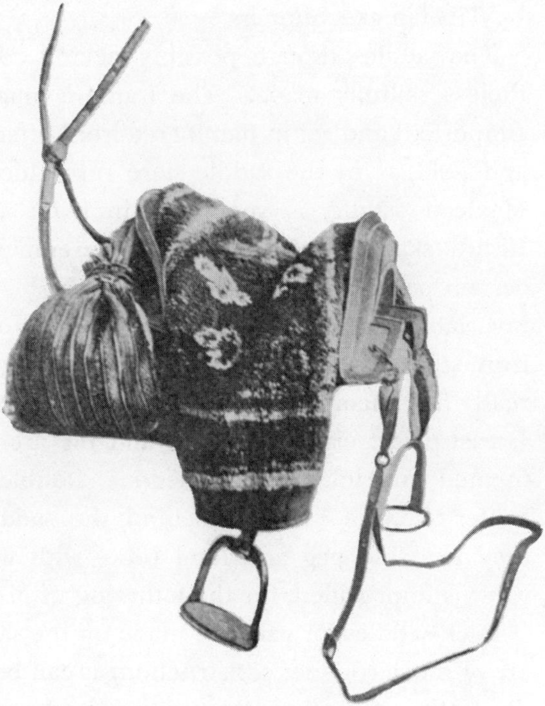

SADDLE

It must not be inferred from the above remarks that there are no steel swords in Tibet, for indeed many fine blades of excellent Chinese steel can be seen all over the country in the possession of the richer officials, such as the huge two-handed, double-edged swords of Chinese importation, used by Tibetan executioners.

The saddles, though possibly lacking comfort, are nevertheless skilfully made. The frame is made of solid wood (imported) and set in hammered iron (often inlaid with silver and gold, as in the saddle here reproduced), which, like a Mexican saddle, is very high in front and at the back. Lizard skin or coloured leather is employed to decorate certain parts, and a pad covers the seat. A rug is, however, invariably placed over this pad for comfort, and the short iron stirrups compel one to sit with legs doubled up, a really not uncomfortable position when one gets used to it. Breast-piece, crupper, bridle and bit are of leather ornamented with inlaid metal pieces. Double bags for *tsamba*, butter, &c. are fastened behind the saddle, together with the inevitable peg and long rope, with which no Tibetan rider is unprovided, for the tethering of his pony at night.

Pack-saddles for yaks are made on the same principle, but are of much rougher construction, as can be judged from the illustrations,* in which the two saddles I used on my journey are represented. The baggage is made fast by means of ropes to the two upper bars. To keep the saddle in position on the yak, and to prevent sores being inflicted, pads and blankets are laid upon the animal's back. Add to this protection the long coat possessed by the beast itself, and it will be clear why it very seldom sustains the slightest injury from these apparently cruel burdens.

* See vol. i. chapter xl.

CHAPTER LIII

Rain in torrents—A miserable night—A gorge—A gigantic inscription—Sheltered under boulders—A fresh surprise—Only two followers left.

WHEN night came on, I did not consider it safe to encamp near the Tibetans. We moved away, driving our yaks before us and dragging the newly purchased sheep. We marched two-and-a-half miles, and then halted in a depression in the ground (16,050 feet), where we had a little shelter from the wind, which blew with great force. To our right lay a short range of fairly high mountains running from North to South, and cut by a gorge, out of which flowed a large stream. At that time of the evening we could not hope to cross it, but an attempt might be made in the morning, when the cold of the night would have checked the melting of the snows. Heavy showers had fallen frequently during the day, and the moment the sun went down there was a regular downpour. Our little *tente-d'abri* had been pitched, but we had to clear out of it a couple of hours later, the small basin in which we had pitched it having been turned into a regular pond. There was no alternative for us but to come out into the open, for where the water did not flood us the wind was so high and the ground so moist that it was not possible to keep our tent up.

The pegs would not hold. The hours of the night seemed very long as we sat tightly wrapped up in our waterproofs, with feet, hands and ears frozen, and the water dripping down upon us. At dawn there were no signs of the storm abating. We had not been able to light a fire in the evening, nor could we light one now, and we were cold, hungry and miserable. The thermometer had been down to 36°. Towards noon, the rain still pouring down in torrents and there being no sign of its clearing, we loaded our yaks and entered the gorge between the snow-covered mountains. With difficulty we crossed the tributary we had so far followed, and then proceeded along the right bank of the main stream to 23° 30″, then to 25°.

We were so exhausted and wet that, when towards evening we came to an enormous cliff, on the rocky face of which a patient Lama sculptor had engraved in gigantic letters the everlasting characters, *Omne mani padme hun*, we halted. The gorge was very narrow here, and we managed to find a dry spot under a big boulder, but as there was not sufficient room for all five, the two Shokas went under the shelter of another rock a little way off. This seemed natural enough, nor could I anticipate any danger, taking care myself of the weapons and the scientific instruments, while the Shokas had under their own sheltering boulder the bags containing nearly all our provisions except tinned meats. The rain pelted all night, the wind howled, and again we could not light a fire. The thermometer did not fall below 38°, but the cold, owing to our drenched condition, seemed intense. In fact, we were so frozen that we did not venture to eat, but, crouching ourselves in the small dry space at our disposal, we eventually fell fast asleep without tasting food. I slept soundly for the

CAMP WITH GIGANTIC INSCRIPTION

first time since I had been in Tibet, and it was broad daylight when I woke up, to find the man Nattoo from Kuti, and Bijesing the Johari, departed from under their sheltering rock, together with the loads entrusted to them. I discovered their tracks, half washed away, in the direction from which we had come the previous night. The rascals had bolted, and there would have been comparatively little harm in that, if only they had not taken with them all the stock of provisions for my two Hindoo servants, and a quantity of good rope, straps, and other miscellaneous articles, which we were bound to miss at every turn and which we had absolutely no means of replacing.

Of thirty picked servants who had started with me, twenty-eight had now abandoned me, and only two remained: faithful Chanden Sing and Mansing the leper!

The weather continued horrible, with no food for my men and no fuel! I proposed to the two to go back also and let me continue alone. I described to them the dangers of following me farther, and warned them fully, but they absolutely refused to leave me.

"Sahib, we are not Shokas," were their words. "If you die, we will die with you. We fear not death. We are sorry to see you suffer, sahib, but never mind us. We are only poor people, therefore it is of no consequence."

CHAPTER LIV

My time fully occupied—Our own yak drivers—A heavy blow —Along the stream—Soldiers in pursuit of us—Discovered.

THIS last disaster should, I suppose, have deterred us from further progress, but it somehow made me even more determined to persist than I was before. It was no light job to have to run afield oneself to capture the yaks, which had wandered off in search of grass; and having found them and driven them back to our primitive camping-place, to tie upon their backs the pack-saddles, and fasten on them the heavy tin-lined cases of scientific instruments and photographic plates. This task was only part of the day's routine, which included the writing up of my diary, the registering of observations, sketching, photographing, changing plates in cameras, occasionally developing them, surveying, cleaning of rifles, revolver, &c. &c. The effort of lifting up the heavy cases on to the pack-saddles was, owing to our exhausted condition, a severe tax on our strength, and the tantalising restlessness of the yaks forced us to make several attempts before we actually succeeded in properly fastening the loads, particularly as we had lost our best pieces of rope and leather straps. Our sole remaining piece of rope seemed hardly long enough to make the final knot to one of the girths; anyhow neither my bearer nor

Mansing had sufficient strength to pull and make it join ; so I made them hold the yak by the horns to keep him steady while I pulled my hardest. I succeeded with a great effort, and was about to get up, when a terrific blow from the yak's horn struck me in the skull an inch behind my right ear

YAK WITH CASES OF SCIENTIFIC INSTRUMENTS

and sent me rolling head over heels. I was stunned for several moments, and the back of my head was swollen and sore for many days, the mark of the blow being visible even now.

We proceeded along the right bank of the river on a course of 85° between reddish hills and distant high snowy mountains to the N.W. and E.S.E. of us, which we saw from time to time when the rain ceased and the sky cleared. The momentary lifting of the clouds would be followed by another downpour, and the marching became very unpleasant and difficult, as we sank deep in the mud. Towards evening, we suddenly discovered some hundred and fifty soldiers riding full gallop in pursuit of us along the river

WITH ONLY TWO MEN I PROCEEDED TOWARDS LHASSA

valley. We pushed on, and having got out of their sight behind a hill, we deviated from our course and rapidly climbed up to the top of the hill range; my two men and the yaks concealed themselves on the other side. I remained lying flat on the top of the hill, spying with my telescope the movements of our pursuers. They rode unsuspectingly on, the tinkling of their horse-bells sounding pleasant to the ear at that deserted spot. They made a pretty picture, and, thinking probably that we had continued our way along the river, they rode past the spot where we had left the path, and, possibly owing to their haste to catch us up, did not notice our tracks up the hillside.

Rain began to fall heavily again, and we remained encamped at 17,000 feet with all our loads ready for flight at any moment; the night being spent none too comfortably. I sat up all night, rifle in hand, in case of a surprise, and I was indeed glad when day dawned. The rain had stopped, but we were now enveloped in a white mist which chilled us. I was very tired, and telling Chanden Sing to keep a sharp watch, tried to sleep for a while.

"*Hazur, hazur! jaldi apka banduk!*" ("Sir, sir, quick, your rifle!") muttered my bearer, rousing me. "Do you hear the sound of bells?"

The tinkling was quite plain. As our pursuers were approaching, evidently in a strong body, there was no time to be lost. To successfully evade them appeared impossible, so I decided to meet them, rather than attempt flight. Chanden Sing and I were armed with our rifles, and Mansing with his Gourkha *kukri*, and thus we awaited their arrival. There came out of the mist a long procession of grey, phantom-like figures, each one leading a pony. The advance guard stopped from time to time to examine the ground; having discovered our footprints only partially washed away by the rain, they were following them up. Seeing us at last on the top of the hill, they halted. There was commotion among them, and they held an excited consultation; some of them unslung their matchlocks, others drew their swords, while we sat on a rock above and watched them with undivided attention.

CHAPTER LV

An interview—Peace or war ?—Gifts and the scarf of friendship—The *Kata*—The end of a friendly visit.

AFTER hesitating a little, four officers signalled to us that they wished to approach.

"You are a great king!" shouted one at the top of his voice, "and we want to lay these presents at your feet," and he pointed to some small bags which the other three men were carrying. "*Gelbo! Chakzal! Chakzal!*" ("We salute you, king!")

I felt anything but regal after the wretched night we had spent, but I wished to treat the natives with due deference and politeness whenever it was possible.

I said that four men might approach, but the bulk of the party was to withdraw to a spot about two hundred yards away. This they immediately did, a matter of some surprise to me after the warlike attitude they had assumed at first. They laid their matchlocks down in the humblest fashion, and duly replaced their swords in their sheaths. The four officers approached, and when quite close to us, threw the bags on the ground and opened them to show us their contents. There was *tsamba*, flour, *chura* (a kind of cheese), *guram* (sweet paste), butter, and dried fruit. The officers were most profuse in their humble salutations. They had removed their caps and thrown them on the ground, and they kept their tongues sticking out of their mouths until I begged them to draw them in. They professed to be the subordinates of the Tokchim Tarjum, who had despatched them to inquire after my health, and who wished me to look upon him as my best friend. Well aware of the difficulties we must encounter in travelling through such an inhospitable country, the Tarjum, they said, wished me to accept the gifts they now laid before me, and with these they handed me a *Kata*, or "the scarf of love and friendship," a long piece of thin silklike gauze, the ends of which had been cut into a fringe. In Tibet these *Katas* accompany every gift, and no caller ever goes about without one, which instantly on arrival he produces for presentation to his host. The high Lamas sell them to devotees, and one or more of these scarves is presented to those who leave a satisfactory oblation after visiting a lamasery and temple. If a verbal message is sent to a friend, a *Kata* is sent with it, and among officials and Lamas small pieces of this silk gauze are enclosed even in letters. Not to give or send a *Kata* to an honoured visitor is considered a breach of good manners and is equivalent to a slight.

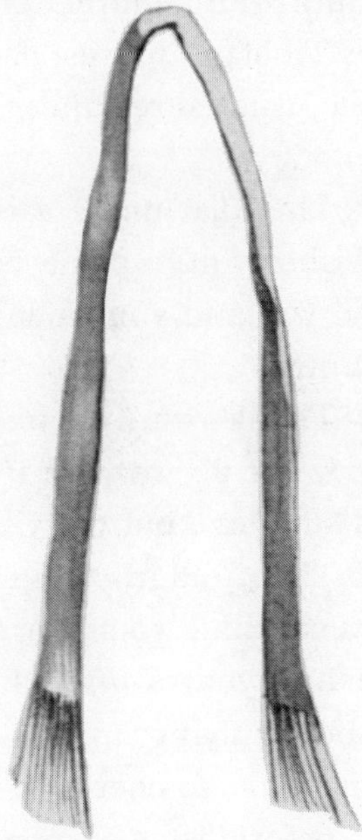

A KATA

I hastened to express my thanks for the Tarjum's kindness, and I handed the messengers a sum in silver of three times the value of the articles presented. The men seemed very pleasant and friendly, and we chatted for some time. Much to my annoyance, poor Mansing, bewildered at the sight of so much food, could no longer resist the pangs of hunger and, caring little for the breach of etiquette and likely consequences, proceeded to fill his mouth with handfuls of flour, cheese and butter. This led the Tibetans to suspect that we must be starving, and with their usual shrewdness they determined to take advantage of it.

"The Tarjum," said the oldest of the messengers, "wishes you to come back and be his guest, when he will feed you and your men, and you will then go back to your country."

"Thank you," I replied; "we do not want the Tarjum's food, nor do we wish to go back. I am greatly obliged for his kindness, but we will continue our journey."

"Then," angrily said a young and powerful Tibetan, "if you continue your journey we will take back our gifts."

"And your *Kata!*" I rejoined, sending first the large ball of butter flying into his chest, and after it the small bags of flour, *tsamba*, cheese, fruit, &c., a minute earlier prettily laid out before us.

This unexpected bombardment quite upset the Tibetans, who, with powdered coats, hair and faces, scampered away as best they could, while Chanden Sing, always as quick as lightning when it was a case of hitting, pounded away with the butt of his rifle at the roundest part of one ambassador's body, as in his clumsy clothes he attempted to get up and run.

Mansing, the philosopher of our party, interrupted in his feed but not put out, nor concerned in what was going on, picked up the fruit and cheese and pieces of butter scattered all over the place, mumbling that it was a shame to throw away good food in such a reckless fashion.

The soldiers, who had been watching attentively from a distance the different phases of the interview, considered it prudent to beat a hasty retreat, and, mounting their steeds with unmistakable dispatch, galloped pell-mell down the hill, and then along the valley of the river, until they were lost to sight in the mist, while the poor ambassadors, who had been unable to rejoin their ponies, followed as quickly as possible under the circumstances, considering the rarefied air and rough ground.

Their cries of distress, caused by fear alone, for we had done them no harm, served to strengthen the contempt in which my men by now held the Tibetan soldiers and their officers.

The scene really was comical, and I made as much capital as I could out of it, laughing with my companions and ridiculing to them the supposed valour of Tibetans.

When the Tibetans were out of sight, Chanden Sing and I pocketed our pride and helped Mansing to collect the dried dates, apricots, the pieces of *chura*, butter and *guram*. Then having loaded our yaks we marched on.

CHAPTER LVI

Rain in torrents—A swampy plain—The sun at last—Our yaks stolen and recovered.

WE were not in luck. The weather continued squally in the morning, and in the afternoon the rain was again torrential. We went towards 78° over uninteresting and monotonous grey country with a chain of snowy peaks stretching from South-West to North-East. We waded through a fairly deep and very cold river, and subsequently rose over a pass 17,450 feet. A number of Hunyas, with flocks of several thousand sheep, came in sight, but we avoided them. They did not see us.

At the point where we crossed it, the main stream turns in a graceful bend to 140° (b.m.). We climbed over hilly and barren country to an altitude of 17,550 feet, where several small lakelets were to be found, and, having marched in all fourteen and a-half miles in a drenching rain, we descended into a large valley. Here we had great difficulty in finding a spot where to rest for the night. The plain was simply a swamp, with several lakes and ponds, and we sank everywhere in mud and water. All our bedding and clothes were soaked to such an extent that it really made no difference where we halted; so we pitched our little tent on the banks of a stream coming out of a valley to the North,

TORRENTIAL RAIN

from which, extending in an easterly direction, rose a series of pyramidal mountains, covered with snow, and all of almost equal height and base. To the South were high peaks with great quantities of snow upon them. This valley was at an elevation of 17,450 feet, and the cold was intense.

At night the rain came down in bucketsful, and our *tente d'abri* gave us but little shelter. We were lying inside in water, and all the trenches in the world could not have kept it from streaming in. In fact, it is no exaggeration to say that the whole valley was a sheet of water from one to several inches deep. Of course, we suffered intensely from cold, the thermometer dropping to 26° at 8 P.M., when a South-East wind blew furiously ; and the rain fell mixed with sleet for a time, and was followed by a heavy snowstorm. We lay crouched up on the top of our baggage, so as not to sleep on the frozen water, and when we woke in the morning our tent had half collapsed owing to the weight of snow upon it. During the day the temperature went up and rain fell afresh, so that when we resumed our marching, we sank into a mixture of mud, snow and water several inches deep. We had to cross three rivers, and to skirt five lakes of various sizes, following a course of 83° 45′.

Seven miles of this dreary marching saw us encamped (17,380 feet) by the foot of a conical hill 17,500 feet, where an almost identical repetition of the previous night's experience took place. The thermometer was down to 32°, but fortunately the wind subsided at eight in the evening. As luck would have it, the sun came out the following day, and we were able to spread out all our things to dry, during which process we had yet another novel experience.

Our two yaks had disappeared. I climbed up to the

summit of the hill above camp, and with my telescope scoured the plain. The two animals were some distance off being led away by ten or twelve men on horseback, who drove in front of them a flock of about five hundred sheep. By their clothing I recognised the strangers to be robbers. Naturally I started post haste to recover my property, leaving Chanden Sing and Mansing in charge of our camp. I caught them up as they marched slowly, though, when they perceived me, they hastened on, trying to get away. I shouted three times to them to stop, but they paid no heed to my words, so that I unslung my rifle and would have shot at them had the threat alone not been sufficient to make them reflect. They halted, and when I got near enough I claimed my two yaks back. They refused to give them up. They said they were twelve men, and were not afraid of one. Dismounted from their ponies, they seemed ready to go for me

HEAD OF BRIGAND

As I saw them take out a flint and steel to light the fuses of their matchlocks, I thought I might as well have my innings first, and, before they could guess at my intention, I applied a violent blow with the muzzle of my rifle to the stomach of the man nearest to me. He collapsed, while I administered another blow to the right temple of another man who held his matchlock between his legs, and was on the point of

BRIGANDS WITH SHEEP

striking his flint and steel to set the tinder on fire. He, too, staggered and fell clumsily.

"*Chakzal, chakzal! Chakzal wortzié!*" ("We salute you, we salute you! Please listen!") exclaimed a third brigand, with an expression of dismay, and holding up his thumbs with his fist closed in sign of approval.

"*Chakzal,*" I replied, shoving a cartridge into the Mannlicher.

"*Middù, middù !*" ("No, no !") they entreated, promptly laying down their weapons.

I purchased from these men about thirty pounds of *tsamba* and eight of butter, and got one of them to carry this to my camp, while I, without further trouble, recovered my yaks and drove them back to where Chanden Sing and Mansing were busy lighting a fire to make some tea.

SADDLE BAGS

CHAPTER LVII

Travelling Tibetans—Over a high pass—A friendly meeting—A proffered banquet—Ascent to 20,000 feet—Looking for the Gunkyo Lake—Surprised by a phantom army.

TOWARDS noon, when our things had got almost dry in the warm sun, the sky became overclouded, and it again began to rain heavily. I was rather doubtful as to whether I should go over a pass some miles off to 93° (b.m.), or should follow the course of the river and skirt the foot of the mountains. We saw a large number of Tibetans travelling in the opposite direction to ours, and they all seemed much terrified when we approached them. We obtained from them a few more pounds of food, but they refused to sell us any sheep, of which they had thousands. I decided to attempt the first-mentioned route and, making our way first over a continuation of the flat plateau, then over undulating, ground, we came to two lakelets, at the foot of the pass in question. The ascent was comparatively gentle, over snow, and we followed the river descending from the top. About half-way up, on looking back, we saw eight soldiers galloping toward us. We waited for them; and as soon as they came up to us, they went through the usual servile salutations, depositing their arms on the ground to show that they had no intention of fighting. A long friendly palaver followed, the Tibetans professing their friendship for us and their willingness to help us to get on in any way in their power. This was rather too good to be true, and I suspected treachery, all the more so when they pressed and entreated us to go back to their tents, where they wished us to remain as their highly-honoured guests, and where we should have all the luxuries that human mind can conceive showered upon us. On further specification, these were found to consist of presents of *chura*, cheese, butter, yak milk, and *tsamba*, and they said they would sell us ponies if we required them. The description was too glowing; so, taking all things into consideration, and allowing for the inaccuracy of speech of my interlocutors as well as of Tibetans in general, I thanked them from the bottom of my heart and answered that I preferred to continue my way and bear my present sufferings.

They perceived that I was not easy to catch, and, if anything, they respected me the more for it. In fact they could not disguise their amazement at my having got so far with only two men. When I had given my visitors some little present, we parted at last, in a very friendly manner.

We climbed up to the pass (18,480 feet), and before us on the other side found a large stretch of flat land, some two thousand feet lower. I could see a lake, which I took to be the Gunkyo. Nevertheless, to make certain of it, I left my men and yaks in the pass and went to reconnoitre from a peak 19,000 feet high, N.E. of us. There was much snow and the ascent was difficult and tedious. When I got to the top another higher peak barred the view in front of me, so descending first and then ascending again, I climbed this second summit, finally reaching an elevation of 20,000 feet, and obtaining a good bird's-eye view of the country all round. There was a long snowy range to the North, and, directly under it, what I imagined to be a stretch of water, judging from the mist and clouds forming above it, and from the grass on the lower portion of the mountains.

A hill range stood in my way, just high enough to conceal the lake behind it. I rejoined my men and we continued

PHANTOM-LIKE VISITORS

our march down the other side of the pass, sinking in deep, soft snow. We pitched our tent at a spot about five hundred feet higher than the plain below us, in a gorge formed by the two mountain sides coming close together. Notwithstanding that I was now quite accustomed to great altitudes, the ascent to 20,000 feet had caused a certain exhaustion, and I should have been glad of a good night's rest.

Mansing and Chanden Sing, having eaten some food,

slept soundly, but I felt very depressed. I had a peculiar sense of unrest and of some evil coming to us during the night.

We were all three under our little tent, when I began to fancy there was some one outside. I do not know why the thought entered my head, for I heard no noise, but all the same I felt I must see and satisfy my curiosity. I peeped out of the tent with my rifle in hand, and saw a number of black figures cautiously crawling towards us. In a moment I was outside on my bare feet, running towards them and shouting at the top of my voice, "*Pila tedan tedang!*" ("Look out, look out!") which caused a stampede among our ghostlike visitors. There were, apparently, numbers of them hidden behind rocks, for when the panic seized them, the number of runaways was double or even treble that of the phantoms I had at first seen approaching. At one moment there seemed to be black ghosts springing out from everywhere, only, more solid than ghosts, they made a dreadful noise with their heavy boots as they ran in confusion down the steep descent and through the gorge. They turned sharply round the hill at the bottom and disappeared.

When I crawled inside the tent again Chanden Sing and Mansing, wrapped head and all in their blankets, were still snoring!

CHAPTER LVIII

A sleepless night—Watching our enemy—A picturesque sight —A messenger—Soldiers from Lhassa—Taken for a Kashmeree —The Gunkyo Lake.

NATURALLY I passed a sleepless night after that, fearing that the unwelcome visitors might return. We speculated much as to how the Tibetans had found us, and we could not help surmising that our friends of the previous afternoon must have put them on our track. However, such was the inconceivable cowardice shown on every occasion by the Tibetans, that we got to attach no importance to these incidents, and not only did they not inspire us with fear, but they even ceased to excite or disturb us much.

We went on as usual, descending to the plain, and when we had got half-way across it, I scoured the hills all round with my telescope to see if I could discern traces of our pusillanimous foes.

"There they are," cried Chanden Sing, who had the most wonderful eyesight of any man I have known, as he pointed at the summit of a hill where, among the rocks, several heads could be seen peeping. We went on without taking further notice of them, and then they came out of their hiding-place, and we saw them descending the hill in a long line, leading their ponies. On reaching the plain they mounted their steeds and came full gallop towards us. They were quite a picturesque sight in their dark-red coats or brown and yellow skin robes and their vari-coloured caps. Some wore bright red coats with gold braiding, and Chinese caps. These were officers. The soldiers' matchlocks, to the rests of which red and white flags were attached, gave a touch of colour to the otherwise dreary scenery of barren hills and snow, and the tinkling of the horse-bells enlivened the monotony of these silent, inhospitable regions. They dismounted some three hundred yards from us, and one old man, throwing aside his matchlock and sword in a theatrical fashion, walked unsteadily towards us. We received him kindly, and he afforded us great amusement, for in his way he was a strange character.

"I am only a messenger," he hastened to state, "and therefore do not pour your anger upon me if I speak to you. I only convey the words of my officers, who do not dare to come for fear of being injured. News has been received at Lhassa, from whence we have come, that a *Plenki* (an Englishman) with many men is in Tibet, and can be found nowhere. We have been sent to capture him. Are you one of his advance guard?"

"No," I replied drily. "I suppose that you have taken several months to come from Lhassa."

"Oh no! Our ponies are good," he answered; "and we have come quickly."

"*Chik, ni, sum, shi, nga, do, diu, ghieh, gu, chu, chuck chick, chuck ni,*" the Tibetan counted up to twelve, frowning and keeping his head inclined towards the right as if to collect his thoughts, at the same time holding up his hand, with the thumb folded against the palm, and turning down a finger as he called each number. The thumbs are never used in counting. "*Lum chuck ni niman!*" "Twelve days," said he, "have we been on the road. We have orders not to return till we have captured the *Plenki*. And you?" asked he inquisitively, "how long have you taken to come from Ladak?"

He said that he could see by my face that I was a

"I AM ONLY A MESSENGER"

Kashmeree, I being probably so burnt and dirty that it was hard to distinguish me from a native. The old man cross-examined me to find out whether I was a *pundit* sent by the Indian Government to survey the country, and asked me why I had discarded my native clothes for *Plenki* (European) ones. He over and over again inquired whether I was not one of the *Plenki's* party.

"*Keran ga naddo ung?*" ("Where are you going?") he queried.

"*Nhgarang ne koroun Lama jehlhuong.*" ("I am a pilgrim," I replied, "going to visit monasteries.")

"*Keran mi japodù.*" ("You are a good man.")

He offered to show me the way to the Gunkyo Lake, and was so pressing that I accepted. However, when I saw the 200 soldiers mount and follow us, I remonstrated with him, saying that if we were to be friends we did not need an army to escort us.

"If you are our friend, you can come alone, and we will not injure you," I gave him to understand; "but if you are our enemy we will fight you and your army here at once, and we will save you the trouble of coming on."

The Tibetan, confused and hesitating, went to confabulate with his men, and returned some time after with eight of them, while the bulk of his force galloped away in the opposite direction.

We went across the plain to 355° (b.m.), until we came to a hill range, which we crossed over a pass 17,450 feet high. Then, altering our course to 56° 30′, we descended and ascended several hills, and at last found ourselves in the grassy sheltered valley of the large Gunkyo Lake, extending from South-East to North-West. With a temperature of 68° (Fahr.) the water in hypsometrical apparatus boiled at 183° 3½′ at 8.30 in the evening. The lake was of extraordinary beauty, with the high snowy Gangri mountains rising almost sheer from its waters, and on the southern side lofty hills forming a background wild and picturesque, but barren and desolate beyond all words. At the other end of the lake, to the North-West, were lower mountains skirting the water.

We encamped at 16,455 feet, and the soldiers pitched their tent some fifty yards away.

THE GUNKYS LAKE

CHAPTER LIX

In pleasant company—Unpopularity of the Lamas—Soldiers —Towards the Maium Pass—Grass—Threats—Puzzled Tibetans—The Maium Pass—Obos.

DURING the evening the Tibetans came over to my camp and made themselves useful. They helped us to get fuel, and brewed tea for me in Tibetan fashion. They seemed decent fellows, although sly if you like. They professed to hate the Lamas, the rulers of the country, to whom they took special pleasure in applying names hardly repeatable in these pages. According to them, the Lamas had all the money that came into the country, and no one but themselves was allowed to have any. They were not particular as to the means used to obtain their aim; they were cruel and unjust. Every man in Tibet, they said, was a soldier in case of emergency, and every one a servant of the Lamas. The soldiers of the standing army received a certain quantity of *tsamba*, bricks of tea and butter, and that was all, no pay being given in cash. Usually, however, they were given a pony to ride, and when on travelling duty they had a right to obtain relays of animals at post-stations and villages, where also they were entitled to claim supplies of food, saddles, or anything else they required, to last them as far as the next encampment. The weapons (sword and matchlock) generally belonged to the men themselves, and always remained in the family; but occasionally, and especially in the larger towns, such as Lhassa and Sigatz, the Lamas provided them: gunpowder and bullets were invariably supplied by the authorities. The arms were manufactured mostly in Lhassa and Sigatz. Although the Tibetans boasted of great accuracy in shooting with their matchlocks, which had wooden rests to allow the marksman to take a steady aim, it was never my pleasure to see even the champion shots in the country hit the mark. It is true that, for sporting purposes and for economy's sake, the Tibetan soldier hardly ever used lead bullets or shot, but preferred to fill his barrel with pebbles, which were scarcely calculated to improve the bore of the weapon. Furthermore, gunpowder was so scarce that it was but very seldom they had a chance of practising.

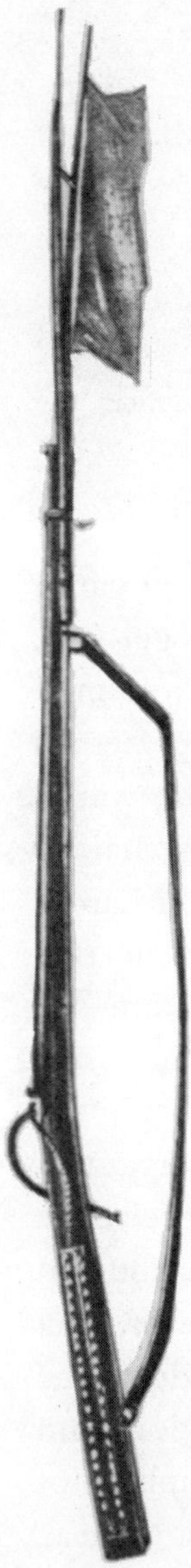

MATCHLOCK

MATCHLOCK

Lithographed by F. A. Brockhaus, Leipzig (Germany).

FLYING PRAYERS ON THE MAIUM PASS.

At sunrise the view of Gunkyo was magnificent, with the snow-covered mountains tinted gold and red, and reflected in their minutest details in the still waters of the lake. We loaded our yaks, the Tibetans giving us a helping hand, and started towards the Maium Pass, following a general course of 109° up the river, which throws itself into the Gunkyo Lake.

The valley was very narrow, and ran in continuous zigzags; but although the altitude was great, there was abundance of grass, and the green was quite refreshing to the eyes, tired as we were of snow and reddish barren mountains and desert-like stretches of land. We came to a basin where, on the opposite bank of the stream, was a large Tibetan camping-ground with a high wall of stones. Behind it I could see smoke rising, which made me suspect that there were people concealed there.

Our Tibetan friends asked what we were going to do, and begged me to stop there to talk and drink tea. I said I had had quite enough of both, and would proceed.

"If you go on we will kill you," said one of the soldiers, getting into a temper, and taking advantage of our politeness towards him and his mates.

"*Nga samgi ganta indah*" ("If you please"), I answered with studied courtesy.

"If you go another step, we will cut off your head, or you will have to cut off ours," cried two or three others, stretching their bare necks towards me.

"*Taptih middù*" ("I have not got a small knife"), I replied, quite seriously, and with assumed disappointment, twirling my hand in the air in Tibetan fashion.

The Tibetans did not know what to make of me, and when I moved towards the pass, on which hundreds of flying prayers flapped in the wind, after politely bidding them good-bye with tongue out, and waving both my hands palms upwards in front of my forehead in the most approved Tibetan style, they took off their caps and humbly saluted us by going down on their knees and putting their heads close to the ground.

We crossed the plain, and slowly wended our way up the pass. Near the top we came to a track, the highway from Ladak to Lhassa *viâ* Gartok, along the northern side of the Rakstal, Mansarowar and Gunkyo Lakes. On the pass itself were planted several poles connected by means of ropes, from which flying prayers waved gaily in the breeze. *Obos*, or mounds of stones, had also been erected here. The slabs were usually white, and bore in many instances the inscription "*Omne mani padme hun.*" Yak skulls and horns, as well as those of goats and sheep, were laid by the side of these Obos, the same words being engraved on the bone and stained red with the blood of the animal killed.

These sacrifices are offered by Tibetans when crossing a high pass, especially if there is a Lama close at hand to commemorate the event. The meat of the animal killed is eaten by the people present, and, if the party is a large one, dancing and singing follow the feast. As I have already remarked, these Obos are found all over the country ; they indicate the points marking the passes or summits of hills, and no Tibetan ever goes by one of them without depositing on it a white stone to appease the possible wrath of their God.

CHAPTER LX

The Maium Pass—Into the Yutzang province—Its capital—The Doktol province—Orders disregarded—The sources of the Brahmaputra—Change in the climate—The valley of the Brahmaputra—Running risks.

THE Maium Pass (17,500 feet), to which from where I started no Englishman had ever penetrated, is a great landmark in Tibet, for not only does one of the sources of the great Tsangpu, or Brahmaputra River, rise on its S.E. slopes, but it also separates the immense provinces of Nari-Khorsum (extending West of the Maium Pass and comprising the mountainous and lacustrine region as far as Ladak) from the Yutzang, the central province of Tibet, stretching East of the pass along the valley of the Brahmaputra and having Lhassa for its capital. The word *Yu* in Tibetan means "middle," and it is applied to this province, as it occupies the centre of Tibet. To the North of the Maïum lies the Doktol province.

I had taken a reconnoitring trip to another pass to the N.E. of us, and had just returned to my men on the Maium Pass, when several of the Tibetan soldiers we had left behind rode up towards us. We waited for them, and their leader, pointing at the valley beyond the pass, cried: "That yonder is the Lhassa territory and we forbid you to enter it."

I took no notice of his protest, and driving before me the two yaks I stepped into the most sacred of all the sacred provinces, "the ground of God."

We descended quickly on the Eastern side of the pass, while the soldiers, aghast, remained watching us from above, themselves a most picturesque sight as they stood among the Obos against the sky-line, with the sunlight

SOURCE OF THE BRAHMAPUTRA

shining on their jewelled swords and the gay red flags of their matchlocks, while over their heads strings of flying prayers waved in the wind. Having watched us for a little while, they disappeared.

A little rivulet, hardly six inches wide, descended among stones in the centre of the valley we were following, and was soon swollen by other rivulets from melting snows on the mountains to either side. This was one source* of the

* I passed the other source on the return journey.

great Brahmaputra, one of the largest rivers of the world. I must confess that I felt somewhat proud to be the first European who had ever reached these sources, and there was a certain childish delight in standing over this sacred stream which, of such immense width lower down, could here be spanned by a man standing with legs slightly apart. We drank of its waters at the spot where it had its birth, and then, following a marked track to 125° (b.m.), we continued our descent on a gentle incline along a grassy valley. The change in the climate between the West and South-east sides of the Maium Pass was extraordinary. On the Western side we had nothing but violent storms of hail, rain and snow, the dampness in the air rendering the atmosphere cold even during the day. The soil was unusually marshy, and very little fuel or grass could be found. The moment the pass was crossed we were in a mild, pleasant climate, with a lovely deep blue sky over us and plenty of grass for the yaks, as well as low shrubs for our fires; so that, after all our sufferings and privations, we felt that we had indeed entered the land of God. Notwithstanding that I expected great trouble sooner or later, I was not at all sorry I had disobeyed the soldiers' orders and had marched straight into the forbidden territory—it was a kind of wild satisfaction at doing that which is forbidden.

The Brahmaputra received three small snow-fed tributaries descending rapidly from the steep mountains on either side of us; and where the main stream turned sharply to 170°, a fourth and important tributary, carrying a very large volume of water, came down to it through a gorge from 20° (b.m.).

We encamped near the junction of these rivers, on the right bank of the main stream, at an altitude of 16,620 feet.

From the Maium Pass a continuation of the Gangri chain of mountains runs first in a South-easterly direction, then due East, taking a line almost parallel to the higher Southern range of the Himahlyas, and forming a vast plain intersected by the Brahmaputra. On the Southern side of the river can be seen minor hill ranges between the river course and the big range with its majestic snowy peaks and beautiful glaciers. This Northern range keeps an almost parallel line to the greater range southward; and, though no peaks of very considerable elevation are to be found along it, yet it is of geographical importance, as its Southern slopes form the Northern watershed of the holy river as far as Lhassa.

The valley enclosed between these two parallel ranges is the most thickly populated valley in Tibet. Grass is abundant, and fuel easily obtainable, and therefore thousands of yaks, sheep, and goats can be seen grazing near the many Tibetan camps along the Brahmaputra and its principal tributaries. The trade route taken by the caravans from Ladak to Lhassa follows this valley; and, as I came to Tibet to see and study the Tibetans, I thought that, although I might run greater risks, I could in no part of the country accomplish my object better than by going along this thickly populated track, which moreover had never before been trodden by a European.

CHAPTER LXI

Expecting trouble—Along the Brahmaputra—A thunderstorm—A dilemma—A dangerous river—Swamped—Saved—Night disturbers—A new friend.

WE slept very little, as we expected the soldiers to attack us during the night to try and stop our progress, but all was quiet and nothing happened; our yaks, however, managed to get loose, and we had some difficulty in recovering them in the morning, for they had swum across the stream, and had gone about a mile from camp on the other side.

The night had been very cold, the thermometer dropping as low as 32½°. We did not pitch our little tent, in case of emergencies, and we were tired and cold after the long march of the previous day. There was a South-westerly breeze blowing and I found it hard to have to cross the river, chase the yaks and bring them back to camp. Then, exhausted as we were, we had in addition to go through the daily routine of loading them. We followed the right bank of the stream to bearings 170° (m.), then to 142° 30′ (b.m.), where it wound in and out between barren hills, subsequently flowing through a grassy valley three-quarters of a mile wide and a mile and a half long. It then went through a narrow passage to 17° 30′ (b.m.) and turned to 103° and farther to 142° through an undulating grassy valley two miles wide, in crossing which we were caught in a terrific thunderstorm, with hail and rain. This was indeed an annoying experience, for we were now before a very large tributary of the Brahmaputra, and the stream was so swollen, rapid and deep that I was much puzzled as to how to take my men across: they could not swim, and the water was so cold that a dip in it would give any one a severe shock. However, there was no time to be lost, for the river was visibly rising, and as the storm was getting worse, difficulties would only increase every moment. We took off every stitch of clothing and fastened our garments, with our rifles, &c., on the pack-saddles of the yaks, which we sent into the water. They are good swimmers, and though the current carried them over a hundred yards down stream, we saw them with satisfaction scramble out of the water on to the opposite bank. Notwithstanding the faith that Chanden Sing and Mansing had in my swimming, they really thought that their last hour had come when I took each by the hand and asked them to follow me into the stream. Hardly had we gone twelve yards when the inevitable took place. We were all three swept away, and Chanden Sing and Mansing in their panic clung tight to my arms and dragged me under water. Though I swam my hardest with my legs, we continually came to the surface and then sank again, owing to the dead weight of my helpless mates. But at last, after a desperate struggle, the current washed us on to the opposite side, where we found our feet, and were soon able to scramble out of the treacherous river. We were some two hundred yards down stream from the spot at which we had entered the river, and such was the quantity of muddy water we had swallowed that we all three became sick. This left us much exhausted, and, as the storm showed no signs of abating, we encamped (16,320 feet) there and then on the left bank of the stream. Though we sadly needed some warm food, there was, of course, no possibility of lighting a fire. A piece of choco-

TIBETAN DOG

late was all I had that night, and my men preferred to eat nothing rather than break their caste by eating my food.

We were asleep under our little tent, the hour being about eleven, when there was a noise outside as of voices and people stumbling against stones. I was out in a moment with my rifle, and shouted the usual "*Paladò*" ("Go away"), in answer to which, though I could see nothing owing to the darkness, I heard several stones flung from slings whizzing past me. One of these hit the tent, and a dog barked furiously. I fired a shot in the air, which had the good effect of producing a hasty retreat of our

SMALL MANI WALL

enemies, whoever they were. The dog, however, would not go. He remained outside barking all night, and it was only in the morning, when I gave him some food and caressed him in Tibetan fashion, with the usual words of endearment, "*Chochu, Chochu,*" that our four-footed foe became friendly, rubbing himself against my legs as if he had known me all his life, and taking a particular fancy to Mansing, by whose side he lay down. From that day he never left our camp, and followed us everywhere, until harder times came upon us.

CHAPTER LXII

Leaving the course of the river—A pass—An arid plain—More vanishing soldiers—Another river—A *mani* wall—*Mirage?*—A large Tibetan encampment—The chain of mountains North of us.

THE river was turning too much towards the South, so I decided to abandon it and strike across country, especially as there were faint signs of a track leading over a pass to 110° (b.m.) from camp. I followed this track, and along it I distinguished marks of hundreds of ponies' hoofs, now almost entirely washed away. This was evidently the way taken by the soldiers we had encountered on the other side of the Maium Pass.

Having risen over the col 17,750 feet, we saw before us an extensive valley with barren hills scattered over it. To the South we observed a large plain some ten miles wide, with snowy peaks rising on the farther side. In front was a hill projecting into the plain, on which stood a *mani* wall; and this latter discovery made me feel quite confident that I was on the high road to Lhassa. About eight miles off to the NNW. were high snowy peaks, and as we went farther we found a lofty mountain range, with still higher peaks, three miles behind it. We had travelled half-way across the waterless plain, when we noticed a number of soldiers' heads and matchlocks popping in and out from behind a distant hill. After a while they came out in numbers to observe our movements, then retired again behind the hill. We proceeded, but when we were still half a mile from them they abandoned their hiding-place, and galloped away before us, raising clouds of dust. From a hill 16,200 feet, over which the track crossed, we perceived a group of very high snowy

AN EFFECT OF MIRAGE

peaks about eight miles distant. Between them and us stood a range of hills cut by a valley, along which flowed a river carrying a large volume of water. This we followed to 126° (b.m.), and having found a suitable fording-place, we crossed over at a spot where the stream was twenty-five yards across, and the water reached up to our waists. We found here another *mani* wall with large inscriptions on stones, and as the wind was very high and cutting, we made use of it to shelter us. Within the angle comprised between bearings 240° and 120° (b.m.) we could observe a very high, snowy mountain range in the distance (the great Himahlyan chain), and lower hill ranges even as near as three miles from camp. The river we had just crossed flowed into the Brahmaputra, and we were now at an elevation of 15,700 feet. We saw plainly at sunset a number of black tents before us at bearings 120°; we calculated them to be two miles distant. We counted about sixty, as well as hundreds of black yaks.

At sunrise the next morning, much to our surprise, they had all vanished; nor, on marching in the direction where we had seen them the previous night, were we able to find traces of them. It seemed as if it must have been *mirage*. Eventually, however, some fourteen miles away, across a grassy plain bounded to the North-East by the range extending from North-West to South-East, and with lofty snowy peaks at 72° some five miles off, we came upon a very large Tibetan encampment of over eighty black tents at an altitude of 15,650 feet. They were pitched on the banks of another tributary of the Brahmaputra, which, after describing a great curve in the plain, passed West of the encampment. Five miles off, in the arc of circle described from 310° to 70° (b.m.), stood the chain of mountains which I had observed all along; but here the elevations of its peaks became gradually lower and lower, so much so that the name of "hill range" would be more appropriate to it than that of "mountain chain." Behind it, however, towered loftier peaks again with their snowy caps.

CHAPTER LXIII

A commotion—An invitation declined—The tents—Delicacies—The *Chokseh*.

WE wanted food, and so made boldly for the encampment. Our approach caused a great commotion, and yaks and sheep were hastily driven away before us, while men and women rushed in and out of their tents, apparently in a state of much excitement. Eight or ten men reluctantly came forward and entreated us to go inside a large tent. They said they wished to speak to us, and offered us tea. I would not accept their invitation, distrusting them, but went on across the encampment, halting some three hundred yards beyond it. Chanden Sing and I proceeded afterwards on a round of calls at all the tents, trying to purchase food and also to show that, if we had declined to enter a particular tent, it was not on account of fear, but because we did not want to be caught in a trap. Our visit to the different *golingchos* or *gurr* (tents) was interesting enough. The tents themselves were very cleverly constructed, and admirably adapted to the country in which they were used; and the various articles of furniture inside attracted my curiosity. The tents, black in colour, were woven of yaks' hair, the natural greasiness of which made them quite waterproof. They consisted of two separate pieces of this thick material, supported by two poles at each end, and there was an oblong aperture above in the upper part of the tent, through which the smoke could escape. The base of the larger tents was hexagonal in shape : the roof, generally at a height of six or seven feet above the ground, was kept

BLACK TENT

very tightly stretched by means of long ropes passing over high poles and pegged to the ground. Wooden and iron pegs were used for this purpose, and many were required to keep the tent close to the ground all round, so as to protect its inmates from the cutting winds of the great plateau. Long poles, as a rule numbering four, with white flying prayers, could be seen outside each tent, or one to each point of the compass, the East being taken for a starting-point. Around the interior of the larger tents there was a mud wall from two to three feet high, for the purpose of further protection against wind, rain and snow. These walls were sometimes constructed of dried dung, which, as time went on, was used for fuel. There were two apertures, one at either end of the tent; that facing the wind being always kept closed by means of loops and wooden bolts.

A DONGBO OR TEA CHURN

The Tibetan is a born nomad, and shifts his dwelling with the seasons, or wherever he can find pasture for his yaks and sheep; but, though he has no fixed abode, he knows how to make himself comfortable, and he carries with him all that he requires. Thus, for instance, in the centre of his tent, he begins by making himself a *goling*, or fireplace of mud and stone, some three feet high and four or five long, by one and a half wide, with two, three, or more side ventilators and draught-holes. By this ingenious contrivance he manages to increase the combustion of the dried dung, the most trying fuel from which to get a flame. On the top of this stove a suitable place is made to fit the several *raksangs*, or large brass pots and bowls, in which the brick tea, having been duly pounded in a stone or wooden mortar, is boiled and stirred with a long brass spoon. A portable iron stand is generally to be seen somewhere in the tent, upon which the hot vessels are placed, as they are removed from the fire. Close to these is the *toxzum* or *dongbo*, a cylindrical wooden churn, with a lid through which a piston passes. This is used for mixing the tea with butter and salt, in the way I have described as also adopted by the Jogpas.

THE INTERIOR OF A TENT

The wooden cups or bowls used by the Tibetans are called *puku, fruh* or *cariel,* and in them *tsamba* is also eaten after tea has been poured on it, and the mixture worked into a paste by means of more or less dirty fingers. Often extra lumps of butter are mixed with this paste, and even bits of *chura* (cheese). The richer people (officials) indulge in flour and rice, which they import from India and China, and in *kassur,* or dried fruit (namely, dates and apricots) of inferior quality. The rice is boiled into a kind

TSAMGO

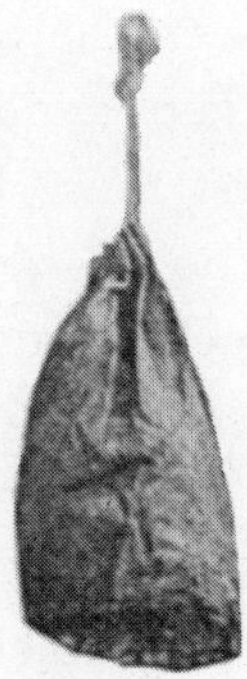

SMALL TSAMBA BAG, CARRIED ON THE PERSON BY TIBETANS

of soup called the *tukpa,* a great luxury only indulged in on grand occasions, when such other cherished delicacies as *gimakará* (sugar) and *shelkara* (lump white sugar) are also eaten. The Tibetans are very fond of meat, though few can afford such an extravagance. Wild game, yak and sheep are considered excellent food, and the meat and bone cut in pieces are boiled in a cauldron with lavish quantities of salt and pepper. The several people in a tent dip their hands into the pot, and having picked up suitable pieces, tug at them with their teeth and fingers, grinding even the bone, meat eaten without bone being supposed to be difficult to digest.

The Tibetan tents are usually furnished with a few *tildih* (rough sitting-mats) round the fireplace, and near the entrance of the tent stands a *dahlo*, or basket, in which the dung is stored as collected. These *dahlos*, used in couples, are very convenient for tying to pack-saddles, for which purpose they are specially designed. Along the walls of the tent are the *tsamgo* or bags of *tsamba*, and the *dongmo* or butter-pots, and among masses of sheepskins and blankets can be seen the little wooden chests in which the store of butter is kept under lock and key.

The first thing that strikes the eye on entering a Tibetan tent is the *chokseh* or table, upon which are lights and brass bowls containing offerings to the *Chogan*, the gilt god to whom the occupiers of the *gurr* (tent) address their morning and evening prayers. Prayer-wheels and strings of beads are plentiful, and lashed upright to the poles are the long matchlocks belonging to the men, their tall props projecting well out of the aperture in the roof of the tent. Spears are kept in a similar manner, but the swords and smaller knives are carried about the person all day, and laid on the ground by the side of their owners at night.

CHAPTER LXIV

Refusal to sell food—Women—Their looks and characteristics—The *Tchukti*—A Lhassa lady.

THE inhabitants of this encampment were polite and talkative. Notwithstanding their refusal to sell us food on the plea that they had none even for themselves, their friendliness was so much beyond my expectation that I at first feared treachery. However, treachery or not, I thought that while I was there I had better see and learn as much as I could. Women and men formed a ring round us, and the fair sex seemed less shy than the stronger in answering questions. I was particularly struck, not only in this encampment but in all the others, by the small number of women to be seen in Tibet. This is not because they are kept in seclusion; on the contrary, the ladies of the Forbidden Land seem to have it all their own way. They are actually in an enormous minority, the proportion being, at a rough guess, backed by the wise words of a friendly Lama, from fifteen to twenty males to each female in the population; nevertheless, the fair sex in Hundes manages to rule the male majority, playing thereby constantly into the hands of the Lamas.

The Tibetan female, whether she be a lady, a shepherdess, or a brigandess, cannot be said to be prepossessing. In fact, it was not my luck to see a single good-looking woman in the country, although I naturally saw women who were less ugly than others. Anyhow, with the accumulated filth that from birth is undisturbed by soap, scrubbing or bathing; with nose, cheeks and forehead smeared with

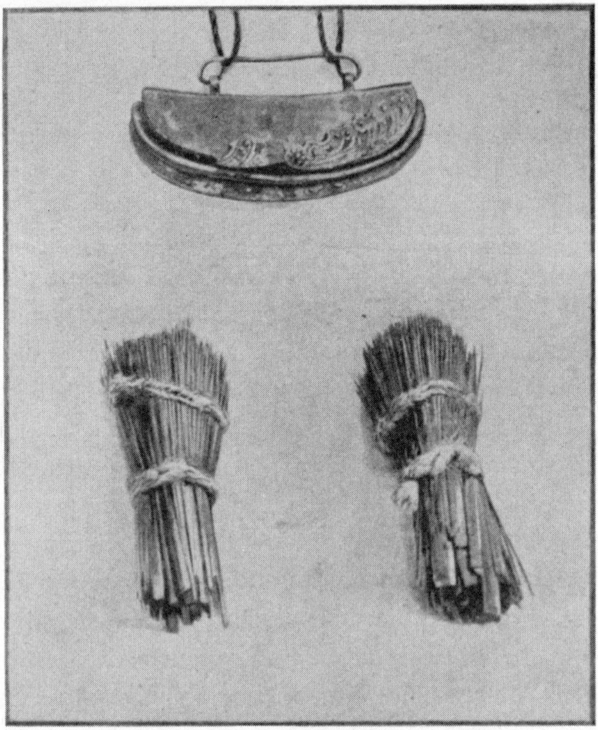

TIBETAN HAIR BRUSHES AND FLINT AND STEEL POUCH

black ointment to prevent the skin cracking in the wind; and with the unpleasant odour that emanates from never-changed clothes, the Tibetan woman is, at her best, repulsive to European taste. After one has overcome one's first disgust she yet has, at a distance, a certain charm of her

TIBETAN WOMEN AND CHILDREN

own. She walks well, for she is accustomed to carry heavy weights on her head; and her skull would be well-set on her shoulders were it not that the neck is usually too short and thick to be graceful. Her body and limbs possess great muscular strength and are well developed, but generally lack stability, and her breasts are flabby and pendent — facts due, no doubt, to sexual abuse. She is generally of heavy frame, and rather inclined to stoutness. Her hands and feet show power and rude strength, but no dexterity or suppleness is noticeable in her fingers, and she has therefore no ability for very fine or delicate work.

THE TCHUKTI

The Tibetan woman is,

nevertheless, far superior to the Tibetan man. She possesses a better heart, more pluck, and a finer character than he does. Time after time, when the males, timid beyond all conception, ran away at our approach, the women remained in charge of the tents, and, although by no means cool or collected, they very rarely failed to meet us without some show of dignity.

On the present occasion, when all were friendly, the women seemed much less shy than the men, and conversed freely and incessantly. They even prevailed upon their masters to sell us a little *tsamba* and butter.

Tibetan women wear trousers and boots like the men, and over them they have a long gown, either yellow or blue, reaching down to their feet. Their head-dress is curious, the hair being carefully parted in the middle, and plastered with melted butter over the scalp as far down as the ears; then it is plaited all round in innumerable little tresses, to which is fastened the *Tchukti*, three strips of heavy red and blue cloth joined together by cross bands ornamented with coral and malachite beads, silver coins and bells, and reaching from the shoulders down to the heels.

They seemed very proud of this ornamentation, and displayed much coquetry in attracting our notice to it. Wealthier women in Tibet have quite a small fortune hanging down their backs, for all the money or valuables earned or saved are sewn on to the *Tchukti*. To the lower end of the *Tchukti* one, two or three rows of small brass or silver bells are attached, and therefore the approach of the Tibetan dames is announced by the tinkling of their bells, a quaint custom, the origin of which they could not explain to me, beyond saying that it was pretty and that they liked it.

A LADY FROM LHASSA

The illustration that I give here of a travelling Tibetan lady from Lhassa was taken at Tucker. She wore her hair, of abnormal length and beauty, in one huge tress, and round her head, like an aureole, was a circular wooden ornament, on the outer part of which were fastened beads of coral, glass and malachite. The arrangement was so heavy that, though it fitted the head well, it had to be supported by means of strings tied to the hair and others passed over the head. By the side of her head, and hanging by the ears and hair, were a pair of huge silver earrings inlaid with malachite, and round her neck three long strings of beads with silver brooches.

Considerable modifications necessarily occurred in these garments and ornaments, according to the locality and the wearer's condition in life, but the general lines of their clothing were practically everywhere the same. Often a loose silver chain belt was worn considerably below the waist, and rings and bracelets were common everywhere.

MONEY BAGS

CHAPTER LXV

Polyandry—Marriage ceremonies—Jealousy—Divorce—Identification of children—Courtship—Illegitimacy—Adultery.

THAT the Tibetans legally recognise polyandry and polygamy is well known. Very little, however, has hitherto transpired as to the actual form of these marital customs, so that the details which follow, startling as they may seem when regarded from a Western standpoint, will be found not without interest.

First of all, I may say that there is not such a thing known in Tibet as a standard of morality amongst unmarried women of the middle classes; and, therefore, from a Tibetan point of view, it is not easy to find an immoral woman. Notwithstanding this apparently irregular state of affairs, the women's behaviour is better than might be expected. Like the Shoka girls, they possess a wonderful frankness and simplicity of manner, with a certain reserve which has its allurements; for the Tibetan swain, often a young man, being attracted by the charms of a damsel, finds that his flirtation with her has become an accepted engagement almost before it has begun, and is compelled, in accordance with custom, to go, accompanied by his father and mother, to the tent of the lady of his heart. There he is received by her relations, who have been previously notified of the intended call, and are found seated on rugs and mats awaiting the arrival of their guests.

After the usual courtesies and salutations, the young man's father asks, on behalf of his son, for the young lady's hand ; and, if the answer is favourable, the suitor places a square lump of yak *murr* (yak butter) on his betrothed's forehead. She does the same for him, and the marriage ceremony is then considered over, the buttered couple being man and wife.

WOMAN WHOSE FACE IS SMEARED WITH BLACK OINTMENT

If there is a temple close by, *Katas*, food and money are laid before the images of Buddha and saints, and the parties walk round the inside of the temple. Should there be no temple at hand, the husband and wife make the circuit of the nearest hill, or, in default of anything else, the tent itself, always moving from left to right. This ceremony is repeated with prayers and sacrifices every day for a fortnight, during which time libations of wine and general feasting continue, and at the expiration of which the husband conveys his better half to his tent.

The law of Tibet, though hardly ever obeyed, has strict clauses regulating the conduct of married men in their marital relations. So long as the sun is above the horizon, no intercourse is permitted; and certain periods and seasons of the year, such as the height of summer and the depth of winter, are also proscribed.

A Tibetan girl on marrying does not enter into a nuptial tie with an individual but with all his family, in the following somewhat complicated manner. If an eldest son marries an eldest sister, all the sisters of the bride become his wives. Should he, however, begin by marrying the second sister, then only the sisters from the second down will be his property. If the third, all from the third, and so on. At the same time, when the bridegroom has brothers, they are all regarded as their brother's wife's husbands, and they one and all cohabit with her, as well as with her sisters if she has any.

The system is not simple, and certainly not very edifying, and were it not for the odd *savoir faire* of the Tibetan woman, it would lead to endless jealousies and unpleasantness: owing, however, largely, no doubt, to the absolute lack of honour or decency in Tibetan males and females, the arrangement seems to work as satisfactorily as any other kind of marriage.

I asked what would happen in the case of a man marrying a second sister, and so acquiring marital rights over all her younger sisters, if another man came and married her eldest sister. Would all the brides of the first man become the brides of the second? No, they would not; and the second man would have to be satisfied with only one wife. However, if the second sister were left a widow, and her husband had no brothers, then she would become the property of her eldest sister's husband, and with her all the other sisters.

It must not be inferred from these strange matrimonial laws that jealousy is non-existent in Tibet among both men and women; trouble does occasionally arise in Tibetan house- or tent-holds. As, however, the Tibetan woman is clever, she generally contrives to arrange things in a manner conducive to peace. When her husband has several brothers, she despatches them on different errands in every direction, to look after yaks or sheep, or to trade. Only one remains and he is for the time being her husband; then when another returns he has to leave his place and becomes a bachelor, and so on, till all the brothers have, during the year, had an equal period of marital life with their single wife.

TIBETAN WOMAN

Divorce is difficult in Tibet and involves endless complications. I inquired of a Tibetan lady what would she do in case her husband refused to live with her any longer.

"'Why did you marry me?' I would say to him," she exclaimed. "'You found me good, beautiful, wise, clever, affectionate. Now prove that I am not all this!'"

This modest speech, she thought, would be quite sufficient to bring any husband back to reason, but all the same a number of Tibetans find it convenient occasionally to desert their wives, eloping to some distant province, or over the boundary. This procedure is particularly hard on the man's brothers, as they all remain the sole property of the abandoned bride. On the same principle, when a husband dies, the wife is inherited by his brothers.

A very painful case came before the court of the Jong Pen at Taklakot. The husband of a Tibetan lady had died, and she, being enamoured of a handsome youth some twenty years younger than herself, married him. Her husband's brother, however, came all the way from Lhassa after her and claimed her as his wife, though he had already a better half and a large family. She would not hear of leaving the husband of her choice, and after endless scenes between them, the case was heard by the Jong Pen of Taklakot. The Tibetan law was against her, as, according to it, she decidedly belonged to her brother-in-law; but money is stronger than the law in the land of the Lamas.

"For the peace of all, you can arrange things this way," was the advice of the Jong Pen. "You can divide your property, money and goods, into three equal parts: one to go to the Lamas, one to your husband's brother, and one to be retained by yourself."

The woman consented; but, much to her disgust, when two parts had been paid out and she was hoping for peace, a question was raised by the Jong Pen as to why she should even retain one-third of the fortune if she no longer made part of the deceased man's family? Thus orders were instantly given that she should be deprived of everything she possessed.

However, the woman was shrewd enough to deceive the Jong Pen's officers, for one night, having bundled up her tent and her goods and chattels, she quietly stepped over the boundary and placed herself under British protection.

THE LADY IN QUESTION

The mode of knowing and identifying children in Tibet is peculiar. It is not by the child's likeness to his parent, nor by other reasonable methods, that the offspring is set down as belonging to one man more than to another, but this is the mode adopted. Supposing that one married man had two brothers and several children, the first child belongs to him; the second to his first brother, and the third to his second brother, while the fourth would be again the first man's child.

The rules of courtship are not very strict in Tibet, yet

intercourse with girls is looked upon as illegal, and in certain cases not only are the parties, if discovered, made to suffer shame, but certain fines are inflicted on the man, the most severe of all being that he must present the young lady with a dress and ornaments. In the case of "gentlefolks" the question is generally solved to the satisfaction of everybody by the man marrying the woman, and by his gracefully presenting "veils of friendship" to all her relations and friends, together with articles of food; but if by mischance she should be placed in an awkward position before the eyes of the world, and the man will not hear of a matrimonial union, then efforts are made to prevent the birth of the child alive. If these are not successful, the mother must be maintained until after the child's birth. In such cases the illegitimate child remains the man's, and suffers the usual indignities of illegitimacy.

Sixteen in the case of women, and eighteen or nineteen in that of men, is regarded as the marriageable age. Motherhood continues until a fairly advanced age, and I have seen a woman of forty with a baby only a few months old. But, as a rule, Tibetan women lose their freshness while still quite young; and no doubt their custom of polyandry not only contributes to destroy their looks but also is the chief cause that limits the population of Tibet.

The Lamas are supposed to live in celibacy, but they do not always keep to their oath, tempted, no doubt, by the fact that they themselves invariably go unpunished. If, on the other hand, in cases of adultery, the culprit be a layman, he has to pay compensation according to his means to the husband, the amount being fixed by the parties concerned and their friends, or by the law if applied for.

In ordinary cases of marital trespass, presents of clothing,

TIBETAN CHILDREN

tsamba, chura, guram, kassur (dried fruit) and wine, accompanied by the never-lacking *Kata*, are sufficient to allay the injured husband's anger and to fully compensate him for any shame suffered.

The only serious punishment inflicted is, however, in the case of the wife of a high official eloping with a man of low rank. Then the woman is subjected to flogging as a penalty for her infidelity, her husband is disgraced, and her lover, after being subjected to a painful surgical operation, is, if he survives, expelled from the town or encampment.

High officials, and a few wealthy people who are not satisfied with one wife, are allowed by the law of the land to keep as many concubines as their means allow them.

CHAPTER LXVI

Tibetan funerals—Disposal of their dead—By cremation—By water—Cannibalism—Strange beliefs—Revolting barbarity—Drinking human blood—The saints of Tibet.

TIBETAN funerals are interesting, but they so closely resemble those of the Shokas, which I have described at length, that any detailed account of them would be a mere repetition of what I have already written.

For the disposal of the dead body itself, however, the Tibetans have curious customs of their own. The most uncommon method, owing to the great scarcity of fuel, is that of cremation, which is only employed in the case of wealthy people or Lamas, and is effected in exactly the same fashion as among the Shokas. Another and more usual plan is to double up the body, sew it into skins, and let it be carried away by the current of a stream. But the commonest method of all is the revolting ceremony which I now proceed to describe.

The body of the deceased is borne to the top of a hill, where the Lamas pronounce certain incantations and prayers. Then the crowd, after walking seven times round the body, retire to a certain distance, to allow ravens and dogs to tear the corpse to pieces. It is considered lucky for the departed and his family when birds alone devour the greater portion of the body; dogs and wild animals come, say the Lamas, when the deceased has sinned during his life. Anyhow, the almost complete destruction of the corpse is anxiously watched, and, at an opportune moment, the Lamas and crowd, turning their praying-wheels, and

A YOUNG LAMA

muttering the everlasting "*Omne mani padme hun*," return to the body, round which seven more circuits are made, moving from left to right.* Then the relatives squat round. The Lamas sit near the body, and with their daggers cut to pieces what remains of the flesh. The highest Lama present eats the first morsel, then, muttering prayers, the other Lamas

* In the case of a sect called Bombos, the circuits are made in the reverse fashion, as also are their prayer-wheels turned from right to left.

partake of it, after which all the relations and friends throw themselves on the now almost denuded skeleton, scraping off pieces of flesh, which they devour greedily; and this repast of human flesh continues till the bones are dry and clean!

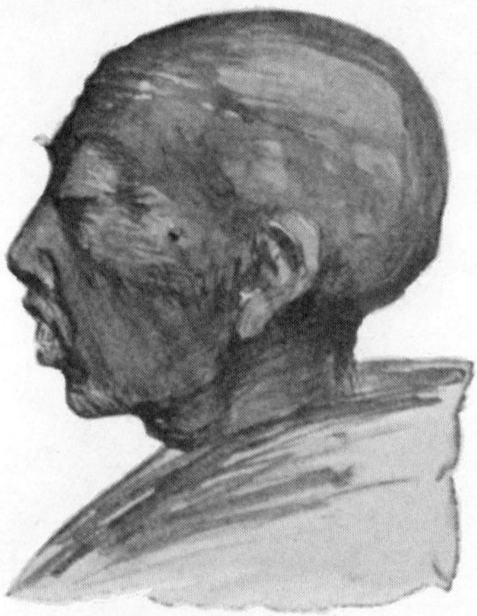

A RED LAMA

The idea of this ghastly ceremony is that the spirit of the departed, of whom you have swallowed a piece, will for ever keep on friendly terms with you. When birds and dogs do not shrink from feeding, it is a sign that the body is healthy, and fit for themselves.

Revolting beyond words is the further fact that, when a man has died of some pestilential disease, and, owing to the odour, the birds will not peck at the body, nor will the famished dogs go near it, then a large number of Lamas, having made the usual exorcisms, sit down by it, and do not get up again until they have devoured the whole of the rotten human flesh! The relatives and friends are wiser and less brutal. They rightly believe that, if voracious animals will not partake of the meal proffered them, it is because the body is that of a sinner against whom God is angry. And who better than the Lamas could make peace between God and him? So let the Lamas eat it all.

CUP MADE OF HUMAN SKULL

In the case of not finding sufficient Lamas to perform these rites, the body is either disposed of by throwing it into the water, or else, the relations having first partaken of a morsel of the flesh, it is bound to a rock to let animals or time do the rest.

CHOKDEN, OR TOMB OF A SAINT

The Lamas are said to have a great craving for human blood, which, they say, gives them strength, genius and vigour. When sucking wounds that are not poisoned, they drink the blood, and also on certain occasions wounds are inflicted for the sake of sucking the blood. At other times the cups cut from human skulls, found in all monasteries, are filled with blood, and the Lamas in turn satisfy their thirst out of them.

But enough of this. It is sickening to set it down, though my book would be incomplete if I had made no mention of the cannibalism of the Lamas.

When a saintly Lama dies, or some old man much respected by the community, either parts of the flesh, or, if cremation has been applied, some of his ashes, are preserved and placed in a *Chokden* erected for the purpose; and, judging by the number of these structures one finds all over Tibet, one feels inclined to think that half the population of the country must have been saints, or else that the standard of saintliness in the sacred land of the Lamas is not prohibitively high.

CHAPTER LXVII

Another commotion—Two hundred soldiers—A stampede—Easy travelling—A long *Mani* wall—Mosquitoes.

COMING out of our tent in the morning, we noticed an unusual commotion among the Tibetans. A number of mounted men with matchlocks had arrived, and others similarly armed immediately went to join them from the tents. They seemed excited, and I kept my eye upon them while I was cooking my food. There were some two hundred in all, picturesquely garbed. They seemed to be good horsemen, and looked well as they rode in a line towards us. A little way off they stopped and dismounted, and the leaders came forward, one stalwart fellow in a fine sheepskin coat marching ahead of the rest. His attitude was very arrogant, and, dispensing with the usual salutations, he approached quite close, shaking his fist at me.

"*Kiu mahla lokhna nga rah luck tiba tangan*" ("I will give you a goat or a sheep if you will go back"), he said.

"*Kiu donna nga di tangon*" ("And I give you this to make you go back!") was my quick answer, while I unexpectedly administered him one straight from the shoulder that sent him flat on his back and sprawling on the ground.

The army, which, with its usual prudence, was watching events from a respectful distance, beat a hasty retreat. The officer, though unhurt, scrambled away, screaming. The Tibetans had so far behaved with such contemptible cowardice that we could hardly congratulate ourselves

"AND I GIVE YOU THIS TO MAKE YOU GO BACK"

on such easy successes. We began to feel that really we had no enemy at all before us, and very likely we became even careless. Anyhow, we ate our food and gave this affair but little thought.

The Tibetans kept their distance, and did not trouble us again that day. Those who had not ridden off retired timidly inside their black tents, and not a soul was to be seen about the encampment—which might have been deserted, so silent and so empty did it appear. I registered

A MANI WALL ON THE ROAD TO LHASSA

my daily observations, made a sketch of one of the black tents, and wrote up my diary; after which we raised camp.

Our progress was now comparatively easy, along a broad grassy plain, and we proceeded without further disturbance in a South-easterly direction, observing a high snowy peak at 20° (b.m.), and a low pass in the mountain range to our North-east at 55° (b.m.). A very high range stood ahead of us in the far distance, with low hills between. In going round one of these lonely hills we found at the foot of it another and more important *mani* wall of some length, with numberless inscriptions of all ages and sizes on stones, pieces of bone, skulls and horns. Farther on, to the South, there were three smaller hillocks and two larger ones. The soldiers we had routed at the encampment had proceeded in the direction we were now following, and we were, in fact, treading all along on the footprints of their ponies.

We had to cross a river and a number of rivulets, and so troublesome was it each time to take off one's shoes and clothes to wade through, that we bundled up our clothes on the yaks, and travelled along for the rest of the afternoon barefooted and with nothing on but a *doti* (loin-cloth), in the style adopted by fakirs.

In an arc of a circle from 120° to 180° (b.m.) we noticed very low hills, and from 160° to 220°, some thirty or forty miles off, could be seen much more clearly now the high range we had observed before. The sun was extremely hot, the ground marshy, the air being thick with huge and very troublesome mosquitoes. We were quickly covered from head to foot with bites, and the irritation caused by them was intense. Halting on the right bank of a large stream at 15,600 feet, we named this spot Mosquito Camp. At sunset the number of mosquitoes around us was such as to drive us nearly mad, but fortunately, the moment the sun disappeared, the thermometer fell to 33°, and we had a peaceful night.

In the evening we saw a number of horsemen riding full speed on a course about one mile south of ours, but converging to the same direction. No doubt they were sent to keep the authorities ahead well informed of our movements.

CHAPTER LXVIII

Washing-day—A long march—*Kiang* and antelope—Benighted —The purchase of a goat—Ramifications of the Brahmaputra —A detour—Through a swamp—Mansing again lost and found.

THE next was for us a great washing-day. The water of the stream was so pleasant and clear that we could not resist the temptation of having a regular cleaning up, washing first our clothing and spreading it to dry in the sun, and then cleansing our faces and bodies thoroughly with soap, a luxury unknown to us for ever so long.

While I was drying myself in the sun—owing to the want of towels—I registered at 211° (b.m.) a very high snowy peak, and a lower one at 213° 30′ forming part of the chain before us. There were mountains on every side of the plain we were traversing ; and another very elevated peak, of which I had taken bearings on a previous occasion, was at 20° (b.m.). A break occurred in the hill range to our North-east, showing a narrow valley, beyond which were high snowy mountains. We made a very long march along the grassy plain, going to 147° (b.m.), and encamped on the bank of the Brahmaputra, here already a wide, deep and very rapid stream. We had passed hundreds of *kiang* and antelopes, and shortly before sunset I took a walk to the hills to try and bring some fresh meat to camp. I stalked a herd of antelopes, and having gone some five miles from camp, I was benighted, and on my return had the greatest difficulty in finding my men in the darkness. They had been unable to light a fire, and as they had both gone fast asleep, I received no answer to my calls. We had selected

KIANG

a sheltered depression in the ground for our camp, and there being hundreds of similar spots everywhere round it, and no landmarks to go by, it was by no means easy to identify the exact place.

Fortunately, at last, after I had shouted for some considerable time, Chanden Sing heard me, and, by the sound of his voice, I found my way back. In the morning we noticed a large encampment about a mile off on the opposite bank of the Brahmaputra, where we might have obtained provisions, but the stream was too rapid for us to cross; moreover, we saw black tents in every direction on our side of the water, and therefore there was no reason to go to the extra trouble and danger of crossing the stream.

Much to our delight, we succeeded in purchasing a goat from some passing Tibetans, who drove before them a flock of several thousand heads, and, as we could not find sufficient

OUR YAKS SINKING IN MUD

dry fuel to make a fire, we entrusted Mansing with the safe-conduct of the animal to our next camp, where we proposed to feast on it.

The Brahmaputra had here several ramifications mostly ending in lakelets, and rendering the plain a regular swamp. The larger branch was very wide and deep, and we preferred following it to crossing it, notwithstanding that we had to deviate somewhat from the course which I would have otherwise followed. We thus made a considerable *détour*, but as it was, even for several miles we sank in mud up to our knees, or waded through water, for although there were small patches of earth with tufts of grass which rose above the water, they collapsed on our attempting to stand upon them.

The whole of the Northern part of the plain was extremely marshy. Our yaks gave us no end of trouble, for when they sank unexpectedly in soft mud-holes, they became restless and alarmed, and in their struggles to save themselves, once or twice shook off their pack-saddles and loads, which we had not been able to fasten properly for want of ropes. Chanden Sing and I, however, managed to keep up with them, and at last, on nearing the hills, the ground showed greater undulations and was rather drier. We saw columns of smoke rising from near the foot of the range to the North of us. We went on another couple of miles, exhausted and dirty, our clothes, which we had spent so much soap and time in washing, filthy with splashes of mud.

"Where are Mansing and the *rabbu?*"* I asked of my bearer.

"He remained behind at the beginning of the swamp. He was too exhausted to drag along the goat you purchased."

I was much concerned, on scouting the country all round from a hillock with my telescope, to see no signs of the poor

* The Tibetans have three distinct kinds of goats: the *rabbu*, or large woolly animal, such as the one I had purchased; the *ratton*, or small goat; and the *chitbu*, a dwarf goat whose flesh is delicious eating. The *rabbu* and *ratton* are the two kinds generally used for carrying loads, and they have sufficient strength to bear a weight not exceeding 40 lbs. for a distance of from five to eight miles daily over fairly good ground.

fellow, and I was angry with myself for not noticing his disappearance before. As there were many Tibetans about the spot where he had remained, I feared foul play on their part, and that he might have been overpowered. Again I imagined that, weak as he was, he might have been sucked down in one of the deeper mud-holes, without a chance of saving himself. I left Chanden Sing to look after the yaks and turned back in search of him. As I hurried back mile after mile, struggling again half across the mud swamp, and yet saw no signs of the poor coolie, I was almost giving up my quest in despair, when my eye caught something moving about half a mile farther on. It was the goat all by itself. I made for it with a sinking heart.

It was only on getting quite close to it that I perceived the poor coolie, lying flat and half sunk in the mud. He had fallen in a faint, and though he was still breathing, he was quite insensible. Fortunately he had taken the precaution of tying the rope of the *rabbu* tight round his arm, and thus not only was it owing to the animal that I had found his whereabouts, but I had also saved our precious acquisition. With some rubbing and shaking I brought the poor fellow back to life, and supported him by the arm until we rejoined Chanden Sing. Not till the middle of the night did we reach Tarbar, a large Tibetan encampment at the foot of the hill range.

CHAPTER LXIX

The alarm given—Our bad manners—A peaceful settlement—
A large river—Gigantic peak—Again on marshy soil.

THE alarm of our arrival, given first by scores of dogs barking at us, then by one of the natives who had ventured to leave his tent to find out the cause of the disturbance, created the usual panic in the place.

"*Gigri duk! gigri duk! Jogpa, Jogpa!*" ("Danger, danger; help, brigands!") cried the Tibetan, running frantically out of his tent; and a few seconds later, black figures could be seen everywhere, rushing in and out of their tents in a state of confusion. It must be remembered that, according to the manners of Tibet, one should time one's arrival at an encampment so as to reach it before sundown, unless notice of one's approach is sent ahead. People who arrive unexpectedly in the middle of the night are never credited with good motives, and their appearance is associated with all sorts of evil intentions, murder, robbery or extortion. I tried to set the minds of the good folk at ease, by stating that I meant no harm; but such was their excitement and confusion that I could get no one to listen to me.

Two old women came to us with a bucket of milk and laid it at my feet, entreating me to spare their lives; and great was their astonishment when, instead of finding themselves murdered, they received a silver rupee in payment. This was the first step towards a peaceful settlement of the disturbance. After some time, calm was restored and, though still regarded with considerable suspicion, we were politely treated by the natives.

Unfortunately, here too we were unable to purchase provisions, the natives declaring that they had not sufficient for themselves. So, having feasted on the *rabbu* which we killed, and on yak's milk, we made preparations to strike camp early next morning.

CARPENTER AND SADDLE-MAKER

At night the thermometer fell to 26°, and the cold was very great; but we purchased a quantity of dung from the natives and made a fine fire in the morning; and, having had a good meal after several days' privations, we felt happier than usual. The natives begged as ever, showing their unrestrained craving for money, to get which they would lower themselves to anything.

North-west of the encampment, through a gorge, flowed

a wide river which skirted the foot of the mountains. It was snow-fed, for in the evening the current was strong and deep, whereas early in the morning the level of the water was several feet lower, being, however, even then hardly fordable. On leaving Tarbar, we followed for a while the course of the river, and, the day being glorious, we were able to admire fully the magnificent panorama of the great rugged mountain-range to our South-west. The higher peaks were nearly all of a pyramidical shape, and at 226° 30′ (b.m.) I observed a gigantic quadrangular peak which I took to be Mount Everest. Next to it, at 225° 30′ (b.m.), is a pyramidical peak, very lofty, but not to be compared in height or beauty to its neighbour. I followed a general course towards 120° (b.m.), and as the river, which we had more or less followed, now described a big bend towards the S.S.E., I decided to cross it. We waded through it successfully with water up to our necks, and again we found ourselves upon marshy land, with a repetition of the previous day's experience.

OLD WOMAN

Farther on, we crossed three more tributaries of the larger stream, all fairly wide and deep ; and then we had once more to get across the main river, now of such depth and rapidity as to cause us much trouble and no small danger. The river traverses the plain in zigzag fashion, and, unless we wanted to follow its banks, and so lengthen the journey by double or treble the distance, this was the only course open to us. Thus, while trying to travel in a straight line, we found ourselves for the third time confronted by this great river, now swollen by other snow-fed streams, and carrying an immense body of water. It was in the afternoon, too, when the water was at its highest. We attempted a crossing at several points, but found it impossible; so I made up my mind to wait for low water early next morning.

CHAPTER LXX

Another Tibetan encampment—Uncontrollable animals—A big stream—Washed away—In dreadful suspense—Rescuing the yak—Diving at great altitudes and its effects—How my two followers got across—A precarious outlook and a little comfort.

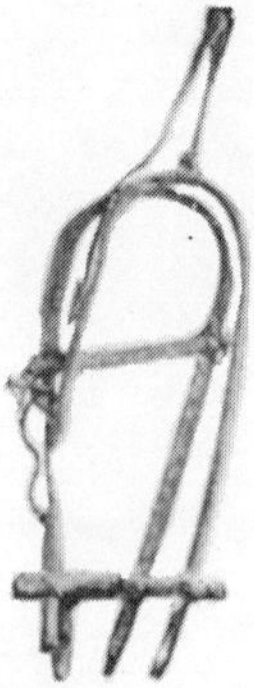

CONTRIVANCE FOR CARRYING LOADS

APPARENTLY my yaks knew this part of the country well; and I noticed that, whenever I lost the track, all I had to do was to follow them, and they would bring me back to it again. Even when I drove them away from the track, they showed a great disinclination to move, whereas they proceeded willingly enough while we were on the high road, which, mark you, is no road at all, for no track is visible except here and there, where the footprints of the last nomads with their sheep, ponies and yaks have destroyed the grass.

Half a mile on the other side of the river was an encampment of some fifty or sixty tents, with hundreds of yaks and sheep grazing near it.

At this point my two yaks, which I noticed had been marching with more than usual smartness, bolted while I was ordering Chanden Sing and Mansing to take down the loads, and went straight into the water.

In attempting to make them turn back, Mansing threw a stone at them, which, however, only sent them on all the faster. The current was so strong, and the bottom of the river so soft, that they both sank, and when they reappeared

RESCUING A YAK

on the surface it was only to float rapidly away down stream. We watched them with ever-increasing anxiety, for they seemed quite helpless. We ran panting along the river bank, urging them on with shouts to drive them to the other side. Alas, in their desperate struggle to keep afloat, and powerless against the current, the two yaks collided violently in mid-stream, and the bump caused the pack-saddle and loads of the smaller yak to turn over. The animal, thus overbalanced and hampered, sank and reappeared two or three times, struggling for air and life. It was, indeed, a terrible moment. I threw off my clothes and jumped into the water. I swam fast to the animal, and, with no small exertion, pulled him on shore, some two hundred yards farther down the stream. We were both safe, though breathless, but, alas ! the ropes that held the baggage had given way, and saddle and loads had disappeared. This loss was a dreadful blow to us. I tried hard, by repeatedly diving into the river, until I was almost frozen, to recover my goods, but failed to find them or even to locate them. Where I suspected them to be the water was over twenty feet deep, and the bottom of the river was of soft mud; so that the weight of the loads would have caused them to sink and be covered over with it.

Diving at such very great elevations gave one a peculiar and unpleasant sensation. The moment I was entirely under water, I felt as if I were compressed under an appalling weight which seemed to crush me. Had the liquid above and around me been a mass of lead instead of water, it could not have felt heavier. The sensation was especially noticeable in my head, which felt as if my skull were being screwed into a vice. The beating at my temples was so strong that, though in ordinary circumstances I can remain under water for over a minute, I could there never hold out for longer than fifteen or twenty seconds. Each time that I emerged from below, gasping for air, my heart beat alarmingly hard, and my lungs seemed as if about to burst.

I was so exhausted that I did not feel equal to conveying across my two men, so I unloaded the stronger yak, and then, with endless fatigue, I drove him and his mate again into the water. Unhampered, and good swimmers as they are, they floated away with the current and reached the other side. Chanden Sing and Mansing, with their clothes and mine tied into a bundle over their shoulders, got on the animals and, after a somewhat anxious passage, they arrived safely on my side, where we camped, my men mourning all night over the lost property. The next morning I made fresh attempts to recover the loads, but in vain! Unhappily they contained all my tinned provisions, and what little other food I had, and they had in them besides eight hundred rupees in silver, the greater part of my ammunition, changes of clothing and three pairs of shoes, my copper hurricane lantern, and sundry knives and razors.

The only thing we recovered was the pack-saddle, which was washed ashore some six hundred yards farther down. Our situation can be summed up in a few words. We were now in the centre of Tibet, with no food of any kind, no clothes to speak of, and no boots or shoes, except those we wore, which were falling to pieces. What little ammunition I had left could not be relied upon, owing to its having been in the water on several occasions; and round us we had nothing but enemies—insignificant enemies if you like, yet enemies for all that.

I got what comfort I could out of the knowledge that at least the water-tight cases with my scientific instruments, notes, sketches and maps were saved, and as far as I was concerned, I valued them more than anything else I possessed.

CHAPTER LXXI

Hungry and worn—A sense of humour—Two buckets of milk—No food to be obtained—Chanden Sing and Mansing in a wretched state—Their fidelity—Exhaustion.

WE went on, hungry, worn out, with our feet lacerated, cheering one another as best we could. We laughed at our troubles; we laughed at the Tibetans and their comical ways; we laughed at everything and everybody, until eventually we even laughed at ourselves. When you are hungry, the sun seems slow at describing its daily semicircle from East to West; yet though involuntary fasting gives you at first an acute pain in the stomach, it doesn't become unbearable until after several days' absolute want of food; that is to say, if you are in a way accustomed, as we were, to extra long intervals between one meal and the next. When we got to our third day's fasting we were keen enough for a meal; and, perceiving some black tents close by the mountain side, about four miles out of our course, we made for them with hungry haste. We purchased two bucketsful of yaks' milk, one of which I drank there and then myself, the second being equally divided between my two servants. That was all we could get. They would sell us absolutely nothing else.

After this we moved forward again, making steady, and, if

one allows for the great elevation we were at, comparatively rapid progress; noting down everything, and holding our own against all comers. We encountered pleasant people, and some unpleasant ones, but, whether their manner was courteous or the reverse, we could nowhere obtain food for love or money.

DRINKING OUT OF A BUCKET

Poor Mansing and Chanden Sing, not having the same interest that I had in my work to keep up their spirits, were now in a dreadful condition. Cold, tired and starved, the poor wretches had hardly strength left to stand on their feet, the soles of which were badly cut and very sore. It really made my heart bleed to see these two brave fellows suffer as they did for my sake; and yet no word of complaint came from them; not once did their lips utter a reproach.

"Never mind if we suffer or even die," said the poor fellows, when I expressed my sympathy with them, "we will follow you as long as we have strength to move, and we will stand by you, no matter what happens."

I had to relieve Chanden Sing of his rifle, as he was no longer able to carry it. I myself, too, felt languid and exhausted as the days went by, and we got scarcely any

SHRINE INSIDE TENT

food. I cannot say that I experienced any very severe physical pain. This was due, I think, to the fact that my exhaustion brought on fever. I had, nevertheless, a peculiar feeling in my head, as if my intellect, never too bright, had now been altogether dulled. My hearing, too, became less acute; and I felt my strength slowly dying down like the flame of a lamp with no more oil in it. The nervous excitement and strain alone kept me alive, and I went on walking mechanically.

CHAPTER LXXII

Eighty black tents—Starved—Kindly natives—Presents—Ando and his promises—A friendly Lama—A low pass—My plans.

WE reached an encampment of some eighty black tents and a mud guard-house. We were positively in a starved condition and it was utterly impossible to proceed farther, owing to the wretched condition of my two men. They begged to be given ponies to ride, for their feet were so sore that, notwithstanding their anxiety to follow me, they could not.

The natives received us very kindly, and, on my applying for them, consented to sell me ponies, clothes and provisions. We encamped about two miles beyond the settlement, and during the evening several persons visited my tent, bringing gifts of flour, butter and *tsamba*, accompanied by *Katas*, the veils of friendship. I made a point of invariably giving the Tibetans, in return for their gifts, silver money to an amount three or four times greater than the value of the articles they presented us with, and they professed to be very grateful for it. A man called Ando, who styled himself a Gourkha, but wore the garb of the Tibetans, came to visit us in our tent, and promised to bring for sale several ponies the next morning. He also undertook to sell me a sufficient quantity of food to enable us to reach Lhassa, and, to show his good faith, brought a portion of the supplies in the evening, and said he would let us have the remainder the next morning.

We next had a visit from a Lama, who appeared both civil and intelligent, and who presented us with some butter and *chura* (cheese). He had travelled in India, he told us, as far as Calcutta, and was on his way from Gartok to

MUD GUARD-HOUSE

Lhassa, where he expected to arrive in four or five days, having an excellent pony. Other Lamas and men who came to see us stated that they had come from Lhassa in that time, and I do not think that they can have been far wrong, as the whole distance from the Lippu Pass on the frontier (near Garbyang) to Lhassa can on horseback be covered in sixteen days.

The natives, as usual, showed great reticence in letting out

the name of the encampment, some calling it Toxem, others Taddju. North of us was a low pass in the hill range, and having already seen as much as I wanted of the Tibetans, it was my intention, if I succeeded in purchasing provisions and ponies, to cross over this pass and proceed towards the Sacred City, following a course on the northern side of the mountain range. Besides, the highway to Lhassa was getting so thickly populated that I thought it advisable to travel through less inhabited regions. I intended proceeding, dressed as a European, until within a few miles of Lhassa. Then I would leave my two men concealed in some secluded spot, and assuming a disguise, I would penetrate alone during the night into the city. This would have been easy enough, as Lhassa has no gates, and only a ruined wall round it.

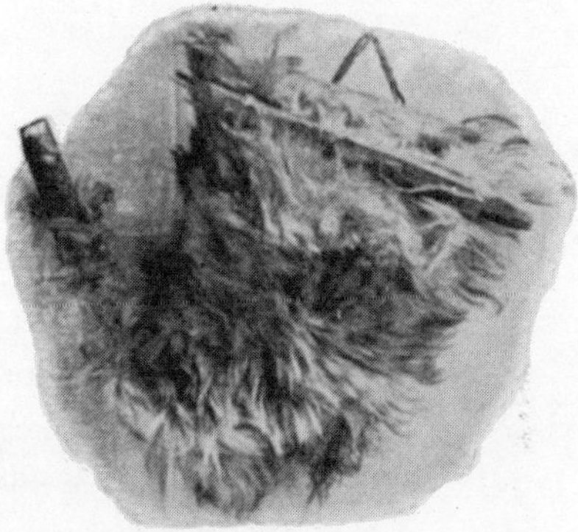

TIBETAN BELLOWS

I succeeded in purchasing some clothing and boots from the Tibetans, and the pigtail that I needed to make me pass for a Tibetan I intended to make myself, out of the silky hair of my yaks. To avoid betraying myself by my inability to speak Tibetan fluently, I thought of pretending to be deaf and dumb.

A good meal brought hope and high spirits, and when I retired to sleep I saw myself already inside the sacred walls.

CHAPTER LXXIII

Strange noises—Ando the traitor—Purchasing provisions and ponies—A handsome pony—Decoyed away from my tent and rifles—Pounced upon—The fight—A prisoner.

DURING the night I was aroused several times by noises, and I went out of my tent to look for the disturbers, but failed to discover any one. This had become my nightly experience, and I attached very little importance to these sounds.

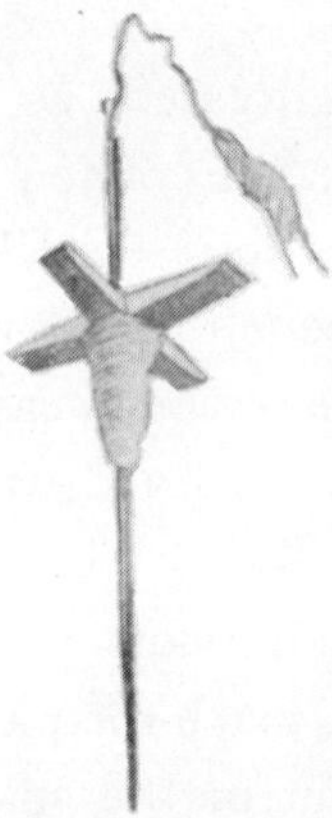

A DISTAFF

In the morning, Ando and two or three Tibetans came to sell us provisions and ponies, and, while my two servants and I were engaged in purchasing what we required, I saw a number of villagers coming up in groups. Some spun their wool, others carried bags of *tsamba* and flour, while others still arrived leading a number of fine ponies. Having purchased provisions to last us a couple of months, we now began the selection of mounts, and naturally my servants and myself were overjoyed at our unexpected piece of luck in finding ourselves, after untold sufferings and privations of all kinds, confronted with abundance of everything we could possibly desire. The demeanour of the Tibetans was so

PURCHASING PONIES

friendly, and they seemed so guileless, that I never thought of suspecting them. Chanden Sing and Mansing, who at bottom were sportsmen of the very first order, delighted at the prospect of getting animals, rode first one pony and then another to suit themselves; and Chanden Sing, having selected a handsome beast for his own use, called me to try it and examine it before paying over the purchase-money. Unsuspecting of foul play, and also because it would not be convenient to try the various lively ponies with my rifle slung over my shoulder, I walked unarmed to the spot, about a hundred yards away from my tent, where the restless animal was being held for my inspection. The natives followed behind me, but such a thing being common in any country when one buys a horse in public, I thought nothing of it. As I stood with my hands behind my back, I well recollect the expression of delight on Chanden Sing's face when I approved of his choice, and, as is generally the case on such occasions, the crowd behind in a chorus expressed their gratuitous opinion on the superiority of the steed selected. I had just stooped to look at the pony's fore-legs, when I was suddenly seized from behind by several persons, who grabbed me by the neck, wrists, and legs, and threw

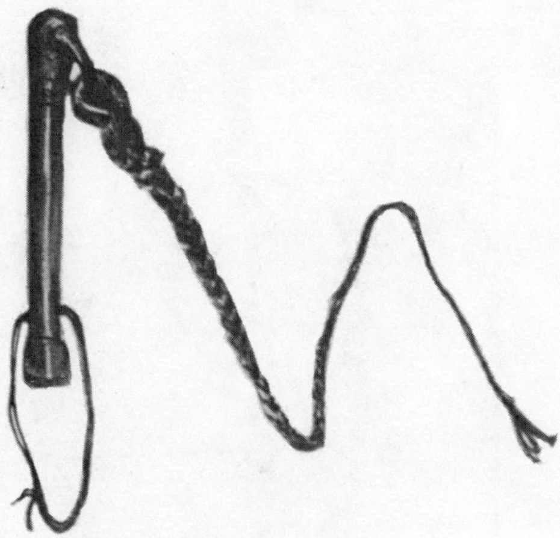

ROPE RIDING-WHIP

me down on my face. I struggled and fought until I shook off some of my assailants and regained my feet; but others rushed up, and I was surrounded by some thirty men, who attacked me from every side, and clinging to me with all their might succeeded in grabbing my arms, legs and head. Weak as I was, they knocked me down three more times, and three more times I regained my feet. I fought to the bitter end with my fists, feet, head and teeth each time that I got one hand or leg free from their clutches, hitting right and left at any part where I could disable my opponents. Their timidity,

I WAS A PRISONER

even when in such overwhelming numbers, was indeed beyond description ; and it was entirely due to it, and not to my strength (for I had hardly any), that I was able to hold my own against them for some twenty minutes. My clothes were torn to bits in the fight. Long ropes were thrown at me from every side, and I became so entangled in them that my movements were impeded. One rope which they flung and successfully twisted round my neck completed their victory. They pulled hard at it from the two ends, and while I panted and gasped with the exertion of fighting, they tugged and tugged to strangle me, till I felt as if my eyes would shoot out of their sockets. I was suffocating. My sight became dim, and I was in their power. Dragged down to the ground, they stamped, and kicked, and trampled upon me with their heavy nailed boots, until I was stunned. Then they tied my wrists tightly behind my back; they bound my elbows, my chest, my neck and my ankles. I was a prisoner !

CHAPTER LXXIV

Chanden Sing's plucky resistance — Mansing secured — A signal — A treacherous Lama — Confiscation of baggage — Watches, compasses and aneroids—Fear and avidity—The air-cushion—Dragged into the encampment.

THEY lifted me and made me stand up. The brave Chanden Sing had been struggling with all his might against fifteen or twenty foes, and had disabled several of them. He had been pounced upon at the same moment as I was, and had fought gallantly until, like myself, he had been entangled, thrown down and secured by ropes. During my struggle, I heard him call out repeatedly: "*Banduk, banduk, Mansing; jaldi, banduk!*" ("Rifle, rifle, Mansing; quick, my rifle!") but, alas, poor Mansing the leper, the weak and jaded coolie, had been sprung upon by four powerful Tibetans, who held him pinned to the ground as if he had been the fiercest of bandits. Mansing was a philosopher. He had saved himself the trouble of even offering any resistance; but he too,

EARRING WORN BY HIGH OFFICIALS

was ill-treated, beaten and tightly bound. At the beginning of the fight a shrill whistle had brought up four hundred* armed soldiers who had lain in ambush round us, concealed behind the innumerable sandhills and in the depressions in the ground. They took up a position round us and covered us with their matchlocks.

All was now over, and, bound like a dangerous criminal, I looked round to see what had become of my men. When I realised that it took the Tibetans five hundred men† all counted to arrest a starved Englishman and his two half-dying servants, and that, even then, they dared not do it openly, but had to resort to abject treachery; when I found that these soldiers were picked troops from Lhassa and Sigatz (Shigatze), despatched on purpose to arrest our progress and capture us, I could not restrain a smile of contempt for those into whose hands we had at last fallen.

My blood boiled when, upon the order of the Lama, who the previous night had professed to be our friend, several men advanced and searched our pockets. They rifled us of everything we possessed, and began overhauling our baggage. The watches and chronometer were looked upon with suspicion, their ticking causing anxiety and curiosity. They were passed round and round and mercilessly thrown about from one person to the other, until they stopped. They were then pronounced "dead." The compasses and aneroids, which they could not distinguish from watches, were soon thrown aside, as "they had no life in them," but great caution was displayed in touching our rifles, which were lying on our bedding when the tent had been torn down.

* The Lamas stated afterwards that this was the number.

† Counting Lamas, villagers and soldiers.

Great fears were entertained lest they should go off by themselves; and it was only on my assurance (which made our captors ten times more cautious) that they were not loaded, that at last they took them and registered them in the catalogue of our confiscated property. I had upon me a gold ring that my mother had given me when I was a child. I asked permission to retain it, and with their superstitious nature they immediately thought that it had occult powers, like the wands one reads of in fairy tales.

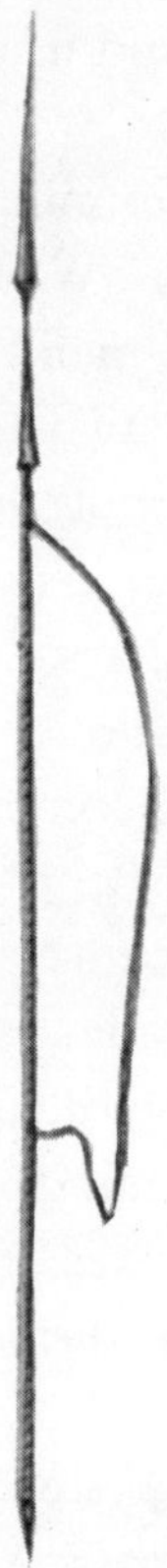

A SPEAR

A man called Nerba, who later on played an important part in our sufferings, was entrusted with it, and warned never to let me see it again. As we three prisoners sat bound and held down by guards it was heartbreaking to see the Lamas and officers handle all our things so roughly as to spoil nearly all they touched; but particularly disgusting was their avidity when, in searching the pockets of the coat I wore daily, and which I had not put on that morning, they found a quantity of silver coins, some eight hundred rupees in all. Officers, Lamas and soldiers made a grab for the money, and when order was re-established, only a few coins remained where the sum had been laid down. Other moneys which they found in one of our loads met with a similar fate. Among the things arousing greatest curiosity was an india-rubber pillow fully blown out. The soft, smooth texture of the indiarubber seemed to catch their fancy, and one after the other they rubbed their cheeks on the cushion, exclaiming

DRAGGED INTO THE SETTLEMENT

at the pleasant sensation it gave them. However, in playing with the brass screw by which the cushion was inflated, they gave it a turn, and the imprisoned air found its way out with a hissing noise. This created quite a panic among the Tibetans, and many were the conjectures of their superstitious minds as to the meaning of the strange contrivance. They regarded it as an evil omen, and naturally I took

TIBETANS OVERHAULING OUR BAGGAGE

advantage of any small incident of this kind to work judiciously on their superstitions and frighten them as much as I could.

The Tibetans, having examined all except my water-tight cases of instruments, photographic plates and sketches, seemed so upset at one or two things that happened, and at some remarks I made, that they hurriedly sealed up all my property in bags and blankets, and ordered the things to be placed on yaks and brought into the guard-house of the settlement. This done, they tied the end of the ropes that bound our necks to the pommels of their saddles, and, having loosed our feet, they sprang on their ponies and rode off, with shouts, hisses and cries of victory, firing their matchlocks in the air, and dragging us prisoners into the settlement.

CHAPTER LXXV

A warning to my men—Calm and coolness—The Pombo's tent—Chanden Sing cross-examined and flogged.

ON reaching the settlement, my last words to my men before we were separated were, "No matter what they do to you, do not let them see that you suffer," and they promised to obey me. We were then conveyed to different tents. I was dragged to one of the larger tents, inside and outside of which soldiers were placed on guard. Those near me were at first sulky, and rough in their manner and speech, but I always made a point of answering them in as collected and polite a fashion as I could. I had on many previous occasions found that nothing carries one further in dealings with Asiatics than to keep calm and cool, and I saw in a moment that, if we were ever to get out of our present scrape, it would be by maintaining a perfectly impassive demeanour in face of anything that might take place. Whether I acted my part well it is not for me to say, but the reader can satisfy himself on that point by perusing the Government inquiry and report made by Mr. J. Larkin, and given in the Appendix to this book.

The tent being kept closed, I was unable to discover what happened outside, but from the noises I heard of people rushing hither and thither, and of shouted orders, besides the continuous tinkling of the soldiers' horse-bells as they galloped past the tent, I concluded that the place must be in a state of turmoil. I had been some three hours in the tent, when a soldier entered and ordered me out.

"They are going to cut off his head," said he to his

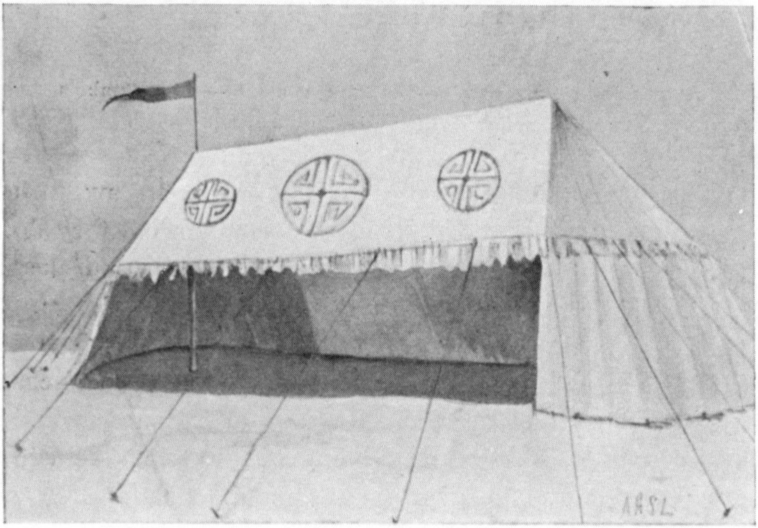

THE POMBO'S TENT

comrades; and, turning round to me, he made a significant gesture with his hand across his neck.

"*Nikutza*" ("All right"), said I drily.

It must not be forgotten that, when a Tibetan himself hears words of this import, he usually goes down on his knees and implores to be spared, with tears, and sobs, and prayers in profusion. So it is not surprising that the Tibetans were somewhat astonished at my answer, and seemed puzzled as to what to make of it. Anyhow, the first ardour of the messenger was sensibly cooled down, and I was led out with more reluctance than firmness.

During the time I had been shut up, a huge white tent with blue ornaments had been pitched in front of the mud-house, and round it were hundreds of soldiers and villagers—a most picturesque sight.

As I was led nearer, I perceived that the front of the tent was wide open, and inside stood a great number of red Lamas, with shaven heads, in their long woollen tunics. The soldiers stopped me when I was about twenty yards from the tent. Additional ropes were added to those already cutting into my wrists, elbows and chest, and the others made tighter. I perceived Chanden Sing led forward, and then, instead of taking me before the Lamas, they pushed me to the rear of the solitary mud-house to preclude my witnessing the scene that followed. I heard Chanden Sing being interrogated in a loud angry tone of voice, and accused of having been my guide. Next I heard wild shouts from the crowd, then a dead silence. A few instants later I distinguished the snapping noise of a lash, followed by hoarse moans from my poor bearer, to whom they were evidently applying it.

I counted the strokes, the sickening noise of which is still well impressed on my memory, as they regularly and steadily fell one after the other to twenty, to thirty, forty, and fifty. Then there was a pause.

CHAPTER LXXVI

Led before the tribunal—The Pombo—Classical Tibetan beyond me—Chanden Sing lashed—The Lamas puzzled—A sudden change in the Pombo's attitude.

A NUMBER of soldiers now came for me, and I was first led, then pushed violently before the tribunal.

On a high seat in the centre of the tent sat a man wearing ample trousers of gaudy yellow and a short yellow coat with flowing sleeves. On his head he had a huge four-pointed hat gilt all over, and with three great eyes painted on it. He was young-looking, and his head was clean shaven, as he was a Lama of the highest order, a Grand Lama and a *Pombo*, or Governor of the province, with powers equivalent to those of a feudal king. On his right stood a stout and powerful red Lama who held a huge double-handed sword, and behind, and at the sides, were a number of other Lamas, officers and soldiers. As I stood silent, and with my head held high before him, two or three Lamas rushed at me and ordered me to kneel. They tried to compel me to do so, by forcing me on my knees, but I succeeded in maintaining an upright posture.

The Pombo, who was furious at my declining to kneel before him, addressed me in words that sounded violent; but, as he spoke classical Tibetan, and I only the colloquial

CHANDEN SING BEING LASHED

language, I could not understand a word of what he said, and I meekly asked him not to use such fine words, as they were unintelligible to me.

The great man was taken aback at this unheard-of request; and, with a frown on his face, he pointed to me to look to my left. The soldiers and Lamas drew aside, and I beheld Chanden Sing lying flat on his face, stripped from the waist downwards, in front of a row of Lamas and military men. Two powerful Lamas, one on each side of him, began again to castigate him with knotted leather thongs weighted with lead, laying on their strokes with vigorous arms from his waist to his feet. He was bleeding all over. Each time that a lash fell on his wounded skin it felt as if a dagger had been stuck into my chest; but I knew Orientals too well to show any pity for the man, as this would have only involved a more severe punishment for him. So I looked on at his torture as one would

THE POMBO

upon a thing of everyday occurrence. The Lamas nearer to me shook their fists under my nose, and explained that my turn would come next, whereupon I smiled and repeated the usual "*Nikutza, nikutza*" ("Very good, very good").

The Pombo and his officers were at a loss what to make of me, as I could plainly see by their faces; so that the more I perceived how well my plan was answering, the more courage I screwed up to play my part to the best of my ability.

The Pombo, an effeminate, juvenile, handsome person, almost hysterical in manner, and likely to make a splendid subject for hypnotic experiments (I had reason to think, indeed, that he had already often been under mesmeric influence), remained with his eyes fixed upon mine as if in a trance for certainly over two minutes.

There was a wonderful and sudden change in the man, and his voice, arrogant and angry a few moments before, was now soft and apparently kindly. The Lamas around him were evidently concerned at seeing their lord and master transformed from a foaming fury to the quietest of lambs; so they seized me and brought me out of his sight to the spot where Chanden Sing was being chastised. Here again I could not be compelled to kneel, so at last I was allowed to squat down before the Pombo's officers.

CHAPTER LXXVII

My note-books and maps—What the Lamas wanted me to say—My refusal—Anger and threats—Ando, the traitor—Chanden Sing's heroism—A scene of cruelty—Rain.

THE two Lamas, leaving Chanden Sing, produced my note-books and maps, and proceeded to interrogate me closely, saying that, if I spoke the truth, I should be spared, otherwise I should be flogged and then beheaded.

I answered that I would speak the truth, whether they punished me or not.

A SOLDIER

One of the Lamas, a great big brute, who was dressed up in a gaudy red silk coat, with gold embroidery at the collar, and who had taken part in the flogging of Chanden Sing, told me I must say "that my servant had shown me the road across Tibet, and that he had done the maps and sketches." If I would say this, they were willing to release me and have me conveyed back to the frontier, promising to do me no further harm. They would cut my servant's head off, that was all, but no personal injury should be inflicted on me.

SOLDIER WITH PIGTAIL WOUND ROUND HIS HEAD

I explained clearly to the Lamas that I alone was responsible for the maps and sketches, and for finding my way so far inland. I repeated several times, slowly and distinctly, that my servant was innocent, and that therefore there was no reason to punish him. He had only obeyed my orders in following me to Tibet, and I alone, not my two servants, was to be punished if anybody was punishable.

The Lamas were angry at this, and one of them struck me violently on the head with the butt-end of his riding-crop.

I pretended not to notice it, though it made my scalp ache and smart.

"Then we shall beat you and your man until you say what we want," the Lama exclaimed angrily.

"You can beat us if you like," I replied with assurance, "but if you punish us unjustly it will go against yourselves. You can tear our skin off, and you can make us bleed to death, but you cannot make us feel pain."

AN OFFICER

Ando, the traitor, who spoke Hindustani fluently, acted as interpreter whenever there was a hitch in our Tibetan conversation, and with what I knew of the language, and with this man's help, everything was explained to the Tibetans as clearly as possible. Notwithstanding this, they continued mercilessly to lash my poor servant, who, in his agony, was biting the ground as each blow fell on him and tore away patches of skin and flesh. Chanden Sing behaved heroically. Not a word of complaint, nor a prayer for mercy, came from his lips. He said that he had spoken the truth and had nothing more to say. Watched intently by all the Lamas and soldiers, I sat with affected stoicism before this scene of cruelty, until, angry at my phlegm, order was given to the soldiers that I should be dragged away. Again they led me behind the mud-house, from where I could distinctly hear the angry cries of the Lamas cross-examining Chanden Sing, and those dreadful sounds of the lash still being administered.

It began to rain heavily, and this was a bit of luck for us, for in Tibet, as in China, a shower has a great effect upon the people, and even massacres have been known to be put a stop to until the rain should cease.

Such was the case that day. The moment the first drops fell, the soldiers and Lamas rushed here, there, and everywhere inside the tents, and I was hastily dragged to the most distant tent of the settlement, which became packed with the guards into whose charge I had been given.

CHAPTER LXXVIII

A high military officer—A likely friend—A soldier and not a Lama—His sympathy—Facts about the Tibetan army.

An officer of high rank was sitting cross-legged at the farther end of the tent. He wore a handsome dark red gown trimmed with gold and leopard skin, and was shod with tall black and red leather boots of Chinese shape. A beautiful sword with solid silver sheath inlaid with large pieces of coral and malachite was passed through his belt.

PURSE

This man, apparently between fifty and sixty years of age, had an intelligent, refined, honest, good-natured face; and somehow or other I felt from the very first moment I saw him that he would be a friend. And, indeed, whereas the soldiers and Lamas treated me with brutality and took every mean advantage that they could, this officer was alone in showing some deference to me and some appreciation of my behaviour. He made room by his side and signed that I might sit there.

FLINT AND STEEL

SNUFF-BOX

"I am a soldier," said he in a dignified tone, "not a Lama. I have come from Lhassa with my men to arrest you, and you are now our prisoner. But you have shown no fear, and I respect you."

So saying, he inclined his head and laid his forehead touching mine, and pulled out his tongue. Then he made a gesture signifying that, though he wished to, he could not then say more, owing to the presence of the soldiers.

Later on we entered into a most amicable conversation, in the course of which he said that he was a Rupun (a grade below that of general). I tried to explain to him all about English soldiers and weapons, and he displayed the keenest interest in all I told him. In return he gave me interesting information about the soldiers of Tibet. Every man in Tibet is considered a soldier in time of war or when required to do duty, but for the regular army all lads that are strong and healthy can enlist from the age of seventeen, those deformed or weakly being rejected as unfit for service. Good horsemanship is one of the qualities most appreciated in the Tibetan soldier, and, after that, unbounded obedience. The Rupun swore by the Tibetan matchlocks, which he believed to be the most serviceable weapons on earth; for, according to him, as long as you had powder enough, you could use anything as a missile. Pebbles, earth, or nails did as good work as any lead bullet.

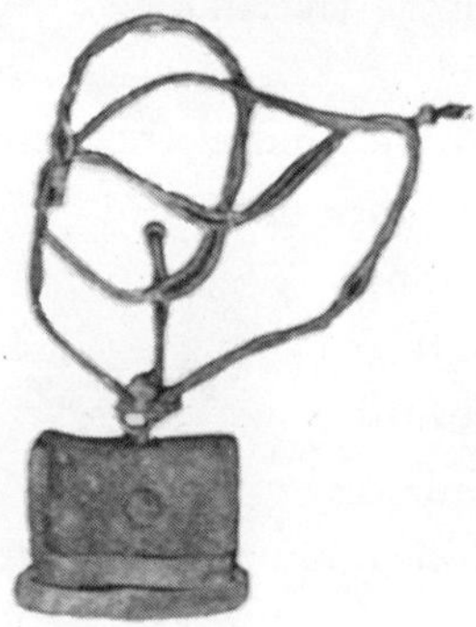

FLINT-AND-STEEL POUCH

He told me that large quantities of these weapons were manufactured at Lhassa and Sigatz (Shigatze), and he stated that the majority of Tibetan men outside the towns possess one. Gunpowder was also made with saltpetre and sulphur found in the country.

The Rupun, seeing how quick I was at picking up words, took a special delight in teaching me, as one would a child, the names of the several grades in the Tibetan army. The *Tchu-pun** was the lowest grade, and only had ten men

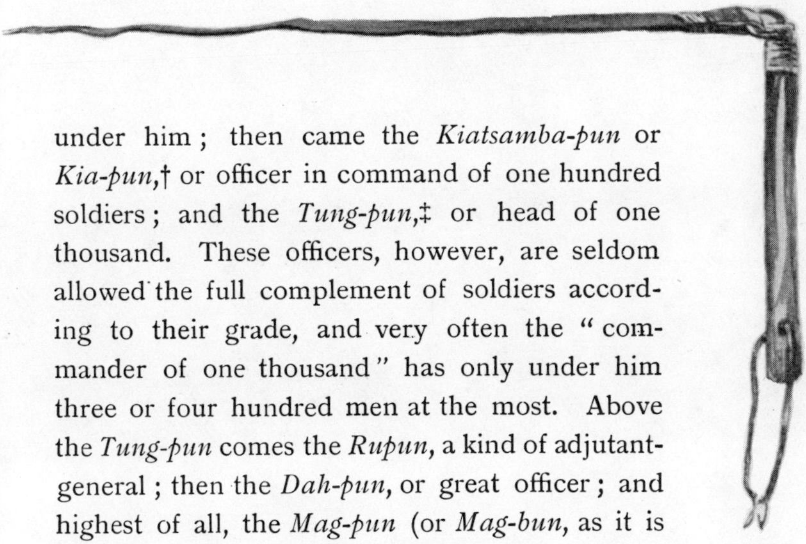

LEATHER HORSE-WHIP

under him; then came the *Kiatsamba-pun* or *Kia-pun*,† or officer in command of one hundred soldiers; and the *Tung-pun*,‡ or head of one thousand. These officers, however, are seldom allowed the full complement of soldiers according to their grade, and very often the "commander of one thousand" has only under him three or four hundred men at the most. Above the *Tung-pun* comes the *Rupun*, a kind of adjutant-general; then the *Dah-pun*, or great officer; and highest of all, the *Mag-pun* (or *Mag-bun*, as it is usually pronounced), the general in chief.

The acquaintance of one of these generals we had already made at Gyanema. Though my informant said that officers are elected for their bravery in time of war and for their strength and aptitude in the saddle and with their weapons, I knew well enough that such was not the case. The posts are mainly given to whoever can afford to pay most for them, and to men

* *Tchu*, ten, *pun*, officer, or officer of ten men.

† *Kiatsamba* or *Kia* = one hundred.

‡ *Tung* = one thousand.

of families under special protection of the Lamas. In many cases they are actually sold by auction.

The method described by the Rupun was nevertheless what is popularly believed by the masses of Tibet to be the way in which military officers are chosen.

CHAPTER LXXIX

Sarcasm appreciated—Kindness—A change for the worse—
The place for an Englishman—Vermin—A Tibetan prayer.

THE Rupun possessed a good deal of dry humour, and I told him how fast the Tibetan soldiers had run away on previous occasions when I had met them and had my rifle by me. But he was quite equal to the situation and exclaimed: "Yes, I know that they ran, but it was not through fear. It was because they did not wish to hurt you." Upon which I answered that, if that were the case, they need not have run so fast.

The Rupun seemed amused and laughed at my sarcasm. He patted me on the back and said I was right. He professed to be grieved to see me tied up, and said he had received strict orders not to give me food or unloose my bonds.

The soldiers, who had been listening open-mouthed to the affable and friendly conversation between the Rupun and myself, a practice not common in Tibet between captor and prisoner, followed their chief's example, and from being harsh and rough, turned quite kindly and respectful. They placed a cushion under me and tried to make me as comfortable as they could in the circumstances.

Towards the evening, however, the Rupun was summoned

before the Pombo, and the guard was relieved by a fresh lot of men. This was a change for the worse. Their manner was extremely rough, and they dragged me away from the dignified seat I had occupied in the place of honour in the tent, and knocked me violently down on a heap of dung which they used for fuel.

CHARM-BOX

"That is the place for *plenkis!*" shouted one of the men, "not in the best part of the tent."

They pounced upon me roughly, and though I made no resistance whatever, they again tied my feet together, and another rope was fastened round my knees. The ends of these ropes were left long, and each was given in charge of a soldier.

No part of a Tibetan tent is over clean, but the spot where I was to rest for the night was the dirtiest. Bound so tightly that the ropes cut channels in my flesh, it was out of the question to sleep; but tenfold worse than this was the disgusting fact that I soon got covered with vermin, which swarmed in the tent. From this time till the end of my captivity, or twenty-five days later, I suffered unspeakable tortures from this pest. The guards, with their swords drawn, were all round me inside the tent, and others were posted outside.

The night was full of strange events. Shouts could be heard at intervals from a distance outside, and some one of the guard in the tent answered them. They were to keep the men awake and make sure that I was still there. One of the soldiers in the tent revolved his prayer-wheel, muttering the following prayer so often that I learned it by heart:

Sangbo, sangbo
Yabni namla dupchenché
Yumni sala lockchendir
Lashin shukpi Kani san
Pashin tagpe Kani san
Yulo parba palui san
Tumlo parba wumboi san
Lassan lussan tamjeh san
Chedan Kordan jindan san
Takpeh yeiki polloh san
Takpeh yonki molloh san
Tzurzu Kaghi Tablah san
Arah, Banza, Nattittì
Jehmi jangla changzalu.

The almost literal translation of the words is this:

Oh, my God, I confess
That my father has gone to heaven,
But my mother is at present alive (*lit.* in the house).
First my mother sinned
And you took all men to heaven,
Then my mother and father sinned and I will go to heaven.
If all other men and I sin, and we withdraw our sins,
We are all liable to sin and the wumboo wood absolves (*lit.* washes all) from all sins.
On the North-west (Lassan) and South-east (Lussan) are the two ways to heaven.
I read the holy book and purify myself,
My arm-bone* is the sacred bone (*lit.* God's bone).

* The Tibetans believe that in men the left, and in women the right, arm belongs to God. They regard it as sacred, because with this arm

And the sign of manhood my left arm.
Oh, my God, who art above my head,
And at the sacred Kujernath, Banzah and Nattittí,
I pray every day for health and wealth (silver and gold).

food is conveyed to the mouth, thus giving life to the body, and also because it is with the arms that one can defend oneself against one's enemies. The bone of the nose is also regarded as sacred.

CHAPTER LXXX

The Rupun as a friend—Treated with respect and deference—Fed by the Rupun and soldiers—Improving my knowledge of Tibetan.

In the middle of the night the Rupun returned. I noticed he seemed very much upset. He sat by my side, and by the light of the flickering fire and a wick burning in a brass bowl filled with butter, I could see in his face an expression of great anxiety. I felt, by the compassionate way in which he looked at me, that he had grave news to give me. I was not mistaken. He moved me from the pestilent place where I had been thrown down helpless by the soldiers, and laid me in a more comfortable and cleaner part of the tent. Then he ordered a soldier to bring me a blanket. Next, to my astonishment, he became very severe, and said he must examine my bonds. He turned quite angry, scolding the soldiers for leaving me so insecurely tied, and proceeded to make the knots firmer, a thing which I felt was impossible. Though he pretended to use all his strength in doing this, I found, much to my amazement, that my bonds were really becoming loosened. He then quickly covered me up with the heavy blanket.

PUKU, OR WOODEN CUP

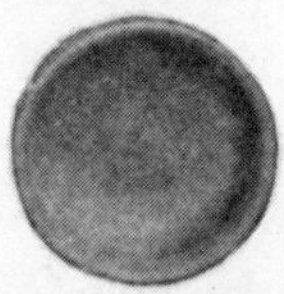

PUKU, OR WOODEN CUP

The soldiers were at the other end of the large tent, and seemed occupied with a loud argument over some paltry matter. The Rupun, stooping low, and making pretence to tuck me in the blanket, whispered :

"Your head is to be cut off to-morrow. Escape to-night. There are no soldiers outside."

The good man was actually preparing everything for my flight. He put out the light, and came to sleep by my side. It would have been comparatively easy, when all the men had fallen asleep, to slip from under the tent and steal away. I had got my hands easily out of the ropes, and should have had no difficulty in undoing all my other bonds; but the thought that I should be leaving my two men at the mercy of the Tibetans prevented my carrying the escape into effect. The Rupun, having risen to see that the guard were asleep, lay down again close to me and murmured :

"*Nelon, nelon ; paladŏ*" ("They are asleep ; go").

Well meant and tempting as the offer was, I told him I must stay with my men.

Having my hands free, I managed to sleep a little during the night; and when the morning came I slipped my hands again inside the ropes.

The Rupun, who seemed much disappointed, tied the ropes round my wrists firmly again, and, though he appeared rather vexed at my not having availed myself of the chance of flight he had given me, he treated me with ever-increasing respect and deference. He even produced his *puku* (wooden bowl), which he filled with steaming tea from the *raksang*,* and lifted it up to my mouth for me to drink.

* *Raksang*, a vessel in which tea mixed with butter and salt is kept boiling over the fire.

On perceiving how thirsty and hungry I was, not only did this good man refill the cup time after time until my thirst was quenched, but he mixed with it *tsamba*, and lumps of butter, which he then stuffed into my mouth with his finger.

It was really touching to see how, moved to kindness, the soldiers imitated his example, and, one after the other, produced handfuls of *tsamba* and *chura*, and deposited them in my mouth. Their hands, it is true, were not over clean, but on such occasions it does not do to be too particular, and I was so hungry that the food they gave me seemed delicious. I had been for two nights and one day without food, and, what with the exertion of the fight and my various exciting experiences, my appetite was very keen.

This great politeness, however, and the sympathy with which not only the Rupun, but even the soldiers treated me now, made me suspect that my end was indeed near. I was grieved not to be able to obtain news of Chanden Sing and Mansing; and the soldiers' reticence in answering questions regarding them made me fear that something awful had happened. Nevertheless, though my gaolers were friendly, I did not betray any anxiety, but pretended to take all that came as a matter of course. I spent the first portion of the day in a lively conversation with the soldiers, partly to divert my thoughts and partly to improve my knowledge of Tibetan.

CHAPTER LXXXI

A bearer of bad news—Marched off to the mud-house—Mansing—Insults and humiliations——Iron handcuffs instead of ropes—The Rupun's sympathy—No more hope—In the hands of the mob.

EARLY in the afternoon a soldier entered the tent, and striking me on the shoulder with his heavy hand, shouted :

"*Ohe!*" (This is a Tibetan exclamation always used by the rougher classes when beginning a conversation. It corresponds to "Look here.")

"*Ohe!*" repeated he; "before the sun goes down you will be flogged, both your legs will be broken,* they will burn out your eyes, and then they will cut off your head!"

The man, who seemed quite in earnest, accompanied each sentence with an appropriate gesture illustrating his words. I laughed at him and affected to treat the whole thing as a joke, partly because I thought this was the best way to frighten them and prevent them from using violence, and partly because the programme thus laid before me seemed so extensive that I thought it could only be intended to intimidate me.

However, the words of the soldier cast a gloom over my

* A form of torture in which, after placing the legs upon two parallel logs of wood, a heavy blow is given with a mallet, fracturing both legs.

friendly guard in the tent, and when I tried to cheer them up, they answered bluntly that I would not laugh for very long. Something was certainly happening, for the men rushed in and out of the tent, and whispered among themselves. When I spoke to them they would answer no more, and on my insisting, they made signs that their lips must from now be closed.

About half an hour later, another person rushed into the tent in a great state of excitement, and signalled to my guards to lead me out. This they did, after making my bonds tighter than ever, and placing extra ropes round my chest and arms. In this fashion I was marched off to the mud-house and led into one of the rooms. A large number of soldiers and villagers assembled outside, and after we had waited some time, Mansing, tightly bound, was brought into the same room. My pleasure at seeing my man again was so great, that I forgot all about what was happening, and paid no attention to the insults of the mob

SOLDIER LAYING BEFORE ME THE PROGRAMME OF TORTURES

peeping through the door. After a while a Lama came in with a smiling face and said he had good news to give me.

"We have ponies here," he said, "and we are going to take you back to the frontier, but the Pombo wishes to see you first to-day. Do not make any resistance. Let us exchange the ropes round your wrists for these iron handcuffs."

Here he produced a heavy pair of them, which he had kept concealed under his coat.

MY HANDCUFFS

"You will not wear them for more than a few moments while we are leading you to his presence. Then you will be free. We swear to you by the Sun and Kunjuk-Sum that we will treat you kindly."

I promised not to resist, chiefly because I had no chance of doing so. For greater safety they tied my legs and placed a sliding knot round my neck; then I was carried out into the open, where a ring of soldiers with drawn swords stood round me. While I lay flat on my face on the ground, held down firmly, they unwound the ropes from around my wrists, and the iron fetters, joined by a heavy chain, were substituted for them. They took some time in fastening the clumsy padlock, after which, all being ready, they unbound my legs.

They made me stand up again, and knowing that I could not possibly get my hands free, they began to load me with insults and offensive terms, not directed to me as an individual, but as a *Plenki*, an Englishman. They spat upon me and threw mud at me. The Lamas behaved worse than any of the others, and the one who had sworn that I should be in no way ill-used if I would submit quietly to be handcuffed was the most prominent among my tormentors and the keenest in urging the crowd on to further brutality.

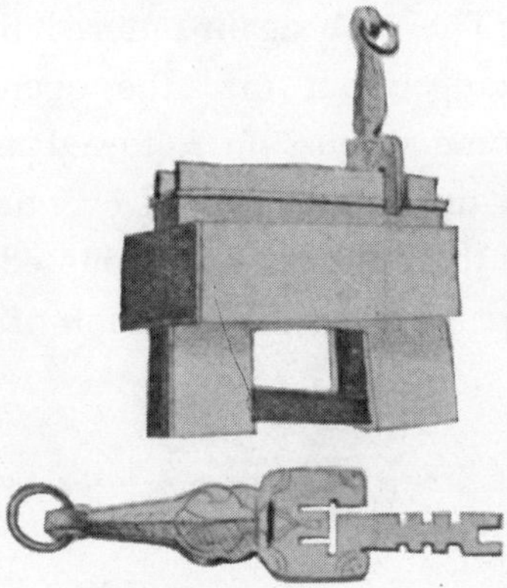

PADLOCK AND KEY

Suddenly the attention of the crowd was drawn to the approach of the Rupun with a number of soldiers and officers. He seemed depressed, and his face was of a ghastly yellowish tint. He kept his eyes fixed on the ground, and, speaking very low, ordered that I should again be conveyed inside the mud-house.

A few moments later he came in and closed the door after him, having first cleared the room of all the people who were in it. As I have mentioned before, Tibetan structures of this kind have a square aperture in the ceiling by which they are ventilated and lighted.

The Rupun laid his forehead upon mine in sign of compassion, and then sadly shook his head.

"There is no more hope," he whispered; "your head will be cut off to-night. The Lamas are bad and my heart is aching. You are like my brother, and I am grieved. . . ."

The good old man tried not to let me see his emotion, and made signs that he could stay no longer, lest he should be accused of being my friend.

The mob again entered the room, and I was once more dragged out into the open by the Lamas and soldiers. Some discussion followed as to who should keep the key of my handcuffs, and eventually it was handed over to one of the officers, who mounted his pony and rode away at a great rate in the direction of Lhassa.

CHAPTER LXXXII

A pitiful scene—A struggle to get to Chanden Sing—Brutally treated—A torturing saddle—Across country at a gallop—A spirited pony—Sand deposits and hills—Speculation—More horsemen coming towards us.

JUST then I heard the voice of my servant Chanden Sing calling to me in a weak agonised tone :

"*Hazur, Hazur, hum murgiaega !*" ("Sir, sir, I am dying !") and, turning my head in the direction from which these painful sounds came, I perceived my faithful bearer with his hands bound behind his back, dragging himself on his stomach towards the door of one of the other rooms of the mud-house. His poor face was hardly recognisable, it bore the traces of such awful suffering.

I could stand no more. Pushing my guards aside with my shoulders, I endeavoured to get to the poor wretch, and had nearly reached him when the soldiers who stood by sprang upon me, grappling me, and lifting me bodily off my feet. They threw me on the back of a pony.

Though I now feared the worst, I tried to encourage my brave servant by shouting to him that I was being taken to Taklakot, and that he would be brought after me the following day. He had exhausted his last atom of strength in creeping to the door. He was roughly seized, and brutally hurled back into the room of the mud-house, so that we could not exchange a word more. Mansing, the coolie, was placed, with his arms pinioned, on a bare-backed pony. The saddle of the pony I had been thrown upon is worthy of description. It was in reality the wooden frame of a very high-backed saddle, from the back of which some five or six sharp iron spikes stuck out horizontally. As I sat

"SIR, SIR, I AM DYING"

on this implement of torture, the spikes caught me in the small of my back.

My guard having been augmented by twenty or thirty mounted men with muskets and swords, we set off at a furious pace. A horseman riding in front of me led my pony by means of a cord, as my hands were manacled behind my back; and thus we travelled across country for miles.

But for those awful spikes in the saddle, the ride would

not have been so very bad, for the pony I rode was a fine spirited animal, and the country around was curious and interesting. We proceeded along an apparently endless succession of yellow sandhills, some of them as high as two or three hundred feet, others not more than twenty or thirty. The sand seemed to have been deposited more by wind than by water, though it is also possible that the whole

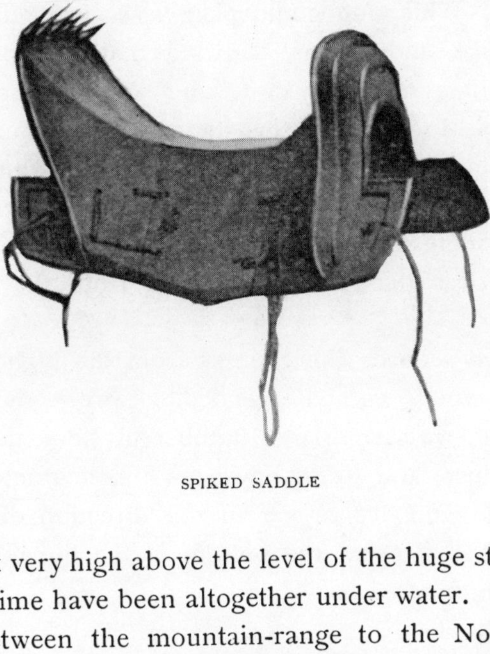

SPIKED SADDLE

basin, not very high above the level of the huge stream, may at some time have been altogether under water. The whole space between the mountain-range to the North of the Brahmaputra and the river itself was covered with these sand mounds, except in certain places where the soil was extremely marshy, and where our ponies sank in deep soft mud. We splashed across several rivulets and skirted a number of ponds. From the summit of a hill to which they led me, I could see that the hills were of much greater circumference and height near the river edge, becoming smaller and smaller as they approached the mountain-range to the North. Moreover, they increased in number and size the farther we went in an easterly direction.

The circumstances under which I was now travelling did not permit me to ascertain the quality of the sand, or make any accurate investigations as to where the sand came from, but a glance at the country all round made me feel sure that the sand had been conveyed there from the South. This one could plainly see from depressions and wavelike undulations, showing that it had travelled (roughly) in a northerly direction; and although, having been unable to ascertain this for a fact, I do not wish to be too certain with regard to the movements and sources of these sand deposits, I was pretty firmly convinced that the sand had been deposited there by the wind, which had carried it over the Himahlyan chain from the plains of India.

My guard scoured the country from the high point of vantage to which we had ascended. Away in the distance to the East, we saw a large number of horsemen raising clouds of dust; and, riding down the hill, the ponies sinking in the soft sand, we set off in the direction of the new comers, the surface at the bottom of the hill being more compact and harder.

CHAPTER LXXXIII

At an unpleasant pace — Drawing near the cavalcade—A picturesque sight—A shot fired at me—Terrible effects of the spikes along my spine—The rope breaks—An ill omen—A second shot misses me—Arrows—The end of my terrible ride.

WE travelled mile after mile at an unpleasant pace, until we arrived at a spot where, drawn up in a line, was the cavalcade we had seen from the summit of the hill. It was a beautiful sight as we approached it, though the pain which I was undergoing rather detracted from the pleasure I should otherwise have taken in the picturesque scene. There were about a hundred red Lamas in the centre, with bannermen whose heads were covered by peculiar flat fluffy hats, and the same number of soldiers and officers in their grey, red and black tunics; some two hundred horsemen in all.

The Pombo, in his yellow coat and trousers and his queer pointed hat, sat on a magnificent pony a little in front of the crowd of Lamas and soldiers.

Curiously enough, when close to this new crowd, the horseman who led my pony let go the rope, and the pony was lashed cruelly and left to its own devices. The soldiers of my guard reined up and drew aside. The pony dashed off in the direction of the Pombo and, as I passed close to him, a man named Nerba (private secretary of the Tokchim

Tarjum), knelt down, and, taking aim with his matchlock resting on its prop, deliberately fired a shot at me.

Although (I learned afterwards) this Nerba was one of the champion shots in the country, and the distance from the muzzle of his matchlock to me not more than four yards, the bullet missed me, whizzing past my left ear. Probably the speed at which my animal was proceeding saved me, as

NERBA FIRING AT ME

the marksman could not take a very steady aim; but my pony, startled at the sudden report of the matchlock at such close quarters, took fright, and began rearing and plunging. I managed to maintain my seat, though the spikes in the saddle were lacerating the lower part of my spine terribly.

Several horsemen now rode up and captured my pony, and preparations were made for another exciting number in the programme of my tortures. In their way these noble Lamas were of a sporting nature, but I swore to myself that,

THE RIDE ON A SPIKED SADDLE

no matter what they did to me, I would not give them the satisfaction of seeing that they were hurting me. Acting on this principle, I pretended not to feel the effect of the spikes tearing the flesh off my backbone; and when they led me before the Pombo to show him how covered with blood I was, I expressed satisfaction at riding such an excellent pony. This seemed to puzzle them.

A cord of yak's hair, about forty or fifty yards long, was now produced, the swivel attached to one end of it fastened to my handcuffs, and the other end held by a horseman. We set off again on our wild career, this time followed not only by the guard, but by the Pombo and all his men. Once or twice I could not help turning round to see what they were about. The cavalcade was a weird and picturesque sight, the riders with their many-coloured dresses, their matchlocks with red flags, their jewelled swords, their banners with long ribbons of all colours flying in the wind; all galloping furiously, shouting, yelling and hissing, amidst a deafening din of thousands of horse-bells.

In order to accelerate our speed, a horseman rode by my side lashing my pony to make it go its hardest. Meanwhile the horseman who held the cord did his utmost to pull me out of the saddle, no doubt in the hope of seeing me trampled to death by the cohort behind me. As I leaned my body forward so as to maintain my seat, and with my arms pulled violently backwards by the rope, the flesh was rubbed off my hands and knuckles by the chain of the handcuffs. In places the bone was exposed; and, of course, every tug brought me into forcible contact with the spikes and inflicted deeper wounds. The cord, though strong, eventually and unexpectedly gave way. The soldier who was pulling at the other end was clumsily unhorsed, and I myself was all but thrown by the unexpected jerk. This ludicrous incident at first provoked mirth among my escort, a mirth which their superstitious minds immediately turned into an ill omen.

When my pony was stopped, as well as the runaway steed of the dismounted cavalier, I took advantage of their fears, and assured them once more that whatever harm they tried to do me would go against themselves. However, the cord was retied with sundry strong knots, and, after an interruption of a few minutes, we resumed our breakneck gallop, I being again sent on in front.

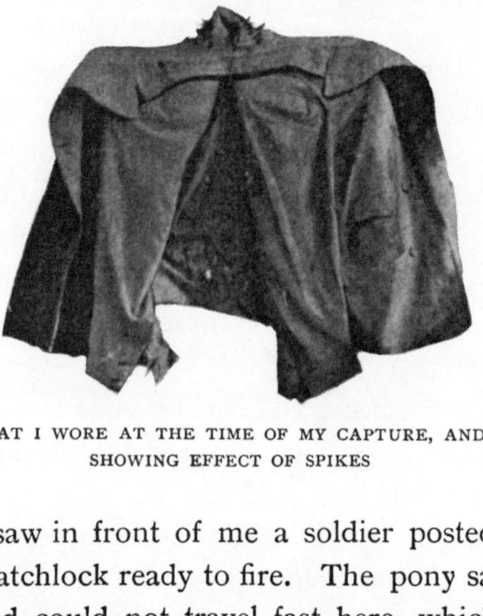
COAT I WORE AT THE TIME OF MY CAPTURE, AND SHOWING EFFECT OF SPIKES

Towards the end of our journey we had to go round the curve of a sandhill, the track between this and a large pond at its foot being very narrow. At this point I saw in front of me a soldier posted in ambush, with his matchlock ready to fire. The pony sank deep in the sand, and could not travel fast here, which I suppose was the reason why this spot had been selected. The man fired as I passed only a few paces from him; but, as luck would have it, this second attempt also left me untouched.

Getting clear of the soft sand, and finding harder ground, we resumed our headlong career. Several arrows were shot at me from behind; but, though some passed very near, not one struck me; and thus, after an interminable ride full of incident and excitement, we arrived, towards sunset, at our destination.

On the crown of a hill stood a fortress and large lamasery, and at its foot, in front of another large structure, the Pombo's gaudy tent had been pitched. The name of this place, as far as I could afterwards ascertain, was Namj Laccé Galshio or Gyatsho.

CHAPTER LXXXIV

Intense pain—Hustled to the execution-ground—Stretched and tied—Thirsting for blood—A parade of torturing appliances —The music—The *Taram*.

TWO or three men tore me roughly off the saddle. The pain in my spine caused by the spikes was intense. I asked for a moment's rest. My captors, however, refused, and, roughly thrusting me forward, said that I would be beheaded in an instant. All the people round jeered and made signs to me that my head would be cut off, and insults of all kinds were showered upon me by the crowd of Lamas and soldiers. I was hustled to the execution-ground, which lay to the left front of the tent. On the ground was a long log of wood in the shape of a prism. Upon the sharp edge of this I was made to stand, and several men held me by the body while four or five others, using their combined strength, stretched my legs as wide apart as they could go. Fixed in this painful position, the brutes securely tied me by my feet to the log of wood with cords of yak-hair. Several men were made to pull these cords, and they were so tight that they cut grooves into my skin and flesh in several places round my ankles and on my feet, many of the cuts* being as much as three inches long.

* Measured some weeks later by Dr. Wilson.

When I was thus firmly bound, one ruffian, the man Nerba, whom I have mentioned before as having fired a shot at me, came forward and seized me from behind by the hair of my head. My hair was long, as it had not been cut for over five months.

The spectacle before me was overwhelming. By the Pombo's tent stood in a row the most villainous brutes I

A DISPLAY OF VARIOUS INSTRUMENTS OF TORTURE

have ever set eyes upon. One, a powerful repulsive individual, held in his hand a great knobbed mallet used for fracturing bones; another carried a bow and arrows; a third held a big two-handed sword; while others made a display of various ghastly instruments of torture. The crowd, thirsting for my blood, formed up in a semicircle, leaving room for me to see the parade of the torture implements that awaited me; and, as my eyes roamed from one figure to the other, the several Lamas shook their various implements to show that they were preparing for action.

A group of three Lamas stood at the entrance of the tent. They were the musicians. One held a gigantic horn which, when blown, emitted hoarse, thundering sounds, and his companions had one a drum and the other cymbals. Another fellow some distance away continually sounded a

LAMA MUSICIANS

huge gong. From the moment I was made to dismount the deafening sounds of the diabolical trio echoed all through the valley, and added to the horror of the scene.

An iron bar with a handle of wood bound in red cloth was being made red hot in a brasier. The Pombo, who had again placed something in his mouth to produce artificial foaming at the lips, and so to show his temper, worked himself up into a frenzy. A Lama handed him the

Lithographed by F. A. Brockhaus, Leipzig (Germany).

THE HOT IRON TORTURE.

implement of torture (the *Taram*), now red hot, and the Pombo seized it by the handle.

"*Ngaghi kiu meh taxon!*" ("We will burn out your eyes!") cried a chorus of Lamas.

The Pombo strode up to me, brandishing the ghastly implement. I stared at him, but he kept his eyes away from me. He seemed reluctant, but the Lamas around him urged him on, lifting the man's arm towards me!

THE TARAM

"You have come to this country to see" (alluding to what I had stated the previous day, viz., that I was a traveller and pilgrim, and had only come to see the country). "This, then, is the punishment for you!" and with these dreadful words the Pombo raised his arm and placed the red-hot iron bar parallel to, and about an inch or two from, my eye-balls, and all but touching my nose.

Instinctively I kept my eyes tightly closed, but the heat was so intense that it seemed as if my eyes, the left one especially, were being desiccated and my nose scorched.

Though the time seemed interminable, I do not think that the heated bar was before my eyes actually longer than thirty seconds or so. Yet it was quite long enough, for, when I lifted my aching eyelids, I saw everything as in a red mist. My left eye was frightfully painful, and every few seconds it seemed as if something in front of it obscured its vision. With the right eye I could still see fairly well, except that everything, as I have said, looked red instead of its usual colour. The hot iron had been thrown down and was frizzling on the wet ground a few paces from me.

CHAPTER LXXXV

Bleeding all over—Insulted and spat upon—"Kill him!"—Urging on the executioner—Refusal to stoop—An unpleasant sword exercise—The execution suspended.

MY position as I stood with my legs wide apart, with my back, hands and legs bleeding, and seeing everything of a ghastly red tinge; amidst the deafening, maddening noise of gong, drum, cymbals and horn; insulted, spat upon by the crowd, and with Nerba holding me so tight by my hair as to tear handfuls of it from my scalp, was one in which I cannot wish even my bitterest enemies to find themselves. All I was able to do was to remain calm and composed and to watch with apparent unconcern the preparations for the next sufferings to be inflicted upon me.

"*Miumta nani sehko!*" ("Kill him with a rifle!") shouted a hoarse voice.

A matchlock was now being loaded by a soldier, and such was the quantity of gunpowder they placed in the barrel that I made sure whoever fired it would have his head blown off; so it was with a certain amount of satisfaction that I saw it handed over to the Pombo. That official placed the weapon against my forehead, with the muzzle pointing upwards. Then a soldier leaning down, applied fire to the fuse and eventually there was a loud report which gave my head a severe shock, and the overloaded matchlock flew clean out of the Pombo's hand, much to every body's surprise. I forced myself to laugh; and their confusion, added to the tantalising failure of every attempt they made to hurt me, drove the crowd to the highest pitch of fury.

A BANNERMAN

"*Ta kossaton, ta kossaton!*" ("Kill him, kill him!") exclaimed fierce voices all round me. "*Ngala mangbo shidak majidan!*" ("We cannot frighten him!") "*Ta kossaton, ta kossaton!*" ("Kill him, kill him!"), the whole valley resounding with their ferocious cries.

A huge two-handed sword was now handed to the Pombo, who drew it out of its sheath.

"Kill him, kill him!" shouted the mob once more, urging on the executioner, who, his superstitious nature not having overcome the ill-omened fact that the matchlock a moment before had jumped out of his hand (which he probably attributed to the doing of some supreme power and not to the over-charge), seemed quite reluctant to come forward.

I seized this moment to say that they might kill me if they wished, but that, if I died to-day, they would all die to-morrow—an undeniable fact, for we are all bound to die some day. This seemed to cool them for a moment, but the excitement in the crowd was too great, and at last they succeeded in working the Pombo up into a passion. His face became quite unrecognisable, such was his excitement, and he behaved like a madman.

At this point a Lama approached and slipped something into the mouth of the executioner, who again foamed at the lips. A Lama held his sword, while he turned up one sleeve of his coat to have his arms free, and the Lamas turned up the other for him. Then he strode towards me with slow, ponderous steps, swinging the shiny sharp blade from side to side before him, with his bare arms outstretched.

The man Nerba, who was still holding me by the hair, was told to make me bend my neck. I resisted with what little strength I had left, and, with the nervous courage of a doomed man, determined to keep my head erect and my forehead high. They might kill me, true enough, they might hack me to pieces if they chose, but never until I had lost my last atom of strength would these ruffians make me stoop before them. I would perish, but it should be looking down upon the Pombo and his countrymen.

The executioner, now close to me, held the sword with his nervous hands, lifting it high above his shoulder. He then brought it down to my neck, which he touched with the blade, to measure the distance, as it were, for a clean effective stroke. Then, drawing back a step, he

THE EXECUTIONER BROUGHT THE SWORD DOWN TO MY NECK

quickly raised the sword again and struck a blow at me with all his might. The sword passed disagreeably close to my neck, but did not touch me. I would not flinch, nor speak, and my demeanour seemed to impress him almost to the point of frightening him. He became reluctant to continue his diabolical performance; but the impatience and turbulence of the crowd were at their highest, and the Lamas nearer to him gesticulated like madmen and urged him on again.

As I write this, their wild shouts, their bloodthirsty countenances, are vividly brought before me. Apparently against his will, the executioner went through the same kind of performance on the other side of my head. This time the blade passed so near that the point cannot have been more than half an inch or so from my neck.

It seemed as if all would soon be over; yet, strange to say, even at this culminating moment I did not seriously realise that I should die. Why this was so I cannot say, because everything pointed towards my end being very near; but I had a feeling all the time that I should live to see the end of it all. I was very sorry, if my end were really at hand, as it seemed likely, that I should die without seeing my parents and friends again, and that they probably would never know how and where I had died. One is naturally at all times reluctant to leave a world in which one has barely had a dull moment, but, after all my wretched experiences, sufferings and excitement, I did not realise my peril so much as I should have done had I, for instance, been dragged from my comfortable London flat direct on to the execution-ground, instead of first having lived through the recent past.

Naturally the scene is one that I am not likely to forget, and I must say for the Tibetans that the whole affair was very picturesquely carried out. Even the ghastliest ceremonies may have their artistic side, and this particular one, performed with extra pomp and flourish, was really impressive.

It appears that the unpleasant sword exercise is sometimes gone through in Tibet previous to actually cutting off the head, so as to make the victim suffer more before the final blow is given. I was not aware of this at the time, and only learnt it some weeks after. It is usually at the third stroke that the victim is actually beheaded.

The Lamas were still clamouring for my head, but the Pombo made a firm stand this time, and declined to go on with the execution. They collected round him and seemed very angry; they shouted and yelled and gesticulated in the wildest fashion; and still the Pombo kept his eyes upon me in a half-respectful, half-frightened manner, and refused to move.

CHAPTER LXXXVI

Mansing arrives—A pretence of killing him—Our execution postponed—Fed by the Lamas

An excited consultation followed, during which, in the midst of this scene of barbarity, my coolie Mansing arrived. He had fallen off his bare-back pony many times, and had been left far behind. The man who held my hair now relinquished his grasp, while another pushed me violently from in front, causing me to fall heavily backward, and putting a painful strain on all the tendons of my legs. Mansing, bruised and aching all over, was brought forward and tied by his legs to the same log of wood to which I was fastened. They informed me that they would kill my coolie first, and one brutal Lama seized him roughly by the throat. I was pushed up in a sitting posture, and a cloth was thrown over my head and face, so that I could not see what was being done. I heard poor Mansing groan pitifully, then there was a dead silence. I called him, I received no answer; so I concluded that he had been despatched. I was left in this terrible suspense for over a quarter of an hour, when at last they removed the cloth from over my head, and I beheld my coolie lying before me, bound to the log and almost unconscious, but, thank God, still alive. He told me that, when I had called him, a Lama had placed his hand upon his mouth to prevent him from answering, while, with the other hand, he had squeezed his neck so tightly as to nearly strangle him. After a while Mansing got better, and the coolness and bravery of the poor wretch during these terrible trials were really marvellous.

We were told that our execution was only postponed till the next day, in order that we might be tortured until the time came for us to be brought out to death.

A number of Lamas and soldiers stood round jeering at us. I seized the opportunity this respite afforded to hail a swaggering Lama and ask him for some refreshment.

"*Orcheh, orcheh nga dappa tugu duh, chuen deh, dang, yak, guram, tcha, tsamba pin*" ("I am very hungry, please give me some rice, yak meat, *ghur*, tea, and oatmeal!") I asked in my best Tibetan.

"*Hum murr, Maharaja!*" ("I want butter, your Majesty") put in Mansing, half in Hindustani and half in the Tibetan language.

This natural application for food seemed to afford intense amusement to our torturers, who had formed a ring round us, and laughed at our appeal, while Mansing and I, both of us famished, were left sitting bound in a most painful position.

The day had now waned, and our torturers did not fail to remind us constantly that the following day our heads would be severed from our bodies, which I told them would cause us no pain, for if they gave us no food we should be dead of starvation by then.

Whether they realised that this might be the case, or whether some other reasons moved them, I cannot say; but several of the Lamas, who had been most brutal, including one who had the previous day taken a part in Chanden

Sing's flogging, now became quite polite and treated us with a surprising amount of deference. Two Lamas were despatched to the monastery, and returned after some time with bags of *tsamba* and a large *raksang* of boiling tea. I have hardly ever enjoyed a meal more, though the Lamas stuffed the food down my throat with their unwashed fingers so fast that they nearly choked me.

"Eat, eat as much as you can," said they grimly, "for it may be your last meal."

And eat I did, and washed the *tsamba* down with quantities of buttered tea, which they poured into my mouth carelessly out of the *raksang*.

Mansing, whose religion did not allow him to eat food touched by folk of a different caste, was eventually permitted to lick the meal out of the wooden bowl. I myself was none too proud to take the food in any way it might be offered, and when my humble "*Orcheh, orcheh tchuen mangbo terokchi*" ("Please give me some more") met with the disapproval of the Lamas, and brought out the everlasting negative, "*Middù, middù*," I was still too hungry to waste any of the precious food: so the Tibetans revolved the wooden bowl round and round my mouth, and I licked it as clean as if it had never been used.

CHAPTER LXXXVII

Happiness checked—Stretched on the rack—Mansing shares my fate—Drenched and in rags—An unsolved mystery.

AFTER all the excitement of the day, we were beginning to feel a little restored and much relieved at being treated rather less roughly, were it only for a few moments, when, small as it was, the improvement in our condition was checked.

A Lama came from the monastery and gave orders right and left, and the place was again in commotion. We were pounced upon and roughly seized, and my legs were quickly untied, a number of men holding me down the while. Again they lifted me until I stood upright on the cutting edge of the prismatic log : two men seized one leg and two the other, and stretched them apart as far as they could possibly go. Then rope after rope was wound round my feet and ankles, and I was made fast as before to the log.

As my legs were much farther apart this time, the pain in the muscles of my legs when they proceeded to knock me down backwards was even greater than it had been on the previous occasion. But before I had time to feel it in full, the Lamas, now as ferocious as I had seen them at first, dragged my manacled arms backwards from under my body and tied a rope to the chain of the handcuffs. This done, they passed the rope through a hole in the top of a high post behind me, and by tugging at it, strained my arms upwards in a way that, had I been less supple, would certainly have broken them. When all their strength combined could not stretch me another inch without tearing my body to pieces, they made the rope fast, and I remained half suspended, and feeling as if all the bones of my limbs were getting, or had got, pulled out of their sockets. The weight of the body naturally tending to settle down would, I felt, every moment increase the suffering of this terrible torture, which was really a primitive form of the rack.

Mansing was likewise suspended on the other side, his feet remaining tied to the log to which my own were fastened, only not quite so wide apart.

The pain was at first intense, the tendons of the legs and arms being dreadfully strained, and the spinal column bent so as nearly to be broken in two. The shoulder-blades forced into close contact, pressed the vertebræ inwards, and caused excruciating pains along the lumbar vertebræ, where the strain was greatest.

As if this were not sufficient, a cord was tied from Mansing's neck to mine, the object of which was to keep our necks stretched in a most uncomfortable position.

It began to rain heavily, and we were left out in the open. The rags to which our clothes had been reduced in our struggle when we were first seized were drenched. Half naked and wounded, we were alternately numbed with cold and burning with fever. A guard encircled us, having with them two watch-dogs tied to pegs. The soldiers were apparently so confident of our inability to escape that they drew their heavy blankets over their heads and slept. One of them in his slumber moved and pushed his sword outside the blanket in which he had now rolled himself tight. This inspired me with the idea of attempting to escape.

Two or three hours later it had become very dark. Thanks to the extremely supple nature of my hands, I succeeded in drawing the right hand out of my handcuffs, and, after an hour or so of stealthy and anxious work I managed to unloose the cord that bound Mansing's feet. Then I whispered to him to get up slowly and to push the sword

THUS ELAPSED TWENTY-FOUR TERRIBLE HOURS

towards me with his foot until I could reach it. If successful in this, I could soon cut my bonds and those fastening Mansing's hands, and with a weapon in our possession we would make a bold dash for liberty.

Mansing, however, was not a champion of agility. In his joy at feeling partly free, the poor coolie moved his stiff legs clumsily. The vigilant watch-dogs detected this, and gave the alarm by barking. The guards were up in a moment, and, timid as they always were, they all hurriedly left us, and went to fetch lights to examine our bonds.

In the meanwhile, protected by the darkness of the stormy night, I had succeeded in replacing my hand inside the iron handcuff. Putting it back was more difficult than drawing it out, but I had just time to effect my purpose. The men who had gone to the monastery returned with lights. I pretended to be fast asleep: a likely thing with every bone in my body feeling as if it were disjointed, every limb numbed and frozen, every tendon and ligament so strained as to drive me mad with pain!

The Tibetans found the bonds round Mansing's feet undone. They examined my hands and saw them just as they had left them. They inspected my feet. The ropes were still there cutting into my flesh. They inspected Mansing's hands, only to find them still fastened to the post behind him.

The Tibetans were so puzzled at this mysterious occurrence that they positively got frightened. They began to shout excitedly, calling for help. In a moment, the alarm having been given, a crowd of men rushed at us, and with their swords drawn, surrounded us. One man, braver than the rest, gave Mansing a few cuts with a whip, warning us that if the ropes were found undone again they would decapitate us there and then. The coolie was again bound, this time more tightly than ever.

CHAPTER LXXXVIII

Mansing partially untied after twelve hours on the rack—Numbed—How the brain works under such circumstances—My scientific instruments—The end of my photographic plates—A paint-box accused of occult powers—An offer refused—Courtesy and cruelty combined.

By way of precaution, a light was set between Mansing and myself, and, as it was still raining hard, the Tibetans placed a canvas shelter over us to prevent the light from being extinguished. At about six or seven in the morning, Mansing's feet were untied, but not his hands. I was left in the same uncomfortable and painful posture. The hours passed very slowly and wearily. My legs, my arms and hands had gradually become quite lifeless, and after the first six or seven hours that I had been stretched on the rack, I felt no more actual pain. The numbness crept along every limb of my body, until I had now the peculiar sensation of possessing a living head on a dead body.

It is indeed remarkable how one's brain keeps alive and working well under such circumstances apparently unaffected by the temporary mortification of the remainder of the system.

The day now dawning was one full of strange incidents. When the sun was high in the sky, the Pombo, with a great number of Lamas, rode down from the monastery, though the distance was very short. He went to his tent, and presently my cases of scientific instruments were brought outside and opened, the soldiers and Lamas displaying an amusing mixture of curiosity and caution over everything they touched. I had to explain the use of each instrument, a difficult matter indeed, considering their ignorance and my limited knowledge of Tibetan, which did not allow of my delivering scientific addresses. The sextant was looked upon with great suspicion, and even more so the hypsometrical apparatus, with its thermometers in brass tubes, which they took to be some sort of firearm. Then came a lot of undeveloped photographic plates, box after box of which they opened in broad daylight, destroying in a few moments all the valuable negatives that I had taken since leaving Mansarowar. The Pombo, more observant than the others, noticed that the plates turned a yellowish colour on being exposed to the light.

"Why is that?" asked he.

"It is a sign that you will suffer for what you are doing to me."

The Pombo flung away the plate, and was much upset. He ordered a hole to be dug in the ground some way off, and the plates to be instantly buried. The soldiers, however, who had been entrusted with the order, seemed loth to touch the plates, and they had to be reprimanded and beaten by the Lamas before they would obey. At last, with their feet, they shoved the boxes of negatives to a spot some distance off, where, in dog fashion, they dug a deep hole with their hands in the muddy ground; and there, alas! I saw my work of several weeks covered for ever with earth.

Now came my paint-box with its cakes of water-colours.

"What do you do with these?" cried an angry Lama, pointing at the harmless colours.

"I paint pictures."

"No, you are lying. With the 'yellow' you find where gold is in the country, and with the 'blue' you discover where malachite is."

I assured them that this was not the case, and told them that, if they would untie me, I would, on recovering the use of my arms, paint a picture before them.

They prudently preferred to leave me tied up.

Their whole attention was now drawn to a considerable sum in silver and gold which they found in the cases, and the Pombo warned the people that not one coin must be stolen.

I took this chance to make an offering of 500 rupees to the lamasery, and told the Pombo that I would like him to accept as a gift my Martini-Henry, which I had noticed rather took his fancy.

Both gifts were refused, as they said the lamasery was very wealthy, and the Pombo's position as an official did not allow him to carry a rifle. The Pombo, nevertheless, was quite touched by the offer, and came personally to thank me.

In a way the rascals were gentlemanly enough in their manner, and I could not help admiring their mixture of courtesy and cruelty, either of which they could switch on at a moment's notice without regard to the other.

CHAPTER LXXXIX

An unknown article in Tibet—My sponge bewitched—A Lama fires my Martini-Henry—The rifle bursts.

THEY had now reached the bottom of the water-tight case, and the Pombo drew out with much suspicion a curious flattened object.

"What is that?" inquired he, as usual lifting the article up in the air.

My sight had been so injured that I could not clearly discern what it was; but on their waving it in front of my nose, I recognised it to be my long mislaid bath-sponge, dry and flattened, which Chanden Sing, with his usual ability for packing, had stored away at the bottom of the case, piling upon it the heavy cases of photographic plates. The sponge, a very large one, was now reduced to the thickness of less than an inch, owing to the weight that had for weeks lain upon it.

The Tibetans were greatly puzzled at this new discovery, which they said resembled tinder; and it was touched with much caution, for some of the Lamas said it might explode.

When their curiosity was appeased, they took it and threw it away. It fell near me in a small pool of water. This was a golden opportunity to frighten my jailers, and I addressed the sponge in English, and with any word that came into my mouth, pretending to utter incantations. The attention of the Lamas and soldiers was naturally quickly drawn to this unusual behaviour on my part; and they could not conceal their terror when, as I spoke louder and louder to the sponge, it gradually swelled to its normal size with the moisture it absorbed.

The Tibetans, who at first could hardly believe their eyes at this incomprehensible occurrence, became so panic-stricken at what they believed to be an exhibition of my

BELT, WITH BULLET AND POWDER POUCHES, DAGGER, NEEDLE-CASE, AND FLINT AND STEEL.

occult powers, that there was a general stampede in every direction.

In a way, all this was entertaining, and anyhow it served to pass away the time. The most amusing scene that afternoon was, however, still to come.

After a time the Lamas screwed up their courage, and returned to where my baggage had been overhauled. One of them picked up my Martini-Henry, and the others urged him to fire it off. He came to me, and when I had explained to him how to load it, he took a cartridge and placed it in the breech, but would insist on not closing the bolt firmly home. When I warned him of the consequences, he struck me over the head with the butt of the rifle.

It is the fashion, when aiming with one of their matchlocks, which have a prop attached to them, to place the butt in front of the nose instead of holding it firmly to the shoulder as we do. So the Lama aimed in this fashion at one of my yaks peacefully grazing some thirty yards off. While everybody watched anxiously to see the results of this marksman's shooting, he pulled the trigger; the rifle went off with an extra loud report, and behold! the muzzle of the Martini burst and the violent recoil gave the Lama a

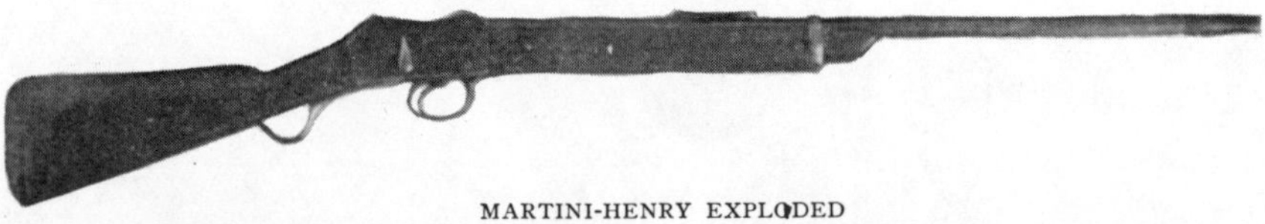

MARTINI-HENRY EXPLODED

fearful blow in the face. The rifle, flying out of his hands, described a somersault in the air, and the Lama fell backwards to the ground, where he remained spread out flat, bleeding all over, and screaming like a child. His nose was squashed; one eye had been put out, and his teeth shattered.

Whether the rifle burst because the bolt had not been properly closed, or because mud had got into the muzzle as well, I could not say; but I give here a photograph of the broken weapon, which the Tibetans returned to me several months later through the Government of India.

The injured Lama, I may say, was the one at the head of the party that wanted to have my head cut off, so that, naturally enough, I could not help betraying my satisfaction at the accident. I was glad they had let me live another day were it only to see his self-inflicted punishment.

CHAPTER XC

A consultation—Untied from the rack—The most terrible twenty-four hours of my life—I lose the use of my feet—Circulation returning—Intense pain—Sports.

THE Pombo, who had been, during the greater part of the afternoon, looking at me with an air of mingled pity and respect, as though he had been forced against his will to treat me so brutally, could not help joining in my laughter at the Lama's sorrowful plight. In a way, I believe he was rather glad that the accident had happened ; for, if he had until then been uncertain whether to kill me or not, he felt, after what had occurred, that it was not prudent to attempt it. The gold ring which had been taken from me on the day of our arrest, and for which I had asked many times, as it had been given by my mother, was regarded as possessing miraculous powers as long as it was upon me ; and was therefore kept well away from me, for fear that, with its help, I might break my bonds and escape. The Pombo, the Lamas and officers held another consultation, at the end of which, towards sunset, several soldiers came and loosed my legs from the stretching log ; and my hands, though still manacled, were lowered from the pillar behind.

As the ropes round my ankles were unwound from the deep channels they had cut into my flesh, large patches of skin came away with them. Thus ended the most terrible twenty-four hours I have ever passed in my lifetime.

I felt very little relief at first as I lay flat on the ground, for my body and legs were stiff and as if dead; and, as time went by, and I saw no signs of their coming back to life, I feared that mortification had set in, and that I had lost the use of my feet for good. It was two or three hours before the blood began to circulate in my right foot, and the pain when it did so was intense. Had a handful of knives been passed slowly down the inside of my leg the agony could not have been more excruciating. My arms were not quite so bad: they also were numbed, but the circulation was more quickly re-established.

In the meanwhile, the Pombo, whether to amuse me or to show off his riches, ordered about one hundred ponies, some with magnificent harness, to be brought up; and, mounting the finest, and holding in his hand that dreadful *taram*, rode round the hill on which the monastery and fort stood.

On returning, he harangued his men, and a series of sports began, the Pombo seating himself near me and watching me intently to see how I was enjoying the performance. First of all the best marksmen were selected, and with their matchlocks fired one after the other at my two poor yaks only a few yards off; but although they aimed carefully and deliberately, they did not succeed in hitting them. I knew that they fired with bullets, for I could hear the hissing sound the missiles made.

Next came a display of fine horsemanship, which was very interesting. I should have enjoyed it more if I had not been suffering agonies all the time. Still, the performance helped to cheer me. First there were races in which only two ponies at a time took part, the last race being run between the two winners of the last heats, and a *kata* was presented to the victor. Next one horseman rode ahead at full gallop flying a *kata*, while some twenty others followed closely behind. The *kata* was left to fly by itself, and when it settled on the ground, the horsemen following the first rode some distance away, and, at a given signal, galloped back wildly, all converging towards the spot, and, bending down from their ponies, attempted to pick up the *kata* without dismounting. Some of the younger men were very clever at this.

Another exercise consisted in one man on foot standing still, while a mounted comrade rode at full gallop towards him, seized him by his clothes, and lifted him on to the saddle.

Though I could not see as well as I wished, I got so interested in the show, and expressed such admiration for the ponies, that the Pombo, becoming quite thoughtful and polite, ordered the best of them to be brought before me, and had me lifted into a sitting posture, so that I could see them better.

CHAPTER XCI

A great relief—The Pombo's attentions—A weird hypnotic dance

THIS was a great relief, for I was suffering more from my humiliating position, being unable to stand, than from the tortures themselves. The Pombo told me that I must now look towards the tent, and then got up and walked towards it.

The opening of the tent was over twenty feet long. Some soldiers came and dragged me close to the front of it, so that I could witness all that went on.

Two big Lamas entered the tent with the Pombo, and a number of other people who were inside were turned out. They closed the tent for a few minutes, and then opened it again. In the meantime a gong summoned the Lamas of the monastery to come down, and, a few minutes later, a string of them came and took their places inside the tent.

The Pombo, in his yellow coat and trousers and four-cornered hat, sat on a kind of high-backed chair in the centre of the tent, and by his side stood the two Lamas who had first entered it with him. The Pombo was beyond doubt in a hypnotic trance. He sat motionless, with his hands flat on his knees and his head erect ; his eyes were fixed and staring. For some minutes he remained like this, and all the soldiers and people who had collected in front of the tent went down on their knees, laid their caps on the ground, and muttered prayers. One of the two Lamas, a fellow with great mesmeric powers, now laid his hand upon the shoulders of the Pombo, who gradually raised his arms

THE POMBO'S CONTORTIONS

with hands outstretched and remained as in a cataleptic state for a long time without moving an inch.

Next the Lama touched the Pombo's neck with his thumbs, and caused the head to begin a rapid circular movement from left to right.

Certain exorcisms were pronounced by the hypnotiser, and the Pombo now began the most extraordinary snake-like contortions, moving and twisting his arms, head, body and legs. He worked himself, or rather was worked, into a frenzy that lasted some time, and the crowd of devotees drew nearer and nearer to him, praying fervently and emitting deep sighs and cries of astonishment and almost terror at some of the more eccentric movements of his limbs. Every now and then this weird kind of dance terminated in a strange posture, the Pombo actually doubling himself up with his head

THE FINALE OF THE DANCE

between his feet and his long flat hat resting on the ground. While he was in this position, the bystanders went one by one to finger his feet, and make low prostrations and salaams. At last the hypnotiser, seizing the Pombo's head between his hands, stared in his eyes, rubbed his forehead, and woke him from the trance. The Pombo was pale and exhausted. He lay back on the chair and his hat fell off his head, which was clean shaven, thus unmistakably showing that he too was a Lama, and, as we have seen, of a very high order, probably of the first rank after the Dalai Lama.

Katas were distributed after this religious performance to all the Tibetans present, and they folded them and stowed them away in their coats.

CHAPTER XCII

Compliments exchanged—A poisoned drink proffered—In acute pain—Uncertainty as to our fate—Working the oracle—Webbed fingers.

THE Pombo came out of his gaudy tent, and I told him that the dance was beautiful, but that I was very hungry. He asked me what I wanted to eat, and I said I would like some meat and tea.

A little later, a large vessel with a delicious stew of yak's meat was brought to me, as well as *tsamba* in abundance. However, though I felt quite famished, I had the greatest difficulty in swallowing even a little food. This I thought must be owing to the injuries to my spine and to the mortification of my limbs, which had apparently affected my whole system.

When the Pombo had retired and night came on, I was again tied to the stretching log, but this time with my limbs not stretched so far apart. My hands, too, were again fastened to the pillar behind, but with no strain on them.

Late in the evening, half a dozen Lamas came from the monastery with a light and a large brass bowl which they said contained tea. The wounded Lama, with his head all bandaged up, was among them, and he was so anxious for me to drink some of it to keep myself warm during the cold night that I became quite suspicious. When they pushed a bowl of it to my lips, I merely sipped a little, and declined to take more, spitting out what they had forced into my mouth. I swallowed a few drops, and a few minutes later I was seized with sharp, excruciating pains in my stomach, which continued for several days after. I can but conclude that the drink proffered me was poisoned.

The following day my left foot, which had remained lifeless since I had been untied from the rack the first time, began to get better, and the circulation was gradually restored. The pain was unbearable.

In the morning indecision again prevailed as to what was to be done to us. A number of Lamas were still anxious to have us beheaded, whereas the Pombo and the others had the previous night almost made up their minds to send us back to the frontier. Unfortunately, it appears* that the Pombo had seen a vision during the night in which a spirit told him that, if he did not kill us, he and his country would suffer some great misfortune. "You can kill the Plenki," the spirit was reported to have said, "and no one will punish you if you do. The Plenkis are afraid to fight the Tibetans."

Among the Lamas no important step is taken without incantations and reference to occult science, so the Pombo ordered a Lama to cut off a lock of my hair, which he did with a very blunt knife, and then the Pombo rode up with it in his hand to the lamasery to consult the oracle. The lock was handed in for inspection, and it seems that, after certain incantations, the oracle answered that I must be beheaded or the country would be in great danger.

* The Tibetan Lamas stated this to the Political Peshkar Karak Sing, our frontier officer.

The Pombo rode back apparently disappointed, and now ordered that one of my toe-nails should be cut ; after which operation, performed with the same blunt knife, the oracle was again consulted as to what should be done, and unhappily gave the same answer.

Three such consultations are usually held by the high court of the assembled Lamas, the Tibetans on the third occasion producing for the oracle's decision a piece of a finger-nail. The Lama who was about to cut this off examined my hands behind and spread my fingers apart, expressing great surprise and astonishment. In a moment all the Lamas and soldiers came round and examined my manacled hands ; a repetition of my experience at the Tucker Monastery. The Pombo, too, on being informed, immediately came and inspected my fingers, and the proceedings were at once stopped.

When some weeks later I was released, I was able to learn from the Tibetans the reason of their amazement. My fingers happen to be webbed rather higher than usual, and this is most highly thought of in Tibet. He who possesses such fingers has, according to the Tibetans, a charmed life ; and no matter how much one tries, no harm can be done to him. Apart from the question whether there was much charm or not in my life in Tibet, there is no doubt that this trifling superstition did much towards hastening the Pombo's decision as to what was to be our fate.

CHAPTER XCIII

Our lives to be spared—An unpleasant march—Chanden Sing still alive—A sleepless night—Towards the frontier—Long and painful marches—How we slept at night—A map drawn with blood.

THE Pombo ordered that my life should be spared, and that I should on that very day start on my return journey towards the Indian frontier. He took from my own money one hundred and twenty rupees, which he placed in my pocket for my wants during the journey, and commanded that, though I must be kept chained up, I was to be treated kindly, and my servants also.

When all was ready, Mansing and I were led on foot to Toxem, our guard consisting of some fifty horsemen riding on ponies. We had to travel at a great speed despite our severely lacerated feet, our aching bones, and the sores and wounds with which we were covered all over. The soldiers led me tied by the neck like a dog, and dragged me along when, panting, exhausted and suffering, I could not keep up with the ponies. We crossed several cold streams, sinking in water and mud up to our waists.

At Toxem, to my great delight, I beheld Chanden Sing still alive. He had been kept prisoner in the mud-house, where he had remained tied upright to a post for over three days, and for four days he had not eaten food nor drunk anything. He was told that I had been beheaded. He was in a dreadful condition; almost dying from his wounds, cold and starvation.

We were detained there for the night, half-choked by smoke in one of the rooms of the mud-house packed with soldiers, who, with a woman of easy morals, gambled the

A WHITE YAK

whole night, and sang and swore and fought, preventing us from sleeping for even a few minutes.

The next day at sunrise Chanden Sing and I were placed on yaks, not on riding saddles, but on pack-saddles such as those shown in the illustration in chapter xl. of vol. i. Poor Mansing was made to walk, and was beaten mercilessly when, tired and worn out, he fell or remained behind. They again tied him with a rope by the neck and

CHANDEN SING TIED TO A POST

dragged him along in a most brutal manner. We had a strong guard to prevent our escaping, and they demanded fresh relays of yaks and ponies and food for themselves at all the encampments, so that we travelled very fast. In the first five days we covered one hundred and seventy-eight miles, the two longest marches being respectively forty-two and forty-five miles; but afterwards we did not cover quite such great distances.

We suffered considerably on these long marches, as the soldiers ill-treated us and would not allow us to eat every day for fear we should get too strong. They let us have food only every two or three days, and our exhaustion and the pain caused by riding those wretched yaks in our wounded condition were terrible.

All our property had been taken away from us, and our clothes were in rags and swarming with vermin. We were barefooted and practically naked. The first few days we generally marched from before sunrise till sometimes an hour or two after sunset; and when we reached camp we were torn off our yaks and our jailers fastened iron cuffs round our ankles, in addition to those we had already round our wrists. Being considered quite safe, we were left to sleep out in the open without a covering of any kind, and often lying on snow or deluged with rain. Our guard generally pitched a tent under which they slept; but even when they did not have one, they usually went to brew their tea some fifty yards or so from us.

Helped by my two servants, who sat by me to keep watch and to screen me, I managed, at considerable risk, to keep a rough record of the journey back, on a small piece of paper that had remained in my pocket when I had been searched by the Tibetans. As I did when on the rack, I used to draw my right hand out of its cuff, and, with a small piece of bone I had picked up as pen, and my blood as ink, I drew brief cipher notes, and a map of the whole route back.

Necessarily, as I had no instruments with which to take careful observations, I had to content myself with taking my bearings by the sun, the position of which I got fairly accurately by constantly watching the shadow projected by my body on the ground. Of course, when it rained or snowed, I was altogether at a loss, and had to reckon my bearings by the observations of the previous day.

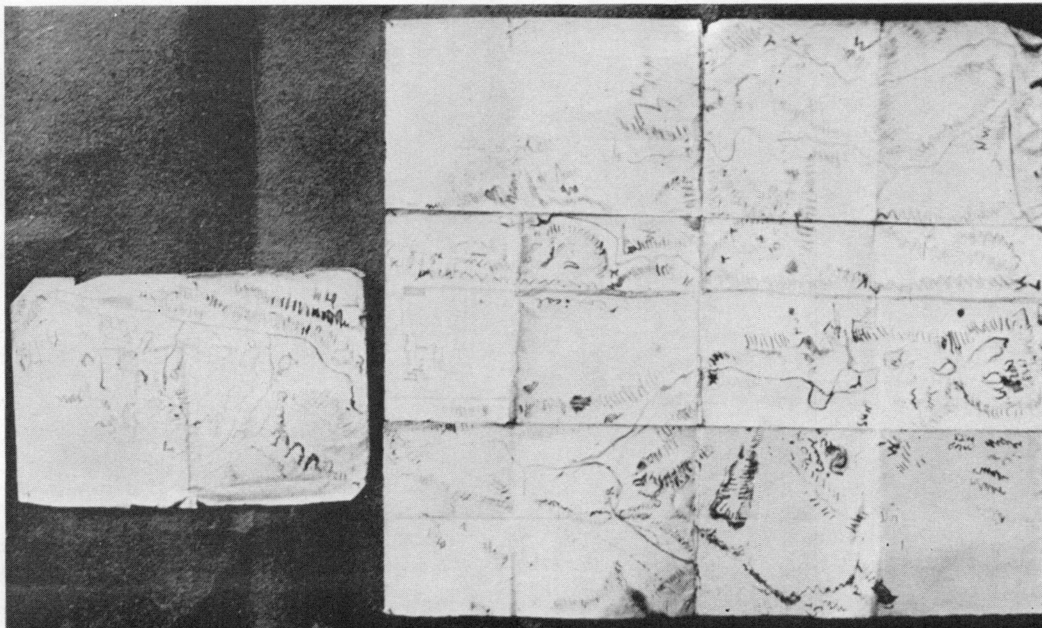

MAP DRAWN IN BLOOD DURING CAPTIVITY

CHAPTER XCIV

South of the outward journey—Severity of our guard—Ventriloquism and its effects—Terrible but instructive days—The Southern source of the Brahmaputra—Leaving Yutzang.

WE travelled, as can be seen by the dotted red line on the map attached to this book, first W. then W.N.W., N.W., W. and N.W., following the Brahmaputra along a course South of the outward journey, until we reached the boundary of the Yutzang * (central, or Lhassa) province. Our guard were not only severe with us, but they also ill-treated us in every possible way. One or two of the soldiers, however, showed kindness and thoughtfulness, bringing us a little butter or *tsamba* whenever they could do so unseen by their comrades. The guard was changed so frequently that we had no chance of making friends with them, and each lot seemed worse than the last.

A very curious incident happened one day, causing a scare among them. We had halted near a cliff, and the soldiers were some twenty yards off. Having exhausted every means I could think of to inspire these ruffians with respect, I resorted to the performance of some ventriloquial feats, pretending to speak and to receive the answers from the summit of the cliff. The Tibetans were terror-stricken.

* Also written U-tzang.

They asked me who was up there. I said it was some one I knew.

"Is it a Plenki?"

"Yes."

Immediately they hustled us on our yaks and mounted their ponies, and we left the place at headlong speed.

ONE OF OUR GUARD

On reaching a spot which from observations taken on my outward journey I reckoned to be in longitude 83° 6′ 30″ E. and latitude 30° 27′ 30″ N. I had a great piece of luck. It is at this point that the two principal sources of the Brahmaputra meet and form one river, the one coming from the N.W., which I had already followed, the other proceeding from the W.N.W. The Tibetans, to my delight, selected the southern route, thus giving me the opportunity of visiting the second of the two principal sources of the great river. This second stream rises in a flat plain, having its first birth in a lakelet in approximate longitude 82° 47′ E. and latitude 30° 33′ N. I gave the Northern source my own name, a proceeding which I trust will not be regarded as immodest in view of the fact that I was the first European to visit it, and of all the circumstances of my journey.

This period of our captivity was dreary, yet interesting and instructive, for, as we went along, I got the soldiers to teach me some Tibetan songs, not unlike those of the Shokas in character, and from the less ill-natured men of our guard I picked up, by judicious questioning, a considerable amount of information, which, together with that collected from my own observations, I have given in this book.

Over a more southerly and lower pass than the Maium Pass, by which, healthy, hopeful and free, we had entered the province of Yutzang, we now left it, wounded, broken down, naked and prisoners.

CHAPTER XCV

Easier times—Large encampments—Suffocating a goat—A Tarjum's encampment—Tokchim—Old friends—Musicians—Charity.

WE now proceeded in a North-westerly direction, and, once clear of the sacred Yutzang province, our guard behaved with rather less cruelty. With the little money the Pombo had permitted me to keep we were allowed to purchase food enough to provide us with more frequent meals, and, while we ate, the soldiers removed our handcuffs, which they temporarily placed round our ankles. Thus, with utensils lent us by our guard, we were able to cook some food ; and, although we had to serve it on flat stones instead of dishes, it seemed indeed delicious.

We crossed over our former track, and then followed it almost in a parallel line, but some miles North of it, along an undulating, clayey plateau, thus avoiding the marshy plain which we had found so troublesome to cross on our journey out. We found large numbers of black tents here and there, and one night, when we were encamped by some small lakes, we were permitted to purchase a goat. A soldier, a good fellow who had been very friendly to us, selected a fine fat one for us, and we were looking forward with pleasure to a solid meal, when we found to our dismay that we had no means of despatching the animal. We could not behead it, as the Tibetans would not trust us with a knife or sword, and the Tibetans themselves refused to kill the animal for us in any other way. Eventually our soldier friend allowed his scruples to be overcome by the payment of a rupee, and proceeded to kill the animal in a most cruel

SOLDIER SUFFOCATING GOAT

fashion. He tied its legs together, and, having stuffed the nostrils with mud, he held the poor beast's mouth closed with one hand until it was suffocated. The soldier during the performance revolved his prayer-wheel with his free hand, praying fervently all the while.

We found ourselves at last in the plain, where a Tarjum's encampment of some two hundred tents was to be seen, and here we remained one night. There was a large assemblage of Lamas and soldiers. In the middle of the night we were suddenly and roughly roused from sleep, and made to move our camp about a mile or so from the settlement; and, early in the morning, having crossed the large stream, we proceeded in a South - westerly direction, reaching the encampment of the Tokchim Tarjum the same night. Here we were met by the officers who had on a previous occasion brought us gifts, and whom we had routed with all their soldiers when they threatened us.

OLD BEGGAR

This time they behaved very decently, the oldest of them showing us every civility, and professing great admiration for our courage in persevering against such heavy odds. The old gentleman did all he could to make us comfortable, and even called up two strolling musicians for our amusement. One man wore a peculiar four-cornered headdress made of skin. He played with a bow on a two-stringed instrument, while his companion, a child, danced and went through certain clumsy contortions, going round every few minutes with his tongue thrust out to beg for *tsamba* from the audience. The Tibetans are very charitable towards beggars, and not only on this, but on other occasions, I

STROLLING MUSICIANS

noticed that they seldom refused, no matter however small their donations might be, to give *tsamba* or pieces of butter or *chura* to the mendicants. The older musician had a square club passed through his girdle, and at intervals he laid down his instrument, and, using the club as a sword, gave an imitation of a martial dance, exactly like the one I have described as performed by the Shokas. Every now and then, too, he applied it to the boy's back and head, to inspire him with fresh vigour, and this generally drew roars of laughter from the audience.

CHAPTER XCVI

Towards Mansarowar—Mansing's vision—Bathing in Mansarowar.

THE next day, amidst repeated good-byes and professions of friendship on the part of our hosts and jailers, we departed towards Mansarowar, and late in the afternoon reached the Tucker village and Gomba, where we put up at the same *serai* in which I had slept on my way out. All our bonds were here removed for good, and we enjoyed comparative freedom, though four men walked by my side wherever I went, and an equal number looked after Chanden Sing and Mansing. Naturally we were not allowed to go far from the *serai*, but we could prowl about in the village. I took this opportunity to have a swim in the Mansarowar Lake, and Chanden Sing and Mansing again paid fresh salaams to the gods and plunged in the sacred water.

The Lamas, who had been so friendly during my former visit, were now extremely sulky and rude ; and, after having witnessed our arrival, they all withdrew into the monastery, banging the gate after them. All the villagers, too, hastily retired to their respective houses. The place was deserted with the exception of the soldiers round us.

Poor Mansing, who, worn out and in great pain, was sitting close by me, looking vaguely at the lake, had an

INTERIOR OF A SERAI

extraordinary vision, the result, probably, of fever or exhaustion.

"Oh, sahib," said he, as if in a dream, though he was quite awake; "look, look! Look at the crowd of people walking on the water. There must be more than a thousand men! Oh, how big they are getting! . . . And there is God . . . Seva. . . . No, they are Tibetans, they are coming to kill us, they are Lamas! Oh, come, sahib, they are so near. . . . Oh, they are flying. . . . !"

A TIBETAN SHEPHERD

"Where are they?" I asked.

I could see that the poor fellow was under an hallucination. His forehead was burning and he was in a high fever.

"They have all disappeared!" he exclaimed, as I placed my hand on his forehead and he woke from his trance.

He seemed quite stupefied for a few moments; and, on my inquiring of him later whether he had seen the phantom crowd again, he could not remember ever having seen it at all.

The natives came to visit us in the *serai* during the evening, and we had great fun with them, for the Tibetans are full of humour and have many comical ways. As for ourselves, now that we were only two marches from Taklakot, it was but natural that our spirits were high. Only two more days of captivity, and then a prospect of freedom.

It was still dark when we were roused and ordered to

start. The soldiers dragged us out of the *serai.* We entreated them to let us have another plunge in the sacred Mansarowar, and the three of us were eventually allowed to do so. The water was bitterly cold, and we had nothing to dry ourselves with.

It was about an hour before sunrise when we were placed on our yaks and, surrounded by some thirty soldiers, rode off.

CHAPTER XCVII

Suna—Wilson and the Political Peshkar across the frontier—A messenger—Our progress stopped—Diverting us over the Lumpiya Pass—Condemned to certain death—We attack our guard—Lapsang and the Jong Pen's private secretary—A document—Nearing Kardam—Retracing our steps—Dogmar.

WHEN we had been marching for several hours, our guard halted to have their tea. A man named Suna, and his brother and son, whom I had met in Garbyang, halted near us, and from them I heard that news had arrived in India that I and my two men had been beheaded, and that thereupon Doctor Wilson and the Political Peshkar Karak Sing had crossed over the frontier to ascertain the facts, and to attempt to recover my baggage, &c. My joy was intense when I heard that they were still at Taklakot. I persuaded Suna to return as fast as he could, and to inform Wilson that I was a prisoner, and tell him my whereabouts. I had barely given Suna this message when our guard seized the man and his brother and roughly dismissed them, preventing them from having any further communication with us. As soon as we were on the march again, a horseman rode up to us with strict orders from the Jong Pen of Taklakot not

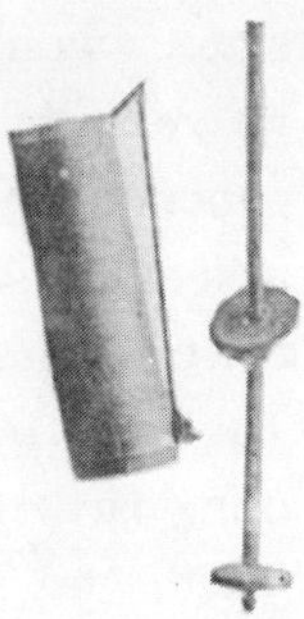

TEA CHURN (OPEN)

to let us proceed any farther towards the frontier by the Lippu Pass, which we could now have reached in two days, but to take us round by the distant Lumpiya Pass. At this time of the year the Lumpiya would be impassable; and we should have to make a further journey of at least fifteen or sixteen days, most of it over snow and ice, during which we, in our starved and weakened state, would inevitably succumb. We asked to be taken into Taklakot, but our guard refused, and in the meantime the Jong Pen of Taklakot had sent other messengers and soldiers to ensure the fulfilment of his orders, and to prevent our further progress.

A BEARER OF BAD NEWS

Our guard, now strengthened by the Taklakot men, compelled us to leave the Taklakot track, and we began our journey towards the cold Lumpiya. This was murder, and the Tibetans, well knowing it, calculated on telling the Indian authorities that we had died a natural death on the snows.

We were informed that we should be left at the point where the snows began, that the Tibetans would give us no food, no clothes and no blankets, and that we should be abandoned to our own devices. This, needless to say, meant certain death.

We determined to stand no more, and to play our last card. After travelling some two and a half miles westward of the Taklakot track, we declined to proceed any more in that direction. We said that, if they attempted to force us on, we were prepared to fight our guard, as whether we died by their swords and matchlocks, or frozen to death on the Lumpiya, was quite immaterial to us.

SHEEP LOADS FOR BORAX AND GRAIN

The guard, in perplexity, decided to let us halt there for the night, so as to have time to send a messenger to Taklakot to inform the Jong Pen, and ask for further instructions.

During the night the order came that we must proceed, so the next morning our guard prepared to start us again towards the Lumpiya. Then we three semi-corpses collected what little strength remained in us, and suddenly made an attack on them with stones; whereupon, incredible as it may seem, our cowardly guard turned tail and bolted! We went on in the direction of Taklakot, followed at a distance by these ruffians, who were entreating us to make no further resistance and to go with them where they wanted us to go. If we did not, they said, they would all have their

A JUMLI SHED

heads cut off. We refused to listen to them, and kept them away by throwing stones at them.

We had gone but a few miles when we met with a large force of soldiers and Lamas, despatched by the Jong Pen to prepare for our death. Unarmed, wounded, starved and exhausted as we were, it was useless attempting to fight against such odds. As it was, when they saw we were at liberty, they made ready to fire on us.

WE ATTACKED OUR GUARD WITH STONES

The Jong Pen's Chief Minister, a man called Lapsang, and the Jong Pen's Private Secretary, were at the head of this party. I went to shake hands with them and held a long and stormy palaver, but they kept firm and insisted on our turning away from the frontier, now that we were almost within a stone's-throw of it, and we must perforce proceed by the high Lumpiya Pass. Those were the Jong Pen's orders, and they, as well as I, must obey them. They would not give us or sell us either animals or clothes which even the small sum of money I had on me would have been sufficient to buy; and they would not provide us with an ounce of food. We emphatically protested, and said we preferred to die where we were. We asked them to kill us then and there, for we would not budge an inch westwards.

LAPSANG AND THE JONG PEN'S PRIVATE SECRETARY

Lapsang and the Jong Pen's Private Secretary now cunningly suggested that I should give them in writing the names of the Shokas who had accompanied me to Tibet, probably with the object of confiscating their land and goods. As I said I could not write Tibetan or Hindustani, they requested me to do it in English. This I did, but substituting for the names of my men and my signature sarcastic remarks, which must have caused the Tibetans some surprise when they had the document translated.

As, however, they refused to kill us there and then, and as Lapsang showed us great politeness and asked us to go by the Lumpiya Pass as a personal favour to him, I reluctantly decided to accept their terms rather than waste any more time, now that we were so near British soil.

Escorted by this large force of men, we had nearly reached Kardam when, in the nick of time, a horseman came up at full gallop and hailed our party. We stopped, and the man overtook us and handed Lapsang a letter. It contained an order to bring us immediately into Taklakot.

We retraced our steps along the undulating plateau above the Gakkon River, and late at night we reached the village of Dogmar, a peculiar settlement in a valley between two high cliffs of clay, the natives of which live in holes pierced in the cliff.

Lapsang, the Jong Pen's Private Secretary, and the greater portion of their soldiers, having changed their ponies, went on to Taklakot; but we were made to halt here, when yet another letter came from the Jong Pen saying he had changed his mind and we must, after all, go by the Lumpiya Pass!

CHAPTER XCVIII

A commotion—The arrival of an army—Elected General-in-chief—How we were to slaughter the Jong Pen's soldiers—My men lay down their arms—Towards Taklakot—Delaling and Sibling—Taklakot at last.

DURING the night there was a great commotion in the place, the people running about and shouting, and a large number of ponies with their riders arriving.

Tibet is farmed out, so to speak, to officials who have become small feudal kings, and these are generally at loggerheads among themselves. To this regal jealousy, and to disputes over the rights of the road, was due the appearance of this new army. There were altogether some hundred and fifty men armed with matchlocks and swords. The chieftain of this band came to me with eight or ten other officers, and spoke so excitedly that I feared there was trouble in store for us. There was indeed. These new arrivals were officers and soldiers from Gyanema, Kardam, and Barca, and they had come with strict orders from the Barca Tarjum that we were on no account to traverse his province or to cross by the Lumpiya Pass. This was very amusing and tantalising, for we had now no way across the frontier open to us. Our guard and some of the Jong Pen's men who had remained behind, finding they were in the minority, thought it prudent to eclipse themselves; and I, anxious as I naturally was to get out of the country as quickly as possible, approved of all that the Gyanema men said, and urged them to fight in case the Jong Pen still insisted on my going through the Tarjum's province. All ways out of the country were barred to us, and unless we resorted to force, I felt we would never escape at all.

JUMLI TRADER AND HIS WIFE IN TIBET

The Gyanema men asked me whether I would lead them in case of a fight with the Jong Pen's soldiers; and I, though not very confident of their courage, accepted the post of General-in-chief *pro tem.*, Chanden Sing and Mansing being promoted there and then to be my aides-de-camp. We spent the greater part of the night in arranging our plan of attack on the Jong Pen's

CLIFF HABITATIONS

troops, and when all was properly settled, the Tibetans, to show their gratitude, brought me a leg of mutton, some *tsamba*, and two bricks of tea.

The morning came, and I was given a fine pony to ride, as were also Chanden Sing and Mansing. Then, followed

CHOKDENS NEAR TAKLAKOT

by my Tibetan troops—a grand cavalcade—we started gaily towards Taklakot. We had been informed that the Jong Pen was concentrating his men at a certain point on the road to bar our way : and it was this point that we must force. My Tibetans said that they hated the Jong Pen's men, and swore they would slaughter them all if they made any stand.

"But they are such cowards," declared one of the Tibetan officers, "that they will run away."

All this talk stopped suddenly when we heard the distant

tinkling of our enemies' horse-bells, and though I encouraged my men as best I could, a panic began to spread among them. The Jong Pen's men came in sight, and presently I witnessed the strange spectacle of two armies face to face, each in mortal terror of the other.

Notwithstanding my remonstrances, matchlocks and swords were deposited on the ground with anxious eagerness by both parties, to show that only peaceful intentions prevailed. Then a conference was held, in which everybody seemed ready to oblige everybody else except me.

While this was still proceeding, a horseman arrived with a message from the Jong Pen, and at last, to everybody's satisfaction, permission was granted for us to proceed into Taklakot.

My army retraced its steps towards the North-west, and, deposed from my high military post, which I had occupied only a few hours, I became again a private individual and a prisoner. With a large escort we were taken along the Gakkon, by barren cliffs and on a rocky road. We passed hundreds of *Chokdens* large and small, mostly painted red, and *mani* walls. Then, having descended by a precipitous track on whitish clay-soil, we reached a thickly inhabited district, where stone houses were scattered all over the landscape. We saw on our left the large monastery of Delaling and, a little way off, the Gomba of Sibling; then, describing a sweeping curve among stones and boulders, we rounded the high graceful cliff, on the top of which towered the fort and monasteries of Taklakot.

Lithographed by F. A. Brockhaus, Leipzig (Germany).

TAKLAKOT FORT.

CHAPTER XCIX

Free at last—Among friends—Forgetting our past troubles—Confiscated baggage returned—A scene with Nerba—Suna's message delivered—How our release was brought about—Across the frontier—Photography at Gungi.

SUCH was our anxiety, when we reached this point, lest something should happen and we should be taken back again, that, as soon as we were across the wooden bridge over the Gakkon, Chanden Sing and I, on perceiving the large Shoka encampment at the foot of the hill, lashed our ponies and ran away from our guard. Thus, galloping our hardest along the high cliff, where hundreds of people live in holes in the clay, we found ourselves at last among friends again. The Shokas, who had come over to this market to exchange their goods with the Tibetans, were astounded when they saw us, recognising us at first with difficulty.

We inquired at once, of course, for Dr. Wilson, and when we found him the good man could, himself, barely recognise us, so changed were we. He seemed deeply moved at seeing our condition.

When the news of our arrival spread in camp, we met with the greatest kindness at the hands of everybody. In a corner of Wilson's tent was a large quantity of candied sugar—several pounds; and so famished was I that I quickly devoured the lot. Later, my Shoka friends brought in all kinds of presents in the shape of eatables, which Rubso, the Doctor's cook, was set to prepare.

The Political Peshkar, Karak Sing, hurried to me with a change of clothes, and other garments were given me by Dr. Wilson. My own ragged attire was literally swarming with vermin; our guard had not allowed us a single change of raiment, nor would they even hear of our washing. It was by a very special favour and on account of its sanctity that we were allowed to plunge in the sacred Mansarowar Lake.

PUNDIT GOBARIA

Later in the day my wounds and injuries were examined by Dr. Wilson, who sent his reports to the Government of India, to the Commissioner of Kumaon, and to the Deputy Commissioner at Almora.

Tenderly nursed by Wilson and Karak Sing, and having partaken of plenty of good food, I found my spirits, which had fallen rather low, reviving as if by magic; and, strange to say, after a few hours of happiness, I was already beginning to forget the hardships and suffering I had endured. I remained three days at Taklakot, during which time part of my confiscated baggage was returned by the Tibetans, and, as can well be imagined, I was overjoyed to discover that among the things thus recovered were my diary, notebooks, maps and sketches. My firearms, some money, the ring I have before referred to as having been a gift of my mother, several mathematical instruments, collections, over 400 photographic negatives, and various other articles were still missing,* but I was glad to get back as much as I did.

DR. WILSON

To Dr. Wilson's tent came the Tokchim Tarjum, of whom I give a portrait, his private secretary Nerba, whom the reader may remember as having played an important part in my tortures, the Jong Pen's secretary, and old Lapsang in a fine green velvet coat with ample sleeves. As can be seen by perusing the Government Enquiry and Report in the Appendix to this book, the above-mentioned Tibetan officers admitted before the Political Peshkar, Dr. Wilson, Pundit Gobaria, and many Shokas, that the account I gave of my tortures—identical with the one in these pages—was

* Some of the articles missing were some months later recovered by the Government of India. See Appendix.

correct in every detail. They even professed to be proud of what they had done, and used expressions not at all flattering to the British Government, which they affected to treat with great contempt.

I nearly got the Political Peshkar and the Doctor into a scrape; for my blood, the little I had left, was boiling with rage at hearing the Tibetan insults. The climax came when Nerba refused to give back my mother's ring, which he had upon him. In a passion I seized a knife that was lying by me, and leaped upon Nerba, the ruffian who, besides, had fired at me and had held me by the hair while my eyes were being burnt prior to my abortive execution. Wilson and Karak Sing seized and disarmed me, but there was a general stampede of the Tibetan officers, and thus our interview and negotiations were brought to an abrupt end.

KARAK SING PAL, THE POLITICAL PESHKAR

In further conversation I now learnt how my release had been brought about. Dr. Wilson and the Political Peshkar, having received the news that my servants and myself had been beheaded, proceeded across the frontier to make inquiries and try to recover my property. They heard then from the man Suna, whom I had sent from Mansarowar with my message, that I was still a prisoner, covered with wounds, in rags and starving. They had not men enough to force their way further into the country to come and meet me; besides, the Tibetans watched them carefully; but they, together with Pundit Gobaria, made strong representations to the Jong Pen of Taklakot, and, by threatening him that an army would be sent up if I were not set at liberty, they at last obtained from the reluctant Master of the fort* a permission that I should be brought into Taklakot. The permission was afterwards withdrawn, but was at last allowed to be carried into execution, and it is entirely due to the good offices and energy of these three gentlemen that I am to-day alive and safe—though not yet sound.

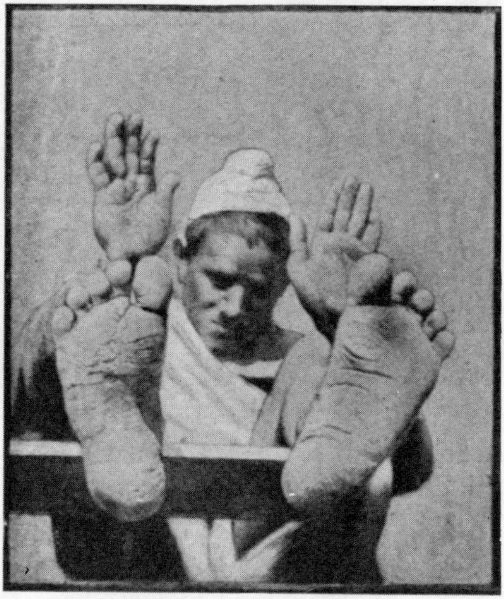

MANSING SHOWING CUTS UNDER HIS FEET

* Jong Pen = Master of the fort.

Pundit Gobaria, who will be remembered as having been mentioned in my early chapters, is the most influential Shoka trader in Bhot, and on very friendly terms with the Tibetans. He was the intermediary through whom negotiations were carried on for my immediate release, and

A GLANCE AT THE FORBIDDEN LAND FROM THE LIPPU PASS

it was largely owing to his advice to the Jong Pen that they resulted satisfactorily.

After a brief rest to recover sufficient strength, I recommenced the journey towards India, and, having crossed the Lippu Pass (16,780 feet), found myself at last again on British soil. We descended by slow stages to Gungi, where, in Dr. Wilson's dispensary, I had to halt for a few days on account of my weak condition.

Wilson had here a quantity of my baggage, instruments,

THE AUTHOR—FEBRUARY 1897

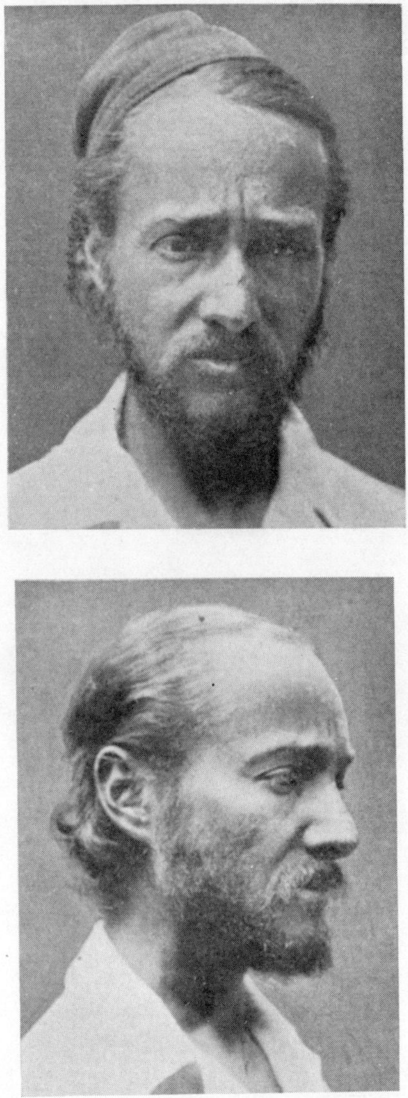

THE AUTHOR—OCTOBER 1897

cameras, plates, &c., which I had discarded at the beginning of my journey, and I immediately had photographs taken of my two servants and myself, showing our wounds and our shocking general condition. Photographs of my feet, taken more than a month after I had been untied from the rack, showed a considerable swelling, as well as the scars round the ankle and on the foot where the ropes had cut into my flesh. In the full-face photograph here reproduced can be noticed the injuries to my left eye, as well as the marks of the hot iron on the skin of my forehead and nose. Chanden Sing's legs, which were photographed on the same occasion, though now practically healed, were still much swollen, and the marks can be seen in the illustration where big patches of skin and flesh had been torn away by the lashes, producing nasty wounds.

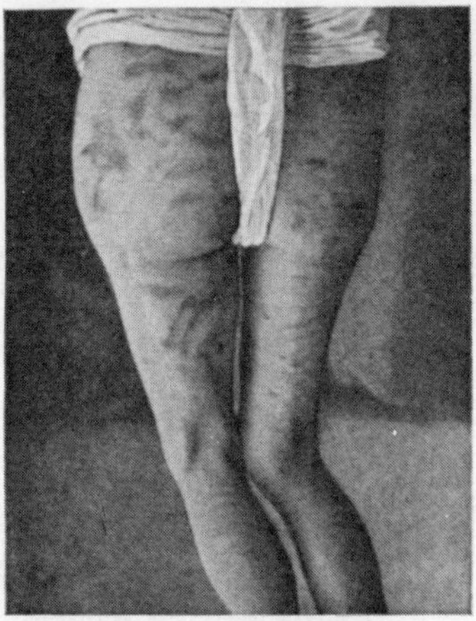

CHANDEN SING'S LEGS, SHOWING MARKS OF LASHES AND WOUNDS HEALED

CHAPTER C

Civilisation once more—Paralysis—The Tinker Pass in Nepal—Kindly natives—Mr. Larkin—Government Inquiry—Back to Tibet—Final good-bye to the Forbidden Land—The return journey—Farewell to Mansing—Home again.

MR. J. LARKIN

It was really wonderful how soon we began to pick up again under the good care of Dr. Wilson and the influence of proper food and clothing. When I saw my face for the first time in a looking-glass, I nearly had a fit, so ghastly did it look ; but I felt more like myself when I had shaved off my beard of several months' growth ; and, after the ever-obliging Wilson, with a pair of blunt scissors, had spent a whole afternoon in performing the functions of hairdresser, I began to look almost civilised again. Clothes were a great nuisance at first, but I soon got into the way of wearing them.

The injuries to my spine were severe, and gave me much trouble. At times the whole of my left side became as if paralysed. Besides, I invariably experienced the greatest

A TIBETAN TEMPORARY SHED

difficulty in sitting down when I had been standing, and in getting up when I had been sitting down. Through the great strain they had undergone, my joints continued stiff and swollen, and remained so for months. I could see comparatively well with my right eye, but was unable to use the left at all.

When slightly better I made an excursion to Tinker, in Nepal, there being a pass in the neighbourhood I had not

CHANDEN SING AND MANSING ENJOYING THEIR FIRST MEAL ACCORDING TO THE RULES OF THEIR CASTES

visited. Having crossed into Nepal at Chongur, I followed a course towards 86° (b.m.), until we came to the Zirri River, descending precipitously between high snowy ridges. Then I kept on the right bank of the Tinker River, first through forests of firs, then among barren rocks and along ravines, the track being extremely bad in some places. The general direction was 88° (b.m.) until the Tinker bridge was reached, by which the stream was crossed, from which point I travelled some three miles to 74° (b.m.), and arrived at the Tinker village, a few Shoka houses perched on the slope of the mountain, having for a background the magnificent snowy peaks dividing Nepal from Tibet. From the village the track to the pass is easy, first to 78° 30′ (b.m.), as far as

A SHAKY PASSAGE ON THE NERPANI ROAD

the Zentim bridge, two miles off, where the Dongon River, descending from 106° (b.m.), meets the Zeyan Yangti,* and, following the latter stream for another four miles, one reaches the Tinker Pass, the distance between here and

* Yangti = River.

TINKER IN NEPAL

Taklakot being twelve miles. At 106° (b.m.) I observed a very high snowy peak, the Dongon.

Having seen all that I wanted to see here I made my way back to Garbyang with all speed, as I was anxious to return to Europe as soon as possible, and I travelled down to Askote in company of Peshkar Karak Sing. The Nerpani

VIEW OF ASKOTE—SHOWING RAJIWAR'S PALACE

road had fallen in two or three places, and rough shaky bridges had been constructed across the deep precipices, one of which can be seen in the illustration on page 206. We met with a hearty reception everywhere, and kindness after kindness was showered upon us by all alike.

At Askote I was the guest of the good old Rajiwar, in whose garden I encamped, and who bestowed upon me every conceivable care and attention. Mr. J. Larkin, hastily despatched by the Government of India to conduct an Inquiry into my case, met me there, and, though still suffering much pain, I insisted on turning back once more towards Tibet, to help him in his task. By quick marches we reached Garbyang, where a deputation of Shokas, who had returned from Tibet, came to me, Mr. Larkin having gone on ahead.

SNAPSHOT OF SHOKA VILLAGERS BEING ROUTED

Among them I noticed several of the men who had betrayed me, and as I was told that there was no way of punishing them for their treachery, I took justice into my own hands, proceeding with a stout stick to teach them some idea of faithfulness, whereupon the whole village ran up to get the fellows out of my clutches. Encouraged by the Tibetans, the Shokas made some insulting remarks about Englishmen; so the fight became general until, ill as I was, and alone against some hundred and fifty men, I succeeded in routing them. The thing might justly be doubted had I not been able to take a snap-shot of them as they fled helter-skelter.

DR. WILSON, MYSELF, MR LARKIN, THE POLITICAL PESHKAR, AND JAGAT SING READY TO ASCEND THE LIPPU PASS

Soon after leaving Garbyang, I overtook Mr. Larkin, and we climbed towards the snows. We intended crossing over the Lippu Pass into Tibet to give the Jong Pen an opportunity of being interviewed, but he refused to meet us.

All the same, to give the Tibetans every chance, we climbed over the Lippu Pass. It had been snowing heavily and it was very cold. A Shoka had only a few days previously been lost in the snow in trying to cross over, and had been frozen to death. There were some twelve feet of snow, and the ascent was by no means easy. However, after toiling for some two hours we reached the summit of the pass, and I slipped once more across the boundary into Tibet. Dr. Wilson, the Political Peskhar, Jagat Sing, and two

ON THE LIPPU PASS

chaprassis were with us. The illustration in which Dr. Wilson appears holding an umbrella to shelter himself from the high wind, with Mr. Larkin and our ponies on his right, and showing also the pile of stones and flying prayers placed there by the Shokas and Tibetans, was taken by me on the pass. Having found a suitable spot where the wind did not cut quite so furiously into our faces, we halted for a considerable time and waited impatiently on the Tibetan

MR. LARKIN'S PARTY AND MINE HALTING NEAR THE LIPPU PASS

side of the boundary for the Jong Pen or his deputies, to whom letters had been sent, to come and meet us; but they did not put in an appearance, so in the afternoon of October 12 I definitely turned my back on the Forbidden

MR. LARKIN LOOKING OUT FOR THE JONG PEN FROM THE LIPPU PASS

Land. I was still far from well, but was glad indeed at the prospect of seeing England and my friends again.

We returned to our camp, a few hundred feet lower than the pass, where we had left our baggage and our men, who had suffered much from mountain sickness.

It was at this camp that the accompanying photograph, which represents me bathing at 16,300 feet, was taken by Mr. Larkin. Chanden Sing, having broken the ice in a stream, poured water from a brass vessel over me, standing, with my feet on snow, in a high wind and with the temperature at 12° Fahr. I reproduce it to show that even in my reduced condition I was able to stand an unusual degree of cold. As a matter of fact, the water that had been taken from under the ice immediately froze on my shoulders, with the result that in a second I had icicles

BATHING AT 16,300 FEET

hanging on each side of my neck and a shawl of ice over my shoulders.

Having fulfilled our mission, Mr. Larkin and I returned by very quick marches to Almora; and it was a great satisfaction to me that in conducting the Government Inquiry in an open Court, Mr. Larkin was able to obtain ample testimony from Shokas and Tibetans as to my treatment, all of which was duly reported to the Government of India, and also to the Foreign Office and India Office in London. A copy of the Inquiry and Government Report will be found in the Appendix.

Winter setting in, the Shokas, who had by now all returned from Tibet, were beginning to migrate to their winter

DHARCHULA. DESERTED HABITATIONS OF SHOKAS

homes at Dharchula, and when we passed the settlement many were already at work repairing the fallen-down roofs of their hibernal habitations. A large number of Tibetans with their sheep had also come over to winter in British territory, and their encampments could be seen all along the road wherever there was sufficient grass for their flocks. The Tibetans—Lamas and officials—maintained a high-handed and insolent demeanour as long as we were in

Bhot, which they regarded as part of their own country; a fact observed not only by Dr. Wilson and the Political Peskhar, who travelled with us up to the frontier and back, as far as Askote, but also by Mr. Larkin, who more than once was astounded at the impudence of Tibetans when on

"I TOLD YOU," EXCLAIMED THE OLD SAVAGE, "THAT WHOEVER VISITS THE HOME OF THE RAOTS WILL HAVE MISFORTUNE"

British soil. It must, however, be said for them that the moment they had come out of Bhot, and had to deal with Hindoos instead of Shokas, their manner changed considerably. Hypocritical deference and servility replaced haughtiness and insolence. Near the frontier we encountered hundreds of yaks and ponies laden with wood which the Tibetans cut from our forests, and compel our natives to take across into Tibet for the consumption of those

Tibetans who do not come over to our side to spend the winter.

At Askote the old Raot who had predicted ill-luck for me when I visited the Raots' dwelling, came to remind me of his prophecy, "I told you," exclaimed the old savage,

A PICTURESQUE BIT OF ALMORA

"that whoever visits the home of the Raots will have misfortune," and I photographed the old scoundrel on the spot, together with his mates, who listened with satisfaction to the words that came from the lips of their prophet.

We proceeded with no delay to Almora, and from there went straight on to Naini Tal, the summer seat of the Government of the North-West Provinces and Oudh, where a conference was held on my case by the Lieutenant-Governor.

Having there enjoyed the unbounded hospitality of that able and energetic officer, Colonel Grigg, Commissioner of Kumaon, I paid off my faithful coolie Mansing, giving him enough for a start in life. He accompanied me to Kathgodam, the terminus of the railway, and showed genuine grief when Chanden Sing and I stepped into the train. As we steamed away from the platform, he salaamed me affectionately, having previously begged that, if ever I should go back to Tibet, I would take him with me; only next time he too must be provided with a rifle! That was the only condition.

Chanden Sing, who remained as my servant, travelled with me to Bombay, and from there we went direct to Florence, the home of my parents, who had suffered in their anxiety at home almost as much as I did in the Forbidden Land.

RAOTS LISTENING TO THE ACCOUNT OF MY MISFORTUNES

APPENDIX

Letter from SIR WILLIAM LEE WARNER, C.S.I., *Political and Secret Department, India Office, London.*

"Honi soit qui mal y pense."

INDIA OFFICE, WHITEHALL, S.W.
August 4, 1898.

DEAR SIR,

With reference to the request contained in your letter of the 27th, and to your interview with me of the same day I forward herewith for your use a copy of Mr. Larkin's "Inquiry and report" into your treatment by the Tibetans.

Yours faithfully,
(Signed) W. LEE WARNER.

A. HENRY SAVAGE LANDOR, Esq.

GOVERNMENT REPORT BY J. LARKIN, ESQ., MAGISTRATE OF THE FIRST CLASS.

Mr. Arnold Henry Savage Landor having been reported to have been captured and tortured by the Tibetans, I was sent up to Garbyang in Byans to ascertain the facts.

Mr. Landor arrived in India on the 10th of April last. He proceeded to Almora, where he arrived on the 27th idem. He stayed there until the 10th of May, to make arrangements for his travels in Tibet. At first he was advised to take some Gurkha soldiers with him, but this fell through, as the military did not accede to his request. He then, on the 27th May, arrived in Garbyang in Byans *patti*. It appears to have been his intention to have entered Tibet by the Lippu Lek Pass. This is the easiest, being about 16,780 feet above sea level. It is the most frequented route taken by the traders of Byans and Chaudans, and is adjacent to Taklakot, a mart for wool, salt, borax, grain, &c. He was, however, frustrated in this, inasmuch as the Jong Pen of Taklakot came to know of Mr. Landor's intention and took steps to prevent it. He caused bridges to be destroyed and stationed guards along the route.

Moreover, he appears to have been kept fully cognisant of Mr. Landor's moves through the agency of his spies in Garbyang.

Under these circumstances Mr. Landor was compelled to resort to some other route, and selected the Lumpia Pass, which stands at an altitude of 18,150 feet.

On the 13th July last, Mr. Landor, with a following of thirty men, entered Tibet. He reached Gyanima, where he was stopped by the Barkha Tarjum. This personage, however, after some persuasion, consented to permit Mr. Landor and seven followers to go forward to the Mansarowar Lake.

Next day the accorded permission was withdrawn, and Mr. Landor and his party were turned back. The party returned three marches, when Mr. Savage Landor determined to go to Mansarowar by the unfrequented wilds.

On the 21st July, Mr. Landor, with nine followers, at midnight in a terrific snowstorm, climbed up the mountain and went off, the bulk of his party continuing their retreat to the Lumpia Lek. By this strategic move Mr. Landor baffled the Tibetan guards (Chaukìdárs). He carefully avoided coming into contact with any of the inhabitants, and in order to do so was obliged to keep to the high mountains and unfrequented wilds.

Travelling thus, with the aid of his compass, sextant and sketch maps, he reached Mansarowar.

Here five of his followers declined to accompany him any farther, so he paid and dismissed them. This was at Tucker. Thus Mr. Landor was reduced to a following of four men. He went on, however, and had accomplished but three marches more when two more of his followers deserted him at night. These went off with some of his supplies, all his servants' food, and ropes.

Mr. Landor was now reduced to the following of a bearer (Chanden Sing) and a coolie (Mansing). Despite his misfortunes he determined to push on : his intention appears to have been to reach Lhassa.

He went over the Mariam La Pass.* This attains an altitude of over 16,000 feet.

Meanwhile the deserters had bruited about the information of Mr. Landor's intention of getting to Lhassa.

While crossing the Nio Tsambo River one of Mr. Landor's yaks went under. The yak was saved, but its valuable load, consisting of all the tinned provisions, Rs. 800 in cash, three pairs of shoes, one slaughtered sheep, wearing apparel, razors, skinning instruments, and some three hundred rifle cartridges, was lost.

This accident was directly the cause of Mr. Landor's capture, as he and his two followers, who were footsore, starving, and disheartened, were driven to seek food and horses from the inhabitants of the country. On the 19th of August 1897 they went to a place called Toxem. The villagers received them well and promised to supply them with food and horses. Next morning, the 20th idem, a number of Tibetans came to Mr. Landor's tent bringing food and ponies.

While Mr. Landor and his servants were engaged trying and selecting ponies, the crowd increased and came up behind its three victims.

Suddenly, without any warning, the Tibetans rushed on Mr. Landor and his two servants, and overwhelming them by numbers, made prisoners of them. They cruelly bound their surprised victims. Then a number of soldiers (who had lain in ambush) arrived and

* Maium Pass

took over the prisoners. The first person to be dealt with was the bearer Chanden Sing. He was accused of having taken his master into Tibet. He was questioned as to this, and also as to the maps and sketches found with Mr. Landor's things. I may mention that when the arrests were made the Tibetans took all of Mr. Landor's property, which they handled very roughly, damaging most of the things. Hearing the Tibetans accuse the bearer, Mr. Landor called out that his servant was in no way responsible for his having entered Tibet. Thereupon a Lama struck him (Mr. Landor) a blow on the head with the butt-end of his riding-whip. Chanden Sing was then tied down and flogged. He received two hundred lashes with whips, wielded by two Lamas. Then the prisoners were kept apart for the night, bound with cords. Next day Mr. Landor was placed on a horse, seated on a spiked pack-saddle. Mansing was put on a bare-backed horse. They still were bound. Mr. Landor's arms were secured behind his back. Thus they were taken off at a gallop towards Galshio. When the party were nearing that place they came up with a party of Lamas, awaiting them by the roadside. Here Mr. Landor's horse was whipped and urged to the front. A kneeling soldier, his musket resting on a prop, fired at Mr. Landor as he went past. The shot failed to take effect. Then they stopped the pony and fastened a long cord to Mr. Landor's handcuffs. The other end was held by a soldier on horseback. The party then continued their career, the Lamas having fallen in. While proceeding at full gallop, the horseman who held the cord attached to Mr. Landor's handcuffs, pulled hard at it to try and unhorse the latter. Had this occurred Mr. Landor must have been trampled to death under the troop of horsemen behind him. Thus they hurried onward till they neared Galshio,* when at a turn in the road a soldier was seen kneeling at the "ready," who fired a shot at Mr. Landor as he came abreast of him. This, like the previous shot, missed its object.

Arriving at Galshio, Mr. Landor was torn off his pony. He was in a bleeding state, the spikes in the pack-saddle having severely wounded his back. He asked for a few minutes' respite, but was

* Galshio = Gyatsho.

jeeringly told by his guards that it was superfluous, as he was to be beheaded in a few minutes. He was then taken, his legs stretched as far as they could be forced apart, and then tied to the sharp edge of a log shaped like a prism. The cords were bound so tightly that they cut into the flesh.

Then a person named Nerba, the secretary of the Tokchim Tarjum, seized Mr. Landor by the hair of his head, and the chief official, termed the *Pombo*, came up with a red-hot iron, which he placed in very close proximity to Mr. Landor's eyes. The heat was so intense that for some moments Mr. Landor felt as if his eyes had been scorched out. It had been placed so close that it burned his nose. The *Pombo* next took a matchlock, which he rested on his victim's forehead and then discharged upwards.

The shock was consequently very much felt. Handing the empty gun to an attendant soldier, the *Pombo* took a two-handed sword. He laid the sharp edge on the side of his victim's neck as if to measure the distance to make a true blow. Then wielding the sword aloft, he made it whiz past Mr. Landor's neck. This he repeated on the other side of the neck.

After this tragic performance Mr. Landor was thrown to the ground and a cloth put over his head and face to prevent his seeing what was being done to his servant Mansing. This must have been done to make Mr. Landor believe that Mansing was being executed. After a short time the cloth was removed and Mr. Landor beheld his servant, with his legs stretched, tied to the same log. Mr. Landor was kept for twenty-four hours in this trying position, legs stretched as far as possible and arms bound to a pole, and Mansing for twelve hours. To add to their misery they were kept in the rain and were afterwards seated in a pool of water. The effect of this torture was to strain the muscles of the legs and arms and injure the spine.

When Mr. Landor's legs were unloosed from their cords, they were so numbed and swollen that for sixteen hours he did not recover the use of them and feared they were mortifying. Mr. Landor's property was overhauled by the officials of Galshio and sealed up. On the afternoon of the third day at Galshio, the two prisoners were taken on foot to Toxem. It was a very trying march, inasmuch as several rivers had to be crossed.

On his arrival at Toxem, Mr. Landor saw his bearer Chanden Sing in a very precarious condition, as the latter had had no food for four days. During all this time the prisoners were firmly bound and carefully guarded. Next day, Mr. Landor and Chanden Sing were placed on yaks. Mansing had to walk. Thus they were taken in the direction of Mansarowar Lake. It was only on arrival at Mansarowar that his guards unbound Mr. Landor.

Arriving at Dogmar the party was stopped by the Jong Pen of Taklakot, who refused to give them passage through his district. This was a very serious affair, as it meant that the worn-out prisoners would have to be taken by a long circuitous route *viâ* Gyanima and into India by the Lumpia Pass. This would probably have done for them. Owing to the intervention of the Rev. Harkua Wilson, of the Methodist Episcopal Mission, *Peshkár* Kharak Sing Pal and Pundit Gobaria, the most influential person among the Bhutias* of Byans, the Jong Pen was compelled to withdraw his prohibition and give his sanction to the prisoners being conveyed to Taklakot.

Arriving at this place the prisoners were hospitably received by the Rev. Harkua Wilson, who is also a medical man. He examined their injuries and attended to them. His statement discloses the dreadful condition he found them in. The Tibetan guards made over some of Mr. Landor's property to him at Taklakot. It was then found that much property had not been restored. Mr. Landor had a list drawn up from memory of his unrestored property. This list (a copy) was handed to the Jong Pen of Taklakot.

I append the list. The Jong Pen has been called upon to restore the missing articles. He urges that the affair did not occur in his district, and that he is in no way responsible for the loss of the property.

He has, however, promised to try to recover them, alleging that the affair has been reported to a superior authority at Gartok. From what I could gather here, it seems probable that all the missing

* Bhutias = Shokas.

property, save the money, will be restored. I tried to see the Jong Pen, but he pleaded illness, and the inutility of a meeting in which he had nothing new to disclose. This personage is notorious in these parts for his implacable hatred to English subjects.

The account of the affair as given by Mr. Savage Landor is fully borne out by his two servants, and, moreover, the Tibetans who took part in it did not try to hide it.

In the Rev. Harkua Wilson's tent at Taklakot, before *Peshkár* Kharak Sing, Gobaria and a large number of Bhutias, several Tibetan officials corroborated the whole account as related by Mr. Landor. The man Nerba, who had held Mr. Landor's hair when about to be beheaded and have his eyes burnt out, admitted he had taken such part in the affair. There can be no doubt that the above account is true and unexaggerated, for the whole of Byans and Chaudans are ringing with it. The Jong Pen of Taklakot was given ample opportunity to explain the affair, but he declined to do so.

Mr. Savage Landor held Chinese passports, and his conduct during his stay in that country did not warrant the officials to have treated him in the barbarous, cruel way they did. I satisfied myself, by careful inquiry from the people here, as to how Mr. Landor behaved.

He is said to have been most munificent in his dealings with all, and invariably affable and courteous. I had seen Mr. Landor just before his entry into Tibet, and when I met him I could scarcely recognise him, though he had then fairly recovered from the terrible treatment he had received. I saw the marks of the cords on his hands and feet, and they are still visible after this lapse of time. He complains that he is still suffering from the injury done his spine, and fears that it may be of a permanent nature.

J. LARKIN.

October 15, 1897.

No. $\frac{645}{\text{N. 277}}$ A. of 189

All communications to Government should give the No., date and subject of any previous correspondence, and should note the Department quoted.

From

THE UNDER-SECRETARY TO GOVERNMENT, N.-W. Province and Oudh.

To

A. H. SAVAGE LANDOR, Esq.,
c/o Messrs. GRINDLAY, GROOM & Co.,
Bankers, Bombay.

Dated ALLAHABAD, *November* 13, 1897.

SIR,

Political Department.

In reply to your letter of November 5, I am desired to send you a printed copy of depositions recorded by Mr. Larkin as noted below:

1. Of yourself;
2. Of Chanden Sing;
3. Of Man Sing;
4. Of Rev. Harkua Wilson;
5. Of Pundit Gobaria;
6. Of Kharak Sing;
7. Of Suna.

I have the honour to be, Sir,
Your most obedient Servant,
H. N. WRIGHT,
Under-Secretary to Government, North-Western Provinces and Oudh. N.M.

ALMORA DISTRICT.

IN THE COURT OF J. LARKIN, Esq., Magistrate of the 1st class.

In re The Matter of the Tortures, Robbery, &c., of A. HENRY SAVAGE LANDOR, Esq., and his servants, by the Thibetan Authorities.

DEPOSITION OF MR. A. HENRY SAVAGE LANDOR; *taken on the 4th day of October* 1897. *Oath administered by me.*

My name is Arnold Henry Savage Landor; my father's name is Charles Savage Landor; I am by caste European. British subject; by occupation artist and traveller; my home is at Empoli (Calappiano), police station Empoli, district Florence, Tuscany, Italy; I reside at London.

Having made up my mind to travel in Turkistan and Thibet, for geographical and scientific purposes as well as to study the manners and customs of those people, I obtained a British passport from the Foreign Office and one from the Chinese Legation in London. I had already a passport granted me by the Chinese Government through the British Consul at Tientsin, China. I also possess letters from Lord Salisbury and the officials of the British Museum. I am prepared to submit all these for scrutiny. I arrived in India by the P. and O. ss. *Peninsular* about the beginning of April. I travelled rapidly up to Almora. I stayed there a short time to make arrangements for my travels in Thibet. I entered that country through the Lumpia Lek. I kept away from the road and paths, passing over several ranges of high mountains, camping at very high altitudes, for nearly three weeks. When I started I had thirty men with me. Twenty-one of them left me when I was only five days in. At Mansarowar Lake five Shokas declined to go any farther. I paid them up and they left. It was they who gave the Lamas of Tucker information of my intention to go to Lhassa. I had proceeded but three marches towards the Maium La Pass when my only two remaining Shokas deserted during the night. They carried off all my stock of provisions for my Hindu servants, ropes, straps, &c. My party had now dwindled down to Chanden Sing (bearer) and Man Sing (coolie). The latter was ill; I fear he is developing leprosy. His feet were in a very sore and cut condition, hence he could scarcely get along. I went over the Maium La Pass and followed the course of the Brahmaputra River for many troublesome marches, until we reached the Neo Tsambo (river), in crossing which one of my yaks sank and its load went down and was lost. I tried hard, by diving and swimming in this very cold and rapid river, to recover my goods, but failed to do so, owing to the depth and muddiness of the water. The load contained all my provisions, some clothes, and all my shoes, cash rupees eight hundred, my lantern, some ammunition, and sundry knives and razors. This misfortune drove me to Toxem, which place we reached in a state of starvation. It had taken us several days to get there. Owing to the weak, fatigued, and starved condition of my two followers, I had to seek to get them food and horses, as it was impossible for them to get on without horses. I would not desert them, as I might have, as I was still prepared to push on despite the many difficulties I had to encounter hourly. Toxem consisted of one mud house and an encampment of about eighty tents. The shepherds received us kindly and consented to sell me horses and provisions. I encamped for the night about two miles beyond the settlement. During the evening several persons visited my encampment, bringing me gifts of provisions. I invariably gave them money in return, certainly three or four times more than the value of the articles presented. During the night I was disturbed several times, and went out into the darkness, but failed to discover any one. This, however, was my nightly experience; hence I grew to attach little moment to these noises. In the morning (August 20), two or three Thibetans came offering to sell me provisions and ponies. While I and my two servants were engaged examining and selecting ponies, I noticed that numbers of villagers came up one by one, spinning their wool or carrying bags of *tsamba* (meal), while others arrived with more ponies. My servants, overjoyed at the hope of getting mounts, rode first one pony and then another to suit themselves, Chanden Sing, having selected one, called me to see it and try it. I walked to the spot, which was about a hundred yards from my tent. Naturally I was unarmed. The demeanour of these people had been so friendly that it gave me no cause to suspect that any treachery was anticipated. While I stood with my hands behind my back, enjoying the delight of my long-suffering servants, I was suddenly seized from the back by several persons. I was seized simultaneously by the neck, arms, wrists, and legs, and was thrown down in a prone position. I fought and struggled and managed to shake off some of my captors, so that I was able to regain my feet; but others rushed up and I was quickly surrounded and overpowered by twenty-five or thirty persons. Ropes were thrown round my neck, legs and body, and thus entangled, I was thrown three several times more to the ground. I fought with my head, teeth, legs, arms, and succeeded in regaining my legs four times. They overcame me at last by strangling me with the rope which they had thrown round my neck. Then they bound me hand, foot, and neck. When I had an opportunity to look round, I saw Chanden Sing struggling against some fifteen or twenty foes. He was quickly entangled, thrown, and secured by ropes. Even Man Sing, the weak and jaded coolie, was overcome by four stout powerful men, though he was not able to offer any resistance. He, too, was bound. While we were struggling against our treacherous foes, some person gave a signal—a shrill whistle—which brought up an ambush of four hundred armed soldiers. These soldiers took up a position round us and covered us with their muskets. Then they searched us and rifled us of any things we had in our pockets. They next proceeded to my tent and took possession of everything I possessed. They sealed up my things in bags subsequent to having overhauled and examined them. Then with shouts and hisses they led us prisoners to Toxem. There we were separated, being placed in separate tents. Guards of many armed soldiers were placed to watch us. In the afternoon of the same day a *Pombo* (a man in authority), with several high Lamas and military officers, held a Court under a gaudy tent. I saw Chanden

Sing led forward to this Court. I was led to the rear of the mud-house to preclude my witnessing the scene. I heard Chanden Sing being interrogated in a loud angry tone and accused of having been my guide. Next I heard Chanden Sing's moans and groans. Then a company of soldiers led me before this tribunal. I was ordered to kneel, and as I would not do so, they tried to compel me to do so by forcing me on my knees. I succeeded in maintaining a standing posture. Then I beheld my servant Chanden Sing lying down, stripped from the waist downwards, in the midst of a number of Lamas and soldiers. I saw two stalwart Lamas, one on each side of him, castigating him with knotted leather thongs. They were laying on him with vigorous arms from his waist to his feet. He was bleeding. As I could not be compelled to kneel, I was allowed to sit down before the *Pombo's* officer. Then my note-books and printed maps were produced, and I was interrogated, first as to the route I had taken, then as to why I had drawn my maps and sketches. I explained as best I could, partly through my servant Chanden Sing and partly through an interpreter (a person who styled himself a Gurkha and who knew a little Hindustani. He wore the garb of the Thibetan). I explained to the officers that Chanden Sing, my servant, did not know the route or anything about the maps and sketches; that I had brought him as my servant, and that I alone was responsible for the route taken by me, and for the maps and sketches; that my servant was not to be punished; that I should be if anybody was punishable. Thereupon one of the Lamas struck me a hard blow on the head with the butt-end of his riding-crop, and they continued to castigate my servant Chanden Sing. I was led away captive, but nevertheless heard the moans of my unfortunate servant. It began raining heavily, and I was taken to a tent, where I was cruelly bound. Soldiers were placed within and without the tent to guard me. I was thus kept the greater part of the night with my arms manacled behind my back and my legs bound. I was so bound that rest or sleep was impossible. The tent was swarming with vermin, which quickly covered me; and I may here remark that I suffered unspeakable tortures from this pest all the time I was in captivity, as I was never permitted to wash, bathe, or change my clothes. In the tent my guard lighted a fire of yak's dung, and the tent was filled with a suffocating smoke, which well-nigh choked me. I was placed near a heap of this stinking fuel. I must say that it was a night full of indescribable misery for me. Though I was fasting all that day and night, yet my cruel jailers gave me no food. I was thus kept a prisoner the following day until about 3 or 4 P.M. Then a soldier entered the tent and informed me that I was to be flogged, my legs broken, my eyes burnt out, and then beheaded. I merely laughed at him; I could not but think that this was said merely to intimidate me. Half an hour later another person arrived and signalled to my guard to lead me out. Not considering me sufficiently secure already, they tightened my bonds and tied others round my body. In this fashion I was taken to the sole house (mud one) in the encampment. Here an enormous pair of heavy handcuffs were put on my hands, which were still kept behind my back. Even in this the treachery of my captors was shown, for they patted me on the back and called me a good man and told me I was to be taken back to Taklakot. This they said fearing I would resist. Then, after locking the handcuffs, they made the key over to one person, who rode away quickly with it lest I might possibly manage to get the key and unlock my handcuffs. For this reason I was never permitted to see or know who carried the key. Just then I heard the voice of my servant, Chanden Sing, calling to me in a very weak tone. He said: "*Hazur! Hazur! Hum murjaiega!*" I endeavoured to get to the poor wretch's assistance. Upon my trying to move towards him my several guards sprang upon me and ruthlessly grappled me and threw me on to the back of a horse. I could only call aloud to my poor servant that I was being taken to Taklakot that day, and that he would be brought after me the following day. I noticed that Chanden Sing was roughly seized and hurled back into one of the rooms of the house, so that we could hold no conversation. My other servant, Man Sing, had his arms pinioned, and he was put on a bare-backed pony. The saddle of the horse I had been thrown upon is worthy of description. It was merely the wooden frame of a very high-backed saddle. From this high projecting back or crupper four or five sharp iron spikes were sticking out. These caught me on the small of my back. My guard was then augmented by some twenty or thirty mounted soldiers with muskets and swords. My pony was held by a horseman, who rode before me. We set off at a furious gallop. Thus we travelled for miles until we arrived at a spot where the *Pombo* with a following of Lamas, banner-men, and soldiers, some two hundred in all, were drawn up. Here my pony was allowed to go on first, and the others reined up and drew aside. As I passed before the *Pombo* and his following a person named Nerba (the Private Secretary of the Tokchim Tarjum) deliberately knelt and fixed his musket on its rest and fired at me from a few paces. The bullet whizzed past me: I was still at a gallop, which no doubt saved my life, as the marksman could not take a steady aim. My pony took fright and reared and plunged, but I maintained my seat, though I was being cruelly pricked by the spikes in the crupper. My pony was then seized and a long cord with a swivel at the end was fastened to my handcuffs. The cord was about fifty yards long. The other end was held by a horseman. In this way we all set off at a hard gallop, and in order to accelerate the speed, a horseman rode by my side and he lashed my pony furiously to make it go at its hardest; meanwhile the horseman who held the cord did his utmost to pull me out of the saddle, so that I would have of a certainty been trampled to death by the cohort behind me. While thus riding furiously with my arms extended backwards I had the flesh rubbed off my hands and knuckles, so much so that the bone was exposed in places, and as the horseman at the back tugged to get me off and I clung hard with my knees, every tug brought me into forcible contact with the spikes in the crupper and wounded me cruelly. The cord was one made of yak's hair. It was strong, but it eventually gave way. The shock unhorsed the soldier. I was all but thrown. This ludicrous incident provoked much mirth among my guards. They stopped my pony and the runaway steed of the dismounted cavalier. The cord was retied with sundry strong knots, and after an interruption of a few minutes we resumed our breakneck gallop, I being in front. When nearing Galshio, and as I was going round the curve of a sandhill, a soldier, who had been posted in ambush, fired a shot at me from a few paces distant. The shot did not strike me. This incident did not stop our headlong career, and we continued on until we arrived at Galshio about sunset. This was the 21st August last. At this place there is a large monastery on the crown of a low hill. At some distance from the base of the hill, and on the plain, was pitched the large white tent of the *Pombo*. Our cavalcade drew up there. I was then roughly torn out of my saddle by two or three men. I requested to stop for one moment. My captors refused me this and, roughly thrusting me forward, said that, as I was about to be beheaded in an instant, it was unnecessary. I was hustled to the left front of the tent, where, on the ground, lay a log of wood in the shape of a prism. Upon the sharp edge of it I was made to stand. I was held by the body by several persons, while others pulled my legs as wide apart as they could be stretched. Then my feet were very securely tied by cords of yak-hair. The cords were so tight that they cut into the flesh in numerous places, some of the cuts or wounds being about three inches long. When I was thus secured one ruffian (Nerba), whom I have alluded to above, came forward and seized me by the hair of my head. He pulled my hair as hard as he could. My hair was long, as I had not had it cut since the day preceding my departure from London about the middle of March. The others formed up in front of me in a semicircle. Then the *Pombo* arose and was handed a bar of iron, which had been made red hot in a brazier, the end grasped by the *Pombo* being bound round with red cloths. He strode up to me, urged on by the Lamas, and said jeeringly that as I had gone to see the country, my punishment would be to have my eyes burnt out. This was in allusion to what I had said at Toxem, viz.—that I was a traveller and merely wished to see the country. He then placed the red-hot bar of iron parallel to and about an inch and a half or two inches from my eyeballs, and all but touching the nose. The heat was so intense that it seemed as if my eyes were desiccated and my nose scorched. There is still a mark of the burn on my nose. I was forced to shut my eyes instinctively. He seemed to me to have kept the bar of heated iron before my eyes for fully thirty seconds or so. After some moments I opened my eyes and beheld the hot iron on the ground. I saw him take a musket from the hands of one of the soldiers standing by He placed this against my forehead and discharged it upwards, giving me a severe shock, though nothing worse. Handing back the discharged weapon to the soldier, the *Pombo* seized a long two-handed sword and came at me. He swung it from side to side all the time foaming from his mouth. This foaming, I believe, was produced artificially. He then motioned to the man who all this time held me by the hair of my head to bend my neck. I resisted with all my might to keep my head erect. Then the *Pombo* touched my neck with the sharp blade of his sword as if to measure the distance for a clean, effective stroke. Then he raised the sword and made a blow at me with all his might. The sword passed disagreeably close to my neck, but did not touch me. I did not flinch ; and my cool indifferent demeanour seemed to impress him, so much so that he seemed reluctant to continue his diabolical performance, but the *posse* of Lamas urged him on by gesticulations and vociferous shouts. Thereupon he went through the same performance on the other side of my neck. This time the blade passed so near that I felt that the blow had not been more than half an inch from my neck. This terminated the sword exercise, much to the disgust of the Lamas, who still continued to urge the swordsman on. Then they held an excited consultation. About this time my coolie, Man Sing, who had frequently fallen off his bare-backed pony, arrived. The person who held my hair then relinquished his hold, and another person came up and gave me a forcible push, which gave me a nasty fall on my back, straining all the tendons of my legs. Then my servant Man Sing was brought forward and tied by his legs to the same log of wood to which I was fastened. Then they made it appear that they were going to behead Man Sing. I was pushed up into a sitting posture and a cloth thrown over my head and face, so that I could not see what was being enacted. I heard Man Sing groan, and I concluded he had been despatched. I was left in this terrible suspense for about a quarter of an hour. Then the cloth was removed, and I beheld my servant lying before me bound to the log. We both asked for food. This seemed to amuse our torturers, for they laughed. In the meanwhile the day was beginning to wane, and our jailers made us understand that our execution was merely put off to the following day. After some time *tsamba* (meal) and tea, were brought in, and it was stuffed into our mouths by our captors. We were kept out in the open without any shelter from the pouring rain. We were sitting in one or two inches of rain and were drenched and numbed with cold. I have already said my hands were manacled from the back; so also were Man Sing's. But at nightfall our captors increased our tortures by straining our manacled arms upwards as high as they could be forced, and then secured them to an upright pole at the back. This caused very severe pain, straining the spine in an incredible way. Then they tied a cord from Man Sing's neck to mine, the effect of which was to make us maintain a most painful position. A guard encircled us, and with them were two watch-dogs tied to pegs. The guard were apparently so confident of our not being able to escape, that they drew their heavy blankets over their heads and slept. One of them left his sword lying by his side. This made me conceive the plan to try to escape. Knowing the extremely supple nature of my hands, I succeeded in drawing the right hand out of my handcuffs. After an hour's anxious and stealthy work I managed to unloose Man Sing's bonds round his feet. In his joy at feeling partly free, Man Sing moved his legs rather clumsily, which the vigilant watch-dogs detected and gave the alarm by barking. The guard were aroused. They went and fetched lights and examined our fastenings. I had succeeded in replacing my hand inside the handcuff. They found Man Sing's bonds loose and, giving him a few cuts with a whip, warned him that if he undid them again they would decapitate him, and refastened them. Then they placed the light between us and put a shelter overhead to prevent the rain extinguishing the light. At about 6 or 7 A.M. the following day they undid Man Sing's feet. I was kept all that day until sunset in the same uncomfortable and painful posture. Thus I was kept fully twenty-four hours. During the day my property had been overhauled and sealed. One of the Lamas picked up my Martini-Henri rifle and put a cartridge in the breach, but failed to push it home firmly. He then discharged the gun. The muzzle of the barrel burst and the face of the Lama was much injured thereby. I laughed heartily at this, and this apparently amused the *Pombo*, for he, too, joined in. About half an hour after this incident my feet were untied. It was then sunset. I found I had lost the use of my feet. It took my right foot some two or three hours before the blood began to circulate freely, but my left foot remained like dead until the following day. That night my feet were secured by cords. A bowl of some boiling steaming liquid, which I was informed was tea, was presented to me to drink. The eagerness of the surrounding Lamas that I should partake of it aroused my suspicion. When it was pushed up to my lips I merely sipped it and declined it. After a short time I felt most sharp, excruciating pains in my stomach, which continued for several days. I could not but conclude that the drink proffered had been poisoned. The following day Man Sing and I were led back on foot to Toxem, our jailers riding on horses. We had to go at a great speed despite our severely lacerated feet. We crossed several cold streams, sinking in mud and water to the waist. At Toxem, to my great delight, I beheld Chanden Sing still alive. We were detained there for that night. On the following day we were placed on yaks' backs and hurried off towards Taklakot. Thus we journeyed at an unpleasantly fast pace for fifteen days, from before daybreak to nightfall. Our guards were bent on taking us *viâ* the Lumpia Pass ; but as this meant a long protracted journey of fifteen or sixteen days, over ice and snow, I knew that we would, in our starved, weakened state, succumb. We were all but naked. This was a day's journey on this side of Mansarowar, where our bonds had been unloosed. We rebelled, and it well-nigh ended in a fight, but our guards consented to halt at Dogmar, until they sent to inquire if the Jong Pen of Taklakot would give us passage through his jurisdiction. After much demur we were eventually taken to Taklakot. This arrangement, I subsequently learnt, was entirely due to the good offices and energy of the *Political Peshkár* Kharak Sing Pal, Rev. H. Wilson, and Pundit Gobaria. On arriving at Taklakot we hastened to Rev. Harkua Wilson's tent, where we were warmly received, attended to, fed, and clothed. My injuries were examined by the Rev. Harkua Wilson, who is a hospital assistant, and who will be able to depose to their nature and extent. In this gentleman's tent, and in the hearing of several persons, among whom were *Peshkár* Kharak Sing, Rev. H. Wilson, and Pundit Gobaria, the man Nerba, above mentioned, the Toxem Tarjum, and the Jong Pen's secretary, and also Lapsang, chief secretary to the Jong Pen, admitted that my account of the affair was perfectly true. Some of my property, more or less damaged, was then restored me by the Tokchim Tarjum. I then gave him two lists, one showing articles restored me, and the other the articles missing. The *Peshkár*, Kharak Sing, has copies of the lists. I was in a very weak state, very exhausted through what I had suffered and little food. It was due to the kind, liberal, and attentive care and treatment of the Rev. H. Wilson and *Peshkár* Kharak Sing Pal that I recovered. The few ragged clothes I had on were literally swarming with lice, as I had no change of raiment, nor was I ever allowed to wash. I contracted the vermin from the tents I was kept in and also from my guards who at first slept round me.

Read over to witness.

A. HENRY SAVAGE LANDOR. J. LARKIN.

DEPOSITION OF CHANDEN SING, *taken on the 9th day of October* 1897.

Solemn affirmation administered by me.

My name is Chanden Sing; my father's name is Bije Singh; I am by caste Thatola; thirty-two years of age; by occupation *kheti;* my home is at That, police station Bisot, district Almora.

I took service as a bearer with Mr. Landor at Almora on the 27th or 28th April last. I accompanied him on his trip to Thibet. We went along through the wilds, encountering many hardships and reached Toxem. There I insisted on my master buying ponies to take us to Darjeeling. This resulted in our capture, for up to then we had vigilantly kept away from the people. The people who brought us ponies to buy played us false. They informed the authorities, who sent soldiers, who lay in ambush behind the sandhills until the crowd of horse dealers and lookers-on, whom we did not suspect of treachery, surrounded and seized us. We were bound with cords by the arms (at back) and legs. My master was more cruelly tied than we two servants. We were taken to the Rája,* who accused me of having brought my master into the country. I was then stretched out and two strong men with whips inflicted two hundred stripes on me. I was questioned as to the maps. My master called out that he, not I, alone understood them, and asked that I should not be beaten. Thereupon a Lama struck him across the head and removed him to a distance, so that I could not communicate with him. They took all our property. Then we were kept separate for the night. I was put in a room and my hands tied to a pole. I could not sleep with the pain I was in. Next day my master, with his hands tied behind his back, was put on a spiked saddle and tied by a long rope held by a horseman. He went at a gallop surrounded by about fifty horsemen armed with guns and swords. Man Sing, our coolie, was also taken with him. My guards informed me my master was to be decapitated at Galshio, and that I was to be beheaded where I was. On the fourth or fifth day my master returned. Meanwhile I was a close prisoner, bound up without food. When I saw my master he was in a pitiful state. He was handcuffed with enormous cuffs, clothes torn to rags, bleeding from his waist, feet and hands swollen. Next day a guard on horseback took us back, bound as we were, on yaks' backs, towards Mansarowar. There I had my cords unloosed. My master was kept bound until we got to Tangchim. We were eventually taken to Taklakot, where the Rev. Harkua Wilson met us and saw our condition. He attended to our wants. My master was well-nigh at death's door. The Thibetans returned some of my master's property, but they have kept about 475 rupees in cash, two rifles, revolver, two files, a lot of soap, medicine, a butterfly dodger, matches, a box of mathematical instruments, a quantity (400) cartridges, a large box of photographic plates and negatives, three bags. We did not molest any one, and paid more than four times the value for any food we bought.

Read over to witness.

J. LARKIN.

* Raja = King.

Deposition of Man Sing, *taken on the 9th day of October* 1897. *Solemn affirmation administered by Pandit Krishnanand.*

My name is Man Sing; my father's name is Sohan Sing; I am by caste Pharswal; twenty-five years of age; by occupation *kheti;* my home is at Sileri, police station Bichla Kattyur, district Almora.

I accompanied Mr. Savage Landor into Thibet. We were surrounded and arrested at Toxem while bargaining and selecting ponies. I was tied up hand and foot, and again tied to a log of wood with my master. When I begged for mercy, they threatened to behead me and struck me on the head with the handle of a *kukri.* We were taken to Galshio. There the Thibetans were on the point of beheading my master. They tried to burn out his eyes. They fired at him twice to kill him. They tried to pull him off his horse to have him trampled upon. He was subjected to many insults and hardships. We were kept bound and guarded until brought to Mansarowar. There our hands were untied. Chanden Sing was with us. He received about two to three hundred lashes at Toxem. I got off most lightly, as when the three of us were captured and examined, I said I was merely the yak driver and not responsible for anything. I lost nothing, but they took my master's property—three firearms, some money, and other things; I cannot enumerate them. We were brought back to Taklakot, where we met friends. My master was made to sit on a spiked saddle and taken from Toxem to Galshio.

Read over to witness.

J. LARKIN.

Deposition of the Rev. Harkua Wilson, *taken on the 9th day of October* 1897. *Oath administered by me.*

My name is Harkua Wilson. By caste Christian; forty-six years of age; by occupation missionary; my home is at Dwarahat, police station M. Dwara, district Almora. I reside at Gunji, Byans.

I am a missionary in the American Methodist Episcopal Society. My work is in the northern *pattis* or Bhot. I accompanied Mr. Savage Landor in July last as far as Gyanima in Thibet. We went through the Lumpiya Pass. It took us four days from Lumpiya to get to Gyanima. At this place the Barkha Tarjam declined to allow me to go on, but he allowed Mr. Landor (who was said to be my brother) with four porters and three servants to go on; but the following day he withdrew this permission. We then returned three marches. At midnight in a snowstorm Mr Landor went up the mountains, determining to go through Thibet by the wilds. He had with him nine followers. He was then in perfect health and strength, and so were his followers. At the end of August I heard that Mr. Landor had been arrested, and, fearing the Thibetans would kill him, I hastened to Taklakot to do my utmost to save him. There I learnt that Mr. Landor and his two servants were being brought back. Hearing that it was the intention of the Thibetans to take them *viâ* the Lumpiya, I, with Pandit Gobaria, Jai Mal, and Lata, induced the Jong Pen of Taklakot to allow Mr. Landor to be brought to Taklakot. On the evening of 7th September *Peshkár* Kharak Sing arrived there. At about 11 A.M. on the 8th September Mr. Landor, Chanden Sing, and Man Sing arrived. I took them to my tent and heard their account of what had happened. I could hardly recognise Mr. Landor; he looked very ill and seemed nearly exhausted. I examined his injuries and found that his forehead had the skin off and was covered with scabs. His cheeks and nose were in the same state. His hair had grown long. He was unshaven and unkempt. He was in rags and dirty, covered with swarms of lice. His hands, fingers, and wrists were swollen and wounded. On his spine at the waist he had an open sore, and the parts around were swollen and red. His seat was covered with marks of wounds caused by spikes. His feet were swollen, and so were his ankles. The flesh about the latter was much hurt and contused, showing marks of cords having been tightly bound round them. He was in a very low condition. I attended to him, having given him a bath and a change of clothes. I gave him food, but though he said he was famished, he could scarcely eat. I am confident, if he had been a few days longer in the hands of the Thibetans and had been taken *viâ* Lumpiya, he would have died. After half an hour the Thibetans brought some of Mr. Landor's things under seal. Some of the Thibetan officials on one side, *Peshkár* Kharak Sing and Gobaria and myself on the other, made out a list of the property, which we took over, and a list was prepared of the articles taken from Mr. Landor and which were missing. Mr. Landor dictated the list from memory. Copies of these lists were furnished to the Jong Pen. I kept Mr. Landor at Taklakot until the afternoon of the 11th September. Then I conveyed him by easy stages to Gunji, where I have a dispensary, and attended to him. I am a hospital assistant. I sent off reports to the Commissioner and Deputy Commissioner. Chanden Sing and Man Sing were also in a wretched state. The former had marks of recent flogging from his waist to above his ankles.

Read over to witness.

J. LARKIN.

DEPOSITION OF PANDIT GOBARIA, *taken on the 13th day of October 1897. Solemn affirmation administered by Pandit Krishnanand.*

My name is Gobaria; my father's name is Jaibania; I am by caste Garbial; forty-eight years of age; by occupation trader; my home is at Garbyang, police station Byans, district Almora.

I heard that Mr. Landor had been arrested and brought down as far as Rungu, and saw that the Jong Pen of Taklakot was sending men to divert Mr. Landor by the long roundabout route *viâ* the Lumpia Pass. I went to the Jong Pen and succeeded in getting him to allow Mr. Landor to be brought to Taklakot. Next morning Mr. Landor and his two servants with two yaks arrived. Mr. Landor was in a very bad state—in a dying state. A list of Mr. Landor's property as received from the Tokchim Tarjum was made. Then Mr. Landor had a list of things taken from him and not returned made out. A Thibetan, named Nerba, who was present, admitted that he had taken part in Mr. Landor's torture and had held him by the hair. The official who had tortured Mr. Landor was the Galjo Changjo and a Lama.

Read over to witness.

J. LARKIN.

DEPOSITION OF THE POLITICAL PESHKAR KHARAK SING, *taken on the 9th day of October* 1897. *Solemn affirmation administered by me.*

My name is Kharak Sing; my father's name is Gobind Sing; I am by caste Pal; twenty-six years of age; by occupation *Peshkár;* my home is at Askot, police station Askot, district Almora.

I am the Political *Peshkár* at Garbyang in Byans. I knew and reported that Mr. Henry Savage Landor had gone into Thibet. On the 5th September I learnt from Bhotias that he had been stopped at Toxem and reported it. I then proceeded to Taklakot in Thibet, to inquire into the matter. On the 7th September, at Taklakot, I learnt that Mr. Landor was a prisoner at Dogmar, and that the Jong Pen would not permit his being brought into Taklakot, as this meant that Mr. Landor would have to go to Gyanima and *viâ* the Lumpia Lek. I then insisted on the Jong Pen allowing Mr. Landor a passage to Taklakot, and warned him of the consequences if he declined. The Jong Pen consented, but gave orders that Mr. Landor should be conveyed hurriedly by night through Taklakot to the Lippu Lek. I protested against this, and eventually Mr. Landor, on 8th September, was conveyed into Taklakot. The Jong Pen had sent two *sawárs* to his guard to admit them. In the Rev. Harkua Wilson's tent Mr. Landor related how he had been tortured. There were several of the Thibetans present who had taken part in the tortures, and they signified that all of Mr. Landor's story was true. Among them was Nerba, of Thokchim Tarjum, who admitted that he had held Mr. Landor by the hair when about to be beheaded, and had cut the nails of his fingers and toes. He admitted he had taken a gold ring from Mr. Landor, which a soldier had taken from him. I made a report of all this and sent (1) a list of Mr. Landor's property restored him by the Thibetans and (2) a list of articles missing. I know Mr. Landor had two rifles and a revolver when he went into Thibet and a considerable amount of money. Mr. Landor was in a very critical position; he was past recognition. He was wounded on the face, body, hands, and legs. I went to the Jong Pen and protested at the treatment given Mr. Landor. The former boldly admitted that Mr. Landor had been treated as alleged, and that it was their duty to act so. The Jong Pen promised to try and have Mr. Landor's missing property restored to him. I know he wrote off to the Garban of Gartok about orders issuing to the Toxem Tarjum. He has engaged to send me anything recovered.

Read over to witness.

J. LARKIN.

DEPOSITION OF SUNA, *taken on the 14th day of October 1897. Solemn affirmation administered by me.*

My name is Suna; my father's name is Gandachiju; I am by caste Khumhar; forty-two years of age; by occupation trader; my home is at Gunji, police station Byans, district Almora.

I saw Mr. Landor and his two servants as prisoners about one and a-half month ago, this side of the Mansarowar Lake. Mr. Landor and Chanden Sing were on yaks; Man Sing on foot. They were well guarded. Tunda and Amr Sing were with me. They went on ahead to Taklakot while I stayed back with the sheep. They went to inform the Rev. Harkua Wilson of the capture. I saw Mr. Landor detained at Dogmar.

Read over to witness.

J. LARKIN.

Statement of property confiscated by the Tibetan authorities, and recovered some months later by the Government of India.

189
DEPARTMENT

From

H. K. Gracey, Esq., C.S.,
The Deputy Commissioner of Almora,

To

A. H. Savage Landor, Esq.,
c/o Grindlay, Groom & Co.
Bombay.

Dated 10*th December*
Received } 1897

No. $\frac{897}{\text{XXII.}}$ of 1897.

File No.

Serial No..

Revolver, 1.
Jewel ring, 1.
Cash—68/12/—in eight-anna pieces.
Cartridges for rifles, 110.
Rifles, 2 (1 damaged).
Cartridges for pistol, 37.
Cleaning-rods for rifles, 2.
Cover for rifle, 1.
" revolver, 1.
Leather strap, 1.
Net to catch butterflies, 1.

File Heading.

Property of Mr. H. Savage Landor.

SUBJECT.

Has the honour to inform him that his marginally noted articles have been received by the Political Peshkar of Garbyang from the Jong-pen of Taklakote.

W. Smith, C.S., *for*
H. K. Gracey, C.S.,
Deputy Commissioner, Almora.
W. J. W.

B. R. Regr. No. 27
Dept. XXII. B.—
1,00,000 of 1896. } P. No. 2131 11–9–96– P. D.

Certificate from DR. WILSON.

DHARCHULA BYAS, BHOT.

I herewith certify that I accompanied Mr. A. Henry Savage Landor in his ascent up the Mangshan mountain, and that Mr. Landor and a Rongba coolie reached an altitude of 22,000 (twenty-two thousand) feet. Owing to the rarefied air, I and the other men accompanying Mr. Landor were unable to go as far as he did. Mr. Landor was at the time carrying on him a weight of thirty seers (60 lbs.), consisting of silver rupees, two aneroids, cartridges, revolver, &c. During the whole time I travelled with Mr. Landor he always carried the above weight on him, and generally carried his rifle besides ($7\frac{1}{4}$ lbs. extra). We all suffered very much during the ascent, as the incline was very steep, and there was deep snow and much troublesome *débris*.

I also certify that I took many photographs * of Mr. Landor and his two servants after they were released, and Mr. Landor looked then very old and suffering, owing to starvation and the wounds that had been inflicted upon him by the Tibetans.

(Signed) H. WILSON,
In charge of Bhot Dispensaries,
American Methodist Episcopal Mission.

DHARCHULA, *April* 27, 1898.

DEAR MR. LANDOR,

Do you remember the night when we separated near Lama Chokden in Tibet, you to proceed towards Lhassa, and I to return to India?

I have in my lifetime seen few such fierce snowstorms. The storm had been raging the whole day and night, and the wind was blowing

* N.B.—Reproductions of some of the photographs mentioned are given in this book.

so hard that we could not hear each other speak. I can only recollect with horror at the dreadful anxiety I was in when you, with a handful of men, escaped from the Tibetan soldiers watching us, and in the dark fearful night proceeded to take your men up the mountain range, with no path, and among loose stones and boulders, a way, indeed, not even fit for goats.

That night, I well remember, you were carrying a weight much greater than the one you usually carried, thirty seers (60 lbs.), for when you left the tent you had in your hand a small bag with 200 extra silver rupees, and you carried your revolver, your rifle, and some extra ammunition. I assure you that I look back with amazement at how you succeeded in pulling through the dangers and difficulties of that night alone.

Yours sincerely,

(Signed) H. WILSON,

American Methodist Episcopal Mission.

DR. H. WILSON'S *Statement.*

I herewith certify that, having heard at Gungi (Byas) that Mr. A. Henry Savage Landor, after losing all his provisions in a large river, had been captured by the Tibetans at Toxem and had there been tortured, I proceeded to Taklakot (Tibet) in the hope of obtaining further news. At Taklakot the news was confirmed, and I heard that Mr. Landor and two servants were brought back under a strong guard. Some uncertainty prevailed as to what route he would be made to follow, and efforts were made by the Tibetans to make him proceed by the long, cold, and dangerous route *via* the Lumpiya Pass, instead of by the shorter and easier route *via* Taklakot. We heard that Mr. Landor and his two men were in very poor health owing to the ill-treatment by the Tibetans, and no doubt the long journey over ice and snow by the Lumpiya Pass left but little chance of their reaching Gungi alive. At the request of Jaimal Bura, Latto

Bura and myself, Pundit Gobaria despatched a man to the Jong Pen at Kujer to explain that we would be thankful and would consider it a great kindness if he would allow Mr. Landor to travel through Taklakot. At last, after much trouble, our request was granted. The officer who brought us the news informed us that Mr. Landor would be made to pass through Taklakot at night, and conveyed directly over the Lippu Pass. The Political Peshkar Kharak Sing Pal arrived in Taklakot that day from India, and we held a consultation. We agreed to keep a watchman in the road all night, but Mr. Landor did not go by. In the afternoon of the 8th, Mr. Landor and his two men arrived. They had been rifled of all they possessed and their clothes were torn and dirty. Mr. Landor and the two men looked very ill and suffering, Mr. Landor's face being hardly recognisable. He and his bearer Chanden Sing gave us an account of the tortures that had been inflicted upon them at Toxem and Galshio, and Mr. Landor showed the Peshkar Kharak Singh, Pundit Gobaria, myself and many Bhotiyas (Shokas) twenty-two wounds on his spine, feet and hands received from the Tibetans. Chanden Sing, who had been administered two hundred lashes, showed numerous black marks and open sores where the skin had been torn on both legs. From Lamas and soldiers who had been present at Mr. Landor's arrest and tortures I heard the following account.

An ambush had been laid, and Mr. Landor and his bearer were caught by treachery when some hundred and fifty yards away from their tent, inside which were the rifles and revolver. They made a desperate resistance and fought for over fifteen minutes, struggling to get at their weapons. Thirty men were on Mr. Landor and twelve or fifteen held Chanden Sing, while four hundred soldiers armed with matchlocks and swords, and who had kept hidden behind sandhills, quickly surrounded them. They were tightly bound with ropes round the neck, chest, and legs, and the arms were pinioned behind their backs. Chanden Sing received two hundred lashes that same day. Mr. Landor and Mansing were taken to Galshio three days later. Ponies were provided for them, Mansing riding bareback, while the wooden frame of a saddle was provided for Mr. Landor, the frame having several iron spikes sticking out of it in the back part of it.

During the long ride to Galshio these nails produced several wounds on Mr. Landor's spine and back. Efforts were made, by means of a rope attached to his handcuffs, to pull him off the saddle and have him trodden to death by the hundreds of ponies of the Lamas, soldiers and officers that came full gallop behind. Moreover, two shots were fired at Mr. Landor. Mansing, unable to use his hands that were bound, fell many times off his steed and remained some two miles behind. When Galshio was reached Mr. Landor was pulled off his saddle, and they told him that his head would be cut off immediately. Dragged mercilessly by soldiers, he was taken to a wooden log. Here they stretched his legs wide apart, and his feet were made fast on the cutting edge of the log by means of tightly bound ropes that cut into his flesh. Then while an officer held him in a standing position by the hair of his head, a hot iron was passed in front of his eyes and a matchlock laid on his forehead and fired. Lastly, the head Lama approached with a long sword and swung it right and left close to Mr. Landor's neck, as if about to cut off the head. Mr. Landor remained composed and spoke no words. After some twenty minutes Mansing arrived, and was tied to the same log in front of Mr. Landor, and pretence was made to behead Mansing, Mr. Landor's face having been covered with a cloth. The Lamas professed to have been very astonished when, after having tied the prisoners' hands high up to poles behind them, Mr. Landor asked for some *tzamba* (oatmeal), meat and rice, and Mansing for some butter.

The amazement of the Tibetans appears to have been even greater when food was brought and Mr. Landor and Mansing partook heartily of it and asked for more. Mr. Landor was kept chained to the log for twenty-four hours, Mansing twelve hours. When they were brought back to Toxem they found that Chanden Sing had been kept four days tied hands and feet to an upright post, and he had been given no food.

At Taklakot, an officer (called Nerba) confessed in my own tent, and before Pundit Gobaria and the Political Peshkar Kharak Sing, that he himself had held Mr. Landor by the hair when he was about to be beheaded. He had also fired a shot at Mr. Landor, and had moreover been ordered by the Lamas to cut off Mr. Landor's toe and finger nails, as well as a lock of his hair. The Taklakot Lamas and the Tokchim Tarjum professed to be sorry at the Galshio Lamas having behaved in such a cruel manner.

At Taklakot we made a list of Mr. Landor's property that was still missing, and we gave a copy to the Jong Pen and one to the Tokchim Tarjum, that they may try to recover what they can.

(Signed) HARKUA WILSON,
Methodist Episcopal Mission.

GUNGI BYAS BHOT, DARMA, *Sept.* 21, 1897.

DR. H. WILSON'S *Certificate of* A. HENRY SAVAGE LANDOR'S *injuries and wounds.*

TAKLAKOT, TIBET, *Sept.* 8, 1897.

I herewith certify that I have examined the wounds that Mr. A. Henry Savage Landor received during his imprisonment at Galshio in Tibet.

There are *five* large sores along the spinal column and the spine itself has sustained severe injuries. At the time they were inflicted these wounds must have caused profuse bleeding.

The feet bear the marks of cruel treatment. On the right foot are still well visible to-day (nineteen days after wounds were inflicted) *six* wounds, viz.—

On the heel one wound one inch long;
Outside ankle ,, half-inch long;
Front of ankle ,, one inch long;
Top of foot, three inches above the toes, one wound one and a-half inch long.
Two small wounds on the upper part of foot.

On the left foot the *four* wounds are of a very severe character, and were produced by ropes cutting into the flesh.

One nasty wound above heel, two and a-half inches long.
One wound below the ankle, one and one-fourth of an inch long.
One wound three inches above the toes, two inches long.
One wound on the heel, half an inch long.

These wounds have caused the feet to be much swollen, the left foot especially having been considerably injured. Its strained tendons give still intense pain when touched and the foot is very heavy, inflamed and swollen.

On the left hand there are *five* wounds.

On middle finger a wound one inch long and deep to the bone.
On root of middle finger, a wound half an inch long.
On small finger, a wound one-fourth of an inch long.
On third „ „ „ „
On first „ „ half an inch long.
The four fingers are still very swollen.

On the right hand there are only *two* wounds.

The first, one half-inch long, on the upper side of the hand.
The second, a quarter of an inch long on the second finger.

Both hands are aching and much swollen, and the wounds upon them were evidently produced by the heavy iron chain of the handcuffs.

On arrival at Taklakot (nineteen days after having been tortured) Mr. Landor is still suffering from strong fever caused by his wounds, and no doubt when they were fresh these must have given Mr. Landor intense pain. His health and strong constitution seem altogether shattered by the sufferings he has undergone.

His face, hands and feet are very swollen, and he appears extremely weak; he himself attributed his great exhaustion to having been unable to sleep for nineteen consecutive nights on account of the bad sores on the spine and legs and because of the heavy iron chains with which he was laden.

H. WILSON,
Hospital Assistant, Methodist Episcopal Mission.

GUNGI BYAS BHOT, DARMA.

N.B.—The numerous smaller wounds, burns, &c., on the face and body are not taken into account.

A copy of this report was despatched from Dr. Wilson direct to the Deputy Commissioner, and was forwarded to the Government of India.

DR. H. WILSON'S *Certificate of* CHANDEN SING'S *injuries.*

TAKLAKOT, *Sept.* 8, 1897.

I herewith certify that I have examined Chanden Sing, Mr. A. Henry Savage Landor's servant who accompanied him to Tibet, where they were arrested and tortured. Chanden Sing has visible to this day on both his legs, and twenty-one days after they were inflicted, innumerable black marks produced by flogging. So severely appears the punishment to have been administered, that large patches of skin and flesh have been torn off by the lashing. Chanden Sing is now in very poor health, and it is evident by his appearance that he suffers greatly from the tortures and ill-treatment received at the hands of the Tibetans.

H. WILSON,

Hospital Assistant, Methodist Episcopal Mission.

GUNGI BYAS, BHOT, DARMA.

A copy of this was sent by Dr. Wilson to the Deputy Commissioner at Almora, and was forwarded to the Government of India.

Certificate by MISS M. A. SHELDON, M.D., *of the Methodist Episcopal Mission.*

M. E. MISSION,
KHELA P. O. DIST. ALMORA.
EAST KUMAON, BHOT.

"All at it and always at it."—WESLEY.

Sept. 28, 1897.

This is to certify that I have seen the wounds inflicted upon Mr. Landor by the Tibetans. It is now about forty days since he was bound and tortured. The wounds are healing well. The scars upon his hands caused by being bound with chains behind his back are plainly visible.

The feet show even more clearly the results of inhuman binding and torture. The wounds have not yet entirely healed, and there is much discoloration. One foot is still swollen.

I have not seen the wounds upon his spine inflicted by a torturing saddle, but he complains of much pain and soreness in that region.

(Signed) MARTHA A. SHELDON, M.D.

Certificate from DOCTOR TURCHINI, *a Director of the Royal Hospital of S.M. Nuova, Florence, Italy.*

D. D. (C. 50) STAMP

R. ARCISPEDALE DI S.M. NUOVA,
GABINETTO
ELETTRO-TERAPICO
DIREZIONE,
FIRENZE.

FIRENZE, 12 *Febbraio*, 1898.

Il sottoscritto Medico Primario Direttore del Turno e Gabinetto elettro-terapico del R^{o} Arcispedale di S. Maria Nuova dichiara quanto appresso: nel mese di Dicembre appena giunto in questa Città visitò il Sig^{re} Henry Savage Landor e lo trovò affetto =

Da *retinite* all' occhio sinistro con suffusione dei mezzi trasparenti, e *da grave iperemia retinica* all' occhio destro. La vista era *abolita* a sinistra, *diminuita* a destra =

La *colonna vertebrale* era dolente, se leggermente compressa con un dito, o se appena percossa col martello da percussione il dolore si faceva intenso, acuto specialmente nelle regioni lombare e dorsale. La deambulazione non era libera ma incerta, la funzionalità degli sfinteri molto difettosa per cui difficolta della mizione e delle evacuazioni.

Presentava poi delle chiazze ecchimobili sopra-malleolari e sopra-carpiche. L'aspetto suo generale era di persona sofferente e molto anemica. Fatte le cure che il caso del Sig^{re} Landor reclamava, oggi 12 Febbraio notiamo; all' occhio destro risoluta la iperemia retinica, aumentato il campo visivo, occhio che serve discretamente alla sua funzione; all' occhio sinistro è molto turbata la circolazione endoculare e quivi la funzione visiva non è ristabilita; non vede gli oggetti e tutto gli fa confusione. La colonna vertebrale presenta sempre dei punti dolenti in specie al rigonfiamento sacro lombare. La deambulazione è più corretta, ma gli sarebbe impossibile fare una passeggiata lunga. La mizione e megliorata, non così la defacazione che è sempre difettosa per impotenza dello sfintere.

Le condizioni generali sono megliorate, ma occorre però al Sig^{re} Landor seguire la cura intrapresa, e specialmente la cura elettrica ed idroterapica.

(Signed) DOTT. TURCHINI.

COMUNE DI FIRENZE.
OFFICIO D'IGIENE.

Visto per la legalizzazione della firma del Sig. Dott. Turchini.
Dal Municipio Firenze
Lira Stamp. *Li 12 Febbraio 1898.*

Il Sindacc.
P. I.
A. Artimini.

Letter from the POLITICAL PESHKAR, KHARAK SING.

Private.

GARBYANG, BHOT,
November 13, 1897.

MY DEAR MR. LANDOR,

I hope that you have received my letter of some time ago and that you may be quite well now. Are you still at Almora? I have not yet got back your things from the Jong Pen, but I hear it is quite true that all your property reached Tokchim a long time ago. I have sent another letter to the Jong Pen, but cannot get an answer as the Lippu Pass is now closed owing to a heavy fall of snow yesterday. It is rumoured that a Tibetan officer is coming from Lhassa to Taklakot to inquire after your case, and probably he may have reached Taklakot yesterday, and after examining your things he will send them down to me. Now I have nearly finished my work at this place. I have collected the dues and paid them to the agents of the Jong Pen. I will go back to Chaudas the day after to-morrow—*i.e.*, on the 15th of this month.

With kind regards and hoping to hear from you soon.

I remain,

Yours sincerely,

KHARAK SING PAL.

Letter from the POLITICAL PESHKAR, KHARAK SING PAL.

HALDWANI, *January* 11, 1898.

MY DEAR MR. LANDOR,

I hope that by this time you have reached safely home. I have been very anxious as I have not heard from you or of your safe arrival there. The dreadful day of the 8th of September is still vivid in my mind, when I first saw you at Taklakot (in Tibet) after you had been tortured by the Tibetans, and where I had come in search of you.

I cannot forget your fearful appearance, with long hair and beard, and your face, body and limbs covered with wounds and bruises. When you arrived at Taklakot, in a few miserable rags stained with blood, dirty and swarming with lice, and surrounded by the guard of Tibetans, I could hardly believe it possible that it was you who stood before me, so much you had changed since I had last seen you.

I am still deeply pained when I think of the pitiable condition you were in, when you showed me 22 (twenty-two) fresh wounds on your hands, feet and spine, without counting the injuries to your face. And indescribable pain gave us too seeing your confiscated baggage under seal of the Tibetan authorities, and to find it, when we opened it, to be full of broken or damaged instruments and other articles of your property.

I think that you may remember my inquiry and consequent anger when the Tibetan officers and soldiers admitted their guilt of tying you by your limbs to the stretching log and of placing you on a spiked saddle; of removing forcibly your toe-nails and pulling you by the hair of your head. You know quite well that I had no power to do more than to report the matter to higher authorities, but I can assure you that it was to me quite unbearable to hear from the Tibetans that they had brought you to execution, and that they boasted of having swung the naked executioner's sword right and left of your neck, and that they had brought a red-hot iron close to your eyes to blind you.

Your servants' condition, especially that of Chanden Sing, whom like yourself the Tibetans kept prisoner for twenty-four days, and who was given two hundred lashes, was pitiable beyond words.

I am anxious to see the photographs taken by Dr. Wilson of you as you were when you arrived at Taklakot. I trust that by now you may feel better and that the pain in your spine may have altogether disappeared. I believe your rifles, revolver, ring, &c., which I succeeded in recovering from the Tibetans, must have reached you by now through the Deputy Commissioner at Almora. The cash and other articles have not been recovered, nor is there any probability of getting them back. Hoping to receive news of you soon and with best salaams,

I am, yours most obediently,

K. KHARAK SING PAL,
Political Peshkar,
Garbyang Dharchula, Bhot.

Letter from COLONEL GRIGG, *Commissioner of Kumaon.*

Commissionership of Kumaon.
Dated December 7, 1897.

MY DEAR LANDOR,

Karak Sing reports that 2 guns (1 damaged), 1 revolver, 1 signet-ring, cash 68/12/-, cartridges (gun) 110, ditto revolver 37, cleaning-rods 2, gun-case 1, leather straps, 1 butterfly-catcher, &c., have been handed to him by the Jong Pen of Taklakot, and he has requested Deputy Commissioner's orders.

I am glad to hear your things are coming on. I hope you are getting stronger.

With our kindest regards,

Yours very sincerely,

E. E. GRIGG.

[NOTE BY THE AUTHOR.—*This letter, as will be seen from the date, reached me after the bulk of the book had gone to press.*]

A PRIVATE LETTER FROM J. LARKIN, ESQ., WHO, DEPUTED BY THE GOVERNMENT, PROCEEDED TO THE FRONTIER TO MAKE AN INQUIRY INTO MY CASE.

ALMORA, *August* 10, 1898.

MY DEAR LANDOR,

Yours of the 21st ult. I am glad to hear that your book on your experiences in Tibet is nearly finished. I wish you may have every success with it, as it is only what you deserve after your trials and hardships in that difficult land of the ultra-conservative Lamas. I am not aware that the Indian papers are attacking you. However, they apparently do not get reliable information if they dispute the fact of your having entered Tibet. We who were in some way connected with your rescue and return have not been "interviewed," or we would give the authentic account of the affair.

I was on a few days' leave at Naini Tal when I heard of your capture, tortures and expulsion from Tibet. I was deputed by the Government to proceed at once to the borders and make an inquiry into the affair. I set off at once, and I met you at Askot, where you were being looked after by the Rajbar. What a change in your appearance! When I saw you standing among some of the Askot natives I could with difficulty identify you. You were bronzed and weather-beaten to such an extent that you were not distinguishable from the natives. I do not think you can blame me for not recognising you readily. Your forehead, nose and the part of your face below your eyes were scarred, and helped to alter your appearance very greatly. You did surprise me when you told me that you would retrace your steps back to the borders on learning from me that I was hastening on to inquire into your case. I had then seen the twenty odd wounds you had on your face, wrists, feet and back. I strongly protested against your undertaking the fatiguing journey back across the perilous and arduous road, as I knew you needed rest and good nourishment, and thought it would be wisest for you to get back to Almora, and be under a good doctor.

You, however, with your characteristic doggedness, meant to accompany me, and I must perforce let you. I was glad in the long run, for you enabled me to make a fuller inquiry than I would otherwise have been able.

As you know, and as I reported to Government, I found after an inquiry on the borders that you had with great difficulty and manœuvring succeeded in entering Tibet, evading the Jong Pen of Taklakot, and the Barca Tarjum at Gyanema, and crossing the Mariam La (Maium Pass) and getting as far as Tuksem (Toxem). You had been deserted by all the mountaineers who had started with you and who had promised to accompany you wherever you went. When you were left with the two Kumaonis, you were surrounded and captured by the *Governor of that part of Tibet* and his men. There, as a sequel to your innumerable fatigues, hardships, desertions, and privations, you and your two followers were ill-treated and tortured *by the Governor*. Have you not got a copy of my official report? I remember you told me you were applying for it. If you possess the copy, surely that will be sufficient to confound your traducers. I saw from the public papers that my report was to be laid on the table of the House of Commons by the Secretary of State for India.

How did the photographs which we took up at the Lippu Pass turn out? I should particularly like to have the one of the group on the pass, and also the one where I am on horseback. I would also like to have the one *I took of you having your matutinal bath when the water froze in your hair and on your body* as it was thrown on you by Chanden Sing; and no wonder it did, as there were ten to twelve feet of snow lying about, and a hardy Bhotia (Shoka) mountaineer had only a few days prior to our arrival been lost in the snow on crossing the pass.

Doubtless it will afford you some pleasure to learn that you have earned quite a reputation among the natives, both Tibetan and Bhotias (Shokas), on account of your universal cordiality, generosity and pluck. They are constantly inquiring about you, and relating your many good traits. Should you ever think of returning here you have made many friends, and you would get a very warm welcome from the natives.

Dr. H. Wilson tells me that, when he took you over from your captors, *the officials of Tibet*, you were in a dying state, and that he only just got you in the nick of time. How are your eyes and spine? I trust they are quite well again. I look back with pleasure to my tour up to the border with you, and our return journey after your journey into Tibet proper, *where you were subjected to tortures by the Governor of the district thereof.*

With every good wish,

Yours very sincerely,

(Signed) J. LARKIN.

INDEX

Printed by BALLANTYNE, HANSON & Co.
London & Edinburgh